PRAYER FROM ALEXANDER TO CONSTANTINE

Prayer from Alexander to Constantine presents and contextualizes approximately fifty prayer texts covering a span of 650 years. It includes prayers from Jewish, Christian and pagan religions. The volume, through individual analysis of each prayer by specialist scholars, provides an invaluably wide study of an area which has, for too long, been fragmented by the specializations of current academic disciplines.

The anthology is the product of an international working group of the Society of Biblical Literature.

While the anthology presents prayers of different religions, it demonstrates the formal similarities of prayers of the Greco-Roman period, whether they be Jewish, pagan or Christian. They include the features of petition, intercession, thanksgiving and adoration.

Prayer from Alexander to Constantine is an invaluable study for any student of theology or the classics. It is also of interest to the more general reader since it may be used as a primary text for theologizing in the twentieth century and beyond. The similarities found within it demonstrate anew the possibilities of finding common turf among the modern-day religions of the world.

Mark Kiley is Assistant Professor in the Philosophy/Theology division in St John's University, New York.

PRAYER FROM ALEXANDER TO CONSTANTINE

A critical anthology

Introduced and edited by
Mark Kiley et al.

London and New York

First published 1997
by Routledge
11 New Fetter Lane, London EC4P 4EE

Simultaneously published in the USA and Canada
by Routledge
29 West 35th Street, New York, NY 10001

Typeset in Garamond by
Solidus (Bristol) Limited
Printed and bound in Great Britain by
Hartnolls Ltd, Bodmin, Cornwall

British Library Cataloguing in Publication Data
A catalogue record for this book is available from the British Library

Library of Congress Cataloguing in Publication Data
A catalogue record for this book has been requested

ISBN 0-415-13234-7
0-415-13235-5 (pbk)

Nothing human is alien to me

Terence

ASSOCIATE EDITORS

CONTENTS

CONTENTS

PART III CHRIST TRADITIONS

CONTENTS

CONTRIBUTORS

Larry J. Alderink is Professor of Religion at Concordia College, Moorhead, Minnesota. Author of *Creation and Salvation in Ancient Orphism* (Scholars, 1981), his research concentrates on ancient Greek religion.

Moshe J. Bernstein, Associate Professor of Bible at Yeshiva University, is co-editor of *Reading 4QMMT: New Perspectives on Qumran Law and Literature* (Scholars, 1996) and *Legal Texts and Legal Issues: Proceedings of the Second Meeting of the IOQS, Cambridge 1995* (Brill, 1997).

Barbara E. Bowe is an Associate Professor of Biblical Studies at Catholic Theological Union, Chicago, IL. She received her Th.D. in New Testament and Christian Origins from Harvard University. At CTU, she teaches courses in NT, early Christianity and biblical spirituality. Her publications include *A Church in Crisis*, a study of the ecclesiology of *1 Clement*.

William Cassidy is Associate Professor and Chair of the Division of Human Studies, Alfred University. Program Chair of the SBL Greco-Roman Religions Section, his research focuses on personal religion and philosophy in archaic and classical Greece.

James H. Charlesworth is Professor of New Testament Languages and Literature at Princeton Theological Seminary and is editor of that institution's Dead Sea Scrolls Project. He edited the first full collection of the Old Testament Pseudepigrapha. He has authored over thirty books (including *Jesus within Judaism*, Doubleday, 1988, and *Jesus' Jewishness*, Crossroad, 1991) and over 200 articles.

Esther G. Chazon, a member of the team editing the Dead Sea Scrolls, teaches Jewish Thought and Second Temple Literature at the Hebrew University. Her thesis, 'A Liturgical Document from Qumran and its Implications: The Words of the Luminaries', will be published by E. J. Brill.

Randall D. Chesnutt is Professor of Religion at Pepperdine University in Malibu, California. His current research interests include the narrative literature of Second Temple Judaism, especially the adaptation of biblical traditions in that literature. Recent publications include *From Death to Life: Conversion in Joseph and Aseneth* (Sheffield Academic Press, 1995).

Angela Russell Christman is Assistant Professor of Theology at Loyola College in Maryland, Baltimore, MD. Her interests include patristic history and theology, especially patristic biblical interpretation, and the relationship between Judaism and Christianity in late antiquity.

John Clabeaux teaches courses in the Bible, Greek and Hebrew at St John's Seminary College in Boston. He authored *A Lost Edition of the Letters of Paul* (Catholic Bible Association of America, 1989). His research is focused on the relationship between Judaism and Christianity in the first and second centuries CE.

Edward M. Cook is Associate Research Scholar at Hebrew Union College, Cincinnati, Ohio. His publications include articles on Aramaic texts from Qumran and *The Dead Sea Scrolls: A New Translation* (with M. O. Wise and M. G. Abegg, Harper, 1996).

Joan E. Cook is Associate Professor of Theology at St Bonaventure University. She is currently working on a book about Hannah in the books of Samuel and in the first century. Her article, 'Hannah's Later Songs: A Study in Comparative Methods of Interpretation' appears in the volume, *Early Christian Interpretation of the Scripture of Israel: Investigation and Proposals*, Sheffield Press, forthcoming.

L. William Countryman is Professor of New Testament at Church Divinity School of the Pacific, Berkeley, CA. He is the author of *Dirt, Greed and Sex: Sexual Ethics in the New Testament and their Implications for Today* (Fortress, 1988).

Toni Craven is Professor of Hebrew Bible at Brite Divinity School, Texas Christian University. With Carol Meyers and Ross Kraemer, she is currently editing *Women in Scripture: A Dictionary of Named and Unnamed Women in the Hebrew Bible, Apocrypha, and New Testament* for Houghton Mifflin Company.

Frederick W. Danker is retired Professor of New Testament at Christ Seminary Seminex/Lutheran School of Theology at Chicago. He specializes in Greek tragedy and New Testament, and loves Pindar. He is the author of *Jesus and the New Age, A Commentary on the Gospel of Luke* (Fortress, 1988) and *Multipurpose Tools for Bible Study* (Fortress, 1993).

Mary Lynnette Delbridge is a doctoral student in New Testament Studies at Union Theological Seminary in New York City. Her research interests focus on kinship language and family relations in early Christianity.

F. W. Dobbs-Allsopp is Assistant Professor of Semitics, Department of Near

Eastern Languages and Civilizations, Yale University. Recent publications include *Weep, O Daughter of Zion: A Study of the City-Lament Genre in the Hebrew Bible* (Editrice Pontificia Istituto Biblico, 1993). Current areas of research include Hebrew poetry, the Book of Lamentations, Semitic linguistics and Northwest Semitic epigraphy.

R. Conrad Douglas holds a Ph.D. from the New Testament Program, Department of Religion, Claremont Graduate School. He is currently a student at the College of Law, University of Iowa.

John C. Endres, S.J. teaches Hebrew Bible and Intertestamental Literature at the Jesuit School of Theology and the Graduate Theological Union in Berkeley, CA. Among his current interests are prayer in the Books of Psalms and Chronicles and the reinterpretation of biblical traditions in the second and first centuries BCE.

Agneta Enermalm is Associate Professor of New Testament at the Lutheran Theological Southern Seminary in Columbia, SC. She has published *Un langage de prière juif en grec. Le témoignage des deux premiers livres de Maccabées*, Coniectanea Biblica, New Testament Series 17 (Uppsala, 1987).

Christopher A. Faraone is Associate Professor of Classics, University of Chicago. Current research interests include Greek poetry and popular religion. He is the author of *Talismans and Trojan Horses, Guardian Statues in Ancient Greek Myth and Ritual* (Oxford, 1992); and with Dirk Obbink, *Magika Hiera: Ancient Greek Magic and Religion* (Oxford, 1991).

Deirdre Good teaches New Testament at the General Theological Seminary in New York City. She is presently working on a translation of the Gospel of Philip with Jorunn Buckley and a book entitled *The Meekness of Jesus.*

Mark Gustafson is Assistant Professor of Classics at Calvin College. His major interests are in late antiquity and in Greco-Roman religions. He has published articles on penal practices in the Roman empire and is currently working on a monograph on bishop Lucifer of Cagliari and his struggle with the emperor Constantius II.

Mark Harding received his Ph.D. from Princeton Theological Seminary in 1993. He is, together with Mark Kiley, associate editor of *The Lord's Prayer and Other Prayer Texts of the Greco-Roman Era* (Trinity, 1994). He is Dean of the Australian College of Theology, Kingsford, New South Wales.

Frances Hickson-Hahn is Associate Professor of Classics at the University of California, Santa Barbara. Her research and teaching interests include Roman historiography and the religion and cult of republican Rome. She has authored a book on *Roman Prayer Language: Livy and the Aeneid of Vergil* (Teubner, 1993).

CONTRIBUTORS

Robert F. Hull, Jun., Ph.D., is Professor and Chair of the Area of New Testament at Emmanuel School of Religion. He is the author of ' "Lucanisms" in the Western Test of Acts? A Reappraisal', *Journal of Biblical Literature*, 1988, vol. 107, pp. 695–707. His research interests include New Testament textual criticism and aspects of early Christian identity.

L. W. Hurtado is Professor of New Testament Language, Literature and Theology, University of Edinburgh. His studies include *One God, One Lord: Early Christian Devotion and Ancient Jewish Monotheism* (Fortress, 1988); *Mark* NIBC (Hendrickson, 1989).

Mark Kiley holds a Ph.D. in the Study of Religion from Harvard University. He publishes primarily in the area of New Testament and Christian origins (see *Colossians as Pseudepigraphy*, JSOT Press, 1986). He teaches in the Philosophy/Theology Division of St. John's University, Staten Island, NY.

Reuven Kimelman is Associate Professor of Near Eastern and Judaic Studies at Brandeis University. He is now writing a book on the Jewish liturgy tentatively titled, *The Liturgy as Literature: A Historical and Rhetorical Commentary to the Jewish Prayerbook*.

Edgar Krentz, Professor of New Testament at the Lutheran School of Theology at Chicago. He is the author of *Galatians* (Fortress, 1985) and of studies of military language in Philippians and hymnody as epideictic literature.

Harry O. Maier is an Associate Professor of NT Studies at Vancouver School of Theology, Vancouver, BC. Dr Maier pursued doctoral studies at Oxford University in the field of early Christianity. His recent publications include *The Social Setting of the Ministry as Reflected in the Writings of Hermas, Clement and Ignatius* (Wilfrid Laurian University Press, 1991) as well as several articles studying heresy and religious dissent in the early Church.

Luther H. Martin is Professor of Religion at the University of Vermont. He has published widely in the area of Hellenistic religions and in theory and method in the study of religion. He is currently working on Hellenistic religious communities.

Carey A. Moore is Amanda Rupert Strong Professor of Religion at Gettysburg College. He has published four volumes in Doubleday's Anchor Bible series, most recently *Tobit: A New Translation, Introduction and Commentary*, 1996. It includes the recently available Hebrew and Aramaic texts of Tobit from Qumran.

Judith Newman received her Ph.D. from the Department of Near Eastern Languages and Civilizations at Harvard. She has taught at both Harvard Divinity School and SUNY-Purchase. She is currently working on a book that explores the uses of scripture in Second Temple prayer.

Carol A. Newsom, Professor of Old Testament at the Candler School of Theology, Emory University, is a member of the team editing the Dead Sea Scrolls. Among her many publications on the Scrolls is *The Songs of the Sabbath Sacrifice: A Critical Edition* (Scholars, 1985).

C. Robert Phillips, III, is Professor of Classics and Ancient History at LeHigh University. He has published widely on Roman religion, Roman history and Greek religion, and is currently completing a book on Roman religion.

Marie-Eloise Rosenblatt teaches at Santa Clara University and wrote *Paul the Accused: His Portrait in Acts of the Apostles* (Glazier/Liturgical, 1995). Her current projects are books on ecology and the Bible, and women in the New Testament.

Jean-Pierre Ruiz (STD, Pontifical Gregorian University) teaches in the Department of Theology and Religious Studies at St. John's University, Jamaica, NY.

Lawrence H. Schiffman, Edelman Professor of Hebrew and Judaic Studies at New York University and a member of the team editing the Dead Sea Scrolls, recently published *Reclaiming the Dead Sea Scrolls: The History of Judaism, The Background of Christianity, The Lost Library of Qumran* (Jewish Publication Society, 1994).

Dan Schowalter is Associate Professor of Religion at Carthage College in Kenosha, Wisconsin. His book, *The Emperor and the Gods: Images from the Time of Trajan*, was published by Fortress Press in 1992. Current research interests include archaeology, apocalyptic literature and the Petrine Epistles.

Philip Sellew is Associate Professor of Classical and Near Eastern Studies at the University of Minnesota. He is editor of *Foundations and Facets Forum* (Polebridge Press), co-editor of *Currents in Research: Biblical Studies* (Sheffield Academic Press) and is currently writing a commentary on the Gospel of Thomas.

Gregory E. Sterling is Associate Professor of New Testament and Christian Origins at the University of Notre Dame. He coordinates Philonic studies for the Society of Biblical Literature and edits related publications. He is series editor for the *Christianity and Judaism in Antiquity* series (University of Notre Dame Press).

Robert Stoops holds a Ph.D. in New Testament and Early Christianity from Harvard University. He has published on the Acts of Peter and other early Christian literature in the *Journal of Biblical Literature, Semeia* and the *Harvard Theological Review*.

Bonnie Thurston is Associate Professor of New Testament at Pittsburgh

Theological Seminary and the author of several books including *Spiritual Life in the Early Church* (Fortress, 1993) and *Reading Colossians, Ephesians, and II Thessalonians* (Crossroad, 1995).

Jeffrey A. Trumbower is an Associate Professor of Religious Studies at St. Michael's College, Colchester, VT. He received his Ph.D. from the University of Chicago in 1989. His dissertation, entitled *Born from Above: The Anthropology of the Gospel of John*, was published in 1992 and he is currently pursuing research on intercessory prayer for the dead in Jewish and Christian traditions.

Richard Valantasis, Associate Professor of Theology at St. Louis University, is currently writing a commentary on the Gospel of Thomas for the Routledge series 'New Testament Readings'.

Annewies van den Hoek is a Lecturer in Greek and Latin at the Harvard University Divinity School. She received her education in the Netherlands. In addition to her lectureship in Greek and Latin at Harvard, she is Fellow for Research at the Museum of Fine Arts in Boston. She has published extensively on Clement of Alexandria and is soon to publish a commentary on *Stromateis IV* in *Sources Chretiennes* (Editions du Cerf).

Frederick W. Weidmann, Assistant Professor of New Testament at Union Theological Seminary in New York, received his Ph.D. at Yale University in 1993. Besides martyrdom, his research interests include the Pauline letters and the early Jesus traditions. Currently, he is completing a monograph tentatively entitled 'Polycarp Remembered: The Harris Fragments and their Challenge to the Literary Tradition'.

Seung Ai Yang (Ph.D., University of Chicago Divinity School) is Assistant Professor of New Testament at the Jesuit School of Theology at Berkeley and the Graduate Theological Union. Her current research is devoted to Jesus' sayings on divorce in the New Testament.

R. Garland Young (Ph.D., Southern Baptist Theological Seminary) is Associate Professor of Religion at Cumberland College, Williamsburg, KY. He currently researches New Testament Hellenistic backgrounds and the parables of Jesus.

PREFACE AND
ACKNOWLEDGEMENTS

This volume is one of the fruits of the Society of Biblical Literature's working group studying prayer in the Greco-Roman period. I have been privileged to chair this group for much of the 1990s and it is now my pleasure to present this anthology of prayer, discussed in a historical-critical mode. It is intended for the general reader and the undergradute student but is also meant not to be tautological for the scholar. This collection displays a broad diversity in formal, chronological and geographical features (and was prevented from displaying an even more finely tuned diversity only by the busy research schedules of some invited authors). The abbreviations used here, and they have been kept to a minimum, conform to those used in the Society of Biblical Literature style sheet.

It is a pleasure for me to thank the many people who have seen the need for this book and worked diligently to make it become a reality. Thanks are due to St John's University, Staten Island, who reduced my teaching load to three courses per term for the duration of the project. Thanks are due also to the individual authors who were intent on creating a first-rate product on schedule, and to the associate editors for their professionalism and generosity. The library staff of Union Theological Seminary, especially Seth Kasten and Drew Kadel, were more than generous in giving me access to the Union collection throughout this time.

I am grateful to Julian Sheffield and to several people at St John's University who provided technical support in the last stages of the manuscript's production: Janet Coppolino, Joe McCauley, Sr. Edna Clark, Scott Bertok, Mark Shapiro, Joe Howard, Mikulas Sikorjak, John LoRusso, Richard Lejeune, Sandy Esposito, Fran Fico, Bethann O'Keefe, and Louise McKenna. My special thanks to my colleague in theology at St John's, Jean-Pierre Ruiz, word-processing warrior and saint-in-progress, and Mr. Richard Stoneman and Kate Chenevix Trench, my gracious editors at Routledge.

Finally, I dedicate this volume to the hundreds of students whom I have taught at St John's University, Staten Island, whose daily needs and interests have kept my discourse about prayer honest.

ABBREVIATIONS

ABD	*Anchor Bible Dictionary*
AGAJU	Arbeiten zur Geschichte des antiken Judentums und des Urchristentums
ALGHJ	Arbeiten zur Literatur und Geschichte des hellenistischen Judentums
ANRW	*Aufstieg und Niedergang der römischen Welt*
ASOR	American Schools of Oriental Research
AV	Authorized Version
b.	Babylonian Talmud
BAGD	W. Bauer, W. F. Arndt, F. W. Gingrich and F. W. Danker, *Greek–English Lexicon of the NT*
Ber.	*Berakot*
BibOr	Biblica et orientalia
BibSac	Bibliotheca Sacra
BJS	Brown Judaic Studies
BZNW	Beihefte zur *Zeitschrift für die neutestamentliche Wissenschaft*
CBQ	*Catholic Biblical Quarterly*
CBQMS	Catholic Biblical Quarterly – Monograph Series
CD	Cairo Damascus (Document)
CH	*Church History*
CRINT	Compendia rerum iudaicarum ad novum testamentum
DJD	Discoveries in the Judaean Desert
DSD	*Dead Sea Discoveries*
EvQr	*Evangelical Quarterly*
ETSE	Estonian Theological Society in Exile
FRLANT	Forschungen zur Religion und Literatur des Alten und Neuen Testaments
GNB	*Good News Bible*
GTV	Göttingen Testamentum Vetus
HNT	Handbuch zum Neuen Testament
HSS	Harvard Semitic Studies

HTR	Harvard Theological Review
HUCA	Hebrew Union College Annual
Ḥul	Ḥullin
j	Jerusalem Talmud
JB	A. Jones (ed.) Jerusalem Bible
JBL	Journal of Biblical Literature
JJS	Journal of Jewish Studies
Jos As	Joseph and Aseneth
JPS	Jewish Publication Society
JPSV	Jewish Publication Society Version
JQR	Jewish Quarterly Review
JSNTSup	Journal for the Study of the New Testament – Supplement Series
JSOT	Journal for the Study of the Old Testament
JSP	Journal for the Study of the Pseudepigrapha
JTS	Journal of Theological Studies
JTSA	Jewish Theological Seminary of America
LCL	Loeb Classical Library
LEC	Library of Early Christianity
LXX	The Septuagint
m.	Mishnah
MasShirShabb	Songs of the Sabbath Sacrifice, or Angelic Liturgy from Masada
Mek.	Mekhilta of Rabbi Ishmael
MSU	Mitteilungen des Septuaginta – Unternehmens
MT	Masoretic Text
NAB	New American Bible
NEB	New English Bible
NHC	Nag Hammadi Codex
NIBC	New International Bible Commentary
NJPS	New Jewish Publication Society
NovT	Novum Testamentum
NRSV	New Revised Standard Version
NTS	New Testament Studies
OBO	Orbis biblicus et orientalis
OL	Old Latin
PGM	Papyri graecae magicae
1Q, 2Q, 3Q, etc	Numbered caves of Qumran, yielding written material; followed by abbreviation of biblical or apocryphal book
QapGen	Genesis Apocryphon
QapPs	Qumran: Apocryphal Psalms
QD	Qumran: Damascus Document
QH	Hodayot (Thanksgiving Hymns)
Q1saa,b	First or second copy of Isaiah

1QM	*Milḥāmah (War Scroll)*
QMMT	*Miqsat Ma^aseh Torah*
QpHab	*Pesher on Habakkuk*
QPs	Qumran: Psalms Scroll
1QS	*Serek ha-Yaḥad (Rule of the Community, Manual of Discipline)*
1QSb	Appendix B (*Blessings*) to 1QS
QT Leviar	Qumran: Testament of Levi in Aramaic
QTob	Qumran: Tobit
Rab.	*Rabbah*
RB	*Revue biblique*
REJ	*Revue des études juives*
RevQ	*Revue de Qumran*
RQ	*Römische Quartalschrift für christliche Altertumskunde und Kirchengeschichte*
RSV	Revised Standard Version
SBL	Society of Biblical Literature
SBLDS	SBL Dissertation Series
SBLRBS	SBL Resources for Biblical Study
SBLSP	SBL Seminar Papers
SBT	Studies in Biblical Theology
SC	Source chrétiennes
SCM	Student Christian Movement (press)
SNTSMS	Society for New Testament Studies Monograph Series
SPB	Studia Patristica et Byzantina
SPh	*Studia Philonica*
STDJ	Studies on the Texts of the Desert of Judah
t.	*Tosefta*
Ta^an	*Ta^anit*
T. Naph.	*Testament of Naphtali*
TU	Texte und Untersuchungen
UF	*Ugaritische Forschungen*
VC	*Vigiliae Christianae*
WUNT	Wissenschaftliche Untersuchungen zum Neuen Testament

GENERAL INTRODUCTION

Mark Kiley

When Homer says that 'prayers are the daughters of great Zeus, and they are lame of their feet, and wrinkled, and cast their eyes sidelong' he is exercising the prerogative of a poet when describing a datum of history.[1] In this present volume, our working definition of prayer is rather more prosaic: 'an address to or celebration of a deity'.[2] The prayers collected here represent only a small sample of the available prayer texts of the period 325 BCE to 325 CE.[3] The period from Alexander to Constantine covered by this volume, some 650 years, may be put in perspective by remembering that 650 years ago, thinkers such as Averroes, Maimonides and Thomas Aquinas had only just begun to lead the way in grappling with the implications of the (for some) newly recovered thought of Aristotle, Alexander's tutor. A lot of water flows under a bridge in 650 years. What can one expect to find in the study of a prayer corpus spanning such a length of time? In this brief introduction, I should like to point out three matrices within which these prayers may be understood: their shared characteristics across ideological lines; some of the most striking of their relations to Hellenistic culture; and some of the avenues which connect them to contemporary concerns.

SHARED CHARACTERISTICS

Hellenistic prayers of all stripes display some formal similarities in that they include petition, intercession, thanksgiving and adoration. They occur alone and in a variety of literary contexts (including narratives as well as more un-abashedly didactic pieces such as letters or tracts). As you will also see, some of the prayers share some other very specific characteristics. For example, the rabbis' use of antiphon as a means of acclaiming the Lord bears a formal resemblance to the use of antiphony in Rev 4 and 5.

Many of these prayers treat similar themes. For example, the genius of Augustus is acclaimed as peacemaker much as is the Christ of Colossians in the New Testament. And many of these prayers ride the undulating waves of that period's ongoing discussion concerning the oneness or multiplicity of deity.[4] In all three groups of prayers discussed here, one can detect several points along a spectrum of attitudes toward existing political realia: from an attitude of perpetuation, to silent or begrudging acceptance, to hope for their transformation, to outright call for their destruction.

The people portrayed in these prayers sometimes give clear voice to the reasons for their complaint or exultation but just as often their personal characteristics are muted by the express concerns of the prayer itself, leaving us the challenging task of divining the social reality behind the prayer. In fact, though I have subdivided these prayers under the headings Judaica, Greeks and Romans, and Christ Traditions, I can supply no guarantee that the hypothetical members of each group never used the prayers of another grouping.

RELATION TO HELLENISTIC CULTURE

I would suggest two aspects of Hellenistic culture fruitful for the further investigation of these and other prayers of the period.

First, this period witnessed an ongoing philosophical critique of the role played by religion in culture. Writers such as Seneca, Plutarch and Lucian made diverse judgements about the degree to which the practices of cult, including prayer, were worthy activities for the knowledgeable cosmopolite. I would particularly recommend that the reader keep an eye trained on the relationship of these prayers to the phenomenon of sacrifice, since sacrifice was one of the most frequently treated objects of philosophical analysis.[5]

Second, the rhetoric of the Hellenistic schools provides the student of the period with some of the conceptual tools and vocabulary with which to discuss these prayers in terms which would have been recognized by people of that period. Rhetoric, the art of persuasion, was a standard part of education of the period, and the components of that rhetoric help one identify a given prayer as, for instance, epideictic, as well as recognize the distinctions between a prayer's invocation, narrative and proposition.[6] One might also consider the degree to which the careful crafting of language by rhetorical rules bears a formal resemblance to sacrifice of the period in that they both may be seen to offer the artful or the special, precisely what is *not* vulgar/profane.[7]

AVENUES TO THE PRESENT

The prayers of this volume may be used as raw material in the theologizing of the twentieth century and beyond. Certainly such a volume as this raises afresh the possibility of finding common turf among present-day Jews, Christians and people of goodwill in other faiths.[8] But within both the Jewish and Christian traditions, those who think in a systematic way about converse with God may find themselves both unable to ignore the formal similarities of their prayers with each other and with the prayers of Greeks and Romans, as well as reluctant to collapse those similarities into substantial equivalence.[9] Second, these prayers raise afresh within each tradition the question of the pertinence of past formulations to present faith-expressions. To take just one example, from within the Christian tradition, recent highly publicized discussions have recognized the fact that worship of Jesus is an accurate expression of traditional Christian faith but have wondered about the degree to which that worship acts as a potential diversion from pursuit of Jesus' own focus in his public/earthly ministry on the reign of God. Contemporary interlocutors who engage in this debate and search for 'the real Jesus' may find in Origen's prayer to Jesus as footwasher a worthy object of contemplation.[10]

Those interested in twentieth-century categories in the philosophy of religion, categories such as *person* or *encounter*, will find in this ancient prayer corpus further stimulus to thinking through the issues associated with those categories.[11] And the practice of addressing deity as *Father*, frequently attested in this corpus, provides some specific data for those interested in human psychology in a post-Freudian era.[12] This corpus may also be useful to those interested in the relation between prayer and broad socio-political currents.[13]

Moreover, this prayer corpus provides raw material for the further propagation and analysis of letters by those who love them. Whether one agrees with Hopkins that prayer is 'a warfare of my lips in truth, battling with God' or with the Spanish poet Unamuno that verse is itself a kind of prayer, or with Pushkin whose creative synthesis moves through prayer and beyond, this collection can serve as a companion/stimulus to the contemporary literary discovery/creation of beauty.[14]

Indeed, the following excerpt from a poem by Amos Wilder celebrating Hadrian's Villa may serve as beneficent sentry facilitating the reader's entry to this collection of ancient prayer. The Roman emperor Hadrian built the villa in the early second century CE in part to capture and propagate some of the beauty of a bygone era. That same goal is part of the rationale for the production of this volume:

> Lavender fumes from sunset's dying torch
> > Mantle the heaven,
> The paling panels of night's western porch
> > So lately riven
> With crimson flares no longer flame and scorch
> > With glowing levin.
>
> The torch is quenched that cast its ruddy flare
> > O'er the Campagna,
> The hosts are vanished and the golden stair,
> > Trump and hosanna,
> The Sabines lose their flush, the dusky air
> > Welcomes Urania.

And all that glory but a silhouette:
    The Villa Hadrian
An acropolis of cypresses like jet
    Against the meridian,
Its ruins gulfed even as its past is set
    Deep in oblivion.
So intimations swarm upon the husk
    Of ancient splendors;
Read in the altered light of history's dusk
    A spirit tenders
More hallowed moods, breathing a fainter musk
    And dreams more tender.

For years distill the eternal from the days
    And leave to silence
All that once raged in time's advancing blaze
    Of lust and violence;
This quiet column marks their holier ways,
    The rest is silence.

Amid the imperial revelry and waste
    And mean appraisal
Of mortal things, this broken tablet chased
    By unknown chisel
With timeless beauty witnesses there paced
    Mid the carousal

Hearts that were bent in those forgotten fetes
    On deeply probing
The granite destinies, the marble fates,
    And on disrobing
That Beauty whose heart therein palpitates,
    The dust ennobling.[15]

NOTES

1 *Iliad* 9.502.ff.
2 An exception is the aretalogy of Isis which has her speaking in the first person but which shares characteristics with other addresses to her and other deities. Also see some of the Songs of the Sabbath Sacrifice. For the propriety of including exceptions to the rule in artistic creations, see Longinus, *On the Sublime* 33.
3 James Charlesworth, ed., with Mark Harding and Mark Kiley, *The Lord's Prayer and Other Prayer Texts from the Greco-Roman Era*, Valley Forge: Trinity, 1994, pp. 101–274 for extensive bibliography to that date. Also see Pieter van der Horst and Gregory Sterling, *Prayers of Antiquity: Greco-Roman, Jewish and Christian Prayers*, translated by John Wm Medendorp, Christianity

and Judaism Series 11, Notre Dame: University of Notre Dame Press, 1997.
4   Robert M. Grant, *Gods and the One God*, Philadelphia: Westminster, 1986.
5   Harold W. Attridge, 'The Philosophical Critique of Religion under the Early
    Empire', *Aufstieg und Niedergang der Römischen Welt* 16.1, ed. W. Haase,
    Berlin, NY: De Gruyter, 1978.
6   D. A. Russell, *Criticism in Antiquity*, Berkeley: Univ. of California, 1981.
    George A. Kennedy, 'The Rhetoric of the Early Christian Liturgy' in David
    Jasper, ed., *Language and the Worship of the Church*, New York: St. Martin's,
    1990, pp. 26–43.
7   The whole question of the relationship of Hellenistic prayer to Hellenistic
    poetry is also ripe for investigation. Barbara Hughes Fowler, *Hellenistic Poetry*,
    Madison, WI: Univ. of Wisconsin, 1990.
8   George Appleton, *The Oxford Book of Prayer*, Oxford: Oxford University
    Press, 1985. Paul Bradshaw and Lawrence Hoffman, eds, *The Making of Jewish
    and Christian Worship*, Notre Dame: University of Notre Dame Press, 1991;
    idem, *The Changing Face of Jewish and Christian Worship in North America*,
    Notre Dame: University of Notre Dame Press, 1991. Herman Slater, ed., *A
    Book of Pagan Rituals*, rpt. York Beach, ME: Samuel Weiser, Inc., 1984.
9   John McKenna, C.M. 'From "Berakah" to "Eucharistia" to Thomas Talley and
    Beyond", *Proceedings of the North American Academy of Liturgy*, Annual
    Meeting, Boston, MA, 5–8 January, 1995, pp. 87–100.
10 Luke Timothy Johnson, *The Real Jesus: The Misguided Quest for the Historical
    Jesus and the Truth of the Traditional Gospels*, San Francisco: Harper, 1996.
    Within the same tradition, see the consistent attempt to integrate dogmatic
    considerations within one's prayer: Karl Rahner, *Prayers for a Lifetime*, New
    York: Crossroad, 1995.
11 John Macquarrie, *Twentieth-Century Religious Thought: The Frontiers of
    Philosophy and Theology 1990-1980*, New York: Scribner's, 1981.
12 John McDargh, *Psychoanalytic Object Relations Theory and the Study of
    Religion: On Faith and the Imaging of God*, New York: Univ. Press of America,
    1983. L. B. Brown, *The Human Side of Prayer: The Psychology of Praying*,
    Birmingham, AL: Religious Education Press, 1994.
13 Enda McDonagh, 'Prayer, Poetry and Politics' in Brian Davies O.P., *Language,
    Meaning and God*, London: Geoffrey Chapman, 1987, pp. 228–43. Perry
    Lefevre, *Radical Prayer*, Chicago: Exploration Press, 1982.
14 W. H. Gardner and N. H. MacKenzie, *The Poems of Gerard Manley Hopkins*,
    Oxford: Oxford University Press, 1984, p. 27. Edited and with an Introduction
    by Stanley Burnshaw, *The Poem Itself*, New York: Horizon, 1981, p. 166. Carl
    Proffer, ed., *Modern Russian Poets on Poetry*, Ann Arbor: Ardis, 1976, pp. 148–
    50.
15 'The Unmenaced Towers. Hadrian's Villa, Tivoli', used with permission of
    Tappan Wilder, for the estate of Amos Wilder. Full text available in Margaret
    Rigg, *Imagining the Real*, Ft Lauderdale, FL: Possum, 1978.

Part I

JUDAICA

1

AN INTRODUCTION TO PRAYER AT QUMRAN

Esther G. Chazon and Moshe J. Bernstein

The Qumran writings, more popularly known as the Dead Sea Scrolls, have, over the past half century, considerably expanded our knowledge of Jewish life and literature during the Second Temple era. The story of the initial discovery of Cave 1 in 1947 and the subsequent discovery of ten more caves containing written documents has frequently been told (see Bibliography). This trove of scrolls covers the gamut of ancient Jewish literature, from the Bible to the common Jewish literature of the Second Temple period to the uniquely Qumranic sectarian works. The subset of texts which can be classified as prayer constitutes a daunting quantity of material in its own right.

In addition to about 100 biblical psalms, well over 200 different non-biblical prayers, hymns and psalms can be counted among the 800 manuscripts from the Judaean desert, with some of them appearing in multiple copies. Texts of prayers are found in liturgical and hymnic collections as well as in other types of works such as pseudepigrapha and sectarian rules (see the list below). Qumran gives us the first historical insight into post-biblical Jewish prayer within a live, liturgical, as opposed to literary, context. Prayer played a major role in the religious life of the Qumran community (*c.* 150–100 BCE to 68 CE), especially in the light of the cultic and spiritual void created by the sect's apparent secession from the Jerusalem Temple. It provided an alternative means of worship as well as an instrument for the atonement of sin. The sectarian documents regularly refer to prayer in sacrificial terms, equating it with sacrifice metaphorically as well as functionally: 'An offering of the lips for judgement is like the sweet fragrance [offered by] the righteous' (1QS 9:5; cf. 11QPs[a] 18:7–8 [= Syriac Psalm 154], 'a person who glorifies the Most High is approved as one offering a meal-offering, as one sacrificing he-goats and cattle').[1]

The development of prayer at Qumran as a substitute for sacrifice appears analogous to the similar process which took place later within rabbinic

Judaism in the wake of the destruction of the Jerusalem Temple in 70 CE. The Qumran sect, like the Rabbis after them, apparently instituted communal prayer at fixed times which were coordinated with the hours of sacrifice at the Jerusalem Temple (twice daily, early morning and late afternoon towards sunset and on Sabbaths and holidays; see Chapter 6, 'Hymn on Occasions for Prayer', Chapter 4, 'Words of the Luminaries', and Chapter 5, the 'Songs of the Sabbath Sacrifice'). There are also parallels in content between certain prayers from Qumran and rabbinic prayer. The 'Daily Prayers' of 4Q503 and the rabbinic 'Benediction on the Luminaries' (*b. Ber.* 11a–12a) both offer praise twice a day, evening and morning, for the creation and daily renewal of the heavenly lights. Both incorporate a description of praise offered by and in unison with the angels, known in later Jewish liturgy as *Qedušat Yoser*. The common presence of this theme may indicate that it was not necessarily Qumranic or rabbinic but was shared by the 'common Judaism' of the Second Temple era.[2]

The regular, fixed liturgy of the community, however central to sectarian religious life, constituted just one of the many facets of prayer at Qumran. Prayer's function as a substitute for Temple worship and as the operative medium for contact with God led to the amassing of a large and rich corpus of liturgical and hymnic material by the Qumran group. The presence of biblical psalms in the corpus demonstrates that not all of the prayers found at Qumran were authored by the sect, and it is likely that many of the extra-biblical prayers which the Qumran sectarians copied and used were also not written by them. A text's Qumranic origin is generally demonstrable only if it exhibits distinctively sectarian terminology, contents and ideas (for example, 'community of God', cosmic dualism, predestination). The distinction between sectarian and non-sectarian works is crucial for understanding the Qumran phenomenon as well as other contemporary Jewish groups and their practices.

At the present stage of publication and research, the psalms, hymns and prayers from Qumran can be classified according to seven major form-critical categories:

1   *Liturgies for fixed prayer times*: evening and morning benedictions for each day of one month (4Q503 cf. 4Q408), prayers for the days of the week (4Q504–506), a cycle of thirteen Sabbath songs for the first quarter of the year ('Songs of the Sabbath Sacrifice'), an annual festival liturgy (1Q34–34*bis*; 4Q507–509; cf. 4Q409, a hymn calling for praise on festivals). The corpus includes other communal prayers whose time of recitation is not explicitly stated (for example, the communal confession of 4Q393 and the lament of 4Q501).

2   *Ceremonial liturgies*: purification rituals (4Q512); liturgies of benediction and malediction for the annual covenant renewal ceremony and other occasions (1QS 1:16–2:26; 4QBerakot; the expulsion

ceremony in 4QDª); marriage (or golden age) ritual (4Q502).

3 *Eschatological prayers*: prayers anticipating or requesting messianic redemption such as the Apostrophe to Zion, as well as prayers and hymns to be recited at the 'end of days' – during the final war against the forces of darkness (1QM 13:1–14:15; cf. 4QM) and at eschatological blessing ceremonies (1QSb, 11QBeraka; cf. 4Q285).

4 *Magical incantations*: a ritual, consisting of Ps 91 and apocryphal psalms, which employs incantation, adjuration and curse formulae (11QapPsª); hymns 'to frighten and terrify' evil spirits (4Q510–511; cf. 4Q444 and 8Q5); an incantation against demons (4Q560).

5 *Collections of psalms*: more than thirty biblical scrolls; a collection of non-biblical *Barki Nafshi* hymns (4Q435–439); a diverse collection of non-canonical psalms (4Q380–381); and several collections which juxtapose biblical and non-biblical psalms such as the large Psalms Scroll from Cave 11 (11QPsª) which has been claimed by some to be a liturgical collection (cf. 11QPsᵇ, 4QPsᶠ).

6 *Hodayot hymns*: individual thanksgiving hymns, often opening with the formula, 'I thank you, Lord', characterize the *Hodayot* collections from Caves 1 and 4. Community hymns also appear in some of the manuscripts (1QHª; 4QHª,ᵇ). It appears that different collections of *Hodayot* texts circulated at Qumran. These hymns are distinctively sectarian in content and language.

7 *Embedded prose prayers*: several prayers found in pseudepigraphical works preserved at Qumran, such as the prayers of Abraham (1QapGen), Levi (4QTLeviarᵇ) and Joseph (4Q372), bear a resemblance to prayers in actual use. For pseudepigrapha in the Qumran library which were already known from existing sources see also Chapter 8 on Tobit and Chapter 10 on Jubilees in this volume.

The list provided above is a descriptive summary. Obviously, an exhaustive account of the hundreds of prayers from Qumran cannot be provided in this brief introduction. This corpus will undoubtedly expand, and categorizations and classifications will change as new editions of scrolls are published and as currently known manuscripts are re-evaluated in light of the new publications. For example, there now seems to be a sub-category of wisdom psalms and prayers (for example, Psalm 154 in 11QPsª and 4Q409).

The prayers presented below have been arranged along a spectrum moving from the most 'biblical' in nature to the most 'Qumranic'. They include two liturgies for fixed prayer times ('Words of the Luminaries' and 'Songs of the Sabbath Sacrifice'), and two representatives of the hymn collections (the *Barki Nafshi* thanksgiving and the Apostrophe to Zion). The Apostrophe to Zion also serves as an example of eschatological prayers although it does not reflect the sect's unique developments in this area. The entry from the personal hymn appended to the *Community Rule* (1QS

10:8b–17) beautifully expresses the religious stance of its author, and is also an important witness for the sectarian concept of prayer.

NOTES

1   Texts from the Judaean desert (including, but not limited to, the Qumran scrolls) are identified by a siglum indicating location, in this case Caves 1 and 11, respectively, from Qumran, and either a document number or an official title, in this case *Serekh ha-Yaḥad*, one of the 'complete' scrolls discovered initially in Cave 1 in 1947, usually referred to as the '*Community Rule*' or the '*Manual of Discipline*', and the 'Psalms Scroll' which is discussed below. For lists of texts and sigla, see J.A. Fitzmyer, SJ, *The Dead Sea Scrolls: Major Publications and Tools for Study*, revised edition, SBLRBS 20, Atlanta, Scholars, 1990 and E. Tov, 'The Unpublished Qumran Texts from Caves 4 and 11', *Biblical Archaeologist*, 1992, vol. 55, pp. 94–104.
2   See further Chapter 18 on Rabbinic Prayer.

SELECTED BIBLIOGRAPHY

General

Schiffman, L.H., *Reclaiming the Dead Sea Scrolls: The History of Judaism, The Background of Christianity, The Lost Library of Qumran*, Philadelphia, Jewish Publication Society, 1994.
VanderKam, J.C., *The Dead Sea Scrolls Today*, Grand Rapids, Eerdmans, 1994.

Specialized

Chazon, E.G., 'Prayers from Qumran: Issues and Methods', in E.H. Lovering (ed.), *SBL 1993 Seminar Papers*, Atlanta, Scholars, 1993, pp. 758–72.
——, 'Prayers from Qumran and Their Historical Implications', *DSD*, 1994, vol. 1, pp. 265–84.
Flusser, D., 'Psalms, Hymns and Prayers', in M.E. Stone (ed.), *Jewish Writings of the Second Temple Period*, Assen/Philadelphia, Van Gorcum/Fortress, 1984, pp. 551–77.
Nitzan, B., *Qumran Prayer and Religious Poetry*, STDJ 12, Leiden, Brill, 1994.
Schiffman, L.H., 'The Dead Sea Scrolls and the Early History of Jewish Liturgy', in L.I. Levine (ed.), *The Synagogue in Late Antiquity*, Philadelphia, JTSA/ASOR, 1987, pp. 33–48.
Schuller, E., 'Some Observations on Blessings of God in Texts from Qumran', in H.W. Attridge, J.J. Collins and T.F. Tobin (eds), *Of Scribes and Scrolls: Studies on the Hebrew Bible, Intertestamental Judaism, and Christian Origins Presented to John Strugnell on the Occasion of His Sixtieth Birthday*, College Theology Society Sources in Religion 5, Latham, University Press of America, 1990, pp. 133–43.
——, 'Prayer, Hymnic and Liturgical Texts from Qumran', in E. Ulrich and J.C. VanderKam (eds), *Community of the Renewed Covenant: The Notre Dame Symposium on the Dead Sea Scrolls*, Notre Dame, IN, University of Notre Dame Press, 1994, pp. 153–74.
Talmon, S., 'Emergence of Institutionalized Prayer in Israel in the Light of the

Qumran Literature', *World of Qumran from Within*, Jerusalem/Leiden, Magnes/ E.J. Brill, 1989, pp. 200–43.
Weinfeld, M., 'Prayer and Liturgical Practice in the Qumran Sect', in D. Dimant and U. Rappaport (eds), *The Dead Sea Scrolls: Forty Years of Research*, STDJ 10, Leiden/Jerusalem, Brill/Magnes, 1992, pp. 241–58.

2

A THANKSGIVING FOR GOD'S HELP (4Q434 II–III)

Edward M. Cook

INTRODUCTION

The 150 poems contained in the biblical Book of Psalms do not exhaust the inventory of Israel's hymns. Undoubtedly there were thousands more, and Jews continued to write them long after the biblical period. A number of these previously unknown psalms have turned up in the ancient library of Qumran (perhaps even in their Book of Psalms!). Some of them represent imitations of the biblical genre with a sectarian twist, while others would not be out of place within the biblical psalter. Some, including the one translated here, are particularly pure examples of the songs of Israel, although their wording is often derived from biblical expressions; occasionally verbatim excerpts from the Bible occur. But, as with the Qumran *Hodayot*,

> It is often difficult to decide to how great an extent it is a question of the individual author himself extracting texts from the Old Testament in his composition, and to how great an extent he is just employing [current] terminology ... which was originally drawn from the Old Testament.[1]

The biblical psalms are of different types, any of which may be either personal or communal. The *lament* focuses on a crisis or calamity suffered by the psalmist or the nation as a whole and usually includes a prayer for deliverance from the affliction. The *praise* emphasizes the greatness of God and what God has done for the psalmist or for the nation and enjoins others to praise the Lord joyfully. The *thanksgiving* emphasizes the goodness of God in delivering the psalmist and/or nation from affliction, and usually contains an expression of thanks or blessing. Mixed types may occur.[2] The following hymn is a thanksgiving, blessing God's goodness as shown to the righteous in Israel. There are no examples in the collection in which it occurs of the other main type of psalm, the individual or communal lament. The scroll editors refer to the collection by the title *Barki Nafshi*: the Hebrew phrase (which occurs in Psalms 103:1, 2, 22; 104:1, 35) means 'bless, O my soul . . .' and occurs several times in the poems.

Judging from the Hebrew Bible, psalms or psalm-like prayers were uttered either during formal occasions of worship (such as making a thanksgiving sacrifice) or informally, outside the sanctuary. The Qumran psalms could have fit either occasion. It is still debated whether the Qumran sect participated in the sacrificial worship of the Temple; if they did not, this expression of thanks could have been composed or recited for a non-sacrificial liturgy or for private devotion.[3]

The hymn contains no clear indication of the time of composition. Since it is written in Hebrew – undoubtedly the original language – it is probably the product of Palestinian Jews of the third or second centuries BCE. None of the vocabulary reflects the technical terminology usually taken to characterize the Qumran sect, nor is the orthography and morphology distinctively 'Qumranian'.[4]

TRANSLATION

Bless, O my soul, the Lord,[5]
for all His wonderful deeds for ever,
and blessed be His name,
for He has saved the life of the poor[6]
and the humble He has not spurned,[7]
and He has not overlooked the needy in trouble,
He has kept His eyes on the weak,
and paid attention to the cry of orphans for help.[8]
He has inclined his ears to their cry,[9]
and because of His abundant mercies, has shown favour to the meek.
He has opened their eyes to see His ways
and inclined their ears to hear His teaching.[10]
He has circumcised their hearts' foreskin[11]
and delivered them for the sake of His kindness.[12]
He has directed their feet to the true path,[13]
and has not abandoned them in their great distress.[14]
He has not given them into the power of oppressors,
nor judged them with the wicked,
nor inflamed His anger against them,[15]
nor annihilated them in His wrath.
His fierce wrath has not blazed out against all,
and He has not judged them in the fire of His zeal.[16]
No, He has judged them by His abundant mercies,
by grievous judgements for the sake of testing them,
that He may increase His mercies [. . .]

15

EDWARD M. COOK

[from the power of] mortals[17] He has saved them,
nor has He judged them by a mass of gentiles.
He has not [abandoned] them within the nations,
and hidden them in [. . .]
He made dark places light in front of them,
and He made rough places smooth.[18]
He revealed to them laws of peace and truth,[19]
[He weighed] their breath in a measure,
He apportioned their words by weight,
and made them sing like flutes.[20]
He gives them a different mind,
so they may walk in [the ways of peace.]
He also brought them near to His heart' s path,[21]
for they had risked their life' s breath.[22]
So He wove a protective hedge around them,[23]
and commanded that no plague should [smite them],
His angels camped around them[24] to protect them,
lest [Belial] attack them [through] their enemies.
[The fire of] His wrath burned [. . .],
His anger [. . .] in them [. . .]
[. . .] in their trouble and [distress],
and You delivered them from every danger.
[Miracles] You have performed for them before mankind,
and You delivered them for Your sake.
[. . .] so that they can examine their sins and their ancestors' sins,
and atone for them [. . .] by Your statutes,
and to the path that You have [taught . . .]

NOTES

1   S. Holm-Nielsen, *Hodayot: Psalms from Qumran*, Acta Theologica Danica II, Aarhus, Universitetsforlaget, 1960, p.303.
2   A short introduction to the genres of the psalter is Claus Westermann, *The Psalms: Structure, Content, and Message*, Minneapolis, Augsburg, 1980.
3   Although 1QS seems to say that the worship of the community is a substitute for sacrificial worship, other Qumran texts such as the Damascus Document, the Temple Scroll and 4QMMT presuppose an audience that engages in animal sacrifice.
4   For a description of the 'Qumran practice' in scribal matters, see Emanuel Tov, *Textual Criticism of the Hebrew Bible*, Minneapolis, Fortress, 1992, pp. 107–11.
5   The call to praise in the imperative mood is characteristic of the hymnic genre (Westermann, op. cit., p. 92).
6   Jer 20:13; cf. 1QH 5:13.
7   cf. Ps 22:24; 1QH 5:20.
8   cf. Ps 34:15: 'The eyes of the Lord are directed toward the righteous, his ears toward their cry'.
9   cf. Dan 9:18.

10   cf. 1QH 7:14.
11   cf. Deut 10:16; 1QpHab 11:13; 1QS 5:5.
12   cf. Ps 6:4; 44:26, etc.; 1QH 2:23.
13   cf. Jer 10:23; Prov 16:9; 1QH 7:25.
14   cf. 1QH 5:12.
15   For 'anger' (^brh) as a flame, see Ezek 22:21, 31; 1QM 14:1.
16   'Fire of his zeal': cf. Ezek 36:5; Zeph 1:18, 3:8; Ps 79:5.
17   Reading [myd bny] \dm.
18   Isa 42:16.
19   'Peace and truth': cf. Jer 33:6.
20   'Their breath by measure (bmdh), he apportioned (tkn) their words by weight
     (bmšql)': These three lines are related in concept and expression to 1QH 1:29–
     30: 'you apportioned (tkn) the fruit of lips ere ever they were; you made . . . the
     expression of lips by measure (bmdh).' Both passages may go back to ancient
     exegesis of Job 28:25: 'when he gave the wind its weight (mšql), and apportioned
     out (tkn) the waters by measure (bmdh)' (NRSV). Echoes of these phrases can
     also be heard in T. Naph. 2:3 and the Hebrew text of Sirach 16:25: 'I will make
     my spirit flow by weight' (\by \^h bmšql ruhy; Syr. \md bmtql\ mly, 'I will
     measure out my words by weight'). See also Leviticus Rabbah 15:2: 'even the
     holy spirit that rests on the prophets is not given except by weight (bmšql) . . .
     even the words of Torah that were given from above were not given except by
     measure (bmdh).'
21   'His heart's path': cf. 1QH 4:21, 24; 6:7; CD 1:11.
22   For the idiom, see Jer 30:21.
23   cf. Job 1:16.
24   Ps 34:7.

SELECTED BIBLIOGRAPHY

Eisenman, R. and Wise, M. O., *The Dead Sea Scrolls Uncovered*, Shaftesbury,
    Element, 1992, pp. 238–40.
García Martínez, F., *The Dead Sea Scrolls Translated: The Qumran Texts in English*,
    trans. W. G. E. Watson, Leiden, E. J. Brill, 1994, p. 436.
Wacholder, B. Z., and Abegg, M. G., *A Preliminary Edition of the Unpublished Dead
    Sea Scrolls, Fascicle 3*, Washington, DC, Biblical Archaeology Society, 1995, pp.
    310–11.

3

APOSTROPHE TO ZION
(11Q PSALMS SCROLL 22:1–15)

Lawrence H. Schiffman

INTRODUCTION

The Hebrew poem translated here has been given the name 'Apostrophe to Zion' by the modern editors of the Dead Sea Scrolls.[1] The rhetorical term 'apostrophe' designates an address to someone not present or to a personified idea. In this case, the poet addresses Jerusalem which he pictures in ideal, almost eschatological terms. This composition is one of a group of poems dealing with Jerusalem which were apparently available to the composers of the sectarian scrolls and which must have been part of the shared literature of the ancient Jewish community.[2]

The example discussed here is the most prominent and the most beautiful exemplar of this genre of poetry found at Qumran. It is difficult to add any comment to this stirring poem which expresses the dreams Jews have had for the city of Jerusalem from the time of King David until the present. Its presence in the liturgically oriented Psalms Scroll shows that the Qumran sect shared in the fundamental Jewish loyalty to the holy city, even though it had withdrawn from participation in the central Temple worship because of disagreements over the conduct of the sacrifices and ritual purity regulations.

The Qumran corpus contains two types of documents loosely termed Psalms Scrolls. In one, all the material is drawn from psalms contained also in the Masoretic Psalter. In the other, both canonical psalms and other poems are included in the same collection. Scholars disagree as to whether this second type of Psalms Scroll is actually a biblical text or not. Those who take these scrolls as actual texts of the book of Psalms see the contents of that book as still not completely fixed at this time – the two centuries BCE when most of the Qumran scrolls were copied. As a result, they maintain that terms such as 'apocryphal' and 'canonical' imply a distinction which was not perceived at Qumran. Others, and we are among them, believe it more likely, however, that the Psalms Scrolls of the second type, containing what from our point of view are apocryphal, non-canonical, compositions, represent liturgical compilations and do not affect our understanding of canon in the Second Temple period.[3]

The Apostrophe to Zion is one of the additional, that is, non-canonical, poems which are found in such expanded Psalms Scrolls. It was first published as part of the edition of the cave 11 Psalms Scroll (11QPs[a]) but is also found in 4Q Psalms[f] as well. The text is virtually complete in the 11Q version, and the 4Q version is much more fragmentary but offers some improved readings.[4]

Literary parallels between our text and other compositions and with the poems which are embedded in the War Scroll[5] indicate that this poem was probably composed before the War Scroll[6] (that is, by the early first century BCE[7]). This would be consonant with the dating of the manuscript of 4Q Psalms[f] to the mid-first century BCE and of the 11Q Psalms Scroll to the early first century CE.[8] Since some time must have elapsed between the composition of this poem and its inclusion in the Psalms Scrolls, we can posit composition by at least the beginning of the first century BCE, but it is possible that the poem reaches back much earlier, even into the Maccabean era. Indeed, there are parallels between this genre of poetry and the poems embedded in 1 Maccabees which were originally composed in Hebrew. Although the links between the Psalms Scroll and the sectarian calendar (11QPs[a] 27:2–11, 'David's Compositions') argue for Qumran sectarian provenance for the scroll as a whole, there is no reason to connect this poem to any particular group of Second Temple Jews.

Content and literary structure

Poems similar to the 'Apostrophe' are found in the Bible in Isa 54:1–8, 60:1–22 and 62:6–8, and these passages have influenced our poem. Some vocabulary is taken from Isa 66:10–11 as well. While the Hebrew of this poem is for the most part that of the Hebrew Bible, it has a distinctively post-biblical flavour. The main themes are that Zion (i.e. Jerusalem) is included in the prayers of those who love her and that these prayers remind God of the promises made to Zion. These promises, it is expected, will be fulfilled in the eschatological era when the city of Jerusalem enjoys her promised glory.

The style of the poem is biblical, and its poetic structure is therefore for the most part composed of bi-cola (two-clause verses) of two three-word units grouped together. Some verses are of tri-cola (three-clause verses) with three units of three words each, and one is a bi-colon of three and four words.

The basic structure is that of an acrostic, with each bi-colon (or in some cases colon) beginning with a successive letter of the Hebrew alphabet. The eighteen-verse poem may be divided into three strophes. Verses 1–6 assure Zion of a future, with children playing in its parks and faithful leading citizens who hope for her redemption. Verses 7–13 refer to Zion's sorrow and promise that God will banish from her violent and sinful people. Verses 14 to the end state that Zion will attain the fulfilment of the prayers said for her by the prophets.[9]

TRANSLATION

I will remember you[10] for a blessing, O Zion,
I have loved you[11] with all my might;[12]
may your memory be blessed for ever!

Great is your hope, O Zion,
that peace and your longed-for salvation will come.

Generation after generation will dwell in you,
and generations of the pious will be your glory.[13]

Those who yearn for the day of your redemption
that they may rejoice[14] in your great glory,

They are nourished from the abundance of your glory,[15]
and in your beautiful squares they promenade.[16]

You will remember the righteous acts of your prophets,
and in the deeds of your pious ones you will glory.

May violence be purged from your midst;
Let falsehood and dishonesty be eradicated from you.

Your children will rejoice[17] in your midst,
and your friends will join together with you.

How much have they hoped for your redemption,
and your pure ones have mourned for you.[18]

Your hope, O Zion, shall not perish,[19]
nor will your longing be forgotten.

Who is it who has ever perished in righteousness;
or who is it that has ever escaped in his iniquity?

A person is tested according to his way(s),
one will be requited according to his deeds.

All around your enemies are cut off, O Zion,
and all those who hate you have scattered.[20]

Praise of you is pleasing,[21] O Zion,
cherished throughout[22] the world.

Many times will I remember you for a blessing;
with all my heart I will bless you.[23]

May you attain everlasting justice,[24]
and may you receive the blessings of magnates.

May you merit the fulfilment of the vision prophesied[25] about you,
the dream[26] of the prophets which was sought[27] for you.

Be exalted[28] and spread far and wide,[29] O Zion,
praise the Most High, your Redeemer;[30]
may my soul rejoice at (the revelation of) your glory!

NOTES

1 J. A. Sanders, *The Psalms Scroll of Qumran Cave 11 (11QPs^a)*, Discoveries in the Judaean Desert (hereafter DJD) 4, Oxford, Clarendon Press, 1965, pp. 43, 85–9; idem, *The Dead Sea Psalms Scroll* (hereafter *DSPS*), Ithaca, NY, Cornell University Press, 1967, pp. 76–7, 123–7; J. Starcky, 'Psaumes apocryphes de la grotte 4 de Qumrân (4QPs^f vii-x)', *RB*, 1966, vol. 73, pp. 353–66. A preliminary translation by Sanders appeared in F. M. Cross, *Scrolls from the Wilderness of the Dead Sea*, San Francisco, American Schools of Oriental Research, 1969, p. 21 and plate 2 (p. 11).

2 Another such poem is to be found in the War Scroll (1QM 12.12–14). For a general discussion of the image of Jerusalem in the Dead Sea Scrolls see L. H. Schiffman, *Reclaiming the Dead Sea Scrolls*, Philadelphia, Jewish Publication Society, 1994, pp. 385–94.

3 In the early stages of the debate, Sanders, 'Cave 11 Surprises and the Question of Canon', *New Directions in Biblical Archaeology*, edited by D. N. Freedman and J. C. Greenfield, Garden City, Doubleday, 1969, pp. 101–30, was led by the differing content and arrangement to argue that the 'canon' of Psalms at Qumran was open-ended and was opposed by S. Talmon, *World of Qumran from Within*, Jerusalem, Magnes, 1989, pp. 244–72 and M. H. Goshen-Gottstein, 'The Psalms Scroll (11QPs^a): A Problem of Canon and Text', *Textus*, 1966, vol. 5, pp. 22–33. For recent discussion, see Schiffman, op. cit., pp. 178–80, and contrast the approach of P. Flint, 'The Psalms Scrolls from the Judaean Desert: Relationships and Textual Affiliations', in G. J. Brooke (ed.) with F. García Martínez, *New Qumran Texts and Studies, Proceedings of the First Meeting of the International Organization for Qumran Studies, Paris 1992*, STDJ 15, Leiden, E. J. Brill, 1994, pp. 31–52.

4 A full list of variants is given in Starcky, op. cit., pp. 359–60.

5 On the poetry in the War Scroll, see B. Nitzan, *Qumran Prayer and Religious Poetry*, trans. J. Chipman, STDJ 12, Leiden, E. J. Brill, 1994, pp. 201–26.

6 cf. especially the Jerusalem poem referred to in n. 2 above. This material is certainly part of an earlier collection as shown by P. R. Davies, *IQM, the War Scroll from Qumran, Its Structure and History*, Rome, Biblical Institute Press, 1977, pp. 91–104, esp. 103. Davies sees these poems as Maccabean in character.

7 The extant manuscripts of the War Scroll have been dated from the last half of the first century BCE to the first half of the first century CE.

8 Starcky, op. cit., p. 355; Sanders, DJD 4, p. 9.

9 Sanders, DJD 4, p. 85; idem, *DSPS*, p. 123.

10 cf. Isa 62:6. But we follow Sanders, *DSPS*, p. 125 n. 1 in reading the *zkwrk* as indicated by the fragmentary 4QPs[f] which reads [\z]*krk*.

11 Alternatively, 'I love you . . .'; cf. Isa 66:10, Ps 122:6. For God's love of Zion, see Ps 78:68, 87:2.

12 cf. Deut 6:5; 2 Kgs 23:25.

13 cf. Isa 62:3.

14 cf. Isa 66:10.

15 cf. Isa 66:11.

16 Literally, 'rattle their bangles'. While this expression has a negative connotation in Isa 3:16 it is positive here.

17 cf. Isa 65:18, 66:10.

18 cf. Isa 66:10. It is possible also to emend *tmyk* to *tmyd*, yielding 'and they have mourned for you always'.

19 cf. Ezek 37:11.

20 cf. Num 10:35, Ps 68:2.

21 Literally, 'pleasing to the nose'. The root ^*rb* is used in the Bible to refer to sacrifices. The notion here is that throughout the world the praise of Jerusalem is cherished by the Jews as incense is pleasing to God (Sanders, *DSPS*, p. 127 n. 20).

22 Sanders, DJD, p. 87, translated, 'ascending through all'. He notes (*DSPS*, p. 127 n. 20) that 4QPs[f] reads *me^al kol tevel*, 'more than the entire world'.

23 4QPs[f] reads, 'Many times will I remember you for a blessing, O Zion, I have [lo]ved you with all my might', but this reading is an error resulting from familiarity with the first verse of the poem (Sanders, *DSPS*, p. 127 n. 21).

24 cf. Dan 9:24 where 'vision' is mentioned as below in the next line.

25 Literally, 'spoken'. 4QPs[f] has 'said'.

26 With 4QPs[f]. 11QPs[a] has 'dreams'.

27 For the usage of the root *b^h* regarding Jerusalem, cf. Isa 21:12. The meaning and grammatical form of this word are uncertain here.

28 cf. Prov 11:11.

29 cf. Isa 54:2.

30 cf. Ps 147:12.

SELECTED BIBLIOGRAPHY

Cross, F. M., *Scrolls from the Wilderness of the Dead Sea*, San Francisco, American Schools of Oriental Research, 1969, pp. 11 (plate 2) and 21.

Sanders, J. A., *The Dead Sea Psalms Scroll*, Ithaca, NY, Cornell University Press, 1967, pp. 76–7, 123–7.

——, *The Psalms Scroll of Qumran Cave 11 (11QPs[a])*, DJD 4, Oxford, Clarendon Press, 1965, pp. 43, 85–9.

Starcky, J., 'Psaumes apocryphes de la grotte 4 de Qumrân (4QPs[f] vii–x)', *RB*, 1966, vol. 73, pp. 353–66.

4

DIBRE HAMME\OROT: PRAYER FOR THE SIXTH DAY (4Q504 1–2 v–vi)

Esther G. Chazon

INTRODUCTION

Dibre Hamme\orot ('Words of the Luminaries') is a collection of prayers for the days of the week, ending with the Sabbath.[1] The six weekday prayers vary from day to day in details of content, but are alike in form and genre. They are all communal supplications motivated by historical recollections. Their basic structure is as follows:

1   Title with date formula, for example, '[Prayer on the] Fourth Day'.
2   Introduction – the opening words, *zekhor \adonay* ('Remember, Lord') formulate a request for God to recall a divine attribute or action.
3   Historical prologue – a lengthy and detailed recitation of specific historical events.
4   Petition – a request for physical deliverance (Tuesday, Wednesday, Friday) or spiritual strengthening in the observance of the Law (Sunday, Thursday).[2]
5   Concluding benediction – a formal benediction praising God for the action requested in the petition.
6   Response – Amen, amen.

Each prayer is an independent, self-contained unit which is tied into a weekly scheme through the chronological progression of the historical reminiscences during the course of the week. This progression begins with the creation of Adam related at the beginning of the prayer for the first day and concludes with the post-exilic troubles described in the prayer for the sixth day translated below. The Sabbath liturgy, which consists of doxological hymns, is not part of the chronological scheme.[3]

The distinction between weekday and Sabbath prayers is one of several features which *Dibre Hamme\orot* shares with the later synagogue liturgy. Others include the use of closing benedictions and the liturgical pattern of petitions for forgiveness, turning from sin, and knowledge of Torah. Supplications generically like the Friday prayer had formerly been recited only *ad hoc* at times of acute distress (cf. Jer 14; Joel 2; 3Macc 2:2–10, 6:2–14). It is a significant shared feature of both *Dibre Hamme\orot* and later Jewish prayer that such petitions are included as a regular liturgy.[4]

The title of the document written on the back of the first column of the scroll (4Q504) probably relates to its liturgical function, with *dibre* referring to the 'words' of the prayers and *hamme\orot*, 'the luminaries', being used as a term for the day, the unit of time for which these prayers are designated (cf. Gen 1:14 and 1QS 10:1–8). Three copies of *Dibre Hamme'orot* (4Q504–506) have survived at Qumran, all in Hebrew. The oldest and most complete manuscript (4Q504) can be dated palaeographically to the middle of the second century BCE. This liturgy is thus likely to have been composed before the settlement at Qumran was founded and belongs to the earlier stratum of the literature of the Dead Sea Scrolls.

The prayer for the sixth day is presented below (unfortunately, the title has not survived). This is the last prayer in the historical scheme of the six weekdays. The final historical period described here, a post-exilic era fraught with 'troubles, blows and trials', probably reflects the author's times and socio-political matrix.

The historical prologue consists of two parallel units which present two consecutive periods according to the same sin–exile–return pattern:

Idolatry–Desolation of the Land–Exile–Repentance–Deliverance from Exile (v 1–17 = lines 2–26 below)
Recent Sin–Punishment (Distress)–Repentance–Atonement (v 17–vi 10 = lines 27–51 below)

Relief from the recent troubles and deliverance from the nations are requested in the petition. Both historical passages draw extensively upon the divine predictions and promises given in Lev 26, while the covenant promises of Deut 30 are quoted in the first part of the prologue and echoed in the petition. This presentation, which casts present suffering and repentance as a repetition of past salvation history and the fulfilment of biblical promises, serves to motivate the petition for deliverance by presenting it as a final step in the divinely ordained process.

TRANSLATION[5]

1 [Remember, Lord . . .][6]
   [. . . They abandoned] the source of living water,[7]
      and worshipped a foreign god in their land.[8]
   Their land was also laid waste for their enemies,

5   because Your rage and Your burning anger
            were poured out in the fire of Your jealousy
            to make it desolate of all passers-by.[9]
        But, in spite of this,
            You did not despise the seed of Jacob
10   and You did not abhor Israel to destroy them utterly
            so as to violate Your covenant with them,
            because You alone are the living God
            and there is none beside You.
        You remembered Your covenant
15   in that You took us out before the nations' eyes,
            and You did not abandon us among the nations.[10]
        You were gracious to Your people, Israel,
            in all the lands to which You banished them
            so that they bethought themselves
20   to return to You and to heed Your command,
            according to all that You commanded them
            through Your servant, Moses.[11]
        For You have poured Your holy spirit upon us[12]
            to bring Your blessings upon us
25   so that we sought You in our distress
            and whispered in the constraint of Your chastisement.[13]

        And we have come into difficult straits, blows and trials[14]
            through the rage of the oppressor
            for we too have tired God with our iniquity,
30   we have caused the Rock to weary with [our] sin;
            but He did [not] weary us
            so that we would profit from walking
            in the way in which [we should walk].
        But we did not obey [Your commandments . . .][15]

35 [You cast aw]ay[16] from us all our transgressions
            and You purified us from our sin for Your sake.
        To You, God, is righteousness[17]
            for You have done all these things.
        Now, today, when our heart is humbled,
40   we have expiated our iniquity
            and the iniquity of our forefathers,
            in our unfaithfulness
            and in that we walked contrarily.[18]
        We did not despise Your trials
45   and our soul did not abhor Your blows
            so as to break Your covenant
            in all the distress of our soul.[19]

For, You who sent our enemies upon us,
    strengthened our heart
50   so that we will recount Your might
    to generations to come.[20]

We entreat You, Lord,
    as You perform wonders from eternity to eternity,
    let Your anger and Your rage be turned back from us,
55   look upon our af[fliction] and our suffering and our oppression,
    deliver Your people from [all] the lands, near and far,
    to which [You have banished them],[21]
    all those written in the book of life.[22]
    [. . .] to serve You and to praise You [. . .][23]
60   from all those who harass them[24]
    [. . .] who cause them to stumble . . .[25]
[Blessed be the Lord]
    who has delivered us from all distress.[26]
    Amen, [amen].

NOTES

1 For the detailed reconstruction and analysis of form, content and function see E.G. Chazon, '4QDIBHAM: Liturgy or Literature', *RevQ*, 1992, vol. 15, pp. 447–55 and ' "Words of the Luminaries" (4QDibHam): A Liturgical Document from Qumran and Its Implications', unpublished Ph.D. thesis, Hebrew University, 1992; forthcoming STDJ 1997.

2 The petition for Monday has not survived.

3 cf. E.G. Chazon, 'On the Special Character of Sabbath Prayer: New Data from Qumran', *Journal of Jewish Music and Liturgy*, 1992–3, vol. 15, pp. 1–21.

4 See Chapter 1, and Chapter 18 on Rabbinic Prayer.

5 The line numeration below is for convenience of reference and does not reflect divisions in the manuscript.

6 The title and opening formula are reconstructed in the lacuna at the end of 4Q504 1–2 iv on the basis of the titles and formulas which have survived for the other days of the week. See Chazon, 'Liturgy or Literature'.

7 The language is reminiscent of Jer 2:13; 17:13.

8 The line describes the sin of idolatry which was perceived as the reason for the Exile and the destruction of the First Temple (cf. Jer 5:19).

9 Zech 7:14, 'I scattered them among all the nations whom they had not known, and the land was left desolate behind them without passers-by.' This is an actualization of the punishment threatened in Lev 26:32–3 (cf. Mic 7:13 and Zeph 3:6–8).

10 A deliberate application of the promise of Lev 26:44–5. The last line has been reworked so that it refers to the deliverance from the Exile (cf. Ezra 9:7–9; Neh 9:30–1).

11 The people's repentance in Exile, which paved the way for the Return to the Land, echoes the covenant promise of Deut 30:1–2.

12 Isa 44:3 applied to repentance and return. Many allusions to Isaiah begin here.

13 A reworking of Isa 26:16 reflecting a distinctive interpretation of this difficult verse, or perhaps a variant reading. Here *lḥš* ('whisper') is rendered as a verb (cf.

1QIsᵃ), and, as in LXX and the Aramaic targum, *ṣaqun*, here rendered 'constraint' (JPSV 'anguish'; NRSV 'they poured out') is taken as a noun parallel to *ṣar* ('distress'). Contrast MT.

14 Description of current troubles. Note the use of the first person plural here as opposed to the third person plural in lines 2–10.

15 Isa 43:22–4 and 48:17–8. There are two possible vocalizations of a key word in the last line: we have translated vocalizing *lo* as suggested by the context of the prayer, but if we vocalize *lu* like MT, the meaning is 'if only we had obeyed'. In any case, this portion of the prayer clearly describes the sin which led to the current troubles and functions as a confession of that sin.

16 I have rendered *wattashlekh* as a past tense, reflecting God's forgiveness as already accomplished, in keeping with the historical mode of this section of the prayer. Alternatively, it could be taken as a simple imperfect (*wetashlekh* = 'may You cast away'), expressing a request for future forgiveness.

17 A formula justifying the divine punishment; cf. Dan 9:7, 14; LXXDan 3:27; Neh 9:33; Tobit 3:2; 1QH xvi 9.

18 Lev 26:40–1 is reworked here to express the worshippers' expiation of their sins upon which their redemption is conditioned.

19 A radical alteration of Lev 26:44–5, which in its original form describes God's long-suffering patience, into a statement about the worshippers' unflinching acceptance of divinely appointed troubles. Compare lines 8–16, 27–8 and see the introduction for the importance of the biblical re-usage here.

20 The promise to recount God's might to future generations is a recurrent theme in the weekday prayers of *Dibre Hamme\orot.*

21 The petition for deliverance appeals to the covenant promise of Deut 30:1–4 (lines 17–21 in the historical prologue). Prayers for the ingathering of the exiles are well documented in Palestinian literature of the Second Temple period: 1Chr 16:35; Ben Sira 36:11; 50:26; 1Macc 1:27; *Pss Sol* 8:28; 1Q34*bis* 2+1; 4Q509 3.

22 cf. Isa 4:3 and Dan 12:1; see also Ps 69:29 and 4Q381 31 8.

23 A promise to praise God when the petition is answered is typical of this type of prayer already in the Bible; cf. Ps 142:8; 106:47 = 1Chr 15:35. At Qumran, cf. 11QPsᵃ xix ('Plea for Deliverance').

24 With the scribal correction, we read *ṣorereihem* ('those who harass them'), but the text before the correction read *ṣore^eihem* (a strange form of the word usually translated 'leprosy' or 'plague') which would be rendered 'from all their plagues'.

25 Reading *hamakhšilim*, but it is also possible that the text is *hamikhšolim* ('the stumbling blocks'). The term refers either to the troubles of the worshippers or to those who caused them.

26 The benediction restates the theme of distress, and offers praise for the deliverance requested in the petition. Note the similarity of the concluding benediction to the rabbinic supplication recited on public fast days, 'Blessed are you, Lord, who answers in time of distress' (*m. Ta^an.* 2:4).

SELECTED BIBLIOGRAPHY

Chazon, E.G., 'Words of the Luminaries' (4QDibHam): A Liturgical Document from Qumran and Its Implications, unpublished Ph.D. thesis, Hebrew University, 1992; forthcoming STDJ 1997.

——, '4QDIBHAM: Liturgy or Literature,' *RevQ*, 1992, vol. 15, pp. 447–55.

——, 'On the Special Character of Sabbath Prayer: New Data from Qumran', *Journal of Jewish Music and Liturgy*, 1992–3, vol. 15, pp. 1–21.

5

SONGS OF THE SABBATH SACRIFICE

Carol A. Newsom

INTRODUCTION

The Songs of the Sabbath Sacrifice is a liturgical cycle of thirteen related compositions. Each of the songs begins with a heading indicating the date of the Sabbath for which it is to be used. The reference in the headings to the Sabbath sacrifice (literally, the 'whole offering') might suggest that the songs were intended as a cultic accompaniment to or even a replacement for the sacrificial offering. If that were the case, however, one would expect a cycle of fifty-two songs, not thirteen.[1] Rather than a cultic function, the Sabbath Songs are better understood in terms of the practice of a type of communal mysticism, specifically a communion with angels in the act of praise. Like certain psalms, the Sabbath Songs open with a call to praise God, addressed to the angels. The body of the song, however, does not record the words of angelic praise but rather describes the angelic priests, and even the heavenly temple, in the act of praise.

The cycle of Sabbath Songs has three distinct sections which differ both in content and style. Songs 1–5, composed in ordinary poetic parallelism, describe God's establishment of angelic priests, their functions and their praise. As far as can be determined, it is only in these initial songs that the human community speaks in the first person and addresses God. Songs 6–8, the central part of the cycle, are strikingly different. The sixth and eighth songs consist largely of repetitious, formulaic accounts of the praises and blessings offered by angels designated as the 'seven chief princes' and the 'seven deputy princes' respectively. The seventh song begins with an elaborately developed sequence of seven calls to praise, addressed to each of the seven angelic priestly councils. Then the song describes how the heavenly temple itself bursts into praise. The third section of the composition, songs 9–13, provides a progressive description of the heavenly temple and the praise uttered by its various parts. This part, and the cycle as a whole, concludes with a description of the divine chariot throne and of the angelic high priests (songs 12–13).

Ten fragmentary copies of the text exist, nine from Qumran and one from Masada. Although the Sabbath Songs were influential within the Qumran community, they do not contain any specifically sectarian characteristics. It is possible that the Sabbath Songs originated in pre-Qumran priestly circles, perhaps related to those responsible for the Book of Jubilees and the Aramaic Testament of Levi.[2]

TRANSLATION

Excerpt from the Song for the Second (?) Sabbath (4Q400 2 1–8)

[. . .] to praise Your glory wondrously with the divine beings of knowledge and the praiseworthiness of Your royal power together with the holiest of the h[oly ones]. They are honoured among all the camps of godlike beings and reverenced by mortal councils, a [wonder] beyond godlike beings and mortals (alike). And they declare His royal splendour according to their knowledge and exalt [. . .] the heavens of His realm. And in all the lofty heights wondrous psalms according to all [. . .] the glory of the King of godlike beings they declare in the habitations where they have their station. But [. . .] how shall we be considered [among] them? And how shall our priesthood (be considered) in their habitations? And our ho[liness . . .] their holiness? [What] is the offering of our mortal tongue (compared) with the knowledge of the heavenly [beings? . . .] our [s]ong, let us exalt the God of knowledge [. . .][3]

The Song for the Sixth Sabbath (composite text from Masada ShirShabb, 4Q403 1 i 1–29, 4Q404 1–2, 4Q405 1–3)[4]

[For the Instructor. Son]g of the sacrifice of the sixth Sabbath on the ninth of the [second] month.
[Praise the G]o[d] of gods, O you inhabitants of the height of heights [. . .] most holy; and exalt His glory [. . .]

(approximately 10 lines missing)

[Psalm of blessing by the tongue of the first chief prince][5] to the [eternal G]od [with its seven wondrous blessings; and he will bless] the Kin[g . . . seven times with seven] words of [wondrous blessing.][6]
[Psalm of magnification by the tongue of the second to the king of] truth and [righteousness with its seven wondrous (songs of) magnification; and he will magnify the God of] all the hea[venly beings . . . seven times with seven words of wondrous] magnification.
[Psalm of exaltation by the tongue] of the third of the chief princes,

29

exalting the God of lofty angels seven times with seven words of wondrous exaltation.

Psalm of praise by the tongue of the fou[rth] to the Warrior who is above all [heavenly beings] with its seven wondrous powers; and he will praise the God of power seven times with seven words of [wondrous] praise.

[Ps]alm of thanksgiving by the tongue of the fifth to the [Ki]ng of glory with its seven wondrous thanksgivings; he will give thanks to the God of glory seven [times with seven words] of wondrous thanksgivings.

[Ps]alm of rejoicing by the tongue of the sixth to the God of goodness with [its] seven [wondrous] songs of joy; [and] he will cry joyously to the King of goodness seven times with [seven words of] wondrous rejoicing.

Psalm of praisesong by the tongue of the seventh of the [chief] princes, a mighty praisesong to the God of holiness with its seven w[on]drous [praisesongs;] and he will sing praise to the King of holiness seven times with [seven wo]rds of wondrous praise[song.]

Seven psalms of His blessings; seven psalms of the magnification [of His . . .], seven psalms of the exaltation of His Kingdom; seven psalms of the [praise of His . . .]; seven psalms of thanksgiving for His wonders; seven psalms of rejoicing in His strength; seven psalms of praise for His holiness [. . .] seven times with seven wondrous words, words of [. . .]

(The sixth Sabbath Song continues with an account of the blessings of the seven chief princes. The seventh chief prince's blessing and the concluding blessing complete the series.)

The [sev]enth among the chief princes will bless in the name of His holiness all the holy ones who establish knowledge with seven words of [His] wondrous holiness; and he will bless all who exalt His statutes with sev[en] wondrous [wor]ds, to be for strong shields; and he will bless all who are app[ointed for] righteous[ness], who praise His glorious kingdom [. . .] forever, with seven wondrous words, for eternal peace.

And all the [chief] princes [will bless togethe]r the godlike hea[ven]ly [beings . . .] all [their] sevenfold appointed testimonies; [and] they will bless those appointed for righteousness; and all the blessed [. . .bles]sed for ever [. . .] to them.

Blessed be the Lord, the K[ing of] all, above all blessing and pr[aise. And he will bless all the holy] ones who bless Him [. . .] in the name of His glory. [And he will] bless all the everlastingly blessed ones.

30

Excerpt from the Song for the Twelfth Sabbath
(4Q405 20ii-21-22 6-14)[7]

For the Instr[uctor. Song of the sacrifice of] the twelfth [Sa]bbath [on the twenty-first of the third month.]
[Praise the God of . . .] wondrous [. . .] and exalt Him before the Glory in the tabern[acle of . . .] knowledge. The cherubim fall before Him and bless. As they rise, the sound of divine stillness [. . .], and there is a tumult of jubilation as their wings lift up, the sound of divine [stillnes]s. The image of the chariot throne do they bless (which is) above the firmament of the cherubim. [And the splendou]r of the luminous firmament do they sing (which is) beneath His glorious seat. And when the wheels move, the holy angels return. They go out from between its glorious [h]ubs. Like the appearance of fire (are) the most holy spirits round about, the appearance of streams of fire like electrum. And there is a radiant substance with glorious colours, wondrously hued, brightly blended, the spirits of living godlike beings which move continuously with the glory of the wondrous chariots. There is a still sound of blessing in the tumult of their movement. And they praise (His) holiness as they return on their paths. As they rise, they rise marvellously; and when they settle, they [stand] still. The sound of glad rejoicing falls silent, and there is a stillness of divine blessing in all the camps of the godlike beings; [and] the sound of prais[es . . .] from between all their divisions on the[ir] si[des . . . and] all their mustered troops rejoice, each o[n]e in [his] stat[ion].

NOTES

1   For contrasting views on this issue see C.A. Newsom, *Songs of the Sabbath Sacrifice: A Critical Edition*, HSS 27, Atlanta, Scholars Press, 1985, pp. 13–21, and J. Maier, 'Shîrê ^Ôlat hash-Shabbat. Some Observations on their Calendric Implications and on their Style', in J. Trebolle Barrera and L. Vegas Montaner (eds), *The Madrid Qumran Congress*, STDJ 11, Leiden, E.J. Brill, 1992, vol. 2, pp. 543–60.

2   See C.A. Newsom, ' "Sectually Explicit" Literature from Qumran', in W. Propp, B. Halpern and D. Freedman (eds), *The Hebrew Bible and Its Interpreters*, Winona Lake, IN, Eisenbrauns, 1990, pp. 167–87 for a discussion of the problems involved in determining the provenance of the Sabbath Songs.

3   This fragment, unfortunately badly broken, contains the only clear first person plural speech in the Sabbath Songs. Despite the reticence of the speaker, the joint praise suggests that the Sabbath Songs are a means of establishing an experience of communion with the angels. Common praise with the angels is an element both of the Jewish synagogue liturgy and of the Christian eucharist.

4   The highly formulaic nature of the sixth Sabbath song makes it possible to restore much of what is not preserved in the manuscripts.

5   The seven 'chief princes' mentioned in the sixth Sabbath song are to be identified with the seven highest ranking angels, sometimes called archangels or

angels of the Presence in other literature (see 1 Enoch 20:1–8; 87:2). In the Sabbath Songs, however, they have specifically priestly functions (cf. T. Levi 3:4–7).

6   In the Sabbath Songs the actual words of the angelic blessing are never revealed; cf., however, Rev 5:12, where a seven-word hymn celebrates 'the Lamb that was slaughtered'.

7   This Sabbath song, describing the praise offered to God by the chariot throne, is formed in large part from an exegetical interpretation of Ezekiel 1 and 10. See C.A. Newsom, 'Merkabah Exegesis in the Qumran Sabbath Shirot', *JJS*, 1987, vol. 38, pp. 11–30 for further discussion.

SELECTED BIBLIOGRAPHY

Maier, J., 'Shîrê ^Ôlat hash-Shabbat. Some Observations on their Calendric Implications and on their Style', in J. Trebolle Barrera and L. Vegas Montaner (eds), *The Madrid Qumran Congress*, STDJ 11, Leiden, E. J. Brill, 1992, vol. 2, pp. 543–60.

Newsom, C. A., *Songs of the Sabbath Sacrifice: A Critical Edition*, HSS 27, Atlanta, Scholars Press, 1985.

——, 'Merkabah Exegesis in the Qumran Sabbath Shirot', *JJS*, 1987, vol. 38, pp. 11–30.

——, ' "He Has Established for Himself Priests": Human and Angelic Priesthood in the Qumran Sabbath Shirot', in L. Schiffman (ed.), *Archaeology and History in the Dead Sea Scrolls*, JSPSupp 8, Sheffield, JSOT Press, 1990, pp. 101–20.

——, ' "Sectually Explicit" Literature from Qumran', in W. Propp, B. Halpern and D. Freedman (eds), *The Hebrew Bible and Its Interpreters*, Winona Lake, IN, Eisenbrauns, 1990, pp. 167–87.

Schiffman, L.H., '*Merkavah* Speculation at Qumran: The 4QSerekh Shirot ^Olat ha-Shabbat', in J. Reinharz et al. (eds), *Mystics, Philosophers and Politicians: Essays in Jewish Intellectual History in Honor of Alexander Altmann*, Duke Monographs in Medieval and Renaissance Studies 5, Durham, NC, Duke University Press, 1982, 15–47.

Schwemer, A., 'Gott als Koenig und seine Koenigsherrschaft in den Sabbatliedern aus Qumran', in M. Hengel and A. Schwemer (eds), *Koenigsherrschaft Gottes und himmlischer Kult im Judentum, Urchristentum und in der hellenistischen Welt*, Tübingen, J.C.B. Mohr (Paul Siebeck), 1991, pp. 45–118.

6

HYMN ON OCCASIONS FOR PRAYER (1QS 10:8b–17)

Moshe J. Bernstein

INTRODUCTION

This prayer is part of the conclusion of 1QS (*Serekh ha-Yaḥad*, often known as the *Community Rule* or *Manual of Discipline*), a work which is a *mélange* of some of the rules and theology of the Qumran sect. The last two columns of this scroll, one of the original seven which were discovered in 1947, differ in their contents from the prose text of the rest of the document. The similarity of the material in this section to that in the *Hodayot* ('Thanksgiving Hymns', 1Q/4QH) has often been noted although significant details prevent us from identifying the 1QS text as merely another representative of *Hodayot*-type poetry. It is clear that these two columns do not constitute a single prayer, and, indeed, the last portion (11:15–22) is introduced by the characteristic 'Blessed are you, my God.' How many separate hymns exist in the entire portion, however, can be debated,[1] and there is not even full agreement as to where the poetic portion begins.[2] The brief section which has been selected for inclusion in this anthology (1QS 10:8b–17) can certainly stand as an independent unit, but it is important to get a sense of its context, particularly its relationship to the preceding segment.

The conclusion of the 'prose' text, 1QS (9:26), asserts that man[3] shall bless God and recite his praises at all times, '[And in distr]ess he shall bless his maker and wheresoever he shall be, he shall recou[nt his mercies with an offering of] (his) lips.' The selection translated here is then preceded by a portion (1QS 10:1-8a) which might be described as a 'Hymn about the Times for Prayer',[4] which gives us insight into how prayer functioned in the overall life of the community. There is an emphasis in this text, not at all unexpected at Qumran, on the regularity and cyclical nature of time, and the author asserts that he will praise God at all times, at regular intervals of the day, the seasons and the years. The Qumran community, as is well known, placed great emphasis on 'time' as is best evidenced from their calendar, the 'perfect' solar calendar of 364 days, 52 weeks, year in and year out. Every significant day of the year fell on the same day of the week each year, and the regularity and flawlessness of the calendar obviously outweighed the fact that it lost slightly more than a day each year and that in thirty years it would be more than a month off from reality. We are therefore unsurprised to find the very regularity of prayer linked with the cycles of time which played such a significant role in the world-view of the sect. If the times indicated in this prayer were actually those at which the group held a fixed liturgy, then the catalogue of times informs us about two very different, but related, phenomena at Qumran: the importance of time and the regularity of prayer. Although it is expressed in the first person singular, the themes presumably reflect the ideology of the larger group.

Certain of the themes in the first hymn are repeated in the one presented here, but the focus in this one is not on the cyclicality of time. The readiness of the author to praise God at fixed intervals is expanded by a list of circumstances, or situations, wherein prayer will be offered. It is tempting, and perhaps even correct, to see parallels between some of the occasions for prayer noted in this poem and situations where rabbinic Judaism demands the recitation of a blessing or a prayer.

This section contains, additionally, more explicit praise of God and submission to His will and His judgement than did the earlier portion. In a series of descriptive terms for God, the author shows how he thought about God as the object of his worship. The poet's declaration that he will constantly praise God, which is a theme occurring frequently in the biblical book of Psalms, is interspersed with enumeration of specific occasions and situations when this praise will take place. This alternation among times for praise, assertions of praise, and submission to God's law and judgement illustrates the complexity which characterizes the post-biblical hymnody as compared with the biblical.

Several fragmentary copies of the *Serekh* survive from Caves 4 and 5 (and are thus known as 4QS[a,b,etc.], 5QS), and some of them preserve fragments of this prayer.[5] The text as it appears in the Cave 1 version, however, is quite sound, and the additional manuscripts offer little in the way of major improvement or correction, although we shall follow their reading against 1QS in at least one instance.

TRANSLATION[6]

(8b) And as long as I live, the statute is engraved on my tongue as a fruit of praise, and the portion of my lips[7] (9) I shall sing with understanding;

All my melody is for the glory of God and I play my lyre[8] in accord with His holy order; and I shall raise the flute of my lips to the tune[9] of His judgement.

(10) With the coming of day and night I shall come into God's covenant[10] and at the going out of evening and morning I shall declare His statutes.[11]

As long as they exist, I shall set (them as) (11) my limit unswervingly;

I shall affirm that He judges me according to my iniquity, and my sin is before my eyes[12] like an engraved statute.

God I call 'My Vindicator',[13] (12) and the Most High 'Preparer[14] of my goodness';

'Source of knowledge' and 'Fountain of holiness'; 'Eminence of glory' and 'Almighty eternal majesty'.[15]

I shall choose what (13) He shall teach me and I shall accept howsoever He judges me;

As soon as[16] I stretch out my hands and feet, I shall bless His name; before going out and entering, (14) sitting down or arising;

And when reclining upon my couch I shall sing joyfully to Him[17] and I shall bless Him with the offering of the utterance of my lips in an assembly[18] of men.

(15) And before I extend my hand to enjoy the pleasures of the world's produce,[19]

At the onset of fear and terror,[20] and in a state of distress and catastrophe, (16) I shall bless Him for His wondrous marvels.[21]

I shall speak[22] about His might and I shall rely upon His kindness all day,

For I know that in His power is the judgement (17) of all living things[23] and that all His deeds are truth.

So at the onset of distress I shall praise Him, and at His deliverance I shall sing out as well.[24]

NOTES

1   Jacob Licht, the author of the most comprehensive commentary to date on 1QS (*The Rule Scroll: A Scroll from the Wilderness of Judaea: 1QS 1QSa 1QSb. Text, Introduction and Commentary* [Hebrew], Jerusalem, Bialik Institute, 1965, p. 202), divides it into four parts, while conceding that there are no other overt signs of division in the manuscript or in the language of the text. He continues, 'Only the logical analysis of the poetic words informs us of the structure of the segment. The segments differ from one another in subject, in poetic style and structure, but the differences are not striking to the reader.' A.R.C. Leaney, *The Rule of Qumran and Its Meaning: Introduction, Translation and Commentary*, Philadelphia, Westminster, 1966, breaks it up into three parts, '10:1–8a Calendar of Worship', '10:8b–11:15a Hymn', and '11:15b–22 Benediction'. A. Dupont-Sommer, *Les Écrits Esséniens découverts près de la Mer morte*, 3rd edition, Paris, Payot, 1968, pp. 112–18 [English version, from the 2nd edition, trans. G. Vermes, *The Essene Writings from Qumran*, repr.

Gloucester, Peter Smith, 1973, pp. 97–103], divides the poem into five parts, and it is his segmentation which we follow in this translation, as we render the second of his five divisions. J. Carmignac, *Les Textes de Qumran Traduits et Annotés*, Paris, Letouzey et Ané, 1961, pp. 70–3, also treats our passage as a unit, calling it 'Résolutions personnelles – Envers Dieu.' The presence of *ḥoq ḥarut*, 'engraved statute', in 10:8b, opening a circle which closes with the same words in 10:11, supports our joining Leaney, Carmignac and others in beginning the prayer with 10:8b rather than 10:9.

2 Thus G. Vermes, *The Dead Sea Scrolls in English*, 4th edition, London, Penguin, 1995, pp. 83–4, prints 10:1–8a as prose (Leaney's 'Calendar') and then begins setting the text as poetry.

3 My employment of masculine forms for the pray-er and the addressee of prayer (God) follows the grammar and convention of the ancient writer.

4 This text is unconnected to a fragment published by E. Qimron, 'Times for Praising God: A Fragment of a Scroll from Qumran (4Q409)', *JQR*, 1989–90, vol. 80, pp. 341–7.

5 One manuscript from Cave 4 (4QSᵉ) apparently did not contain any of the poetic material corresponding to 1QS 10–11 since it seems to continue from the equivalent of 9:26b directly into a calendrical composition called 4QOtot (S. Metso, 'The Primary Results of the Reconstruction of 4QSᵉ', *JJS*, 1993, vol. 44, pp. 306–7).

6 This translation is based on the text of 1QS and 4QS manuscripts in J.H. Charlesworth *et al.* (eds), *The Dead Sea Scrolls: Hebrew, Aramaic and Greek Texts with English Translations. Volume 1: Rule of the Community and Related Documents*, Tübingen/Louisville, J.C.B. Mohr (Paul Siebeck)/Westminster John Knox Press, 1994, pp. 44–5. Material in parentheses has been added to allow the terse diction of the Hebrew poetry to be more comprehensible in English. The original text is not laid out as poetry, and my attempt in that direction should not be taken as prescriptive.

7 The peculiar idioms 'fruit of praise' and 'portion of lips' appear to be analogues of idioms found elsewhere at Qumran. 'Offering of the lips' (*terumat śefatayim*), is found several times in 1QS (cf. below 10:14). At 9:4–5 it is employed in indicating the superiority of prayer to sacrifice. 'Fruit of the lips' (*peri śefatayim*) is found at 1QH 1:28 and appears to be related to the verse in Hos 14:3 (LXX) 'we shall repay the fruit of our lips' (an hypothetical *peri [[mi] śefatenu]*, where MT reads *parim śefatenu*).

8 Reading *akkeh nivli* with at least one, and probably two, Cave 4 manuscripts. 1QS reads 'my lyre-harp (accords with?) his holy order', with no verb expressed, and could very well be original.

9 Lit. 'measuring cord', although in Ps 19:5 *qawwam*, if not emended to *qolam*, seems to have the meaning 'tune' or 'sound', parallel with *millehem*, 'their words'. The use of the term here together with *mišpaṭ*, 'judgment, law' recalls Isaiah 28:17 'I shall make justice the measuring line' and it is possible that both biblical usages lurk behind the poet's choice of the term.

10 It has been suggested that this phrase refers to the twice-daily recital of the *Shemaʿ* (Deut 6:4). If so, the author of this text, like the Rabbis, may interpret Deut 6:7 'you shall speak of them . . . when you lie down and when you arise' as mandating the times for this aspect of worship. See also Josephus, *Ant.* 4.212. Scholars disagree as to whether the phrases 'beginning of day and night' and 'conclusion of evening and morning' refer to the same two prayer times or to four.

11 Note the characteristic juxtaposition of praise and obedience to the laws of God.

12 cf. Psalm 51:5 'For I know my iniquities and my sin is before me always.'

13   Lit., 'my vindication'. This form of the root *ṣdq* is more often rendered 'right-
      eousness'.
14   Reading *mekhin*, but the distinctions between *waw* and *yod* are not always
      certain, and we could read *mekhon*, 'Foundation of'.
15   This string of epithets for God is typical of Qumran prayer literature. Both
      knowledge and sanctity are seen to flow from God.
16   The poet returns to the theme of when to praise God which he continues
      virtually to the end of our selection. There are possible allusions here to
      Deut 6:7: 'You shall teach them to your children and *speak about them when
      you sit in your house and when you walk on the road, when you lie down and
      when you arise.*' The Rabbis of the Mishnah and Talmud saw this language as
      establishing the parameters for the recitation of the *Shema^*. Licht, op. cit., p.
      217, calls our text 'the slightest hint to the recitation of the *Shema^*', while
      pointing out that some of the language is likely to derive from other biblical
      texts such as Ps 121:8 and 139:2. But, regardless of scriptural source, this passage
      would seem to point to fixed times for prayer at the beginning and end of the
      day. Others have attempted to delineate lines of connection between this text
      and rabbinic prayer other than the *Shema^*, such as the *birkhot hašaḥar*
      ('morning benedictions') which are associated with the initiation of physical
      activities, and, although none of these assertions can be proven, it is tempting to
      see commonality of forms of worship in different manifestations of Judaism in
      late antiquity.
17   Perhaps based, as Licht suggests, on Ps 149:5, 'they sing joyfully upon their
      couches'.
18   Lit., 'array'; the phrase might mean 'in public assembly' and allude to public
      prayer, referred to by the Rabbis as *tefillah beṣibbur*. Leaney, op. cit., p. 234
      (following Carmignac and Dupont-Sommer) renders (based on the Hebrew
      idiom *^rk šlḥn* = 'set a table') 'from the table set for my companions'. Although
      I have translated more neutrally, Leaney's very strong reading of the difficult
      mm^rkt or *bm^rkt* fits very well with the following line which apparently deals
      with blessings before consuming food.
19   If this phrase refers to the recitation of a benediction before eating, we have
      another striking similarity between Qumran thought and rabbinic. The Talmud
      (*b. Ber.* 35a) cites R. Akiba, 'A man is forbidden to taste anything before saying
      a blessing over it', and an anonymous tannaitic opinion, 'It is forbidden to a man
      to enjoy anything of this world without a benediction.'
20   In tandem with the preceding, this phrase may indicate man's obligation to
      praise God both when he enjoys life as well as in time of distress. *M. Ber.* 9:5
      reads: 'We recite blessings over evil as we recite them over good.'
21   The Hebrew *bhpl\ mwdh*, with the latter word an alternative Qumran spelling
      of *m\d* = 'very', appears to be confirmed by 4Q^f. Licht, Dupont-Sommer and
      others, however, take it to be a noun or participle from *ydh* = 'giving thanks
      wondrously'.
22   Although often translated 'meditate', the basic meaning of Hebrew *śyḥ* is
      'speak'. In 1QH 11:5, the same idiom ('speak of his might') found here is
      employed in parallelism with *\azammera*, 'I shall sing'. Rabbinic interpretation
      (*b. Ber.* 26b) draws attention to the parallelism between *tefillah* and *śi^ḥ* in
      Ps 102:1, and associates the latter root with prayer.
23   Job 12:10, with 'judgement' replacing 'soul'.
24   This line forms a sort of chiasmus with the earlier one on blessing God whether
      matters are good or bad. This structure enables the section to end on a positive
      note.

7

PRAYERS IN THE APOCRYPHA AND PSEUDEPIGRAPHA

Randall D. Chesnutt and Judith Newman

The Apocrypha is a collection of approximately fifteen ancient Jewish writings not found in the Hebrew Bible but included in the Septuagint, or Greek translation of the Hebrew Bible.[1] These works were written during the last two centuries BCE and the first century CE. Although most were written in Hebrew or Aramaic, they are now fully preserved only in Greek. The works of the Apocrypha represent various overlapping literary genres, including historical narrative, moralistic novels, wisdom writings, liturgical pieces, embellishments of biblical stories, and an epistle. In Roman Catholic tradition most of the apocryphal works are considered authoritative but are called '*deutero*canonical' because their canonicity was not formally declared until very late (the Council of Trent in 1546). Eastern Orthodox churches regard even more of these writings as authoritative. Protestant tradition follows the Jewish exclusion of these books from the canon of scripture, although many Protestant editions of the Bible do print them as a separate section between the Old and New Testaments. In Roman Catholic usage, the term 'Apocrypha' is usually reserved for the works which most others now label 'Pseudepigrapha'.

An amorphous group of additional Jewish and Jewish-Christian texts from antiquity is now usually assembled under the heading 'Old Testament Pseudepigrapha'. Although the term 'pseudepigrapha' literally means writings with a false claim to authorship, relatively few of the works so classified actually make any such claim. What the works in this collection have in common is simply that they are Jewish or Jewish-Christian writings which originated within the last three centuries BCE and the first two centuries CE but which do not fit conveniently into any other collection. Included in this catch-all category are various kinds of apocalyptic works, testaments, embellishments of biblical stories, wisdom and philosophical works, and poetic compositions. Many of these works incorporate earlier materials and have long and complex compositional histories. Some have survived in two or more quite different forms. In these cases it is difficult or impossible to recover the original form of the text and determine its date or provenance. The existence of many Pseudepigrapha in various ancient and medieval languages (often not in the original language) adds to the complexity of tracing the origins of a given work, and even of distinguishing among its Jewish, Christian and non-Judaeo-Christian elements.

Embedded in the works of the Apocrypha and Pseudepigrapha are numerous and diverse prayers, only a small sampling of which are included in this anthology. Among the prayers not included are: the Apocryphal Prayer of Manasseh, a beautiful penitential prayer of fifteen verses which was apparently written to supply the prayer mentioned in 2 Chronicles 33:12–13 in connection with the repentance by the exiled King Manasseh of Judah; the prayers preserved in the Apocryphal Additions to Esther and Additions to Daniel and designed to fit various situations described in the biblical books of Esther and Daniel; prayers preserved in other works which expand biblical narratives (such as those in Jubilees, Baruch, Pseudo-Philo's *Book of Biblical Antiquities*, 4 Baruch, Prayer of Jacob, and Joseph and Aseneth); prayers embedded in various historical narratives and fictional tales (such as those in 1 Maccabees, 2 Maccabees, 3 Maccabees and Tobit); prayers found in wisdom texts (such as the prayer for deliverance and restoration of Israel in Ben Sirach 36:1–7 and Solomon's prayer for wisdom in Wisdom of Solomon 9:1–18); prayers within the context of apocalyptic visions (such as Enoch's prayer for his posterity in 1 Enoch 84, Ezra's prayer for God's mercy toward creation in 4 Ezra 8:20–36, and Baruch's prayers and laments in 2 Baruch); and the synagogal prayers partially preserved in books 7 and 8 of the Christian *Apostolic Constitutions*. Related to these 'prayers' in the strictest sense of the term are numerous psalms and hymns, including both entire works (*Psalms of Solomon, Odes of Solomon*, and the Syriac *Psalms of David*) and hymnic units within larger works (e.g., Ben Sirach 51:1–12; 51:13–30; 39:12–35; 1 Maccabees 3:50–3; Baruch 3:9–5:9; Judith 16:1–17; Wisdom of Solomon, *passim*; Pseudo-Philo's *Book of Biblical Antiquities, passim*; Testament of Job 25:1–7; 32:1–12; 43:4–17; 53:1–4; and Testament of Moses 10:1–10).[2]

The seven prayers from the Apocrypha and Pseudepigrapha which are included in the following pages give only a flavour of the much larger corpus from which they have been selected. In view of the diversity of these prayers and the works in which they appear, generalizations about their form and theology would be hazardous. The reader is referred instead to the entries on the individual prayers. Two matters of general interest about these prayers do call for special comment: (a) the degree to which they provide information about the actual liturgical practice and private devotion of ancient Jews; and (b) their pervasive use of biblical forms, language, motifs and imagery.

RANDALL D. CHESNUTT AND JUDITH NEWMAN

PRAYER PRACTICE AND RITUAL

Were the prayers that we find in the books of the Apocrypha and Pseude-pigrapha actually prayed by Jews in public or private worship? This seems unlikely. The seven prayers included in this anthology are all intimately bound to their narrative contexts and generally play an important role in the progression of the plot. Yet despite their clear composition as stylized literary pieces, the prayers do reveal information about the actual practice of prayer among ancient Jews and about the history of liturgy.

These prayers do not provide explicit information about the origins and development of fixed daily prayer in Judaism, which came to be a prescribed part of Jewish practice only in the second century CE after the synod at Jamnia. Nevertheless, the literary contexts in which the prayers appear probably reflect situations similar to those in which individuals actually offered prayer.[3] Many of the prayers are in the form of petitions offered at times of distress when Israel or a particular person is in need of divine help. Such petitionary prayers often include elements of lament, confession and praise of God. There are also a number of confessions or prayers of penitence in these books (Additions to Esther 14, Prayer of Manasseh, Joseph and Aseneth 12-13). These confessions often have certain ritual acts associated with them, including donning sackcloth, putting ashes on the head, and fasting.[4]

Another feature of prayer evidenced in these books is the distinction between public and private/individual prayer. Public prayer was offered by a priest or other leader in the Temple in an official capacity and on behalf of others. 3 Maccabees 1: 22 refers to the 'varied prayers' of the Jews who were worried that the Temple was about to be desecrated. These 'varied prayers' are set in contrast to the 'lawful prayer' of petition offered by the high priest Simon on behalf of all the people. The 'lawful prayer' represents a standard form for prayers of help and intercession which includes an address or invocation to God, remembrance of God's help in the past, and a petition.[5]

THE SCRIPTURALIZATION OF PRAYER

Perhaps the most striking feature of the prayers in this section is that they are all heavily indebted to scripture. Such 'scripturalization' is a general pattern in the ancient Jewish prayers which have survived. Indeed, it is a sub-category of the much larger developments in Jewish interpretation of scripture during the Greco-Roman period. Jews of this era appealed to scripture in increasingly profound and elaborate ways to define their self-identity and guide various aspects of their lives,[6] including their prayers. Although the beginnings of this trend can be traced within the Hebrew Bible itself, it comes to full flower in the Greco-Roman period. Here we can note only two prominent aspects of this broad trend. One is that prayers include increasingly elaborate and formulaic language for God. The language in certain biblical passages such as Exodus 34:6, which expresses God's mercy and compassion, and Isaiah 6:3, which expresses God's holiness, reappear in many prayers of this period. Both passages are used also in later Jewish and Christian liturgies.[7]

Second, the language of these prayers is full of biblical allusions and citations. Imagery and concepts, as well as specific language, are all heavily influenced by biblical precedents. Many of the prayers also contain midrashic interpretations of the Bible; that is, they contain interpretive motifs that do not appear in the Bible itself. The prayer in Judith 9 contains a phrase from the 'Song of the Sea' in Exodus 15 as well as an interpretation of the Rape of Dinah in Genesis 34. Baruch's prayer in Baruch 54 contains a theological interpretation of the meaning of the Fall; the author wishes to assert that although Adam's original sin (interestingly, Eve is not blamed here) did bring about human mortality, each individual is none the less 'his own Adam', that is, responsible for his or her own sin.

The pervasive use of scripture in prayers indicates that Jews of the Greco-Roman period were very much 'backward looking'. They were interested in retrieving sacred traditions from the past in order to address God in tried and true language, at times even reminding God of divine promises made in the past. This scripturalization of prayer becomes a hallmark of traditional Jewish and Christian liturgies. For this and many other reasons, the prayers in the Apocrypha and Pseudepigrapha deserve much more attention than they have received.

Convenient English translations of the Apocrypha can be found in many versions of the Bible, such as Bruce M. Metzger (ed.), *The New Oxford Annotated Bible with the Apocryphal/Deuterocanonical Books*, New York, Oxford University Press, 1991. The most comprehensive collection of the Pseudepigrapha in English translation is James H. Charlesworth (ed.), *The Old Testament Pseudepigrapha*, 2 vols, Garden City, NY, Doubleday, 1983–5.

NOTES

1 The number varies slightly among different editions, depending on whether certain works are included here or in the Pseudepigrapha and whether some closely related works are combined or counted separately.

2 For more comprehensive lists of the prayers and other liturgical and devotional forms preserved in the Apocrypha and Pseudepigrapha, see James H. Charlesworth, 'A Prolegomenon to a New Study of the Jewish Background of the Hymns and Prayers in the New Testament', *Journal of Jewish Studies* 33, 1982, pp. 265–85; and idem, 'Jewish Hymns, Odes, and Prayers (*ca.* 167 BCE–135 CE)', in Robert A. Kraft and George W. E. Nickelsburg (eds), *Early Judaism and Its Modern Interpreters*, Atlanta, Scholars Press, 1986, pp. 411–36.

3 Scholars disagree on whether or not thrice-daily prayer was common practice during the Second Temple period. From references in the Hebrew Bible, it

would seem that some pious Jews prayed three times a day in the direction of Jerusalem at least by the early second century BCE (Dan 6:10–13; Psalm 55:17) and that these times were connected to the time of sacrifice (Ezra 9:5, Dan 9:20, Jdt 9:1, Luke 1:10). On this point, see for instance Joseph Heinemann, *Prayer in the Talmud: Forms and Patterns*, Studia Judaica, vol. 9; Berlin, deGruyter, 1977, pp. 13–14. Others have argued that these biblical references refer to occasional, private prayer and cannot be understood to represent a universal practice of prescribed prayer. Ezra Fleischer, 'On the Beginnings of Obligatory Jewish Prayer', *Tarbiz* 59, 1990, pp. 397–441 (in Hebrew), argues that fixed daily prayer was not instituted until after the destruction of the Second Temple.

4   See also the biblical precedents for this in the confessions of Dan 6:10 and Ezra 9:5.

5   For the origins of these elements in prayers of the Hebrew Bible, see Appendix I, 'A Structural Outline of Prayers for Help and Intercession in Prose Texts', in Patrick D. Miller, *They Cried to the Lord: The Form and Theology of Biblical Prayer*, Minneapolis, Fortress, 1994, pp. 337–57.

6   For a good general introduction to this phenomenon, see James L. Kugel and Rowan A. Greer, *Early Biblical Interpretation*, LEC 3, Philadelphia, Westminster Press, 1986.

7   Isaiah 6:3 is redeployed in the Qedushah, a part of the Amidah, the Jewish statutory prayer. The Qedushah, also known as the Sanctus or Trishagion, was adopted for use in Christian eucharistic liturgies from an early date. For more on the later use of Isaiah 6 in Jewish and Christian liturgies, see David Flusser, 'Sanktus und Gloria', in O. Betz, M. Hengel and P. Schmidt (eds), *Abraham Unser Vater: Juden und Christen im Gespräch über die Bibel*, Otto Michel Festschrift, Leiden, E. J. Brill, 1963.

8

IN MISERY, TOBIT PRAYS FOR DEATH (3:1–6)[1]

Carey A. Moore

INTRODUCTION

The Book of Tobit tells the story of a pious and well-to-do Naphtalite who was exiled in Nineveh. There he experienced blindness and poverty as the direct result of his performing one of his most characteristic good deeds: burying the dead. Thanks to the courageous efforts of his son Tobiah, who was assisted by the angel Raphael, Tobit not only recovered his sight and fortune but also gained a virtuous daughter-in-law, Sarah, a wealthy Ecbatanian relative from whom Tobiah exorcized the demon Asmodeus. (Asmodeus had claimed the life of each of her seven previous husbands on their wedding night.)

Although the book has all the outer trappings of an historical account, the story is fictitious: a diaspora romance centring on a successful quest. A pastiche consisting of three well-known Near Eastern folktales,[2] the designs and colours of Tobit are also distinctly biblical, patterned as they are after the betrothal stories of Isaac and Jacob (Genesis 24 and 29), the theology of Deuteronomy and the model of Job.

The discovery at Qumran of four Aramaic texts of Tobit (designated as 4QTob[a,b,c,d]) and one Hebrew (4QTob[e]) has resolved some of the Tobit problems of lower and higher criticism debated over the last 150 years. Thanks to the excellent *editio princeps* of Tobit by Fitzmyer (1995), it is now certain that the Greek text of Tobit had a Semitic *Vorlage*. But whether that *Vorlage* was Hebrew or Aramaic is still debatable, although the evidence tends to favour the latter. The matter, however, is complicated.[3] Of the two Greek text attestations of Tobit, G[I] and G[II], G[II] better represents a Semitic text; however, as the prayer of Tobit in 3:1–6 shows (as do other portions of the book), G[I] *does* sometimes preserve the more original reading.[4]

Why Tobit was never regarded as canonical by Jews is unknown. The presence of a Semitic version of Tobit at Qumran, which dates to at least the late second century BCE, refutes the old arguments that the book was rejected because either it had originally been composed in Greek or had been written too late. Among Christians, Tobit received a mixed reception. In the Eastern Church, it was regarded as canonical by Clement of Alexandria, John Chrysostom and Junilius; but many more rejected it. In the west, however, Tobit was virtually always regarded as canonical, Hippolytus of Rome being the first to refer to Tobit as such.

The four prayers in Tobit (two by Tobit [3:1–6; 13:1–17], and one each by Sarah [3:11–15] and Tobiah [8:5–8]) play a major role in the Book of Tobit; for prayer is a principal means of expressing the author's theology as well as a major way of advancing the plot.[5] Of course, this is not peculiar to the prayers in Tobit; for in the Apocrypha, in the absence of the prophets who could proclaim 'Thus says the Lord', the prayers of believers were a major literary vehicle for expressing the truths of the faith and future of Judaism.

Although a portion of Tobit's prayer is preserved in both the Aramaic and Hebrew texts of Qumran (namely, vv. 5–6),[6] they are so fragmentary that the following English translation must be based upon G[II].

The prayer is divided into three distinct parts: 1) the doxology (v. 2); 2) Tobit's recognition of his sins and those of his ancestors as well as their deserved punishment (vv. 3–5); and 3) his fervent petition to be released from his suffering, probably through death (v. 6). There is no formulaic conclusion.

The prayer's models are like those found in Ezra 9:6–15; Neh 1:5–11; 9:6–38; Dan 9:4–19; and Bar 1–3. Its basic theology, especially in vv. 2–5, is deuteronomistic, i.e., 'Do good and prosper; do evil and be punished' (see Deut 7:12–16; 28:1–30:20; Judg 2:11–15).

True character, it is said, is what a person says and does when no one else is around. If so, then Tobit is a good and faithful man who is at his wits' end. Tobit makes no exalted claims for himself. Instead, he seeks only relief from his emotional and psychological anguish. While Tobit's blindness and poverty are the long-term causes of his depression, the immediate reason for his anguish is his wife's biting retort (2:14) after Tobit had, quite unfairly, accused her of stealing from her employers. Hannah's accusations had been the last straw. He has abandoned any hope of a good death as defined, for example, in Qoh 6:3, that is, many children, a long life, wealth, and a decent burial.

The doxology's emphasis on mercy (v. 2), as well as such petitions as 'remember me' and 'look favourably upon me' (v. 3) and 'Lord, do not turn your face from me' (v. 6) express what Deselaers calls 'a glimmer of hope'.[7] Tobit's petition in v. 6 is admittedly inconsistent, alternating as it does between hope and despair: 'deal with me as you please . . . it is better for me to die . . . Lord, do not turn your face from me . . . it is better for me to die.'

The narrator's primary concern here, as elsewhere, was to tell a tale that would keep the reader's interest by providing him or her with insight into the character and theology of Tobit and to move the story along. For the first-time reader unfamiliar with the tale, Tobit's prayer immediately raises the question: 'What's going to happen to Tobit now?'[8]

TRANSLATION

1 Deeply depressed,[9] I sobbed; and with groaning I began to pray.[10]

2 You are righteous, Lord;[11]
And all your doings are just;
All your ways are merciful and true;[12]
You are the judge of the world.

3 Therefore, Lord,[13] remember me
And look favourably upon me.
Do not punish me for my sins and oversights[14]
And for those of my ancestors.
They sinned against you,[15]

4 And disobeyed[16] your commandments.
So you gave us over for spoil, exile, and death,
To become the talk, a byword,[17] and the object of reproach
Of all the nations among whom you have scattered us.

5 Therefore, your many judgements are true
In dealing with me concerning my sins and those of my ancestors.[18]
For we have not kept your commandments
Nor walked the paths of truth before you.

6 So now, deal with me as you please.
Command that my life be taken from me[19]
So that I may be released from the face of the earth[20] and become dust.
For it is better for me to die than to live[21]
Because I have to hear undeserved insults,
And I am overwhelmed with grief.
Command, Lord,[22] that I may be free from this suffering.
Release me to the eternal resting-place![23]
Lord[24], do not turn your face from me![25]
For it is better for me to die
Than to endure such great distress in my life,
Than to hear such insults.[26]

NOTES

1 My translation of the Greek is taken from my Anchor Bible commentary, *Tobit* (1996), and is used with the permission of Bantam Doubleday Dell Publishing Group, Inc. of New York.

2 The Tale of the Grateful Dead, The Monster in the Bridal Chamber and the Ahiqar Tale. The last-named, known from a fifth-century BCE Aramaic papyrus from Elephantine, Egypt, is the story of a wise man who, though betrayed by his adopted son, is ultimately vindicated.

3 On the one hand, G^II (the Greek text used here) better represents a Semitic text than does G^I (the Greek text used by the King James Bible and the RSV). G^II is represented by LXX^S (MSS 319 and 910 also preserve portions of it). G^I is the Greek version attested to by LXX^BAN and many minuscules, as well as all the ancient versions except the *Vetus Latina* (and Vulgate). However, most recent translations have used G^II, including the JB (1966), the NAB (1970), the NEB (1971) and the NRSV (1989). On the other hand, the *Vorlage* of G^II appears to be a Hebrew text rather than an Aramaic one (Moore 1996: 57–60).

4 Inasmuch as Jerome based his translation on an Aramaic text which was *orally* translated for him into Hebrew by a Jewish Aramaist, the Vulgate is of little help in interpreting the Greek text of Tobit. Evidently, that Aramaic text was quite different from the Greek. The Old Latin of Tobit, which Jerome also used, much more resembles G^II than G^I.

5 For a more thorough discussion of this issue, see the doctoral dissertation of P.J. Griffin, 1984.

6 Verse 5 of 4QTob^a (frg. 5, line 1) has *l]m^cbd by*, 'to deal with me'; and v.6 of 4QTob^b (frg. 1, line 1) has *m[n dylm[hzh*, 'th]an to se[e'. Verse 6 in 4QTob^c has four lines, but, unfortunately, they are just as imperfectly preserved as the above; see frg. 1 i in '200. 4QTob^e' (Fitzmyer 1995: 1).

7 Deselaers 1982: 82.

8 For a much more detailed treatment of Tobit's prayer, with special emphasis on word study, see Griffin 1984.

9 OL adds 'I entered my courtyard [*atrium* (cf. v.17 of LXX and OL where Tobit leaves the *atrium*)].'

10 Here, as elsewhere in Tobit (3:11–15; 8:4–8, 15–17; 13:1–17), major turning points in events are foreshadowed by someone praying. Such a literary technique is also found in Jdt 9:1–14; 12:4-9; Addition C[= 14]:1–11, 12–30 of the Greek Esther; and 1 Macc 7:37–38.

11 Given Tobit's present circumstances, this doxology here at the beginning of Tobit's prayer and in v. 5 is most ironic.
   Lord: In his prayer Tobit uses only God's personal name (vv. 3, 6[*bis*]). Elsewhere Tobit (both as character and narrator) uses a variety of terms for the Deity.

12 *merciful [eleēmosunē] and true [alētheia]*; cf. Ps 24[MT 25]:10 of the LXX; also Deut 32:4. Elsewhere in Tobit *eleēmosunē* designates a human virtue or an outward expression of it.

13 G^I omits 'Therefore, Lord'.

14 *oversights [agnoēmasin]*; cf. Gen 43:12 of the LXX. Although most modern translations emphasize here the absence of intentionality (so JB, GNB, NAB and NRSV), this error of ignorance (OL *negligentia*) is indeed grievous (cf. Jdt 5:20, where Achior says that *agnoēma* can lead to *skandalon*, 'an offence' deserving of the total destruction of Jerusalem).

15 That is, Tobit's ancestors. Were it not for vv. 4 and 5 where Tobit includes himself among the sinners, he could be accused here of self-righteousness, that is, blaming his exile on others (cf. Ezek 18:2b).

16 So G^I [*parēkousan*] and OL; LXX^S 'I disobeyed'. The reading of G^I has been adopted here to keep it consistent with the other plural forms in this verse and the next.

17 G^I omits.
18 G^I and OL read 'and those of my ancestors'. A willingness to be identified (and even punished) with one's Jewish compatriots is a characteristic feature of post-exilic piety (cf. Isa 59:12, Ezra 9:6–7, Neh 1:6, Dan 9:4–19 and Bar 1–3).
19 G^I omits 'from me'.
20 G^I omits 'from the face of the earth'.
21 Cf. a similar conclusion in Job 7:15, 1 Kings 19:4 (by Elijah) and Jonah 4:3; cf. also Sirach 30:17 ('Death is better than a life of misery, and eternal sleep than chronic sickness').
22 G^I omits.
23 *the eternal resting-place.* Literally 'to the eternal place' (cf. Qoh 12:5). In keeping with the deuteronomistic character of the book, Tobit has no hope of rewards or punishment except in *this* life – all of which makes Tobit's present plight seem all the more tragic. The reference here is either to the grave *per se* (Job 21:26, 34:15; Ps 104:29; Qoh 3:20) or to Sheol (= Gk 'Hades'), a place of no return (cf. Job 7:9–10, 14:12; Pss 30:9, 88:10–12; Isa 14:15, 26:14; Ezek 26:20). Unfortunately, the Hebrew word here is not preserved by 4QTob^c. Hades *is* mentioned, by name, in Tob 3:10 and 13:2.
24 G^I omits.
25 This idiom can refer either to God's indifference toward someone (Pss 13:1; 22:24; 27:9; 30:7; 44:24) or to his anger (Deut 31:17–18, 32:20; Ps 88:14; Mic 3:4).
26 G^I omits 'For it is better for me to die . . . than to hear such insults.'

SELECTED BIBLIOGRAPHY

Dancy, J. C., 'Tobit', *The Shorter Books of the Apocrypha*, Cambridge Bible Commentary, Cambridge University Press, 1972.
Deselaers, P., *Das Buch Tobit*, Freiburg Schweiz/Göttingen, Vandenhoeck & Ruprecht, 1982.
Fitzmyer, J. A., 'Tobit', in Magen Broshi *et al.* (eds), *Discoveries in the Judean Desert*, vol. XIX (*Qumran Cave 4. xiv*), Oxford, Oxford University Press, 1995.
Griffin, P. J., 'The Theology and Function of Prayer in the Book of Tobit', doctoral dissertation, Catholic University of America, Washington DC, 1984.
Hanhart, R., *Tobit*, Septuaginta, GTV 8/5, Göttingen, Vandenhoeck & Ruprecht, 1983.
—— *Text und Textgeschichte des Buches Tobit*, MSU 17, Göttingen, Vandenhoeck & Ruprecht, 1984.
Moore, C. A., 'Scholarly Issues in the Book of Tobit Before Qumran and After: An Assessment', *Journal for the Study of the Pseudepigrapha*, vol. 5, 1989, pp. 65–81.
—— 'Tobit, Book of', *Anchor Bible Dictionary*, New York, Doubleday, 1992, vol. 6, pp. 585–94.
—— *Tobit: A New Translation with Introduction and Commentary*, Anchor Bible 40A, New York, Doubleday, 1996.
Nickelsburg, G. W. E., 'Tobit', *Harper's Bible Commentary*, ed. James L. Mays, New York, Harper & Row, 1988, pp. 791–803.
Nowell, I., 'The Book of Tobit: Narrative Technique and Theology', Ph.D. dissertation, the Catholic University of America, 1983. Ann Arbor, MI, University Microfilms International, No. 8314894.
Zimmermann, F., *The Book of Tobit*, Dropsie College Edition, Jewish Apocryphal Literature, New York, Harper & Brothers, 1958.

9

GOD CONDEMNS THE ARROGANCE OF POWER: THE PRAYER IN 3 MACCABEES 6:2–15

Judith Newman

INTRODUCTION

The book of 3 Maccabees is misnamed because it does not concern the Maccabees at all, but rather the period of Ptolemaic rule in the late third century BCE some fifty years before the desecration of the Jerusalem Temple by Antiochus IV Epiphanes and the rise of the Hasmoneans. The book combines two reworked legends. The first (chapters 1–2) takes place largely in Palestine and describes the supposed threat to the Jerusalem Temple by Ptolemy IV Philopater (221–203 BCE). The setting for the second (chapters 3–7) is Egypt during a time in which the Jews are being persecuted by the king for their refusal to abandon the Torah and its dictates. Each of the two parts of the book contains a long prayer coming at a climax of the narrative action.

Date and provenance

3 Maccabees is generally held to date from the late second or early first century BCE. The earliest possible date of the book's composition can be inferred from the reference in 3 Macc 6:6 to the Greek Additions to Daniel, which would of course date sometime after Daniel's composition, *c.* 165 BCE. Similarities in style and vocabulary among 2 Maccabees, the Letter of Aristeas, and 3 Maccabees also suggest a second-century date. It is hard to know how widely the book was circulated. The book and this prayer seem to have had little, if any, lasting influence because to all religious communities except the Eastern Orthodox, the book is considered apocryphal.[1]

Almost certainly composed in Greek, 3 Maccabees is contained in some of the manuscripts of the Greek Septuagint (Alexandrinus and Venetus, but not Vaticanus or Sinaiticus) and also in expanded form in the Syriac Peshitta, but the book does not appear in the Latin Vulgate. The style of Greek employed in the prayer, as well as its use of classical Greek rhetorical forms and biblical allusions, suggest that the author was a well-educated member of diaspora Jewry, perhaps from Alexandria. Although the narrative parts of the book were written in an elevated style and exhibit a thorough Hellenization, the book as a whole and its two long prayers show an intimate knowledge of scripture and traditional biblical interpretation.

The circumstances that prompted the prayer in 3 Maccabees 6:2–15 are dramatic and undoubtedly reflect artistic licence on the part of the author. Ptolemy IV Philopater has rounded up all the Jews in Egypt to kill them for their unwillingness to join the cult of Dionysus.[2] They are herded to a great hippodrome not far from Alexandria and are about to be trampled to death by 500 elephants that have been drugged with wine and frankincense. A leading priest among the Jews, Eleazar, orders all the elders to cease from their petitions and he offers a formal prayer. In response, God 'shows his holy face' by sending two angels, visible to all except the Jews (3 Macc 6:18), and as a result the elephants turn on the Greek troops. This startling turn of events causes the king to have a change of heart. He releases the Jews and provides them with everything necessary for a seven-day feast.

Literary style and theology

Unlike other prayers embedded in narratives (e.g., 1 Samuel 2), this prayer is intimately tied to its context and written in the same florid Greek style, with strong similarities to the prayer in 3 Maccabees 2, which suggest it was not originally used in public or private worship, but was composed deliberately for narrative effect. The purpose of the prayer, and indeed the book itself, was to bolster the morale of Jews in the diaspora who lived frequently under the threat of persecution.

The author's use of biblical characters as examples of virtue and vice in 3 Macc 6:4–8 reflects the borrowing of a Greek rhetorical device.[3] The author uses them to illustrate not only the punishments God has brought upon arrogant rulers (Pharaoh and Sennacherib), but also the ways God has helped Israelites living among foreigners in the past (the three men, Daniel, Jonah). The common element governing the choice of all of these 'exempla' is the dire condition of Israelites/Jews among foreigners, a circumstance in which the Jews in this story found themselves anew.

The essential theology of the prayer is that God is the omnipotent and just ruler of the world who will safeguard Israel from its arrogant enemies throughout history. This theology is clear both from the divine epithets employed and from the divine actions in history described in the exempla list. God is first addressed as 'King of Great Power' in contradistinction to the abuse of great power wielded by the arrogant human rulers Pharaoh,

Sennacherib, and more immediately, Ptolemy Philopater.[4] Verse 9 contains both the petition for help and a capsule summary of the theology of the prayer as a whole. The divine epithets in the prayer display a three-fold emphasis on divine omnipotence, compassion and dislike of arrogance.

The prayer's use of the title 'Father' to address God (6:3, 4, 8) is notable.[5] This epithet summons up the Jews' special relationship to God, and emphasizes God's mercy, as one who cares for the Jews like a parent. God's compassionate character is connected specifically with this parent metaphor in verse 4. God is referred to as 'Father' several times throughout the book, most significantly by King Ptolemy Philopater himself (3 Macc 7:6) when he states that God protects the Jews, 'like a father with his children'. Coming as it does after the episode in the hippodrome, Ptolemy's affirmation under-scores the larger point in the narrative, that Israel's God is omnipotent and will protect pious Jews wherever they may find themselves, which will in turn cause the gentiles to recognize the supreme power of the God of Israel.

TRANSLATION

(2) King of Great Power, Most High, Almighty God, who governs all creation in compassion. (3) Look upon the seed of Abraham, upon the children of the holy Jacob, the people of your holy inheritance in a strange land, who are unjustly perishing, Father.[6]

(4) O Father, when Pharaoh, the former ruler of this Egypt, exalted by lawless arrogance and boastful tongue, was increasing his chariots, you destroyed him in the engulfing sea along with his arrogant army and you manifested mercy to the people of Israel. (5) When Sennacherib the fierce king of the Assyrians, priding himself with his innumerable soldiers, had already seized the whole world by the sword and was lifted up against your holy city speaking in boasting and arrogance, you broke him in pieces, plainly showing to many people your might. (6) When the three companions in Babylonia voluntarily gave up their lives to the fire in order not to serve vain idols, you moistened the fiery furnace and delivered them from the flame even to their hair and sent flames on all their enemies.[7] (7) When on account of slanderous judgements, Daniel was cast below the ground as food for wild beasts, you brought him up to the light unscathed.[8] (8) When Jonah was languishing ignored in the maw of the sea monster from the depths, you revealed him unharmed to all the members of his household, O Father.[9] (9) And now, O hater of hubris, all merciful, protector[10] of all, quickly manifest yourself to the people of Israel who are being outrageously treated by the lawless and arrogant gentiles. (10) And if our life has become ensnared by impiety during our foreign sojourn, rescue us from the hand of hostile forces, O Lord, and destroy us by a fate of your choosing. (11) Do not let the ones who think empty

thoughts bless vain idols for the destruction of your beloved people saying, 'Their God cannot save them.' (12) But you, who have all strength and all power, O Eternal, now watch over us and show mercy to us who are being deprived of life as treasonous plotters because of the unreasoning hubris of the lawless. (13) Let the gentiles fear your invincible power this very day, O Esteemed One, who has power for the salvation of the people of Jacob. (14) The whole multitude of infants and their parents beseech you with weeping. (15) Make known to all the nations that you are with us, O Lord, and do not turn your face from us, but just as you said, 'Not even in the land of their enemies have I in truth disregarded them'; so accomplish it, Lord.[11]

NOTES

1 H. Anderson, '3 Maccabees', in J. H. Charlesworth (ed.), *The Old Testament Pseudepigrapha* Garden City, NY, Doubleday, 1985, vol. 2, p. 516.

2 3 Macc 2:30 mentions that as part of Ptolemy's census, the Jews were to be 'branded by fire on their bodies with an ivy leaf, the emblem of Dionysus'. For a description of the Dionysus cult, consult Marvin Meyer (ed.), *The Ancient Mysteries: A Sourcebook*, San Francisco, Harper, 1987, pp. 61–110.

3 cf. also such exempla lists in 3 Macc 2, Sir 16, 1 Macc 2:49–64 and Wis 10:1–21. See a discussion of this Greek rhetorical feature in Devorah Dimant, 'Use and Interpretation of Mikra in the Apocrypha and Pseudepigrapha', in M. J. Mulder (ed.), *Mikra: Text, Translation, Reading and Interpretation of the Hebrew Bible in Ancient Judaism and Early Christianity*, Compendia Rerum Iudaicarum ad Novum Testamentum, Assen, Van Gorcum/Philadelphia, Fortress, 1990, pp. 391–5.

4 The theme of divine punishment of arrogant rulers is also central in the prayer of 3 Macc 2:2–20. Human arrogance is frequently condemned in the Hebrew Bible (Pss 31:18, 94:4; Prov 16:5, 18:12; Isa 2:11-17, 5:15). The arrogance of human rulers in attempting to upstage the kingship of God is considered even more of an abomination (2 Kgs 19: 22–8; Isa 10:12, 13:11; Add Esth 4:22–4; Sir 9:17–10:18, 48:18; Jdt 9:9–10; 2 Macc 9:4–11).

5 For more on God as 'Father', see the entry *'pater'* in Gerhard Kittel (ed.), *Theological Dictionary of the New Testament*, vol. V (English translation), Grand Rapids, MI, Eerdmans, 1967; and James H. Charlesworth, 'A Caveat on Textual Transmission and the Meaning of *abba'*, in *The Lord's Prayer and Other Prayer Texts from the Greco-Roman Era*, Valley Forge, PA, Trinity Press International, 1994, pp. 1–27.

6 Three other Second Temple prayers address God as 'Father'; Isaiah 63:16, Ben Sira 51:10 and the recently published 4Q372, the Prayer of Joseph. For a discussion of the Qumran fragment, see E.M. Schuller, 'The Psalm of 4Q372 1 within the Context of Second Temple Prayer', *Catholic Biblical Quarterly*, 54, 1992, pp. 67–79.

7 This is a reference to Shadrach, Meshach and Abednego in Daniel 3. God's 'moistening' of the furnace seems to derive from Additions to Daniel 1:27 or 3:50 (LXX) in which the same Greek word is used. So, too, the interpretive elaboration found in verse six that their enemies were punished by the same flames that threatened to consume the three companions derives from Additions to Daniel 1: 24–5 or 3: 47–8 (LXX).

8 Daniel 6.
9 Jonah 2. Jonah's restoration to his family is not contained in the biblical account, but compare the account in *Lives of the Prophets* 10 in which he returns to his district after the fish spews him out and his mother accompanies him on his subsequent travels.
10 Alexandrinus reads *dikasta*, or 'judge'.
11 The statement quoted is almost an exact reproduction of the divine promise in Leviticus 26:44. Quotations of divine speech from scripture, especially divine promises, is a common literary device in many apocryphal and pseudepigraphical prayers.

SELECTED BIBLIOGRAPHY

Anderson, H., '3 Maccabees', in J. H. Charlesworth (ed.), *The Old Testament Pseudepigrapha*, vol. 2, Garden City, NY, Doubleday, 1985, pp. 509–29.
Emmet, C.W., 'The Third Book of Maccabees', in R. H. Charles (ed.), *Apocrypha and Pseudepigrapha of the Old Testament*, New York, Oxford, Clarendon Press, 1913, vol. 1, pp. 155–73.
Hadas, Moses, *The Third and Fourth Books of Maccabees*, New York, Ktav, 1976 reprint of New York, Harper & Brothers, 1953.
Rahlfs, A., *Septuaginta*, vol. 1, Stuttgart, Deutsche Bibelgesellschaft, 1935.

10

PRAYER OF NOAH: JUBILEES 10:3–6

John C. Endres, S.J.

INTRODUCTION

In the Book of Jubilees there is a remarkable prayer in which Noah prays to God to preserve him and his descendants from the influence and the power of the evil spirits, known as the Watchers. Known from old traditions about Enoch (now found in the Books of Enoch), these Watchers were fathered through the offspring of the improper sexual unions between divine beings and human women, described in Genesis 6:1–4 (with parallels in 1 Enoch 15:8–16:1 and in Jubilees 10:1–2, 8–11). In this prayer Noah reminds God of the pattern of divine mercy already shown to the patriarch's offspring and then he implies that God should live up to that image in the present generation. Specifically, he wants God to neutralize the power of evil spirits and even to imprison them; he also prays that God bless his sons that they might continue to populate the earth and may not be corrupted, as the Watchers were before them.

The Book of Jubilees contains a retelling of the story of Israel's origins, paralleling the Book of Genesis and the early chapters of Exodus. It presents an adapted version of the stories of the creation, the patriarchs and matriarchs, and Moses' life in Egypt. Jubilees expands the biblical version in several ways, often including rationales for Israel's festivals and laws in events before the revelation at Sinai. This author also composed some prayers for important biblical personages, which amplify one Jewish view of these figures and their theology of prayer. Written in the second century BC, probably between 170 and 140 BC,[1] this Palestinian work provides an important witness to early biblical interpretation, especially by its inclusion of prayer texts.

Attestation

The Book of Jubilees is attested in Hebrew, Greek, Syriac, Latin and Ethiopic manuscripts, though the complete text appears only in Ethiopic versions. Prior to the discovery of the Dead Sea Scrolls many thought that Jubilees was written in Hebrew, and the remnants of fourteen or fifteen Hebrew manuscripts of Jubilees found at Qumran made a Hebrew original much more likely.

The Prayer of Noah (10:3–6) is attested only in Ethiopic manuscripts, since the extant portions of other versions do not contain this section of the text. There are also allusions to Noah's actions (in ch. 10 of Jubilees) in George Syncellus' *Chronographica*, but there is no trace of the prayer text.

Three editions of Ethiopic Jubilees have appeared:

(1) August Dillmann (1859), based on 2 MSS (38 and 51);
(2) R. H. Charles (1895), based on Dillmann's MSS 38 (D, d) and 51 (C, c) plus 2 additional MSS 12 (A, a) and 25 (B, b), which he favoured;
(3) James VanderKam (1989) based on a collation of 15 MSS (9, 12, 17, 20, 21, 25, 35, 38, 39, 42, 44, 47, 48, 58, 63), with special preference given to MS 25 (= B in Charles). This translation relies on the critical edition of VanderKam (1989).

Sources of this prayer

Jubilees 10:1–17 incorporates traditions which probably developed parallel to those in the Bible but which were not directly derived from the Genesis account of Noah. R. H. Charles claimed that much of the narrative surrounding this prayer developed from an ancient book, the Book of Noah.[2] Some contemporary scholars agree, based on analysis of fragments of several manuscripts at Qumran about Noah.[3] Although there are remnants of this hypothetical book in a Hebrew text[4] as well as in a Greek version,[5] neither of them contains a prayer text as we have it in Jubilees. However, both the Greek and Hebrew witnesses to the story indicate that Noah prayed on this occasion, so this prayer has been deftly introduced into a traditional story. Davenport suggests that 'the prayer in v. 3 may originally have been a part of a collection of prayers and blessings of the ancestors.... A liturgical fragment has been expanded.'[6] Whether the prayer is a composition by the author of Jubilees or whether it derives from an earlier stream of tradition is difficult to determine; in either case it well represents an early Jewish awareness of the malignant effect of active evil spirits descended from the offspring of the Watchers.

Literary context in Jubilees

Noah is a very important figure in Jubilees. After his birth notice in 4:28, Jubilees lists his sons and progeny and then describes the Flood and the subsequent covenant, his celebration of the Feast of Shebuot, reasons for using the solar (364-day) calendar, the problems faced by his descendants, and the partitioning of the land between Shem, Ham, Japheth and Cainan. It concludes with Noah's death in 10:15–17. In Jubilees 10:1–17, the narrative deals with the problem of evil spirits active in the world; they present grave difficulties for human beings. Noah begs God to remove their influence (10:3–6) and God responds by restricting nine-tenths of them. At the conclusion of this arrangement Noah died and 'slept with his fathers' (10:15).

Comparison with biblical and other Jewish prayers

The tone of these requests seems milder than the brusque, concrete language of many biblical Psalms, especially the Laments. Noah appeals to God's abundant mercy (v. 3) and God's knowledge of the lives of those humans saved from the Deluge: these sentences remind us of the confession of trust found in many Psalms of Lament.

In this prayer Noah responds to the terrible corruption of human beings by these unclean demons spawned by the Watchers. He begs God to remove these agents of corruption to humans, evils that are externalized by this imagery of the Watchers and their offspring. His appeal to God encompasses the great motifs from the scriptures, God's 'mercy and compassion' as well as the fulfilment of the divine blessing and commandment 'to increase and multiply' on the face of the earth.

Prayer to restrict the power of evil spirits is otherwise attested in Jewish literature from this era.[7] First, there are two texts of rewritten Bible, like Jubilees, which contain prayers against demons as they retell stories of Israel's heroes, David and Solomon. In the *Biblical Antiquities* of Pseudo-Philo (#60), David utters a prayer against the evil spirits affecting Saul. Josephus attributes to Solomon prayers (incantations and exorcisms) against demons, 'for the benefit and healing' of human beings (*Antiquities* VIII, 45–7). Also, at the end of the Qumran Psalms Scroll the writer attributes to David four songs 'for making music over the stricken' (11QPs[a] xxvii. 9–10); these have been considered prayers against evil spirits. Other Qumran texts, the *Songs of the Maskil* (4Q510 and 4Q511) also contain language against evil spirits, but their literary genre is quite different from the prayer of Noah. Similarly, a Greek papyrus from Cairo, dated to first or second century CE, contains a prayer requesting God to send the saving angel (from the time of Exodus onward) to ward off the power of evil spirits.[8]

TRANSLATION OF JUBILEES 10:3–6

3. [Noah] prayed in the presence of God his Lord and he said: 'Lord of the spirits[9] which are in all flesh, You, who have shown me mercy and saved me and my sons from the water of the Flood and did not make me perish (as You did to the children of destruction) since Your kindness toward me has been great, and great has been

Your mercy to my soul.

May Your kindness be raised high over Your children's children,[10] and may the evil spirits not rule over them lest they destroy them from the earth.

4 Now bless me and my sons so we might increase and grow numerous and fill the earth.[11]

5 And You know how Your Watchers acted – the fathers of these spirits – during my days.

Now these spirits who are still alive – lock them up and keep them captive in the place of judgement, so they may not cause corruption among the children of Your servant, my Lord, since they are vicious and were created for corrupting.

6 Do not let them rule over the spirits of the living since You alone know their judgement.[12]

Let them have no power over the children of the just from now on and for evermore.'

NOTES

1 James VanderKam, 'Jubilees, Book of', in D. N. Freedman (ed.), *Anchor Bible Dictionary*, vol. III, New York, Doubleday, 1992, p. 1030.

2 R. H. Charles (ed.), *The Book of Jubilees or the Little Genesis, Translated from the Editor's Ethiopic Text*, London, Adam & Charles Black, 1902, pp. 78–80.

3 Florentino García Martínez, *Qumran and Apocalyptic: Studies on the Aramaic Texts from Qumran*, Leiden and New York, E. J. Brill, 1992, pp. 36–43.

4 cf. Charles, *Jubilees*, 1895, p. 179.

5 cf. Charles, *Jubilees*, 1902, p. 78n.

6 Gene L. Davenport, *The Eschatology of the Book of Jubilees*, Leiden, E. J. Brill, 1971, p. 86 n. 5.

7 cf. Bilhah Nitzan, *Qumran Prayer and Religious Poetry*, Studies on the Texts of the Desert of Judah, vol. XII, Leiden, E. J. Brill, 1994, especially ch. VIII, 'Magical Poetry', pp. 227–72. She provides the summary of Jewish prayers for protection against evil and demonic spirits.

8 Pierre Benoit, 'Fragment d'une prière contre les esprits impurs?' *Revue Biblique* 58, 1951, pp. 549–65.

9 'Lord of the spirits': an expression known from the Torah as well as early Jewish literature and Greek Christian inscriptions from Egypt and Nubia. For example Num 16:22, 'They fell on their faces, and said, "O God, the *God of the spirits* of all flesh, shall one person sin and you become angry with the whole congregation?" ' Num 27:16, ' "Let the LORD, the *God of the spirits* of all flesh, appoint someone over the congregation." ' NJPS: 'LORD/ God, Source of the breath of all flesh.' In *Numbers*, The JPS Torah Commentary, p. 135, J. Milgrom explains this epithet: '*elohei*, literally "God of" '. He translates it as 'Source of' and comments: 'God gives man His breath at birth, and withdraws it at death . . . since God is Creator of life, He alone determines who is to live and who is to die.' Compare Klaus Berger, *Das Buch der Jubilaen*, Juedische Schriften aus hellenistich-roemischer Zeit, Band II, Lieferung 3, Guetersloh, Verlagshaus Gerd Mohn, 1981, p. 378 n. 3c. Revelation 22:6 'And he said to me, "These words are trustworthy and true, for *the Lord, the God of the spirits* of

the prophets, has sent his angel to show his servants what must soon take place." '

10 'Your children's children.' O. S. Wintermute, 'Jubilees', in J. H. Charlesworth, *The Old Testament Pseudepigrapha*, Garden City, NY, Doubleday and Co., 1985, vol. 2, p. 76, translates 'Let your grace be lifted up upon my sons', following the critical text of Charles (*Jubilees*, 1895). Charles had emended his base text at this point, but VanderKam considers the manuscripts which feature this reading to be of inferior (12 = A) or nondescript quality (35, 58). VanderKam's reading (*weluda weludeka*), which I have translated, derives from MS 25 (= B in Charles), which was Charles's base text and which VanderKam describes as 'the greatest authority' for his edition, since 'none of the newer copies surpasses 25 in textual value' (VanderKam, *The Book of Jubilees*, translated by James C. VanderKam, Louvain, E. Peeters, 1989, p. xxi). The present translation might suggest God's care for all humankind ('your children'), rather than understanding Noah as praying for his own grandchildren, as the context of the prayer might suggest. See James VanderKam (ed.), *The Book of Jubilees: A Critical Text*, Louvain, E. Peeters, 1989, p. 58, ad loc.

11 Berger, op.cit, p. 378 n. 4a: 'In the Prayer against the Demons this clause/ sentence is a conspicuous insertion in the form of a common blessing formula. Its citation simply indicates protection and blessing.'

12 'their judgement'. O. S. Wintermute, op. cit., p. 76, translates: 'because you alone know their judgement'. VanderKam, *The Book of Jubilees*, p. 59: 'for you alone know their punishment'. Berger, op. cit., p. 379: 'Since you alone know their power. And you should maintain no power over the children of the righteous.' Charles (1902 and 1913) emended *ta'mr kuennanehomu* to *ta'mr kuanneno lomu*, translating: 'for Thou alone canst exercise dominion over them.'

SELECTED BIBLIOGRAPHY

Berger, Klaus, *Das Buch der Jubilaen*, Juedische Schriften aus hellenistich-roemischer Zeit, Band II, Lieferung 3, Guetersloh, Verlagshaus Gerd Mohn, 1981.

Charles, R. H., *The Ethiopic Version of the Hebrew Book of Jubilees*, Oxford, Clarendon Press, 1895.

——, *The Book of Jubilees or the Little Genesis, Translated from the Editor's Ethiopic Text*, London, Adam & Charles Black, 1902.

——, *The Apocrypha and Pseudepigrapha of The Old Testament in English*, vol. 2, *The Pseudepigrapha*, Oxford, Clarendon Press, 1913.

Davenport, Gene L., *The Eschatology of the Book of Jubilees*, Leiden, E. J. Brill, 1971.

Dillmann, August, *Mashafa kûfalê sive Liber Jubilaeorum, qui idem a Graecis 'H Λεπτη ενεσις inscribitur, aethiopice ad duorum librorum manuscriptorum fidem primum edidit Dillmann*, 1859.

Endres, John C., S.J., *Biblical Interpretation in the Book of Jubilees*, CBQMS 18, Washington, DC, Catholic Biblical Association of America, 1987.

García Martínez, Florentino, *Qumran and Apocalyptic: Studies on the Aramaic Texts from Qumran*, Leiden and New York, E. J. Brill, 1992.

Nitzan, Bilhah, *Qumran Prayer and Religious Poetry*, Studies on the Texts of the Desert of Judah, vol. XII, Leiden, E. J. Brill, 1994.

VanderKam, James (ed.), *The Book of Jubilees: A Critical Text*, Scriptores Aethiopici, tomus 87, Louvain, E. Peeters, 1989.

VanderKam, James, *The Book of Jubilees*, Scriptores Aethiopici, tomus 88, Louvain, E. Peeters, 1989.
Wintermute, O. S., 'Jubilees', in J. H. Charlesworth (ed.), *The Old Testament Pseudepigrapha*, vol. 2, Garden City, NY, Doubleday and Co., 1985.

11

JUDITH PRAYS FOR HELP (JUDITH 9:1–14)

Toni Craven

INTRODUCTION

Judith is an anonymous fictional story, probably written by a Palestinian Jew. Written in Greek that imitates Hebrew idiom and syntax, Judith intermingles uncertain and even imaginary details with facts drawn from Palestinian, Assyrian, Babylonian, Persian, and Greek history and geography, and most especially Jewish religious customs of the second century BCE.

Texts

Judith is extant in four Greek codices: Vaticanus (LXX^B), Alexandrinus (LXX^A), Basiliano-Vaticanus (LXX^N) and Sinaiticus (LXX^S); four translations: Old Latin, Syriac, Sahidic and Ethiopic; and other relatively late abridged and modified Hebrew versions. Despite Jerome's claim in the Vulgate to have translated an Aramaic text, no ancient Aramaic or Hebrew manuscripts have been found. The oldest extant text of Judith is probably a third-century CE potsherd on which Jdt 15:1–7 is preserved.

Date

Although the exact date of the book's composition cannot be determined, Judith was probably written in the first century BCE, during the late Hasmonean period. A reference to Judith in the first epistle of Clement of Rome in the first century CE makes it clear that the story was composed before this time.

Narrative organization and prayer

Prayer is important throughout the sixteen chapters of the Book of Judith. Part I (1:1–7:32) is like a communal lament gone awry. Faced with the political and religious threat of Assyrian aggression under the leadership of Nebuchadnezzar and his general Holofernes, the fearful Israelites nearly surrender. At the instruction of their high priest Joakim, the Israelites fortified the passes that led to the hilltop towns blocking Holofernes' advance to Jerusalem (4:7–8), and then cried out to God, fasted, sprinkled ashes on their heads and put sackcloth everywhere (4:10–11). They petitioned God to 'look with favour upon the whole house of Israel' (4:15).[1]

The narrative records that God 'heard their prayers and looked upon their affliction' (4:13), but the Israelites, not knowing this, lost heart. Blockaded by the Assyrian army for thirty-four days, the people in Bethulia cried out, 'We have no one to help us; God has sold us into their hands' (7:25). Their town leader Uzziah urged courage, but vowed to surrender to the Assyrians if God did not rescue them within five days (7:30–1).

Part II (8:1–16:25) details how a childless wealthy widow (8:2; 16:22), Judith, a woman of habitual and daily prayer (see 8:5–6), delivered the Israelites from their own fears and the Assyrian enemy. As Judith tells Holofernes, she 'serves the God of heaven day and night' (11:17). Indeed, it is her nightly practice of going outside the enemy camp to bathe and pray that provides the ruse for her escape after she has beheaded the enemy general (see 11:17–19; 12:6–9; 13:10).

Context and structure

Judith's personal lament in Judith 9, is embedded in a narrative unit detailing Judith's plan to save Israel (8:9–10:8). Concatenated uses of the verb 'hear' underscore the importance of hearing and being heard. Judith, who has 'heard' of the five-day compromise (8:9), insisted that the leaders of Bethulia, Uzziah, Chabris and Charmis 'hear' her judgement (8:11, 32) for they had put themselves in the place of God, who is not like a 'mortal to be threatened, nor like a human being to be won over by pleading' (8:18). Declaring that God is free to deliver or destroy (8:17) and that God will 'hear', if God so pleases (8:17), Judith challenged the leaders: 'let us set an example' (8:24); 'let us give thanks to the Lord our God, who is putting us to the test' (8:25). She argued that God's chastisement was pedagogical, not punitive (8:26–7).

When the leaders have left her house, Judith prays her longest prayer in the book (9:1–14). She asks that God crush the foreigners who have threatened the safety of the Jerusalem Temple (9:1, 8). Recalling that God empowered Simeon to annihilate those who defiled Dinah by means of a sword given into his hand by God (9:2–4a), Judith begs God to 'hear' her (9:4, 12). Like Simeon, Judith prays to carry out heaven-sent vengeance against Israel's enemies.[2] Crediting God with control of past, present and future events (9:5–6) and quoting Exod 15:1, Judith implores 'the Lord who crushes wars; the Lord is your name' to destroy the Assyrians (9:7–8) by giving her – a widow and a female – a 'strong hand' and 'deceitful words' (9:9–10).[3] She prays a five-fold request that God 'look on their arrogance', 'send fury on their heads, 'give into my hand – a widow's – the strength I need', 'strike down' the enemy, and 'crush' their pride (9:9–10). God's 'strength' does not depend on numbers, nor God's 'might' on the powerful (9:11).

Then in a litany of ten titles for God, arranged in two groups of five titles on either side of the repeated Greek particle, *nai nai* ('yea', 'verily', 'please'), Judith prays, 'God of the lowly, helper of the oppressed, supporter of the weak, protector of those in despair, saviour of the hopeless – please, please – God of my father [unclear whether Judith's own father or her ancestor Simeon], God of the heritage of Israel, ruler of heaven and earth, creator of the waters, king of all your creation, hear my prayer!' (9:11b–12). Petitions that God 'hear' her prayer (9:12) and grant her success in deceiving the enemy (9:13–14) close her prayer.

Theological uniqueness

Judith's prayer and her understanding of God rise like a phoenix out of the ashes of the community's despair (see 7:32). Having defended the radical freedom and foreknowledge of God to the town leaders, she asks that God hear her prayer (9:4, 12), destroy the Assyrians (9:8) and crush the enemy through the deceit of her lips, by the hand of a female (*theleia*; 9:10, 13). Judith is not concerned for her own safety. God's holiness and the safety of the Temple motivate her lament.

The story is not critical of her petition that God arm her with the unusual weapon of murderous deceit (compare Ps 149:7–8), although some interpreters are offended that Judith intentionally lies and murders.[4] In fact, when Holofernes has been beheaded, the high priest Joakim and the Israelite elders praise Judith, saying, 'You are the glory of Jerusalem, you are the great boast of Israel, you are the great pride of our nation! You have done all this with your own hand; you have done great good to Israel, and God is well pleased with it' (15:9b–10a).

As it turns out, the petitions and theology of chapter 9 are fundamental to the plot and success of the entire narrative. Neither Assyria's military aggression nor Israel's manipulative lament wins in the end. Judith, alone, successfully deceives and destroys the enemy, because God heard her prayer. As the last words of chapter 9 make clear, all power and might belong to the Lord who protects and delivers Israel (9:14).

Artistic representations

Judith's story has been celebrated in music, literature, theatrical versions, statuary and paintings.[5] Judith holding the severed head of Holofernes is featured in works by Donatello, Cristofano Allori, Michelangelo, a sixteenth-century bronze Hanukkah lamp, Caravaggio, Gentileschi, and numerous others have highlighted the dimensions of the story dealing with sex and death. Ruskin, in his 1877 *Mornings in Florence*, tellingly writes: 'Do you happen to know anything about Judith yourself, except that she cut off Holofernes' head; and has been made the high light of about a million vile pictures ever since.'

TRANSLATION

(1) Then Judith fell on her face, put ashes on her head and uncovered the sackcloth she was wearing. Just as the evening's incense offering was being offered in the house of God in Jerusalem, Judith cried aloud to the Lord and said,

(2) 'Lord, God of my ancestor Simeon, into whose hand you put a sword to take vengeance on the foreigners who had violated a virgin's womb to defile her,[6] uncovering her thighs to shame her, and polluting her womb to dishonour her. You said, 'This shall not be done!' Yet they did it. (3) On account of this, you gave over their rulers to be slaughtered, and their bed, which blushed for shame for her deceived,[7] to bloodshed. You struck down slaves with princes and princes on their thrones. (4) You gave up their wives to plunder and their daughters to captivity, and all their booty for division among your beloved children, whose zeal for you was great and who abhorred the pollution of their blood and had called on you for aid.

'God, my God, hear me also – a widow! (5) It is you who do these things and what preceded and what follows them. You have planned the present and the future. What you have in mind comes to pass. (6) The things you decide come forward and say, "Here we are!" For all your ways are ready and your judgement is with foreknowledge.

(7) 'Here are the Assyrians, greatly increased in power, boasting horses and riders, priding themselves in the power of their infantry, trusting in shield and spear, bow and sling! They do not know that you are the Lord who crushes wars; (8) Lord is your name.[8] Shatter their might by your power and bring down their force in your anger! For they plan to pollute your sanctuary, to defile the tabernacle where your glorious name rests, to break off the horns of your altar with the sword. (9) Look on their arrogance! Send your fury on their heads! Give into my hand – a widow's – the strength I need. (10) By the deceit of my lips,[9] strike down the slave with the ruler and the ruler with his servant. Crush their pride by the hand of a female! (11) For not on numbers does your strength depend, nor on the powerful your might.

'You are God of the lowly, helper of the oppressed, supporter of the weak, protector of those in despair, saviour of the hopeless – (12) please,

please – God of my father, God of the heritage of Israel, ruler of heaven and earth, creator of the waters, king of all your creation, hear my prayer![10] (13) Make my deceitful words wound and bruise those who have planned harsh things against your covenant, your sacred house, Mount Zion, and the house your children possess. (14) Make every nation and every tribe know clearly that you are God, the God of all power and might, and that there is no other who protects the people of Israel but you.'

NOTES

1 See especially Samuel E. Balentine, *Prayer in the Hebrew Bible: The Drama of Divine–Human Dialogue*, Overtures to Biblical Theology, Minneapolis, Fortress Press, 1993, pp. 118–98.

2 James Kugel, 'The Story of Dinah in the *Testament of Levi*', *Harvard Theological Review*, 1992, vol. 85, compares Jdt 9:2 to Gen 34:25, showing that Simeon and Levi 'were not armed with ordinary weapons', pp. 4–6.

3 The text is ironic. In patriarchal society, there was no greater dishonour than that a man be brought down by a female's hand (see Judg 9:53–4). The Greek work *theleia* (female) is used in 9:10; 13:15; and 16:5, rather than the more common *gyne* (woman).

4 On lying, see O. Horn Prouser, 'The Truth About Women and Lying', *Journal for the Study of the Old Testament*, 1994, vol. 61, pp. 5–28, and Toni Craven, 'Women Who Lied for the Faith', in Peter Paris and Douglas Knight (eds), *Justice and the Holy: Essays in Honor of Walter Harrelson*, Atlanta, Scholars Press, 1989, pp. 49–60.

5 For recent selected summaries see Nira Stone, 'Judith and Holofernes: Some Observations on the Development of the Scene in Art', in James VanderKam (ed.), *'No One Spoke Ill of Her': Essays on Judith*, Atlanta, Scholars Press, 1992, pp. 73–93; Mieke Bal, 'Head Hunting: "Judith" on the Cutting Edge of Knowledge', *Journal for the Study of the Old Testament*, 1994, vol. 63, pp. 3–34; and Carolyn Collette, 'Judith', in David Lyle Jeffrey (ed.), *A Dictionary of Biblical Tradition in English Literature*, Grand Rapids, Eerdmans, 1992, pp. 423–4.

6 Meaning of the Greek is unclear. Lit. 'who loosened the virgin's womb' (*metran*). Perhaps 'headdress' or 'girdle' (*mitran*). See Carey A. Moore, *Judith: A New Translation with Introduction and Commentary*, Anchor Bible 40, Garden City, NY, Doubleday, 1985, pp. 190–1; and Morton S. Enslin, *The Book of Judith*, Jewish Apocryphal Literature VIII, Leiden, E. J. Brill, 1972, p. 123.

7 Uncertain how to translate the two Greek references to 'deceit' (*apate*). NAB has both: 'Therefore you had their rulers slaughtered; and you covered with their blood the bed in which they lay deceived, the same bed that had felt the shame of their own deceiving.' Most, as above, omit one reference. See Enslin, *The Book of Judith*, p. 123.

8 Compare with Exod 15:3, 'YHWH is a man of war; YHWH is his name' and Jdt 16:2, 'The Lord is a God who crushes wars.' Toni Craven, *Artistry and Faith in the Book of Judith*, Society of Biblical Literature Dissertation Series 70, Chico, CA, Scholars Press, 1983, p. 106.

9 Three references to deceit (*apate*) in all: two in 9:3; one in 9:10.

10 See Craven, *Artistry and Faith in the Book of Judith*, p. 91.

TONI CRAVEN

SELECTED BIBLIOGRAPHY

Craven, Toni, *Artistry and Faith in the Book of Judith*, Society of Biblical Literature Dissertation Series 70, Chico, CA, Scholars Press, 1983.
—— 'Judith', in Raymond E. Brown, Joseph A. Fitzmyer and Roland E. Murphy (eds), *The New Jerome Biblical Commentary*, Englewood Cliffs, NJ, Prentice Hall, 1990, pp. 572–5.
Enslin, Morton S., *The Book of Judith*, Jewish Apocryphal Literature VIII, Leiden, E. J. Brill, 1972.
Moore, Carey A., *Judith: A New Translation with Introduction and Commentary*, Anchor Bible 40, Garden City, NY, Doubleday, 1985.

12

PRAYER OF A CONVERT TO JUDAISM (JOSEPH AND ASENETH 12–13)

Randall D. Chesnutt

INTRODUCTION

A long prayer uttered in connection with a gentile's conversion to Judaism appears in Joseph and Aseneth, a Hellenistic Jewish romance written in Greek in the first century BCE or CE and now often included among the Old Testament Pseudepigrapha. The fictional story recounts the conversion of the gentile girl Aseneth to the God of Israel, her marriage to the patriarch Joseph (a marriage mentioned only in passing in Genesis 41:45, 50–2; 46:20), and the conflicts surrounding that conversion and marriage. Having at first arrogantly spurned her father's suggestion that she be given to Joseph in marriage, Aseneth falls madly in love with Joseph immediately upon seeing him, and penitently turns to his God. Secluding herself in her ornate penthouse, she repudiates her idols, renounces all her valuables, and fasts and repents in sackcloth and ashes for seven days. Following two soliloquies in which she laments her wretched situation and musters the courage to address the true God, she offers the prayer translated below (Joseph and Aseneth 12–13). An angelic visitor then arrives to authenticate Aseneth's conversion, and the story continues with her marriage to Joseph and the resulting conflicts.

Whether Aseneth's ascetic rigour and prayer echo any fixed ritual practices is unknown; the narrative itself presents her actions as autonomous and gives no indication that she is following prescribed ritual. Her prayer is so closely related to the particulars of the story in which it appears that it is not likely to have had an independent liturgical life in the form in which we have it. Nevertheless, extensive formal, verbal and thematic parallels with other ancient Jewish prayers, both canonical and extra-biblical, suggest that this prayer has much in common with the actual liturgical practice and private prayer life of ancient Jews. Careful form-critical and traditio-historical analyses of the prayer are needed in connection with the surprisingly large group of other prayers of confession, lament and petition which are embedded within narrative works from the post-exilic and Second Temple periods (Ezra 9:6–15; Nehemiah 9:6–37; Daniel 9:4–19; Judith 9:2–14; Tobit 3:2–6, 11–15; Additions to Esther 13:9–17; 14:3–19; 1 Baruch 1:15–3:8; 1 Maccabees 3:50–3; 4:30–3; 3 Maccabees 2:2–20; 6:2–15; Jubilees 10:3–6; 2 Baruch 48:2–24; 54:1–22; Prayer of Manasseh; Josephus, *Antiquities* 4.3.2; 2.16.1).

The Greek text translated here is from the long version of Joseph and Aseneth edited by C. Burchard (published most conveniently in an appendix in A.-M. Denis, *Concordance grecques pseudépigraphes d'Ancien Testament*, Louvain, Université Catholique de Louvain, 1987, pp. 851–9). Another recension of the story which is about one-third shorter overall and which contains a version of Aseneth's prayer correspondingly shorter than the one translated here is believed by most scholars to be a later abridgement of the original.

TRANSLATION

12

1   Lord, God of the ages,[1]
who created all things and brought them to life,[2]
who gave the breath of life to all your creation,
who brought the invisible things out into the light,

2   who made the things which exist and which appear out of those
      which do not appear and do not exist,
who raised up the heaven and laid its foundation on a dome upon the
      back of the winds,
who laid the earth's foundation upon the waters,
who placed great stones upon the watery abyss.
And the stones will not sink
but are like oak leaves on top of the waters,
and they are living stones,
and they hear your voice, Lord,
and they keep your commandments which you commanded them,
and from your ordinances they do not deviate,
but do your will to the end.
For you, Lord, spoke and they were made alive,
for your word, Lord, is life for all your creatures.[3]

3   To you I come for refuge, Lord,
and to you I will cry out, Lord,
to you I will pour out my plea,
to you I will confess my sins,
and to you I will reveal my transgressions.[4]

4   Spare me, Lord,
for I have sinned often in your sight.
I have transgressed and committed sacrilege,
and I have spoken evil and unspeakable things in your sight.

5   My mouth is defiled from sacrifices to idols
and from the table of the gods of the Egyptians.[5]
I have sinned, Lord,
in your sight I have sinned often in ignorance,[6]
and I have worshipped dead and deaf idols.[7]
And now I am not worthy to open my mouth to you, Lord.
And I, Aseneth, daughter of Pentephres the priest,
the virgin and princess,
who was at one time pompous and arrogant
and thriving in my riches beyond all people,[8]
am now an orphan and desolate and forsaken by all people.[9]

6   To you I come for refuge, Lord,
and to you I bring my plea,
and to you I will cry out.

7   Rescue me before I am seized by those who pursue me.

8   For as a frightened little child flees to his father,
and the father stretches out his hands and picks him up from the
    ground
and embraces him against his breast,
and the child clutches his hands tightly around his father's neck
and recovers from his fear
and rests against his father's breast,
while the father smiles at his childish confusion,
so you also, Lord, stretch out your hands to me as does a father who
    loves his child,
and pick me up from the ground.[10]

9   For behold, the wild old lion pursues me,[11]
because he is the father of the Egyptians' gods,
and his children are the gods of the frenzied idolaters.
And I have come to hate them,
for they are the lion's children,
and I threw them all away from me and destroyed them.

10   And their father the lion pursues me ferociously.

11   But you, Lord, rescue me from his hands,
and from his mouth remove me,
lest he snatch me away like a lion[12]
and tear me to pieces,
and throw me into the flame of fire,
and the fire will throw me into the storm,
and the storm will envelop me in darkness

and throw me out into the depths of the sea,
and the great eternal sea monster will consume me,
and I will perish eternally.

12 Rescue me, Lord, before all these things come upon me.
Rescue me, Lord, the desolate and isolated one,
because my father and mother have disowned me and said,
'Aseneth is not our daughter',[13]
because I destroyed and shattered their gods
and came to hate them.

13 And now I am an orphan and desolate,
and I have no other hope except in you, Lord,
and no other refuge besides your mercy, Lord,
because you are the father of orphans
and a protector of the persecuted
and a helper of the oppressed.[14]

14 Have mercy on me, Lord, and keep watch over me,
the chaste virgin who is forsaken and an orphan,
because you, Lord, are a sweet and good and gentle father.

15 What father is as sweet as you, Lord?
And which one is as quick in mercy as you, Lord?
And which one is as patient toward our sins as you, Lord?
For behold, all the gifts[15] of my father Pentephres,
which he has given to me for an inheritance are temporary and
    vanishing,
but the gifts of your inheritance, Lord, are imperishable and eternal.

13

1 Consider my lowliness, Lord,
and have mercy on me.
Observe my orphanhood
and have pity on me, the oppressed one.
For behold, I fled from all others
and came to you for refuge, Lord, the only benevolent one.

2 Behold, I abandoned all the earth's goods,
and to you I came for refuge, Lord,
in this sackcloth and ashes,[16]
naked and an orphan and left all alone.

3 Behold, I put aside my royal robe of violet linen interwoven with
    gold
and put on a black mourning tunic.

4 Behold, I loosened my golden girdle and threw it away from me
and girded myself with a rope and sackcloth.

5 Behold, my tiara and my diadem I threw off my head
and sprinkled myself with ashes.

6   Behold, the floor of my chamber,
      which is covered with multi-coloured and purple stones,
      which was formerly sprinkled with perfumes
      and wiped with bright linen cloths,
      is now sprinkled with my tears
      and has been disgraced by being strewn with ashes.

7   Behold, my Lord, from my tears and from the ashes,
      there has come to be as much mud in my chamber as in a broad
          street.

8   Behold, Lord, my royal dinner and provisions
      I have given to the stray dogs.

9   And behold, for seven days and seven nights I fasted,
      and I neither ate bread nor drank water,
      and my mouth has become as dry as a drum,
      and my tongue as a horn,
      and my lips as a potsherd,
      and my countenance is fallen,
      and my eyes have become shamefully inflamed from my many tears,
      and all my strength has left me.[17]

11   Behold, therefore, all the gods whom I formerly worshipped in
         ignorance:
      now I know that they were deaf and dead idols,
      and I have given them up to be trampled by people,
      and thieves plundered those which were silver and gold.[18]

12   And to you I came for refuge, Lord, my God.
      But you, rescue me from my many acts of ignorance,

13   and be understanding towards me,
      because I sinned against you in ignorance, being a virgin,
      and I have been led astray unwittingly,
      and I have spoken blasphemous things against my lord Joseph,[19]
      because I, the wretched one, did not know that he is your son,
      since people had told me that Joseph is a shepherd's son from the land
         of Canaan.
      And I, the wretched one, came to believe them and was led astray.
      And I scorned him and spoke evil things about him,
      and I did not know that he is your son.

14   For what person will engender such beauty
      and so much wisdom and virtue and power
      as does the most wonderful Joseph?

15   Lord, I commit him to you
      because I love him more than myself.
      Watch closely over him in the wisdom of your grace.
      And you, Lord, commit me to him as a maidservant and slave.
      And I will make his bed

and wash his feet
and wait on him
and be a slave to him
and serve him forever.[20]

NOTES

1 The epithet 'God of the ages' (or 'eternal God') is traditional. Among the extra-biblical Jewish prayers, it appears in Sirach's prayer for deliverance in Sirach 36:17 and with slight variations in Tobit's prayer of thanksgiving in Tobit 13 and Isaac's prayer for Jacob in Josephus, *Antiquities* 1.18.6. See also 1 Clement 35:3; 55:6; 61:2.

2 Direct address to God followed by various attributions of praise in the third person or participial form is a standard feature of blessings in the statutory prayers in rabbinic tradition. Invocation of God as creator is typical of petitionary and other kinds of prayers and hymns in diverse Jewish and Jewish-Christian sources. In addition to numerous instances in the Hebrew Bible, see Prayer of Manasseh 2; 2 Baruch 21:4–5; 1 Enoch 18:1–2; 84:2–3; Jubilees 12:19; Josephus, *Antiquities* 1.18.6; the blessings before the morning and evening Shema; Acts 4:24; 1 Clement 59.3.

3 The creation language which dominates the first two verses abounds with echoes of both biblical and extra-biblical Jewish sources and articulates many of the fundamental tenets of Jewish cosmology (cf. Genesis 1–2 [LXX]; Isaiah 48:13; Psalms 24:2; 33:9; 136:6; 148:5–6; Wisdom of Solomon 9:1; 11:25; Judith 16:14; Sirach 16:27–8; 1 Enoch 18:2; 2 Baruch 21:4–5; 48:8; 2 Enoch 24–8; Philo, *Special Laws* 4.35; *Dreams* 1.13; Qumran *Community Rule* 3.15–16; Josephus, *Antiquities* 1.18.6; John 1:3–4; Acts 17:25; Romans 4:17; Hebrews 11:3; 2 Peter 3:5; and the synagogal prayers preserved in *Apostolic Constitutions* 7.34.1–8; 8.12.7–15. Creation imagery is not only a conventional element of prayer but is especially suited to Aseneth's case. Conversion to Judaism is conceived throughout Joseph and Aseneth as an act of creation, a transition from darkness to light, from death to life, from nothingness to blessed existence (8:9; 15:5, 12; 20:7; 27:10). It is therefore appropriate that Aseneth appeals to God as the creator who gives life, who forms being out of non-being, who transforms darkness into light. God's salvific activity is analogous to his creative activity.

4 Aseneth's profuse confession of sin and desperate appeal for mercy and deliverance which begin here are closely parallel in language and imagery to the penitential psalms and other individual laments in the Hebrew Bible (e.g., Psalms 25 [LXX 24], 51 [LXX 50] and 103 [LXX 102]), the apocryphal Prayer of Manasseh, and the Prayer of Azariah in the apocryphal Additions to Daniel 3–22.

5 Avoidance of the contamination of idolatry is one of the most definitive features of Jewish self-identity in Joseph and Aseneth (2:3; 7:1; 8:5–7; 11:7–9, 16; 21:13–15). The predicament which Aseneth's conversion resolves, though couched here in the language of 'sins' and 'transgressions' and 'sacrilege', boils down to the single fault of rejecting the true God by participating in the defiling worship of idols. Accordingly, the story of her conversion stresses her utter repudiation of idolatry and everything associated with it (9:2; 10:12–13; 19:5).

6 The refrain 'I have sinned, Lord, ... I have sinned' appears repeatedly in Aseneth's psalm in Joseph and Aseneth 21 and in Prayer of Manasseh 12.

7 The word translated 'deaf' could also be translated 'dumb'. The same

description of idols appears in 8:5; 11:8; and 13:11. The inability of idols to see, hear, speak or act is stressed repeatedly in both biblical and extra-biblical polemics against idolatry (Psalms 115:3–8; 135:16–17; Isaiah 40:18–20; 44:9–20; 46:6–7; Jeremiah 10:2–10; 3 Maccabees 4:16; Jubilees 12:1–5; 20:7–8; Sibylline Oracles 3.31; 2 Enoch 10:16; Apocalypse of Abraham 1–7; Testament of Job 2–5; Letter of Jeremiah, *passim*).

8   Aseneth's beauty and virginity, her plush palatial quarters and her arrogance toward suitors – all standard features in Hellenistic romances – are described in 1:4–2:12; 4:9–12.

9   The language used here and in 12:13–14; 13:1–2 to describe Aseneth's familial and social ostracism owes much to the biblical passages on the sojourner, the orphan and the widow (e.g., Deuteronomy 10:18; 16:11-14; 24:17–21; 27:19), and to extra-biblical traditions about the desperate situation of the proselyte (see especially Philo, *Special Laws* 1.57; 4.34; *Virtues* 20).

10 The content and wording of verse 8 are very uncertain because of wide variations among the Greek manuscripts and early versions. The imagery of God's lifting Aseneth up from the ground may reflect Roman practices surrounding birth and adoption (as Mark Kiley has suggested in private correspondence). A Roman father literally 'lifted' a newborn infant from the ground to indicate his intent to 'raise' (rather than expose) the child (see P. Veyne, *A History of Private Life*, 5 vols, trans. A. Goldhammer, Cambridge, MA, Harvard University Press, 1987–91, vol. 1, p. 9). The possible use of this metaphor in the account of Aseneth's conversion deserves careful study; certainly it would accord nicely with the new creation/new birth imagery which is employed in the narrative (see R. D. Chesnutt, *From Death to Life: Conversion in Joseph and Aseneth*, Journal for the Study of the Pseudepigrapha Supplement Series 16, Sheffield, Sheffield Academic Press, 1995, pp. 145–9, 172–6) and with Aseneth's lament that she is 'an orphan and desolate and forsaken by all people' unless she is 'lifted up' by an adoptive father, God (12:5, 8).

11 The depiction of the persecutor as a lion appears in prayers for deliverance both in the Psalter (7:1–2; 10:9; 17:12; 22:13, 21; 35:17; 57:4) and in extra-biblical prayers (Additions to Esther 14:13). If Joseph and Aseneth was composed in Egypt, as most scholars believe, the metaphor is especially appropriate because Re, the Egyptian sun-god and 'father of all the gods', is often depicted in ancient sources as a lion (*Book of the Dead*, Spell 62b; Plutarch, *Table-Talk* 4.5.2; Aelian, *Animals* 12.7). The image of the ferocious and vengeful lion thus vividly expresses the new convert's fear that the supreme Egyptian deity will retaliate against her for renouncing Egyptian religion.

12 Other witnesses read 'like a wolf'.

13 No such rancour is reported in the narrative, where Aseneth's parents treat her cordially. The language here rather reflects the traditional motif of the gentile convert's social and familial ostracism. See Philo, *Special Laws* 1.9; 1.57; 4.34; *Virtues* 20; Josephus, *Antiquities* 20.2.4; 20.4.1–2; Numbers Rabbah 8.2.

14 The motif of the Lord as the sole refuge and helper of those otherwise defenceless is frequent in the Psalms (e.g., 91:9) and in extra-biblical prayers (Judith 9:11, 14; Additions to Esther 13:9-17; 14:3; Josephus, *Antiquities* 2.16.1)

15 The reading 'gifts' (domata) is doubtful both here and later in this verse. 'Houses' (dōmata) has considerable textual support.

16 Aseneth's acts of penitence alluded to here and in the lines following are narrated in chapters 9-11. Fasting, wearing sackcloth or other mourning garments, and sprinkling oneself with or sitting in ashes are well-known signs of grief, humiliation, and penitence in the Hebrew Bible and become standard

RANDALL D. CHESNUTT

accoutrements for prayers of confession and petition in late biblical and apocryphal writings (Ezra 9:5; Nehemiah 9:1; Daniel 9:3; Additions to Esther 14:2; Judith 9:1; Pseudo-Philo, *Biblical Antiquities* 30:4–5).

17 Verse 10 is omitted from Burchard's Greek text and from this translation because it is very poorly attested in the manuscript tradition.

18 In the narrative of Aseneth's disposal of her idols there is no reference to thieves plundering the gold and silver (cf. 10:12–13; 11:4). But as elsewhere in polemics against idolatry, the vulnerability of idols to thievery serves to demonstrate their utter helplessness (see Letter of Jeremiah 57–8; Aristides, *Apology* 3.2; and note 7 above).

19 See 4:9–12.

20 Aseneth's prayer is answered in the remainder of the story in the sense that the couple marry, bear children and enjoy God's beneficent protection against their antagonists.

SELECTED BIBLIOGRAPHY

Burchard, C., *Untersuchungen zu Joseph und Aseneth: Überlieferung-Ortsbestim-mung*, WUNT 8, Tübingen, Mohr, 1965.

——, 'Joseph and Aseneth', in J. H. Charlesworth (ed.), *The Old Testament Pseudepigrapha*, New York, Doubleday, 1983–5, vol. 2, pp. 177–247.

——, 'The Present State of Research on Joseph and Aseneth', in J. Neusner *et al.* (eds), *Religion, Literature, and Society in Ancient Israel, Formative Christianity and Judaism*, Langham MD, University Press of America, 1987, vol. 2, pp. 31–52.

Chesnutt, R. D., *From Death to Life: Conversion in Joseph and Aseneth*, Journal for the Study of the Pseudepigrapha Supplement Series 16, Sheffield, Sheffield Academic Press, 1995.

——, 'Joseph and Aseneth', *Anchor Bible Dictionary*, ed. D. N. Freedman, 6 vols, New York, Doubleday, 1992, vol. 3, pp. 969–71.

Nickelsburg, G. W. E., *Jewish Literature Between the Bible and the Mishnah*, Philadelphia, Fortress Press, 1981, pp. 258–63, 271–2.

Philonenko, M., *Joseph et Aséneth: Introduction, texte critique, traduction et notes*, SPB 13, Leiden, E. J. Brill, 1968.

13

THE SONG OF HANNAH IN PSEUDO-PHILO'S *BIBLICAL ANTIQUITIES*

Joan E. Cook

INTRODUCTION

Biblical Antiquities (*Bib. Ant.*) is a rewritten Bible, a work that expands the biblical narrative by adding various details such as oral legends, lessons important to the community, or items to catch the reader's attention. Some scholars think rewritten Bibles were used in synagogues for teaching purposes. *Bib. Ant.* recounts the biblical narrative from the time of Adam to the death of Saul. It expands the character and role of several biblical women, including Hannah.[1]

Manuscript profile

Of the twenty-one Latin manuscripts, eighteen complete and three fragmentary, that are witnesses to the text of *Bib. Ant.*, two are particularly important for reconstructing the original version of *Bib. Ant.*: Fulda-Cassel Theol. 4°,3 (eleventh century) and Phillipps 461 (twelfth century). The sixteenth-century *editio princeps* by John Sichardus appears to be based on Fulda-Cassel and a now lost earlier version. A sixteenth-century Hebrew version, *Chronicles of Jerahmeel*, seems to be a translation from Latin with biblical quotations that resemble the Masoretic text. Biblical quotations in the Latin versions follow the Vulgate in some instances and the Septuagint in others.[2]

Original and translation languages

The Semitisms in the Latin text, errors in translation and independence from the Greek Old Testament lead to the conclusion that the book was composed in Hebrew. The possibility that it was composed in Aramaic is unlikely: a few translation errors can be explained from Hebrew vocabulary but not from Aramaic, and there is no positive reason to favour Aramaic. The Latin versions are most likely translations from Greek, into which the original Hebrew was translated.[3]

Date and provenance

The date of composition remains uncertain. Two schools of thought date the work to either before or after 70 CE. Those who favour the earlier date point to the book's genre, 'rewritten Bible',[4] which fell into disuse after 70 CE; and to the references to sacrifice (e.g. 32:3) and the Temple ('Unto this day', 22:8), which suggest that the Temple was still standing at the time of composition. Those who prefer the later date note the book's parallels to 2 Baruch and 4 Ezra, in spite of their different theological concerns. The issue remains unclear, but the latest possible date of composition is around 100 CE because the biblical text on which the author relies is, according to F. M. Cross's categories, Palestinian rather than Babylonian or Egyptian. Palestinian texts were probably suppressed around 100 CE.[5] The earliest possible date of composition is probably around 135 BCE if the reference to Getal (39:8) refers to Zenon, ruler of Philadelphia (Ammon).[6]

The book's provenance is most likely Palestine, based on its original composition in Hebrew, dependence on the Palestinian biblical text and concern for Temple-related issues. Its author is an anonymous person(s) known as Pseudo-Philo, but not likely to be Philo. The book's use of the Bible differs from Philo's, and it contradicts Philo's work in several instances. Philo does not seem to have known the Hebrew language well enough to compose in Hebrew.[7]

The work's cultural setting cannot be precisely identified. Its political setting appears to be the period shortly before the Roman destruction of the Temple in 70 CE, and its perspective is that of mainstream Judaism among the scribes in Palestine.[8]

Relation to other works

Pseudo-Philo's work shares with other rewritten Bibles the characteristic of expansion (see for example *The Jewish Antiquities* of Josephus and *The Book of Jubilees*). Another expanded Song of Hannah can be found in *Targum of the Prophets*, in which the Song is enlarged into a prediction of divine guidance throughout Israel's early military history. And references to several characters in *Bib. Ant.* appear elsewhere in Intertestamental literature. One who figures in the narrative of Samuel's birth is Kenaz, whom Pseudo-Philo (25:2) and Josephus (*Ant.* 5.3.3. par. 182) identify as Israel's first judge. But Judg 3:9 identifies Othniel, son of Kenaz, as the first judge. The book does not seem to have influenced other, later works.[9]

Function in literary context

The Song of Hannah appears in the same context as the biblical version, in the account of Hannah's dedication of Samuel at the Shiloh shrine after she had weaned him. Pseudo-Philo's version of Hannah's role differs from that of the Bible in so far as all the people were promised that Elkanah's barren wife would bear a son who would serve as judge and prophet. Unaware of the promise, Hannah requested a son of Eli the priest. After Samuel was weaned and Hannah took him to the Shiloh shrine as she had promised, Eli told her of the earlier promise. He confirmed that she, as Samuel's mother, would nourish the twelve tribes. In response Hannah prayed her Song. The extent of the expansions in the Song is unusual but not unique. The Song most likely served in the synagogue for homiletic and study purposes, rather than as a hymn.

Structure of the prayer

The Song takes the form of a testament, through which Hannah proclaims the beginning of a new era of divine protection of the people with Samuel as their human leader. Its introductory verse contains two parts: Hannah's call to the nations and kingdoms to listen to her words followed by her proclamation of her authority to speak, a result of her new role as Samuel's mother. The body of the Song also has two parts, corresponding to the two points of view from which Hannah speaks. In verses 4–5 she speaks as the mother of Samuel the light-giver and law-giver, developing the motifs of light and law introduced metaphorically in the previous verse. She teaches the people about life after death as a reward for the quality of one's present life. In verse 6 she speaks as mother of Samuel the prophet and priest, giving genealogical and predictive details. The Song concludes with Hannah's request that Samuel remain at the shrine.[10]

Theology

The prayer, as well as the entire work, highlights divine guidance of the people, particularly their leaders, throughout their early history. Judgement and afterlife figure prominently, particularly in the Song of Hannah, Deborah's hymn in 32:3 and Jonathan's words to David in 62:9. The Song reflects the community's questions about the nature of life after death, such as: whether all or only some people are evil, whether all people will die or only the evil ones, and whether the good will actually be *raised* from the dead or will be *transformed* from continued earthly existence into another mode of life.[11]

Translation

51:3 And Hannah prayed,[12] 'Come to my voice, all nations, and listen to my speech, all kingdoms, because my mouth has been opened to speak,[13] and my lips have been commanded to sing a hymn to the Lord. Drip, my breasts, and proclaim your testimony, because you have been commanded to give milk. For the one who is filled with your milk[14] will be established, and the people will be illuminated by his words, and to the nations he will show the ordinances,[15] and his horn will be exalted[16] very high.

4 Therefore I will speak my words openly, because from me will come forth the ordering[17] of the Lord, and all people will learn the truth.[18] Do not hasten to say great things or to let lofty words come forth from your mouth,[19] but take delight in glorifying [God]. For when the light from which wisdom is born comes forth, not those who possess many things will be called wealthy, nor will those who have born in abundance be called mothers. For the barren one who has given birth has been filled, but the one with many children has been emptied.[20]

5 For the Lord puts to death in judgement and brings to life in mercy.[21] For the evil ones live in this world, and he gives life to the just when he wills. For he confines the evil ones in darkness, and preserves his light for the just. And when the evil ones die they will perish, but when the just go to sleep they will be set free.[22] In this way every judgement will remain until the one who upholds it is revealed.

6 Speak, speak, Hannah, and do not be silent; sing a hymn, daughter of Batuel, about the marvellous things that God has performed with you. Who is Hannah that a prophet is born of her?[23] Or who is the daughter of Batuel that she should give birth to the light of the people?[24] And you, Elkanah, get up and gird your loins;[25] sing a hymn about the signs of the Lord, for Asaph prophesied in the wilderness concerning your son, saying, "Moses and Aaron are among his priests and Samuel is among them."[26] See, the word has been fulfilled according to the prophecy.[27] And these things will endure until the horn is given to his anointed one, and [until] power is present at the throne of his king.[28] So let my son stay here and serve[29] until he is made a light for this nation.'

NOTES

1 The complex topic of women in *Bib. Ant.* is discussed in Pieter Willem van der Horst, 'Portraits of Biblical Women in Pseudo-Philo's *Liber Antiquitatum Biblicarum*', *Journal for the Study of the Pseudepigrapha* 5, 1989, pp. 29–46, and Joan E. Cook, 'Females and the Feminine in

Pseudo-Philo', *Proceedings* 13, 1993, pp. 151–9.

2   Charles Perrot and Pierre-Maurice Bogaert, with the collaboration of D. J. Harrington, *Pseudo-Philon: Les Antiquités bibliques,* Paris, Les Éditions du Cerf, 1976, vol. 1, pp. 15–57 contains a detailed analysis of the extant manuscripts and their relationship to one another, written by Perrot.

3   Harrington details this information in D. J. Harrington, Charles Perrot and Pierre-Maurice Bogaert, op. cit., vol. 2, pp. 75–7.

4   See explanation in first paragraph.

5   Harrington discusses this question further in 'Pseudo-Philo' in James H. Charlesworth (ed.), *The Old Testament Pseudepigrapha*, vol. 2, Garden City, NY, Doubleday, 1985, p. 299; see also F. M. Cross, Jun., 'The History of the Biblical Text in the Light of the Discoveries in the Judaean Desert', *Harvard Theological Review* 57, 1964, pp. 281–99.

6   Bogaert in Harrington, Perrot and Bogaert, op. cit., vol. 2, pp. 66–74.

7   See Harrington's synthesis in Charlesworth, op. cit. pp. 299–300.

8   Frederick J. Murphy, *Pseudo-Philo: Rewriting the Bible,* New York, Oxford University Press, 1993, p. 7.

9   Harrington gives a detailed discussion of the relation of *Bib. Ant.* to canonical and apocryphal works in Charlesworth, op. cit., pp. 301–2.

10 The structure of the Song is discussed in detail in Joan E. Cook, 'Pseudo-Philo's Song of Hannah: Testament of a Mother in Israel', *Journal for the Study of the Pseudepigrapha* 9, 1991, pp. 103–14.

11 See Charles Perrot's comprehensive treatment of the book's theological themes in Harrington, Perrot and Bogaert, op. cit., vol. 2, pp. 39–65.

12 These words occur verbatim in 1 Sam 2:1.

13 The Latin reads, *ut loquar*, 'that I may speak'.

14 The Latin reads, *qui lactatur de vobis*, who is given milk by you'.

15 The Latin word *terminos* can be traced back to the Hebrew *hwqym*, 'limits, boundaries, laws, statutes'. It occurs in *Bib. Ant.* both here and in 15:6. See Harrington in Charlesworth, op. cit., p. 323 n. 15d. The word 'ordinances' highlights the relationship between the word and 'ordering' in the following verse.

16 These words are similar to 1 Sam 2:10.

17 The Latin reads *constitutio*.

18 These words allude to Isa 51:4.

19 These words are similar to 1 Sam 2:3.

20 These words are similar to 1 Sam 2:5. See also Harrington's note that the Latin depends on the Hebrew sb 'h of 1 Sam 2:5, which alludes to the number 'seven' (in Charlesworth, op. cit., p. 365).

21 These words are an expansion of 1 Sam 2:6.

22 The contrast between the just and the wicked is similar to the opposition between the faithful and the wicked in 1 Sam 2:9.

23 Literally, 'that a prophet is from her', followed by 'that she gave birth'. This translation respects the parallel meaning, and might also reconcile the similarities in the Greek *egenēthē* (was) and *egennēthē* (was born). See Harrington's note in Charlesworth, op. cit., p. 366 n. 51l.

24 These words recall Isa 51:4.

25 These words are similar to Jer 1:17 and Job 38:3.

26 These words are similar to Ps 99:6.

27 Literally, 'the prophecy agrees'.

28 These words are similar to 1 Sam 2:10.

29 These words are similar to 1 Sam 2:11.

SELECTED BIBLIOGRAPHY

(All these works contain exhaustive bibliographies.)

Harrington, D. J., 'Pseudo-Philo', in James H. Charlesworth (ed.), *The Old Testament Pseudepigrapha*, vol. 2, Garden City, NY, Doubleday, 1985, pp. 297–377.

——, Perrot, Charles, and Bogaert, Pierre-Maurice, *Pseudo-Philon: Les Antiquités bibliques*, 2 vols, trans. by Jacques Cazeaux, Paris, Les Éditions du Cerf, 1976.

James, M. R., with Prolegomenon by Louis H. Feldman, *The Biblical Antiquities of Philo*, New York, KTAV Publishing House, Inc., 1971.

Murphy, Frederick J., *Pseudo-Philo: Rewriting the Bible*, New York, Oxford University Press, 1993.

14

2 BARUCH 54:1–22

F. W. Dobbs-Allsopp

INTRODUCTION

Provenance, date and language

The Syriac Apocalypse of Baruch (hereafter 2 Baruch), from which the prayer below is taken, comes down to us in a sixth-century Syriac manuscript, presumably translated from the Greek.[1] Opinion is divided concerning whether the original language is Greek or Semitic.[2] Most agree that 2 Baruch was written in the late first century or the early second century CE[3] as a response to the destruction of the Second Temple in 70 CE and the theological challenge that this catastrophe posed to the poet's community. The anonymous poet casts himself as Baruch the scribe of Jeremiah, and the apocalypse itself is set fictionally in the period following the destruction of Jerusalem in 587/6 BCE.

Earlier scholars were inclined to see the text as an amalgam of various sources,[4] but most recent scholars concur that it represents a unified literary work, even if it draws on a variety of traditions.[5] It tells a story about the spiritual journey of Baruch and his community as they move from grief over the Temple's destruction to a consolation which takes hope in God as manifested through the Law.[6] The story divides into seven subsections,[7] which are held together by a narrative prose framework into which various other kinds and genres of literature are interwoven, for example conversations (usually between Baruch and God, or Baruch and his community), prayers and laments, speeches, visions and a letter.[8] In each of the five central subsections, a prayer or lament from Baruch figures prominently: 10:6–12:5; 21:4–25; 35:2–4; 48:2–24; 54:1–22. These prayers and laments embody the major themes and issues treated in 2 Baruch and highlight major junctures in the narrative journey from grief to consolation.

Literary context, structure and theology

The prayer of 2 Baruch 54 functions in its immediate context (2 Baruch 53:1–77:16)[9] as a structural hinge binding the vision of the clouds in chapter 53 with the vision's interpretation (explicated through the figure of Ramael) in chapters 55 and following. The prayer itself asks God to reveal the meaning of the vision of the clouds (see v. 6). As a petitionary prayer, 2 Baruch 54 bears a clear resemblance to many of the prayers in the Hebrew Psalter: address to God accompanied by praise (vv. 1–5), petition (v. 6) and affirmation of trust (vv. 20–2).[10] The prayer may be outlined as follows:

1 Opening address and praise (vv. 1–5)
2 Petition (v. 6)
3 Baruch's personal testimony and praise (vv. 7–11)
4 Transition (v. 12)
5 Individual responsibility (vv. 13–16)
6 Address to the wicked (vv. 17–19)
7 Concluding address to God (vv. 20–22)

The prayer itself is cast in verse,[11] and thus its message is inextricably bound to its poetic form.

The opening section of the poem (vv. 1–5) addresses God through an extended declaration of praise (cf. Ps 85:2–4; 89:9-11; 2 Baruch 21:7–14; 48:2–8). The repeated and expansive declarations of praise directed toward God here and again in vv. 7–12[12] are striking. This surfeit of praise functions as the structural balance to the lament in 10:6–12:5 with which the main body of the book opens. Lament and praise serve as symbolic guideposts marking the book's narrative trajectory from grief to consolation. In Baruch's first prayer[13] all he can do is utter complaint, while in his final prayer all he can do is utter praise.[14] This balance of lament and praise is evidenced in yet another way. Baruch begins chapter 3 with the rhetorical question: 'O Lord, my Lord, have I come into this world to look on the evil things of my mother?' (3:1). He then answers his own question: 'No! I cannot bear to look at the destruction of my mother' (3:2). Although some have supposed that Baruch is here taking up the attitude expressed by Job in his great lament ('Perish the day on which I was born', Job 3:3; cf. vv. 10–12), it seems rather that the mother being referred to and eventually lamented ('this mother', 10:16) is mother Zion. Here Baruch uses the biblical personification of the city as a woman to lament Jerusalem's destruction.[15] Any literal allusions to Baruch's actual mother (and there certainly are some, see 10:6–7, 14–16) are only secondary.

By contrast, in 54:10, after having been consoled, Baruch is freed to celebrate and praise 'my mother' who bore me. The words once used in lamentation are now sung in praise. This time, however, Baruch's literal mother is foregrounded, while personified mother Zion is very much in the background. The latter is present only to signal the transformation which has taken place within Baruch and to give the book a sense of closure. After all, one of Baruch's central theological aims is to show his community how they can get along without the Temple. The intention of chapter 4 is to deconstruct the traditional assumptions about the significance of Zion. The earthly Zion, the Zion that was destroyed, is not the true heavenly Zion, which is with God. There is no indication that the poet expected the Temple to be rebuilt. The Law replaces Zion as the focus of worship (at least for this poet, 32:1; 38:1–2; 48:22, 24; 44:3, 5–7; 46:5; 51:3; 54:5, 15; 82:6).[16]

The transition to the poem's wider focus occurs over a span of four lines in vv. 5–6. In v. 6 the actual petition appears. Baruch asks God to interpret the vision of chapter 53. Then follows the aforementioned section of praise which begins as an affirmation of trust (vv. 7–11). Baruch believes God will answer his prayer and reveal to him the vision's meaning because God has done this in the past (v. 7; cf. chapters 36–7, 39–40). Verse 12 is another transitional verse. It summarizes the praise of God that has been rendered by Baruch to this point in the poem, while the reference to God's 'deep thoughts of life' ushers in the praise of God's intelligence which follows directly in v. 13.

The next two sections of the poem (vv. 13–16, 17–19) develop the theme of individual responsibility. While manifesting an obvious belief in the 'two world conception', the hope in an eschatological future does not obviate the need to address life in this world. Baruch is crucially interested in providing his community with the means necessary to carry on in the present world while waiting and hoping for the next. Thus, for Baruch, the two worlds are connected. The Law is the community's hope in this world. It is through the Law that individuals gain entrance into the next world (esp. 44:3, 7; 46:5). Observance of the Law in this world gains greater urgency because it is viewed from the perspective of the future world. The Law is the central theme of the prayer in chapter 48. If the community's hope is in the Law, individuals must nevertheless choose to serve God and his Law. It is this sense of individual responsibility which gains thematic importance in 2 Baruch 54, especially in the last twenty-one lines of the poem (54:13–22). Those perish who do not love God's Law, but those who do will be glorified in the next world.

The Adam theme is introduced in v. 15 in a deconstructionist mode. One of the then contemporary readings of the creation stories in Genesis held that all were fated to sin because Adam sinned first and all of humanity was descended from Adam (48:42; 54:15; cf. 4 Ezra 3:22, 25–6; 7:63–72).[18] Baruch wants to show that this understanding is wrong. To be sure, Adam was responsible for his own sinful acts, but the rest of us are our own Adams (54:19). Thus, Baruch's positive notion of how the Law operates and the centrality of individual responsibility allow him in 48:19 to implore God 'not to make short our times of help', that is, the present world. This need not be construed as manifesting a conflicted eschatology.[19] Rather, Baruch's apocalyptic thinking has an existential component which prizes human flourishing in this world and demands ethical responsibility.

As noted, vv. 17–19 continue the general theme of individual responsibility, only now the theme is framed as a fictive address to the wicked – fictive because the intended audience is, of course, Baruch's community (note the inclusive 'us' in v. 19). The address to the wicked is couched in negative terms, namely, such and such will happen if you do not do this. In v. 17 the responsibility to choose is again underscored ('since you rejected'). In v. 18 reference is once again made to creation. And in v. 19 the Adam imagery is employed for a final time.

In the final section of the prayer (vv. 20–2), Baruch addresses God directly once again, and thus formally closes the poem as he had opened it. The mention of 'the consummation of the world' adds to the sense of closure created by the return to direct address by semantically underscoring the end of the poem through reference to the end times. Reprises of the petition and the theme of individual human responsibility add to the poem's sense of closure.

TRANSLATION

1 I prayed to the Mighty One:
   You, you alone, O Lord, know from of old the far reaches of this world,
   And whatever passes through time does so at your word!
   According to human deeds you hasten the beginning of every era,
   And the end of the ages are known by you alone!
2 You are that one for whom nothing is hard,
   And what is more, everything easy you do with a nod;
3 You are that one whom the depths and the heights alike attend,
   Even the start of every age is set by your word;
4 You are that one who reveals the future to the fearful,
   And who cares for them in the present;
5 You are the one who shows wonders to the ignorant,
   You are the one who overcomes obstacles for the incapable;
   You are the one who lights the darkness and reveals what is hidden to the faultless,
   Those who in faith submit to you and your Law!
6 You showed your servant this vision,
   So reveal to me also its interpretation!
7 For I know that whatever I have prayed about I have received an answer,
   And everything I have requested of you you have revealed to me.
   You disclosed to me in what voice I should praise you,
   And with what members I should lift up your praise and glory!
8 For if my members were mouths, or the hairs of my head voices,

Even then I could not honour you with praise, or praise you properly;
Nor could I recount your splendour, or tell of the glory of your
    beauty!

9   For who am I among people,
Why am I reckoned among those who are far worthier,
That I should hear all of these marvellous things from the Most High,
The innumerable promises from that one who created me?

10   Blessed is my mother among mothers!
And praised among women is she who bore me!

11   I will not stop extolling the Mighty One!
And what is more, in a voice of praise I will recount his wonders!

12   For who can imitate your wonders, O God,
Or apprehend your deep thoughts of life!

13   For you intelligently lead all the creatures your right hand created,
And you set every source of light beside you,
And you prepare the storehouses of wisdom beneath your throne!

14   Rightly, those perish who have not loved your Law,
And the torment of the judgement awaits those who have not
    submitted themselves to   your power!

15   Even if Adam first sinned and brought death upon all those who were
    not of his time,
Still those who were born from him, either each one among them
    prepares himself for the coming torment,
Or each one from among them chooses for himself the coming glory.

16   For truly, that one who believes receives a reward!

17   Now embrace destruction, O wicked of today,
Because instantly you will be punished for having rejected the
    understanding of the Most High.

18   For his deeds have not taught you,
Nor has the handiwork of his everlasting creation persuaded you.

19   Therefore, Adam is not the cause but for himself alone,
And all of us, each one is our own Adam.

20   And, you, O Lord, what you have revealed to me, interpret for me!
And everything about which I have prayed to you, make known to
    me!

21   At the consummation of the world, there is punishment for the
    wicked according to their wickedness,
But you glorify the faithful according to their faith!

22   For those who are yours you lead,
But for those who sin you blot out from among yours.

NOTES

1   *Bibliotheca Ambrosiana* B. 21 Inf. in Milan, fols 257a–265b. The latest edition of

this Syriac text has been edited by S. Dedering, *Apocalypse of Baruch*, Old Testament in Syriac 4.3, Leiden, E. J. Brill, 1973 and is used as the textual basis for the present translation. For further discussion about the Syriac text, as well as the Greek fragments and the Arabic version, see P.-M. Bogaert, *L'Apocalypse de Baruch: Introduction, traduction, du syriaque et commentaire*, Sources Chrétiennes 144, Paris, Les Éditions du Cerf, 1969, pp. 38–40; Dedering, op. cit., pp. ii–iv; A. F. J. Klijn, '2 Baruch', in J. H. Charlesworth (ed.), *The Old Testament Pseudepigrapha*, vol. 1, Garden City, NY, Doubleday, 1983, pp. 615–16; G. B. Sayler, *Have the Promises Failed? A Literary Analysis of 2 Baruch*, SBLDS 72, Atlanta, Scholars Press, 1984, pp. 1-3; F. J. Murphy, *The Structure and Meaning of Second Baruch*, SBLDS 78, Atlanta, Scholars Press, 1985, p. 1; F. Leemhuis *et al.*, *The Arabic Text of the Apocalypse of Baruch*, Leiden, E. J. Brill, 1986.

2   Whatever the original language, it seems clear that the prayers and laments in 2 Baruch draw consciously on the tradition of prayer and poetry known from the Hebrew Bible.

3   See R. H. Charles, *The Apocalypse of Baruch*, London, Anden Charles Black, 1896, pp. lxiv–lxv; Bogaert, op. cit., pp. 272–80, 294–319; Klijn, op. cit., pp. 616–17; Sayler, op. cit., pp. 103–10; Murphy, op. cit., p. 2.

4   Charles, op. cit., pp. liii–lxv.

5   Bogaert, op. cit., pp. 56–81; Sayler, op. cit., esp. pp. 11–39; Murphy, op. cit., esp. pp. 11–29.

6   Sayler, op. cit., p. 12.

7   However, there is some dispute over the precise boundaries of each subsection.

8   See esp. Sayler, op. cit., pp. 13, 38.

9   Bogaert, op. cit., I, pp. 66–7, Sayler, op. cit., pp. 33–5. Murphy, op. cit., pp. 22–4, J. H. Charlesworth, 'Baruch, Book of 2 (Syriac)', in *ABD* 1, p. 621, and J. J. Collins, *The Apocalyptic Imagination*, New York, Crossroad, 1984, p. 170 understand these basic chapters as comprising a cohesive subsection of 2 Baruch.

10 For a convenient discussion of the basic elements in petitionary prayers, see P. D. Miller, Jun., *They Cried to the Lord: The Form and Theology of Biblical Prayer*, Minneapolis, Fortress, 1994, pp. 44–130. One should note that 2 Baruch 54, like the other prayers in 2 Baruch, is a literary composition, by which I mean that it was composed as an integral part of the argument of the book as a whole. This is not to suggest that it bears no relation to actual prayers used liturgically or privately. It surely does. But one cannot treat 2 Baruch 54 simply as an exemplar of an actual prayer.

11 A quick perusal of several translations of 2 Baruch 54 suggests that not all are agreed that this prayer is in fact poetry. The confusion results from a failure to appreciate the nature of the poetry. To be sure, 2 Baruch 54 does not exhibit the isosyllabic metre which comes to dominate later Syriac poetry. Nor is it reminiscent of the classical Greek or Latin metrical traditions. Rather, Baruch's prayer bears many of the features which characterize the poetic tradition known best from the Hebrew Bible, e.g., free-verse-like lines, the prevalence of parallelism (of various kinds), the play of variation, and frequent use of lexical repetition. This is not to say that the prayer was originally composed in Hebrew, but only that it shares the characteristics of the Hebrew poetic tradition.

12 Verbs and nouns built from the root *sbh*, 'to praise', occur eight times in vv. 7–11.

13 For the idea that laments are in fact prayers directed to God, see Miller, op. cit., pp. 55–6.

14 However, Baruch does not win through to consolation as easily as some have supposed. The opening lament is powerful; the pain and grief is real. In 21:4–25 Baruch is still very much exercised by the pain and suffering of this world, and in vv. 19–25 in particular he is still in complaint mode. Verse 19 opens with the classic complaint thrice repeated: How long? Another lament is uttered in 35:2–4, and even in 48:14–15 Baruch's anger at the destruction of the Temple and the suffering of the community remains, however briefly articulated, close to the surface. It is only in the prayer in chapter 54 that Baruch can hymn God's praises without complaint or lament.

15 See esp. the book of Lamentations; F. W. Dobbs-Allsopp, *Weep, O Daughter of Zion: A Study of the City-Lament Genre in the Hebrew Bible*, BibOr 44, Rome, Editrice Pontificio Istituto Biblico, 1993, pp. 75–90; idem, 'The Syntagma of *bat* Followed by a Geographical Name in the Hebrew Bible: A Reconsideration of Its Meaning and Grammar', *CBQ* 57, 1995, pp. 451–70.

16 See Charlesworth, op. cit., p. 620.

17 For this terminology see Murphy, op. cit., pp. 31–70.

18 See the convenient discussion with references to other literature by M. E. Stone, *Fourth Ezra*, Hermeneia, Minneapolis, Fortress, 1990, pp. 63–6.

19. See W. Harnisch, *Verhängnis und Verheissung der Geschichte*, FRLANT 97, Göttingen, Vandenhoeck & Ruprecht, 1969, pp. 249–67; Collins, op. cit., pp. 171–2, 176.

SELECTED BIBLIOGRAPHY

Bogaert, P.-M., *L'Apocalypse de Baruch: Introduction, traduction, du syriaque et commentaire*, Paris, Les Éditions du Cerf, 1969.

Charles, R. H., *The Apocalypse of Baruch*, London, Anden & Charles Black, 1896.

Charlesworth, J. H., 'Baruch, Book of 2 (Syriac)', in *ABD* 1, pp. 620–1.

Collins, J. J., *The Apocalyptic Imagination*, New York, Crossroad, 1984.

Dedering, S., *Apocalypse of Baruch*, Old Testament in Syriac 4.3, Leiden, E. J. Brill, 1973.

Harnisch, W., *Verhängnis und Verheissung der Geschichte*, Göttingen, Vandenhoeck & Ruprecht, 1969.

Klijn, A. F. J., '2 Baruch', in J. H. Charlesworth (ed.), *The Old Testament Pseudepigrapha*, vol. 1, Garden City, NY, Doubleday, 1983, pp. 615–52.

Murphy, F. J., *The Structure and Meaning of Second Baruch*, Atlanta, Scholars Press, 1985.

Sayler, G. B., *Have the Promises Failed? A Literary Analysis of 2 Baruch*, Atlanta, Scholars Press, 1984.

15

JOSEPHUS AND PHILO

Mark Harding

JOSEPHUS

Josephus was born in Israel in *c.* 37 CE into an aristocratic priestly family descended from the Hasmonean priest-princes, descendants of the Maccabean heroes who prosecuted the revolt against Antiochus Epiphanes in 167–164 BCE and served as high priests in the Temple in Jerusalem from the middle of the second century till the reign of Herod the Great (40[37]–4 BCE). Josephus died in Rome in *c.* 100 CE, having enjoyed the patronage of the three Flavian emperors, Vespasian (69–79), and his sons Titus (79–81) and Domitian (81–96).

In his autobiography (the *Life*) Josephus presents himself as a precocious and gifted child. As a teenager, he made a thorough examination of the three major groups within Judaism, learning as much as he could about the Pharisees, Sadducees and Essenes. He spent three years as the 'zealot', or close follower, of Bannus, an otherwise unknown hermit. After this time he entered political life representing the interests of the most influential Jewish group, the Pharisees.

At the outbreak of the Jewish War in 66, Josephus was appointed by the aristocratic leadership in Jerusalem as the general in charge of organizing resistance to the Romans in Galilee. However, in the campaign of 67 Vespasian quickly subdued the fortified cities and towns of the region and besieged Josephus in Jotapata. The wily Josephus survived a suicide pact among his staff, claiming that God had revealed to him the fact that the Jewish cause was lost and the Roman emperors were destined to rule the world. When taken to Vespasian, he was prompted by the spirit of prophecy to pronounce the Roman general and his son, Titus, future emperors. By 69 Vespasian was in fact emperor in Rome. After his capture, Josephus spent the remainder of the war as a guest of and adviser to the Romans.

He wrote four works in the following order: the *Jewish War*, the *Jewish Antiquities*, the *Life* and *Against Apion*. Each of these has survived in great part because early Christian writers, such as Origen (*c.* 185–254 CE) and Eusebius (*c.* 260–339 CE), closely identified with his tendentious presentation of the reasons for the destruction of Jerusalem and the Temple. They perceived in his works confirmation of what they regarded as a providential eclipse of the Jews and the passing of the status of 'chosen people' to the Christians. The works of Josephus were thus copied and circulated in Christian, not Jewish, circles. There are some Christian interpolations in texts of Josephus, though not every element in these may be secondary. Indeed his references to John the Baptist and the death of James the 'Lord's Brother' in *Antiquities*, 18.116–19 and 20.200 respectively appear to be genuine as they stand in the text. The same cannot be said of the discussion of Jesus in *Antiquities*, 18.63–4. Moreover, Josephus not only mentions Christian heroes, such as John the Baptist and James, but wrote about people and events that figure in the New Testament, such as Herod the Great (Matthew 2), Pontius Pilate, the rebellion of Judas the Galilean (Acts 5:37), the death of Agrippa I (Acts 12:20–3) and the movement led by the unnamed Egyptian (see Acts 21:38).

His first work, a history of the Jewish War in seven books, was completed in the mid-70s CE. In it he chronicles the progressive breakdown of law and order in Israel under Roman rule. Josephus clearly indicts the hotheads among the Jews, blaming them for the revolt, and claiming that God himself had deserted to the cause of the Romans against the impious and recalcitrant Jews.

The *Antiquities* is an extensive presentation and elaboration of the historical traditions of the Jews in twenty books. The first eleven books are devoted to a re-presentation of the biblical traditions. Books 12–20 carry the story of the Jews down to the outbreak of the Jewish War. The whole work has a decided apologetic thrust directed to gentile readers. One notes the editing out of the account those matters which might have proved prejudicial to his intent such as the divine promise to Israel of exclusive possession of the land of Canaan, the occasional moral failings of the patriarchs and the Israelite heroes, and the tradition that Moses had murdered an Egyptian overseer. Josephus demonstrates the venerable nature of Jewish traditions, and commends Jewish morality and the reasonableness of the Jewish conception of God. Although one could call Josephus a defector, he never assimilated his Jewish heritage to that of Greco-Roman culture. He sought to offer his readers an account of Judaism which was calculated to increase respect during the aftermath of the first revolt. Consequently, Josephus' voice seems out of step with Jewish sentiment expressed in the Jewish apocalypses 4 Ezra and 2 Baruch, and in the succession of revolts in Egypt, Cyrene, Cyprus and Babylon in 115–17 CE, and in Israel itself in 132–5. Two shorter works, the autobiographical *Life* and his polemical *Against Apion* (an Egyptian anti-Jew), were written at the same time as the *Antiquities*.

The prayers Josephus incorporated into his works are confined almost exclusively to the first eight books of the *Antiquities*. These play a significant part in his purpose of presenting to his gentile readers the worthy and lofty conception of God, free of mythology and idolatry (see *Antiquities*, 1.15). The six major prayers of these books are literary creations on Josephus' part. Two of them, Moses' prayer at the sea (2.335–7) – discussed in this book (see pp. 92-8) – and Moses' prayer when confronted by the rebellion of Korah and the Reubenites (4.40–50), have no biblical parallel. The other four, Isaac's blessing of Jacob (1.272–3), Joshua's prayer after the defeat at Ai (5.38–41) and the two prayers of Solomon at the consecration of the Temple (8.107–8, 111–17) are elaborations of prayers already found in the biblical text.

SELECTED BIBLIOGRAPHY

P. Bilde, *Flavius Josephus Between Jerusalem and Rome*, Sheffield, JSOT Press, 1988.
S. J. D. Cohen, *Josephus in Galilee and Rome: His Vita and His Development as a Historian*, Leiden, E. J. Brill, 1979.
L. H. Feldman and G. Hata (eds), *Josephus, Judaism, and Christianity*, Leiden, E. J. Brill, 1987.
—— and —— (eds), *Josephus, the Bible, and History*, Leiden, E. J. Brill, 1989.
M. Harding, 'Making Old Things New. Prayer Texts in Josephus's *Antiquities:* A Study in the Transmission of Tradition', in J. H. Charlesworth with M. Harding and M. Kiley (eds), *The Lord's Prayer and Other Prayer Texts from the Greco-Roman Era*, Valley Forge, Trinity Press International, 1994, pp. 54–72.
S. Mason, *Flavius Josephus on the Pharisees*, Leiden, E. J. Brill, 1991.
——, *Josephus and the New Testament*, Peabody, MA, Hendrickson, 1992.
T. Rajak, *Josephus: The Historian and His Society*, Philadelphia, Fortress, 1984.
S. Schwartz, *Josephus and Judaean Politics*, Leiden, E. J. Brill, 1990.
H. St J. Thackeray, *Josephus: The Man and the Historian*, New York, KTAV, 1967.
Pere Villalba i Varneda, *The Historical Method of Flavius Josephus*, Leiden, E. J. Brill, 1986.

PHILO

Philo was a wealthy and well-educated Jew born in Alexandria in *c.* 20 BCE. He died in *c.* 50 CE. His apostate nephew, Tiberius Alexander, served a term as procurator of Judaea in 46–8 CE, was later Prefect of Egypt and led Titus' Roman troops at the siege of Jerusalem in 70 CE. Tiberius' father, Alexander, Philo's brother, served as alabarch in Alexandria and had gilded the doors of the Temple in Jerusalem.[1] We know little of Philo's life. He was an integral member of an embassy which appealed to the emperor Gaius (Caligula) in 40 CE regarding the bloody pogroms against the Jews in Alexandria in 38 (see his *On the Embassy to Gaius*). In *Against Flaccus*, he mentions the famous Prefect of Judaea, Pontius Pilate (26–36), approvingly citing Agrippa I's description of him as an evil, rapacious man who furthered the anti-Jewish policies of Sejanus, Pilate's patron in Tiberian Rome at least until the former's execution in 31 CE. Philo made at least one pilgrimage to the Temple in Jerusalem.

Like Josephus, but for different reasons, Philo was an influential writer in later Christian circles in which his works were copied and circulated. His allegorical manner of interpreting the biblical text was emulated in the early Church. Platonic thinking was a major influence on Philo, and was also a significant contributor to the scholarly tradition as it developed in the early Christian writers.

Philo's genius lies in his philosophical presentation of the Jewish faith and scriptural deposit. He achieved a synthesis of philosophical insight redolent chiefly of Platonic, but also Stoic, influence and the Jewish scriptural heritage. He was the first to achieve this in any major way. Such a task had been undertaken to a lesser extent in the Jewish diaspora by earlier writers, such as the second-century BCE Aristobulus (for extant text, see J. H. Charlesworth (ed.), *Old Testament Pseudepigrapha*, Garden City, NY, Doubleday, vol. 2, pp. 837–42), eager to mount an apologetic for Judaism in the midst of Greco-Roman culture, perhaps even to persuade potential Jewish apostates to remain within the fold. Josephus' *Antiquities* and most of Philo's works are, therefore, similar in thrust. Both writers set about commending the Jewish legacy to their sophisticated Greco-Roman contemporaries in a manner that would further its respect and esteem.

Most approximate to Philo's purpose is the apocryphal *Wisdom of Solomon* written, perhaps, in Egypt in the first century BCE. In this work the claim is made that wisdom is not in the hands of Greek philosophers – a very misleading conclusion – but in the hands of faithful Jews. This wisdom is identified with the law of God mediated to Moses. Sirach 24 also makes this identification.

It is evident that Philo had a thorough education in the literature and thought of the Hellenistic world. His knowledge of the Jewish scriptures is derived from his familiarity with the Septuagint (LXX). He did not know Hebrew. For him, the LXX (an Alexandrian production) is fully authoritative.

Philo's writings have been well preserved, though some of his treatises have been lost. Peder Borgen divides Philo's considerable output into the following categories:

1 *Exposition of the Laws of Moses.* The works in this category underscore the superiority of the Jewish Torah, enshrining the most noble virtues such as piety, courage and self-control (see *On the Creation of the World, On Abraham, On the Decalogue, On the Special Laws*).
2 *Allegorical interpretations.* These works, resembling the midrashim, are verse-by-verse expositions of passages in Genesis. Like the works in the first category, these also stress the moral excellence of the great Israelite heroes such as Abraham and Moses. Their example guides the pious and faithful into an ever-deepening relationship with God (*On the Sacrifices of Abel and Cain, On the Migration of Abraham, On Dreams*).

3   *Thematic works.* In this group, Philo treats various philosophical principles (e.g. *On the Contemplative Life, On Providence*), as well as apologetic matters which arise out of concrete historical circumstances (e.g. *Against Flaccus, On the Embassy to Gaius*).
4   Philo also wrote commentaries on the books of Genesis and Exodus, entitled *Questions and Answers*, which outline the literal as well as allegorical meaning of the biblical text. These appear to be intended for a synagogue audience. Helmut Koester describes them as 'exegetical and homiletical lectures'.[2]

In Philo, the offering of sacrifices and prayers represents the two modes of expressing religious devotion to God. Nevertheless, for most Jews, Philo included, prayer and praise has become a substitute for the offering of sacrifice owing to geographical remove from Jerusalem and the Temple. After the destruction of the Temple in 70 CE, prayer replaced sacrifice for all Jews.

Philo, in common with many of his Jewish contemporaries, stresses right conduct as a necessary prerequisite of worship, prayer included (see *On Moses*, 2.107–8). Indeed, the honour due to God is better rendered by prayer and praise from a devoted heart than by literal sacrifices. Reflecting biblical and Greek philosophical traditions, Philo is fully persuaded that the only rightful response of people to the providential care bestowed on them by God is the activity of prayer and praise. No other 'gift' will suffice since all things are God's (*On Noah's Work as a Planter*, 130; *On the Special Laws*, 1.271; cf. Psalm 50:12–13; Acts 17:24–5; Seneca [citing Plato], *Epistles*, 65.8). Those who pray aright, Sharyn Dowd concludes, cast themselves in absolute dependence on the providence of God, confessing their sins, and, on that basis, making their petitions to him ('The Theological Function of Petitionary Prayer in the Thought of Philo', p. 254).

While Philo's works return frequently to discussion of the propriety and theology of prayer, there are very few prayers in his works. In addition to the two discussed in this volume (*On the Migration of Abraham*, 101; *On the Special Laws*, 2.198-9), others occur in *On Dreams*, 1.164 (prayed by Philo himself) and *Who is the Heir*, 24–9 (prayed by Abraham).

NOTES

1   Katherine G. Evans, 'Alexander the Alabarch: Roman and Jew', SBLSP 34, 1995, pp. 576–94.
2   *Introduction to the New Testament*, Philadelphia/Berlin and New York, Fortress/de Gruyter, 1982, vol. 1, p. 275.

SELECTED BIBLIOGRAPHY

P. Borgen, 'Philo of Alexandria', in M. E. Stone (ed.), *Jewish Writings of the Second Temple Period*, Compendia rerum iudaicarum ad novum testamentum, Section 2,

Assen/Philadelphia, Van Gorcum/Fortress, 1984, pp. 233–82.
S. E. Dowd, 'The Theological Function of Petitionary Prayer in the Thought of Philo', *Perspectives in Religious Studies*, 1983, vol. 10, pp. 241–54.
E. R. Goodenough, *An Introduction to Philo Judaeus*, New Haven, Yale University Press, 1940.
J. Laporte, *Eucharistia in Philo*, New York, Edward Mellen Press, 1983.
C. W. Larsen, 'Prayer of Petition in Philo', *Journal of Biblical Literature*, 1946, vol. 65, pp. 185–203.
S. Sandmel, *Philo of Alexandria: An Introduction*, New York/Oxford, Oxford University Press, 1979.
D. Winston, *Logos and Mystical Theology in Philo of Alexandria*, Cincinnati, Hebrew Union College Press, 1985.
H. A. Wolfson, *Philo: Foundations of Religious Philosophy in Judaism, Christianity, and Islam*, 2 volumes, Cambridge, MA, Harvard University Press, 1947.

16

THE PRAYER OF MOSES IN JOSEPHUS, *ANTIQUITIES* 2.335–7

Mark Harding

INTRODUCTION

Before his capture by the Romans, Josephus (*c.* 37–100 CE) had been a participant on the Jewish side in the first year of the First Revolt (66–70). His major work, the *Antiquities of the Jews*, was written to inform a sophisticated Greco-Roman audience of the origin, historical traditions and superior antiquity of the Jews. Given the difficulties faced by Roman administrators in the province of Judaea culminating in the large-scale revolt of 66–70 CE, the literary task undertaken by Josephus is decidedly apologetic in its tone.

The historian's model in terms of scope and intent was the twenty-book *Roman Antiquities* of Dionysius of Halicarnassus, completed in 7 BCE.[1] Urged on by those who were 'curious' about the Jews (*Ant.* 1.8), Josephus set out to show in his own twenty books that the Jews have a venerable and glorious history, and that Moses, their lawgiver (*nomothetēs*) has imparted a 'pure' conception of God free of the 'unseemly mythology' that bedevils the religious traditions of other nations (*Ant.* 1.15–16).[2]

Josephus also has a moral purpose in writing. He sets out to show that those who live in accordance with the will of God and keep his laws prosper in all things whereas the disobedient end in disaster (see *Ant.* 1.14). Those who follow the path of virtue laid out by God receive from him a life of bliss (*eudaimōn bios*), while those who 'step outside the path of virtue' are justly punished (*Ant.* 1.20). Faithful Jews and their leaders receive divine blessing. The recalcitrant, even among the Jews, receive just condemnation for their moral failings.

The *Antiquities* may be regarded as a monumental exercise in the transmission and actualization of tradition. To render the Jewish heritage intelligible to his Roman audience is pre-eminently Josephus' grand design. His intent can be traced not only in the presentation of the course of Jewish history under divine providence but also in the prayers he devised for his characters in the first eleven books which re-tell the biblical story down to the time of Ezra and Esther.[3]

The prayer translated here is one of six substantial prayers in direct speech in the Josephan corpus, all of them in books 1–11 of the *Antiquities*.

Attestation

At an early stage in the manuscript tradition, the *Antiquities* was divided neatly into two sections, books 1–10 and 11–20. The text of the prayer of Moses is settled in the manuscript tradition. Apart from the variant at the beginning of the prayer (see n. 22 below), there are no significant textual variants or corruptions.[4]

The Greek text translated here is that printed in the ten-volume Loeb Classical Library edition of the works of Josephus.[5] This text is based on that adopted by Benedict Niese, whose edition of the Works was published in Berlin in 1887. The divisions of the text into sections are those introduced by Niese. The translation is my own.

Provenance, date and language

Josephus wrote the four works which have come down to us in Greek.[6] Though Greek was not his native language, he writes that he has laboured zealously in Greek grammar, as well as poetry and prose (see *Antiquities* 20.263; cf. 1.7). According to his final paragraph (20.267), the completed work can be dated to the thirteenth year of Domitian's reign (81–96 CE), i.e., 93–4 CE, when Josephus himself was 56.

Josephus wrote the work in Rome under the patronage of the Flavian emperors. According to the *Life* 428–30, this patronage actually increased under Domitian who punished Josephus' Jewish accusers and exempted him from taxation on his property in Judaea.

Relation to other works

Josephus, like some other early Jewish writers of the era, approaches the task of actualizing the biblical and historical heritage of the Jews consciously aware of the philosophical and cultural milieu in which he and his audience are situated. In the Preface to the *Antiquities* he has already signalled the worthy contribution of Moses to religious thinking and his disdain for 'unseemly mythology'. Thus Moses, the patriarchs and the great heroes of the Jewish heritage are presented as enlightened and, of course, eminently virtuous and venerable philosopher-Jews. Their conception of God, as expressed by Josephus, owes much to current philosophical, especially Stoic, thinking.[7] To this extent Josephus' historical presentation is reminiscent of the more thorough-going philosophical treatments of the Jewish heroes in the corpus of Philo.

The prayer of Moses is an invocation of God as totally sovereign.⁸ This point is underscored again and again in the prayers of early Judaism, and is flagged by the epithet 'Master of the Universe'. This epithet is used not only by Josephus, but found elsewhere in early Jewish literature and in the rabbinic deposit.⁹ While it is not present in the prayer of Moses, the concept of divine lordship over creation is expressed in the prayer – especially in section 337: 'sea and mountain which surround us are yours,' Moses prays for the benefit of the terrified and despairing Israelites.

The prayer is offered by Moses in the fullest confidence that God is well able to help, not on the basis of any contract initiated by the pray-er since no one could have a claim on God because he is totally self-sufficient, but on the ground that God is Israel's helper (boēthos) and ally (symmachos).¹⁰ Harold W. Attridge is right to argue that these terms, used commonly enough in Greco-Roman literature of the benefits bestowed by the gods on nations and people, become in Josephus replacements for the biblical concept of an exclusive covenant relationship with Israel.¹¹ Attridge proceeds to demonstrate that the alliance bestowed on Israel has been granted on account of her virtue, and, as a consequence, is potentially available to all nations.¹² The reality of God's alliance is expressed in his providential care for this people of Israel in miraculous deliverances, such as that at the Sea, and the raising up of religious and ethical guides such as Moses. Moreover, the people left Egypt in accord with his will. God, Moses prays, can do whatever it takes to extricate his special people, as long as they continue to be found pursuing the path of virtue.

The term *pronoia* ('providence'), used frequently in Josephus, demonstrates his preparedness to invoke the terminology of the philosophical traditions of Plato and the Stoics in mounting his apologetic for Judaism. In the Greek philosophical writers, the term denotes God's care in his rational ordering and superintending of the created order.¹³ The term is found both in the prayer of Moses (*Ant.* 2.336) and twice in the exhortation which precedes it (*Ant.* 2.330, 331).

However, in Josephus *pronoia* is no mere reflection of the Greek idea of divine forethought. God exercises providence in accordance with the moral truth and religious conceptions he has revealed most fully to Moses, and in which Abraham and the patriarchs also participated. Thus when Moses urges the people to entrust themselves to divine *pronoia* as the only hope they might reasonably entertain in their present extremity (see *Ant.* 2.330–3), he can appeal to the fact that God does in fact favour them on the grounds of their attainments in the pursuit of virtue. Indeed their total lack of power and ingenuity to escape from their predicament allows Moses to affirm that God delights to work for the benefit of those he favours when they have lost all hope. In other early Jewish writers *pronoia* is also manifest both in God's care bestowed upon the Jewish people, often in dire circumstances, and in his frustration of the purposes of the wicked.[14]

The frequent use of *pronoia* in early Jewish writings in Greek testifies to the wide dissemination and attractiveness of this key philosophical idea in early Judaism, especially in the diaspora. That the concept is also encountered in early Christian writings underscores the considerable commonality of terminology that existed between Greek (and Roman) philosophy and early Jewish and Christian theological expression. In contrast both to the Stoic's concept of a rational ordering of the universe and to the Greek concept of deterministic fate (*heimarmenē*), the idea of providence in the early Jewish and Christian writers spoke, on the one hand, of divine moral purpose expressing itself in saving deeds bestowed upon the virtuous and retribution visited upon the wicked and, on the other, implied human responsibility to be oriented to the will of God as it had been expressed in the scriptures, chiefly in the moral code delivered to Moses.[15] To this extent *pronoia* was a congenial term for those standing in the biblical tradition who, like Josephus, sought to commend that tradition to the world.

Literary context in the *Antiquities*

The presentation of the career of Moses begins in *Ant.* 2.205 and concludes at the end of book 4 (section 331). One of the Egyptian 'sacred scribes' (*hierogrammateis*) predicts, prior to Moses' birth, that he would govern the Egyptians, exalt the Israelites, and would surpass all humanity in virtue (*aretē*). Moreover, he would be revered not only by the Jews but by all nations (2.216). Josephus has already anticipated Moses' unprecedented contribution to the religion of the Jews in his Preface to the *Antiquities* (1.15).

The immediate context of the prayer is the familiar story of the plagues, the Passover and the Exodus. The pursuing Egyptian army has hemmed in the Israelites between mountainous cliffs on one side and sea on the other. The Israelites are fearful, forgetful of the miracles performed in Egypt on their behalf by God, and, as a consequence, despairing of their salvation. Indeed, Josephus dramatically magnifies the terror of the Israelites.[16] In sections 330–3, Moses exhorts them to entrust themselves to the providence (*pronoia*) of God their great helper (*boēthos*), confident that God is about to demonstrate to them his power (*ischys*) to save them on the one hand and confound their enemies on the other. The prayer, which follows immediately, juxtaposes the themes of fear and despair on the part of the Israelites with the providence of God expressed in the miraculous deliverance.

Once delivered, the Israelites express their response to the miraculous divine intervention with joy, their confidence and assurance re-kindled just as Moses had foreshadowed in his prayer.

Use and effect in later writings

With respect to the prayer of Moses and the other prayers of the *Antiquities*, it is difficult to gauge their effect in specific terms on later writers. We have already seen that Josephus' corpus of works was copied and circulated in Christian circles. This phenomenon has much to do, as I indicated in the introductory essay on Josephus and Philo, with the early Christians' developing sense of a self-identity over against the Jews. They found much that was useful in the historian's rehearsal of the biblical tradition in the *Antiquities*, and his mention of New Testament people and events.[17] As far as I am aware, however, early Christians do not cite the prayer of Moses at the Sea.[18]

As models of the marriage of philosophical insight in biblical context, the prayers of Josephus, like this prayer of Moses, might have served as fruitful models for early Christian expressions of spirituality since the philosophical terminology, which the early Christians found congenial as a medium of their own theological insights, is shared by Josephus.[19]

TRANSLATION

(335) (When Moses reached the shore, he took his staff and invoked God as ally[20] and helper,[21] crying out with these words:) You[22] are not ignorant of the fact that for us to escape from the present situation lies neither in our power nor in human ingenuity. Indeed, if there is any salvation for this host which left Egypt in accordance with your will, you can provide it.[23] (336) We despair of any other hope and resource.[24] To you alone we flee for refuge. If there is anything to come from your providence enabling us to escape from the wrath of the Egyptians we look to you. May this aid come quickly which will underscore your power to us.[25] By your hand[26] raise the people who have fallen into despair to contentment and confidence concerning their salvation. (337) The dire straits into which we have fallen are not outside your domain, for sea and mountain which surround us are yours. If you command, it shall be opened, or the deep become dry land. Why, we might escape through the air should you, in your strength, decide to save us in this way.[27]

NOTES

1 For a brief summary of the similarities of Josephus' *Jewish Antiquities* and the *Roman Antiquities* of Dionysius of Halicarnassus, see H. W. Attridge, *The Interpretation of Biblical History in the Antiquitates Judicae of Flavius Josephus*, Missoula, Scholars Press, 1976, pp. 43–57.
2 See H. St J. Thackeray, Introduction to vol. IV of the Loeb edition of Josephus' Works, p. vii.

3 The biblical story actually concludes at *Ant.* 11.303.
4 On the text of the Josephan corpus and the use of Josephus in the early and medieval Church, see H. Schreckenberg, *Rezeptionsgeschichtliche und textkritische Untersuchungen zu Flavius Josephus*, Leiden, E. J. Brill, 1977) and his *Die Flavius-Josephus-Tradition in Antike und Mittelalter*, Leiden, E. J. Brill, 1972 respectively.
5 Translated and edited by H. St J. Thackeray, A. Wikgren, R. Marcus and L. H. Feldman, Cambridge, MA, Harvard University Press, 1926–65.
6 An earlier edition of the *Jewish War* was written for Jews in Aramaic. See *War* 1.3.
7 See especially L. H. Feldman, 'Mikra in the Writings of Josephus', in J. Mulder and H. Sysling (eds), *Mikra: Text, Translation, Reading and Interpretation of the Hebrew Bible in Ancient Judaism and Early Christianity*, Assen/Philadelphia, Van Gorcum/Fortress, 1988, p. 499 where he discusses Josephus' presentation of Abraham (see *Ant.* 1.225) and Moses (see *Ant.* 2.229). Note also Clement of Alexandria's citation of the observation of the Pythagorean philosopher Numenius: 'For what is Plato, but Moses speaking in Attic Greek?' *Stromata* 1.22.
8 The freedom of God in relation to his creation, a corollary to his sovereignty, is expressed by the term *aprosdeēs* ('self-sufficient'), a term used in Greek philosophy as well as in works of early Judaism in Greek. See Plato, *Timaeus* 33D; Letter of Aristeas, 211; 1 Macc 12:9; 2 Macc 14:35; 3 Macc 2:9; Philo, *On the Unchangeableness of God* 56; see also Josephus, *Ant.* 8.111; cf. Acts 17:25; 1 Clem 52:1.
9 See, e.g., *Ant.* 1.272; 4.46 (both occurring in prayers); 3 Macc 2:2; Sirach 23:1; cf. m. Abot 4.22.
10 See *Ant.* 2.335.
11 See H. W. Attridge, op. cit., pp. 78–92.
12 ibid., p. 81 and n. 2.
13 It first occurs in a philosophical/theological context in Herodotus, *Histories* 3.108. See also Plato, *Timaeus* 30B; Plutarch, *On the Obsolescence of Oracles* 426A, 436D.
14 See 3 Macc 4:21; 5:30; 4 Macc 9:24; 13:19; 17:22.
15 See L. H. Martin, 'Josephus' Use of *heimarmenē* in the *Jewish Antiquities* XIII, 171–3', *Numen*, 1981, vol. 28, pp. 127–37 and H. W. Attridge, op. cit., p. 157.
16 See ibid., p. 77.
17 See H. Schreckenberg, 'The Works of Josephus and the Early Christian Church', in L. H. Feldman and G. Hata (eds), *Josephus, Judaism, and Christianity*, Leiden, E. J. Brill, 1987, pp. 315–24.
18 It is absent in H. Schreckenberg's register of citations of Josephus in the Fathers and the medieval writers (*Die Flavius-Josephus-Tradition in Antike und Mittelalter*).
19 Josephus' conception of the working of *pronoia* as just government of the universe is paralleled in Irenaeus, *Against Heresies* 3.25 and Recognitions of Clement 8.10.
20 For the use of the word *symmachos* ascribed to God as 'ally' see also 2 Macc 8:24; Philo, *On the Migration of Abraham* 62; Herodotus, *Histories* 8.143; Josephus, *Antiquities* 4.2.
21 The Greek word used here, *boēthos*, is also used of God quite frequently in the LXX. See, e.g., Exod 15:2; 18:4; and 2 Macc 3:39. According to R. Marcus, it is also used of God in Greek inscriptions. See his 'Divine Names and Attributes in Hellenistic Literature', *American Academy for Jewish Research*, 1931–2, p. 58.

The terms *symmachia* and *boētheia* both occur in Dionysius of Halicarnassus, *Roman Antiquities* 6.6.3 as benefits of the gods in their relations with the Romans.

22 The direct speech of the prayer begins without the pray-er invoking an epithet of God, though, of course, Josephus has reported that Moses invoked God as 'ally and helper'. According to Rengstorf's *Concordance* of Josephus' works, however, the 'inferior' manuscript group (following Niese's assessment) – S (Codex Vindobonensis), P (Codex Parisinus) and L (Codex Laurentianus) – does interpolate the extremely common invocation '(*ō*) *despota*' at this point in the text. Any absence of epithet would have struck both Jewish and non-Jewish audiences as odd. For the ubiquity of epithets in invocations of the gods in Greek prayers, see K. von Fritz, 'Greek Prayers', *Review of Religion*, 1945, vol. 10, pp. 16–17. The Hebrew Bible does afford a few examples of prayers in which there is no epithet of God. See, e.g., Exod 17:3–4; Num 16:15.

23 cf. Philo, *Life of Moses* 1.174 in which Moses, in the same context, exhorts the people: 'It is God's special property to find a way where no way is.'

24 cf. Psalm 124; Job 19:10.

25 cf. Psalm 77:14; 90:16.

26 Josephus usually avoids the anthropomorphisms of the biblical text. See A. Schlatter, *Wie sprach Josephus von Gott?*, Beitraege zur Foerderung christlicher Theologie 14, Guetersloh, Bertelsmann, 1910, vol. 14, p. 22.

27 The three-fold means of escape – mountain (*oros*), deep (*pelagos*) and air (*aeros*) – are adduced as evidence of Josephus' predilection for triads. See H. St J. Thackeray's Introduction to vol. 4 of the Loeb edition of the works of Josephus, p. xvi. There is no mention of the mountain in the biblical account. For the pliability of the created order in the hands of God, see Ps 97:5; 104 *passim*; 144:5–7.

SELECTED BIBLIOGRAPHY

H. W. Attridge, *The Interpretation of Biblical History in the Antiquitates Judicae of Flavius Josephus*, Missoula, Scholars Press, 1976.

L. H. Feldman, 'Mikra in the Writings of Josephus', in J. Mulder and H. Sysling (eds), *Mikra: Text, Translation, Reading and Interpretation of the Hebrew Bible in Ancient Judaism and Early Christianity*, Assen/Philadelphia, Van Gorcum/Fortress, 1988, pp. 455–518.

M. Harding, 'Making Old Things New. Prayer Texts in Josephus's *Antiquities* 1–11: A Study in the Transmission of Tradition', in J. H. Charlesworth with M. Harding and M. Kiley (eds), *The Lord's Prayer and Other Prayer Texts from the Greco-Roman Era*, Valley Forge, Trinity Press International, 1994, pp. 54–72.

R. A. Marcus, 'Divine Names and Attributes in Hellenistic Literature', *American Academy for Jewish Research*, 1931–2, pp. 43–120.

J. A. Montgomery, 'The Religion of Flavius Josephus', *Jewish Quarterly Review*, 1920–1, N.S., vol. 11, pp. 277–305.

A. Schlatter, *Wie sprach Josephus von Gott?*, Beitraege zur Foerderung christlicher Theologie 14, Guetersloh, Bertelsmann, 1910.

17

PHILO OF ALEXANDRIA: TWO PRAYERS

Gregory E. Sterling

The selections from Philo are from the two most important series of treatises in his corpus: the first is from the Allegorical Commentary (AC) and the second from the Exposition of the Law (EL). The former is a running allegorical commentary on Gen 2:1–41:24 which is largely built on two structural devices: (a) the use of questions and answers, and (b) elaborate expansions through the citation and analysis of related biblical texts.[1] The latter is a systematic interpretation of the law which uses allegorical exegesis sparingly.[2] Since each series is an independent work, we will consider the texts separately.

On the Migration of Abraham 101

INTRODUCTION

On the Migration of Abraham is Philo's interpretation of Gen 12:1–3, 4, 6 in the AC.[3] The Jewish commentator begins with a citation of the promises to Abraham in Gen 12:1–3 (§1) which he analyses in §§2–126. He works his way through the biblical text by taking his cue from the verbs: he opens with an allegorical reading of the command to Abraham in Gen 12:1 (§§2–35); then interprets the five 'gifts' (five phrases containing verbs in the future tense) which God promises to Abraham in Gen 12:1–2 (§§36–108); and finally sets out the gifts to others expressed in Gen 12:3 (§§109–18, 119–26). Philo then proceeds to take up and interpret the three phrases of Gen 12:4 (§§127–47, 148–75, 176–215). He concludes with a brief treatment of Gen 12:6 (§§216–25).

Attestation

The Greek text is attested by four major families of manuscripts: MAHP.[4] M is represented by *Laurentianus plut.* X.20, an early thirteenth-century parchment manuscript. A is best evidenced by *Monacensis gr.* 459, another thirteenth-century parchment.[5] The most adequate witness to H is *Venetus gr.* 40, a fourteenth-century paper manuscript. The manuscript contains both the whole treatise and another text of §§1–12 and the first seven words of §13 (= H²).[6] The final family is P which *Petropolitanus* XX A a1, a thirteenth- or fourteenth-century paper manuscript, represents. It is closely related to *Venetus gr.* 40 (family H). We therefore have relatively good textual evidence for the treatise.

Cultural setting

Philo's work should be read as the apex of a long and impressive tradition of Jewish literary activity in Alexandria.[7] Beginning with the LXX in the third century BCE, Alexandrian Jews experimented with various Hellenistic literary traditions. Some worked in historiography: Demetrius, Artapanus, Aristeas, Pseudo–Hecataeus and the author of 3 Maccabees. Others expanded the LXX in works such as *Joseph and Aseneth, Jannes and Jambres* and the *History of Joseph*. Still others wrote testaments: *Testament of Job, Testament of Abraham, Testament of Isaac* and *Testament of Jacob*. Some composed apocalypses, for example, *Apocalypse of Zephaniah*. Yet others experimented with various types of poetry: Philo the Epic Poet, Theodotus and Sosates with epic; Ezekiel with tragedy; the anonymous collectors and composers of authentic and spurious Greek poetry set to apologetic purposes (Gnomologion of Pseudo-Greek Epic Poets, Gnomologion of Dramatic Verses, Pseudo-Phocylides); and a number of anonymous authors who wrote *Sibylline Oracles*. More directly relevant to Philo are his philosophical predecessors and contemporaries: Aristobulus, the Pseudo-Orphic fragments, Pseudo-Aristeas and the Wisdom of Solomon. We may even have a couple of later liturgical documents: prayers such as the *Prayer of Jacob* and the *Prayer of Joseph*; and homilies such as Pseudo-Philo, *On Sampson* and *On Jonah*. Nor should we consider this list exhaustive. The metrical inscriptions from Tell el-Yehoudiyeh suggest that Egyptian Jews enjoyed an unusually high degree of literary sophistication.[8] Philo stands at the pinnacle of this rich tradition. He certainly knew the work of Aristobulus, Pseudo-Aristeas, Ezekiel, possibly Philo the Epic Poet, and probably many others.

There is a second, largely anonymous tradition to which he owed an even greater debt: the exegetical tradition. Unfortunately, apart from some of the literary works above, Philo's oblique references to other exegetes constitute our evidence for this tradition.[9] He identifies both literalists who fail to appreciate the deeper meanings of Torah, and radical allegorists who undermine the community by rejecting customs.[10] Philo argues for an inclusivistic viewpoint which incorporates both. It is not difficult to see how his intellectual and political roles within the Alexandrian Jewish community reinforce one another.

Literary setting

Our prayer occurs in Philo's discussion of the fourth gift to Abraham, 'I will make your name great.' The Alexandrian begins with the thesis that both reality and reputation ('name') are essential for true happiness (§§86–8). His concern for reputation leads him to a critique of the radical allegorizers who forfeit reputation for reality by valuing symbol over observance, the soul of the law over the body of the law (§§89–93). As a counter he offers five scriptural examples of those who championed both: Abraham who had both the realities or natural laws and gifts or conventional laws (§§94), Leah who received praise from both masculine mind and feminine sense–perception (§§95–6), the women who contributed to the tabernacle demonstrating that the senses as well as the intellect should be included (§§97–100), Isaac who prayed for both (§101), and the high priest who as *Logos* wears garments relating to both the intelligible world, the realm of the real, and the sense–perceptible, the realm of reputation (§§102–5).

Isaac's prayer is taken from the blessing of Jacob in Gen 27:27–9. Philo has only cited two lines from the blessing because they contain the two key words for his argument: 'heaven' and 'earth' (Gen 27:28). He explains their significance in the *Questions on Genesis* when he interprets the same verse: 'In man the mind is like heaven, for they are both rational parts, the one of the world, the other of the soul. But sense-perception (is like) the earth, for both are irrational.'[11] Philo offers his allegorical interpretation by offering a paraphrase of the prayer, a common technique in his corpus.[12] He signals his understanding of each phrase through 'former' and 'second'.[13] His point is that while the intelligible has precedence, Isaac prayed for both heavenly wealth (an experience of the reality of the intelligible realm) and earthly wealth (a reputation for blessedness in the sense-perceptible realm).

Social setting and theology

The use of a biblical blessing/prayer as a secondary text in the AC is hardly surprising since for Philo prayer and exegesis belong together: both are essential aspects of the soul's ascent to God.[14] The text is a classic expression of Philo's commitment to both Platonism and Judaism. As part of the AC, this text was probably written for advanced students in Philo's school. He may have conducted this as a private school or, like Samoe in Sardis (fifth century CE), in a school located in a synagogue.[15] Whatever the precise social setting, the text was designed for religious formation through reflection.

Use and affect on later periods

Philo's spirituality had a significant impact on Christian spirituality, in particular on the Alexandrian school and the traditions it influenced.[16] Philo taught later Christians how to connect Platonism and biblical exegesis. So Origen also interpreted 'the dew of heaven' in Gen 27:28 to refer to intelligible, spiritual blessings, not earthly dew. Unlike Philo, however, he argued that it is improper to pray for earthly things.[17] Whether he modified Philo's exegesis or made the identification of heaven with the intelligible in this context himself,[18] he – like Philo – believed prayer was part of the mystical ascent.

TRANSLATION[19]

For this reason[20] the self–taught Isaac prays on behalf of the lover of wisdom that he will receive good things both with respect to the intelligible world and the sense-perceptible. He says: 'May God give you from the dew of heaven and from the richness of the earth' (Gen 27:28). This is equivalent to saying in the case of the former phrase, 'May he shower you continually with intelligible and heavenly rain – not so furiously that it floods, but softly and gently like dew so that it benefits'; and in the case of the second, 'May he graciously give you sense-perceptible and earthly wealth in its lustre and richness and dry up the opposing poverty of both the soul and its parts.'

On the Special Laws 2.198–9

INTRODUCTION

On the Special Laws is Philo's exposition of particular laws within the EL.[21] After presenting creation as an argument for natural law and the patriarchs (Abraham, Isaac and Jacob) as embodiments of the unwritten law,[22] Philo comes to the written law. He opens his exposition with *On the Decalogue* in which he works through each of the ten commandments. He then uses each of these as a heading to subsume the other laws within the Torah in *On the Special Laws*.[23] He goes on to include a series of appendices in which he collects miscellaneous laws under the headings of various virtues (*On the Virtues*) and completes his discussion with *On Rewards and Punishments*.

Philo organizes the four books *On the Special Laws* symmetrically: two books for each set of five commandments (he counts the fifth as a trans-itional commandment between duties to God and duties to fellow humans since human parents stand in the place of God) with the first and third books devoted to two commandments and the second and fourth to three. The second book therefore deals with the third (§§2–38), fourth (§§39–223) and fifth commandments (§§224–41).

Attestation

Unfortunately, this treatise is very poorly attested in the manuscript tradition.[24] There are only six manuscripts in four families: *Vaticanus gr.* 316, a ninth- or tenth-century parchment, is the sole witness to R and contains §§1–94 and seven words of §95; *Laurentianus plut.* X, 20, a thirteenth-century parchment, is the representative of M and the only manuscript which contains the entire book; family F has three fifteenth- to sixteenth-century manuscripts containing §§1–123 in whole or in part;[25] and *Parisinus gr.* 433, a sixteenth-century paper manuscript which includes §§1–38, is the only evidence for L. We also have some abbreviated excerpts from §§41–214 in a commentary on Luke by Nicetas Serranus, an eleventh-century metropolitan of Heraclea.[26] Our selection therefore depends entirely on M and the catena of Nicetas.

The fragmentary nature of the manuscripts has resulted in a complicated history of printed editions. The *editio princeps* of A. Turnebus (1613) depended on L and therefore only printed §§1–38. A year later, D. Hoeschel added §§39–123 based on two additional manuscripts (*Monacensis gr.* 113 [family F] and one which remains undetermined) and §§140–214 based on the excerpts in Nicetas. When T. Mangey accepted Hoeschel's reconstruction for his 1742 edition of Philo's works, it became the accepted text until A. Mai recognized that part of the book was missing as a result of reading M. He therefore edited §§214–62 in 1818. A full edition of the book did not, however, appear until C. Tischendorf published his *Philonea inedita altera* in 1868. Readers should therefore be very careful when using old editions or translations based solely on older editions of Philo for this treatise.

Literary context

Our prayer is part of Philo's discussion of the laws under the heading of the fourth commandment, the Sabbath commandment in his system of counting the ten. The Alexandrian has used the Sabbath command as a heading for ten Jewish feasts. The prayer is part of his explanation of Yom Kippur (§§193–203), the most important Jewish feast in Alexandria. Philo wrote that this is the feast about which his compatriots 'are in deadly earnest, not only those who are zealous for religion and holiness, but even those who do nothing pious the rest of their life'.[27]

He begins his discussion with an explanation of the oxymoron created by calling a fast a feast, even 'Sabbath of Sabbaths' (§§193–4). He offers three reasons for this name: the fast demonstrates self-control (§195); permits the worshippers to devote the day to prayer (§196); and is a sign of piety since by refraining from consuming the recent harvest, the celebrants demonstrate their dependence on God as the source of life rather than the harvest (§197). He then articulates the inarticulate prayer of the worshippers as a model expression of piety for the celebration of the fast.[28]

Setting and theology

It is impossible to know whether this prayer was ever used. EL was addressed to a wider Jewish audience than the AC. All that we can safely say is that Philo thought it captured the essence of Yom Kippur and presumably would have been suitable for public worship. The thrust of the prayer is the recognition of God as the basic source of human existence, a fundamental axiom in Philonic thought.[29] The use of the wilderness traditions leads him to accentuate complete dependence in this text; in other passages, he concurs with the Stoics that good management of resources is a virtue.[30] The prayer is a good example of how exegesis can shape Philo's line of thought.

TRANSLATION[31]

Those who abstain from food and drink after the ingathering of the fruits all but openly – even if they do not utter a single sound with their voice – cry out with their souls and say these things:

'Gladly have we received and stored up the gifts of nature. Yet we do not ever ascribe our keeping to any corruptible cause, but to God, the Creator and Father and Saviour of both the world, and the things in the world, whose prerogative it is to nourish and carefully protect both through these and without these. Look at how he continually nourished our ancestors in their countless thousands as they traversed the trackless and totally barren desert for the life of a generation – forty years, as if they were in a most fertile and productive land. He cut open brand new springs for a generous supply of drinking water.[32] He rained nourishment from heaven,[33] neither more nor less than was sufficient for each day so that as they used what could not be stored for their essential food supply, they would not sell their good hopes for lifeless items which they could store, but would care little for the supplies and marvel at and worship the Supplier, honouring him with appropriate hymns and benedictions.'

NOTES

1   For recent analyses of the structure of the AC see D. T. Runia, 'The Structure of Philo's Allegorical Treatises: A Review of Two Recent Studies and Some Additional Comments', *VC*, 1984, vol. 38, pp. 209–56 and idem, 'Further Observations on the Structure of Philo's Allegorical Treatises', *VC*, 1987, vol. 41, pp. 105–38. Both articles are reprinted in idem, *Exegesis and Philosophy: Studies on Philo of Alexandria*, Collected Studies Series 332, Aldershot, Variorum, 1990, IV and V.
2   Some of the most important essays on this large commentary are E. R. Goodenough, 'Philo's Exposition of the Law and His De Vita Mosis', *HTR*, 1933, vol. 26, pp. 109–25, who implausibly argued that the EL was intended for a Gentile readership; R. D. Hecht, 'Preliminary Issues in the Analysis of Philo's *De specialibus legibus*', *SPh*, 1978, vol. 5, pp. 1–55; and N. G. Cohen, *Philo*

Judaeus: His Universe of Discourse, Beiträge zur Erforschung des Alten Testaments und des antiken Judentums 24, Frankfurt am Main, Peter Lang, 1995, esp. pp. 1–32, 72–85.

3 For an extensive structuralist analysis of this treatise see J. Cazeaux, *La trame et la chaîne: ou les Structures littéraires et l'Exégèse dans cinq des Traités de Philon d'Alexandrie*, ALGHJ 15, Leiden, E. J. Brill, 1983, pp. 37–152.

4 For details see P. Wendland in L. Cohn, P. Wendland, S. Reiter and I. Leisegang (eds), *Philonis Alexandrini opera quae supersunt*, 7 vols, Berlin, George Reimer, 1886–1930, 2nd edn 1962, 2:xxxi (Latin). Hereafter abbreviated PCW.

5 There are four other manuscripts in this family which contain *Migration: Matritensis Est.* 11, *gr.* 2a, 40 (sixteenth century); *Palatinus gr.* 183 (fouteenth century) which are both derived from *Monacensis*; *Vaticanus gr.* 378 (fifteenth century), a companion to *Vaticanus* 380, both of which stem from *Palatinus gr.* 183; and *Vaticanus gr.* 2174 (sixteenth century), a copy of *Vaticanus gr.* 378.

6 There are nine other manuscripts which contain *Migration* in this family: *Vaticanus gr.* 382 (fifteenth century); *Monacensis gr.* 124 (sixteenth century); *Venetus gr.* 39 (fifteenth century); *Parisinus gr.* 434 (early sixteenth century); *Genuensis Bibl. Congregationis Missionis urbanae* 39 (late fourteenth century); *Escurialensis* Y, I, 5 (fifteenth century); *Ottobonianus gr.* 48 (sixteenth or seventeenth century); *Vaticano–Palatinus gr.* 311 (fifteenth to sixteenth centuries); and *Oxoniensis Collegii Novi* 143 (sixteenth century).

7 For details see G. E. Sterling, *The Jewish Plato: Philo of Alexandria, Greek-speaking Judaism, and Christian Origins*, Peabody, Hendrickson, forthcoming. Almost all of the following texts appear in English translation in J. H. Charlesworth, *The Old Testament Pseudepigrapha*, 2 vols, Garden City, Doubleday, 1983–5.

8 On the metrical inscriptions see P. van der Horst, 'Jewish Poetical Tomb Inscriptions', in J. W. van Henten and P. van der Horst (eds), *Studies in Early Jewish Epigraphy*, AGAJU 21, Leiden, E. J. Brill, 1994, pp. 129–47 and D. Noy, 'The Jewish Communities of Leontopolis and Venosa', in van Henten and van der Horst, pp. 162–82, esp. 168–9. The standard critical edition is W. Horbury and D. Noy, *Jewish Inscriptions of Graeco-Roman Egypt: With an Index of the Jewish Inscriptions of Egypt and Cyrenaica*, Cambridge, Cambridge University Press, 1992.

9 cf. W. Bousset, *Jüdisch–Christlicher Schulbetrieb in Alexandria und Rom: Literarische Untersuchungen zu Philo und Clemens von Alexandria, Justin und Irenäus*, Göttingen, Vandenhoeck & Ruprecht, 1915; reprint, Hildesheim, Georg Olms, 1975; R. G. Hamerton-Kelly, 'Sources and Traditions in Philo Judaeus: Prolegomena to an Analysis of His Writings', *SPh*, 1972, vol. 1, pp. 3–26; B. L. Mack, 'Exegetical Traditions in Alexandrian Judaism: A Program for the Analysis of the Philonic Corpus', *SPh*, 1974–5, vol. 3, pp. 71–112; idem, 'Philo Judaeus and Exegetical Traditions in Alexandria', in W. Haase (ed.), *Religion (Hellenistisches Judentum im römischer Zeit: Philo und Josephus)*, ANRW 2.21.1, Berlin/New York, de Gruyter, 1984, pp. 227–71; T. H. Tobin, *The Creation of Man: Philo and the History of Interpretation*, CBQMS 14, Washington, DC, The Catholic Biblical Association, 1983; and R. Goulet, *La philosophie de Moïse: Essai de reconstitution d'un commentaire philosophique préphilonien de Pentateuque*, Histoire des Doctrines de l'Antiquité Classique 11, Paris, Vrin, 1987.

10 M. J. Shroyer, 'Alexandrian Jewish Literalists', *JBL*, 1936, vol. 55, pp. 261–84; D. M. Hay, 'Philo's References to Other Allegorists', *SPh*, 1979–80, vol. 6, pp. 41–75; idem, 'References to Other Exegetes', in D. M. Hay (ed.), *Both Literal*

and Allegorical: Studies in Philo of Alexandria's Questions and Answers on Genesis and Exodus, BJS 232, Atlanta, Scholars Press, 1991, pp. 81–97.

11 QG 4.215. The translation is that of R. Marcus in F. H. Colson, G. H. Whitaker, and R. Markus, *Philo*, 10 vols and 2 supplementary vols, LCL, Cambridge, Harvard University Press, 1929–62, Suppl. 1. Hereafter abbreviated PLCL.

12 He does the same thing with a prayer of Moses later in this treatise (§§171–2, citing and paraphrasing Exod 33:15).

13 Philo frequently uses 'former' and 'second' to refer back to a text or two points of his exegesis, e.g., *Alleg. Laws* 2.36; *Sacrifices* 132; *Drunkenness* 163; *Names* 78; *Decalogue* 106; *Spec. Laws* 1.32; 4.35, 137–8; *Eternity* 40–1; cf. also *Posterity* 94; *Agriculture* 178; *Moses* 2.46, 231; *Spec. Laws* 1.217; 2.135; 3.129; *Virtues* 130; *Eternity* 65.

14 E.g., *Sobriety* 62–4. See also his description of the Therapeutae, *Contempl. Life* 27–8, for the coupling of the two.

15 On Samoe see A. T. Kraabel, 'Impact of the Discovery of the Sardis Synagogue', in G. M. A. Hanfmann (ed.), *Sardis from Prehistoric to Roman Times: Results of the Archaeological Exploration of Sardis 1958–1975*, Cambridge, Harvard University, 1983, pp. 189–90, and plate 267.

16 The most important work is J. Laporte, *Eucharistia in Philo*, Studies in Bible and Early Christianity 3, New York, Mellen, 1983, pp. 93–7. For an overview of recent assessments see D. T. Runia, *Philo in Early Christian Literature: A Survey*, CRINT 2.3.3, Minneapolis, Fortress, 1993, pp. 132–83, esp. 178–80.

17 Origen, *On Prayer* 16.2–3; cf. also *Homilies on Leviticus* 16.3.

18 cf. also Tertullian, *Against Marcion* 3.24.7–9, who has an interpretation close to Philo's. It is questionable whether Tertullian knew Philo's works, so Runia, *Philo in Early Christian Literature*, pp. 277–81. For a different interpretation which still recognizes the distinction between heaven and earth see Irenaeus, *Against Heresies* 5.33.3.

19 I have used the edition of PCW, 2:288. See also Colson and Whitaker, PLCL, 4:190–1 and J. Cazeaux, *De migratione Abrahami*, Les œuvres de Philon d'Alexandrie 14, Paris, Cerf, 1965, pp. 156–7 (hereafter abbreviated PAPM).

20 The final word of the previous section, 'most properly', may go with either the verb of the preceding section or with the opening prepositional phrase here.

21 For Philo's own statements on the structure of these treatises see *Abraham* 1–6; *Moses* 2.45–7; *Decalogue* 1; and *Rewards* 1–3.

22 cf. *Sobriety* 65; *Prelim. Studies* 34–8; *Names* 12, 88; *Dreams* 1.168; *Abraham* 52–4; *Joseph* 1; *Moses* 1.76; *Rewards* 24–51, 57–66.

23 For explicit statements see *Heir* 173; *Decalogue* 18–20, 154–75; *Spec. Laws* 1.1; 3.7; 4.132, 133; *Rewards* 2.

24 For details see Cohn in PCW 5:xx–xxv (Latin) and Colson in PLCL, 7:xv–xvii.

25 *Laurentianus plut.* LXXXV.10 (fifteenth to sixteenth centuries); *Vaticanus gr.* 379 (fifteenth century); and *Monacensis gr.* 113 (sixteenth century).

26 For details of the manuscripts for Nicetas Serranus see H. L. Goodhart and E. R. Goodenough, *The Politics of Philo Judaeus: Practice and Theory*, New Haven, Yale University Press, 1938; Hildesheim, Olms, 2nd edn, 1967, pp. 169–71.

27 *Spec. Laws* 1.186.

28 On silent prayer see *Spec. Laws* 1.272.

29 E.g., *Creation* 171–2.

30 E.g., *Spec. Laws* 2.187; *Drunkenness* 91–2. For the Stoic view see I. von Arnim, *Stoicorum veterum fragmenta*, 4 vols, Leipzig, Teubner, 1903–24, 3.267, 623, where the '*oikonomike* virtue' is defined as 'the theoretical and practical use of

what is beneficial to the household'.

31 I have used the edition of PCW, 5:135–6. See also Colson, PLCL, 7:430–1 and S. Daniel, *De specialibus legibus I et II*, PAPM 24, pp. 354–7.
32 He appears to have in mind the waters of Meribah (Exod 17:1–7//Num 20:2–13).
33 This is a reference to the manna (Exod 16:1–36//Num 11:1–35).

18

THE SHEMA AND THE AMIDAH: RABBINIC PRAYER

Reuven Kimelman

According to the *Mishnah* (*c.* 200 CE and hereafter abbreviated *m.*), the daily liturgy, in Hebrew, consists of two distinct units: the Shema and its blessings, and the eighteen-benediction Amidah. Both are recited morning and evening, whereas the Amidah is recited also in the afternoon. During the course of the third century they became welded together for the morning service and later for the evening service.

Attestation

Although the *Mishnah* and its two commentaries, the Palestinian and Babylonian Talmud, discuss the motifs, concluding perorations, structures and sequence of the Shema and Amidah liturgies, they fail to provide a full text. Such a text becomes available in the ninth century in the *Order of Prayers* by Amram Gaon and in the fragments of the Genizah of the synagogue of Fostat, Cairo, built in 882 CE. No sweeping generalization on which came first is possible. Both, in the main, hark back at least to the period of Constantine as their structure and motifs pervade early liturgical poetry (*piyyutim*) whereas their angelology and Qedushah/Sanctus are linked to Second Temple literature.[1]

THE SHEMA

Structure of the Shema liturgy[2]

The Shema liturgy has the following components: blessing for creation with angelic acclamation; blessing for Torah – 'With eternal love'; three biblical paragraphs headed by Shema verse; covenantal pledge – 'True and firm'; blessing for redemption with Song of the Sea.

Structurally, it adheres to the chiasmus, or X pattern, as does so much of ancient Jewish literature. By balancing the second part with the first part, albeit through inversion, the chiasmus comprehensively accounts for all the parts while underscoring the centrality of the Shema as follows:

A¹ – blessing for creation and angelic acclamation
    B¹ – blessing for Torah: 'With eternal love'
        C – Shema verse and three biblical paragraphs
    B² – covenantal pledge: 'True and firm'
A² – blessing for redemption and Song of the Sea

The pyramidal or chiastic structure makes the point that the Shema is the literary as well as the theological apex of the unit.[3] The core composed of B¹, C and B² constitutes the original covenantal ceremony. By flanking it with A¹ and A², there emerged a comprehensive liturgical rite for the realization of divine sovereignty.

The Shema liturgy

The Shema liturgy derives its name from its first word: – 'Shema [= Hear] O Israel, the Lord our God, the Lord is one' (Deut 6:4). This verse heads a constellation in the *Mishnah* of three biblical paragraphs, the first two from the Book of Deuteronomy (6:4–9; 11:13–21) and the third from the Book of Numbers (15:37–41). The first paragraph, and possibly the second, may be alluded to, along with the Decalogue, already in Pss 50:7 and 81:9–11,[4] and the third by Josephus.[5] All three appear in the report of the Temple service in *m. Tamid* 5:1 along with the Decalogue and other selections. As a distinct unit, they first appear in *m. Ber.* 2:2. and in *Sipre Deut.* 34–5. Thus in the tannaitic period between 70 CE and 200 CE the three Shema paragraphs achieved their present liturgical status and formulation.

Shema and Decalogue

The first paragraph of the Shema and the Decalogue were linked very early. They appear together in Deut 5–6, the Nash Papyrus,[6] Qumran phylacteries,[7] albeit not in early Christianity.[8] The Shema alone appears in a dispute between the Houses of Hillel and Shammai,[9] in Mark 12:29–30, in the phylacteries of the caves of Murabba\at, and by allusion in the *Manual of Discipline* (1QS 1:12) as well as in *Pseudo-Aristeas* 160.

However, in the tannaitic period the Decalogue no longer appears in the liturgy, purportedly because Jewish Christians made the offensive claim that the Decalogue alone was given at Sinai. It is difficult to attribute such serious surgery of the liturgy to such a cavil for two reasons. First, it is unlikely that the Decalogue's presence in the liturgy along with the three paragraphs of the Shema with their emphasis on compliance with all the commandments would be open to such a charge. The charge could only apply were the Decalogue recited alone. Second, trinitarian explanations for the Qedushah/ Sanctus or the Shema verse did not lead to similar excisions.

More likely, the Decalogue fell into disuse because its liturgical role was assumed by the first two paragraphs of the Shema. According to tannaitic opinion, the uniqueness of the Shema verse consists in the combination of the 'acceptance of the authority of divine sovereignty' and the exclusion of idolatry just as is the case in the first two sayings of the Decalogue.[10] Also the sequence of the Decalogue and the two Shema paragraphs reflect the priority of the acceptance of divine sovereignty over the acceptance of the commandments.[11] The inclusion in the *Mishnah* of this explanation for the sequence of the Shema confirmed it as the Decalogue's theological and liturgical replacement.

Once the Shema became the liturgy for the realization of divine sovereignty, the Temple response to prayer – 'Blessed be the name of His glorious sovereignty for ever and ever' – was interpolated between its first and second verse to underscore this function.

The blessings of the Shema liturgy

The organizing theme of the Shema and its blessings is the realization of God's sovereignty. Each of the three blessings contributes a distinctive motif to the theme which is encapsulated in the concluding peroration. The first morning blessing celebrates creation by blessing God for creating the luminaries, and in the evening blesses God for bringing on the dusk. The second blessing, in both the morning and evening, celebrates revelation by blessing God as lover/chooser of Israel. The third blessing celebrates redemption by blessing God for the Exodus. This tripartite structure was inspired by Psalm 19 and Neh 9:5-37.[12]

The creation motif of the first morning blessing appears as follows:

1   Blessed are You; Lord our God, Sovereign of the universe
2   (Who) forms light and creates darkness
3   (Who) makes peace and creates all.
4   Who illumines the earth and its denizens with mercy.
5   And with His goodness renews every day regularly the work of creation.
6   'How great are Your works O Lord, all of them You fashioned in wisdom, the earth is full of Your masterpieces' (Ps 104:24).
7   O Sovereign (who) alone was exalted from then,
8   Praised, glorified and elevated from days of old ...
9   Blessed are You, Creator of the luminaries.

In order to persuade the worshipper that God is creator and hence sovereign, the blessing attunes the worshipper to the diurnal renewal of the wonders of the universe. It works at engendering astonishment at the ingeniously formed creation by noting God's compassion in bringing about the light and warmth of the daily sunrise.

The thesis of divine sovereignty is seconded by the opening blessing of the evening service:

1 Blessed are You, Lord our God, Sovereign of the universe
2 Who with His word *brings* on evening [night]
3 Who in wisdom *opens* the gates (of dawn) and in understanding *changes* the times (i.e., of the day) [day, night]
4 *Alternates* the times, and *arranges* the stars in their watches according to His will [day, night]
5 He *creates* day and night [day, night]
6 He *rolls away* light before darkness and darkness before light [day/ night, night/day]
7 He *causes* day to pass and *brings* night [day, night]
8 And *distinguishes* between day and night [day, night]
9 Lord of (the heavenly) Hosts is His name[13]
10 May Enduring, Living God constantly reign over us forever[14]
11 Blessed are You, Lord, Who brings on evening [night].

This dusk or tellurion prayer is marked by repeated variations on the cyclical changes from light to darkness. The framing strophes with their repetition of 'brings on evening' (2 and 11) mark the onset of night, whereas each internal strophe, as noted in the square brackets, mentions day followed by night. The pervasive redundancy serves to point out the regularity and predictability of the heavenly changes at dusk in order to allay apprehensions of chaos in the face of the enveloping darkness. The measured quasi-symmetrical lines reflect the symmetry and regularity of the universe. The ten (italicized) transitive verbs point to an all-pervasive divine activity redolent of the ten-fold repetition of 'God said' in the creation narrative. As the morning version, so the evening associates divine creation with divine sovereignty.

The change of the evening guard stars, as it were, a cast of thousands. In order to produce a splendidly orchestrated twilight spectacle, every role is synchronized exclusively by divine speech (line 2). Presenting such an orderly change of stage and scenery bestirs in the worshipper the desire to have the great Designer extend His reign of the natural world over the human one (line 10).

The second blessing makes the case for the election of Israel as an expression of God's love. It opens with the declaration of the beloved, '*With everlasting love have You loved us, O Lord our God.*' This inversion of God's profession of love in Jer 31:3 – '*With everlasting love have I loved you*' – becomes Israel's acknowledgement of divine love. The liturgy, following Jeremiah, grasps revelation as God falling forever in love with Israel. In the morning version, such love is attested to by the gift of the Torah pointedly

111

called 'the statutes of life'. God is entreated to teach Israel these statutes as graciously as He taught their forebears. Based on the reception of the Torah and the imbibing of its teaching, the blessing concludes that God 'chooses His people Israel in love'.[15]

The parallel blessing of the evening service replicates the link between love and teaching. Adhering to the syntax of the Hebrew, it translates as follows:

1   With everlasting love the house of Israel, Your people, have You loved.
2   Torah and commandments, statutes and laws, us have You taught.
3   Therefore, Lord our God, when we lie down and when we rise up,
4   we shall speak of Your statutes and rejoice in the words of Your Torah and in Your commandments forever,
5   for they are our life and the length of our days,
6   and we will recite them day and night.
7   May Your love never depart from us.
8   Blessed are You, O Lord, who loves [His people][16] Israel.

The parallel syntax and Hebrew rhyme scheme of lines 1 and 2 converge to make the point that God's election-love is expressed through teaching Torah and commandments. The idea is reinforced by lines 3 and 4 where God's everlasting love as expressed through such teaching is reciprocated by a commitment on Israel's part to rejoice and study the teaching and commandments forever. As the morning version, so the evening version presents the loving God as a teaching God.

In the first and third blessing (for which, see below), the theme of Divine sovereignty is reinforced by the testimony of celestial and terrestrial choirs. Through the orchestration of these heavenly and earthly realms, divine sovereignty is attested to throughout the universe. By including references to past as well as present, heaven as well as earth, the liturgy reflects the perspective of an omniscient narrator.

In sum, the first blessing serves as the liturgical overture to the opening verse of the Shema through linking up creation with God's exclusive sovereignty, making the point that the creator God is the one God. By portraying God's love as inspiring human love and compliance, the second blessing serves as the prelude to the continuation of the first paragraph of the Shema ('And you shall love the Lord your God . . .') as well as to the second paragraph ('And if you heed my commandments . . .') . The third blessing with its theme of redemption corresponds to the third paragraph ('And He said . . .'). The full correspondence may be diagrammed as follows:

Blessing	Shema	Blessing
1 Creator of lights	'Hear . . . One'	
2 Lover of Israel	'Love . . . Heed . . .'	
3	'And He said . . .'	Who Redeemed

Although the linkage of the 'Love' and 'Heed' units precludes an exact correspondence between the three blessings and the three Shema paragraphs, the second blessing's use of the love motif to induce Israel to reciprocate divine love and to heed the commandments allows for their being grasped as two parts of the same continuum.

The Qedushah/Sanctus and the Song of the Sea

The theme of divine sovereignty receives vivid reinforcement in the middle of the first blessing by the congregation reciting antiphonally Isa 6:3 – 'Holy, Holy, Holy, is the Lord of Hosts; the whole earth is full of His glory', and Ezek 3:12 'Blessed be the glory of God from His place.'[17] According to the blessing, this constituted the angels' acclamation of the divine sovereignty. This celestial acclamation of God serves as a model to Israel to follow suit.

Similarly, in the third blessing the congregation echoes the words of the redeemed acclaiming the divine sovereignty by re-enacting the antiphonal rendition of the Song of the Sea:

> Moses and Israel sang the Song [of the Sea] antiphonally to You with great joy, but all together said, 'Who is like You O Lord among the celestials? Who is like You glorious in holiness?' (Exod 15:11).

After rendering the first half of the Song of the Sea antiphonally, Exod 15:11 is sung in unison as the finale of the part of the Song that deals with the fate of the Egyptians.

The enactment, in the Ashkenazic rite, continues with:

> Your children beholding Your sovereignty as You divided the sea before Moses, responded saying, 'This is my God' (Exod 15:2). And they said, 'The Lord shall reign for ever and ever' (Exod 15:18).

The import of saying, 'This is my God' is spelled out in the re-enactment of the choral response of the Song in the morning service:

> The redeemed sung praises at the seashore of [this] new song to You [antiphonally], but all together acclaimed Your sovereignty by saying, 'The Lord shall reign for ever and ever' (Exod 15:18).

By citing both the initial response of Israel of the Song of the Sea from Exod 15:2 – 'This is my God' – and the final one sung in unison from Exod 15:18 – 'The Lord shall reign for ever and ever' – the whole Song is summarized in this divine acclamation of sovereignty.

The covenantal pledge of the Shema liturgy: 'True and firm'

Besides the three blessings, the angelic model and the Israelite precedent for the realization of divine sovereignty, there is a section called 'True and firm' after its opening two words. It is recited following the three paragraphs of the Shema just as it was in the Second Temple service. This sequence witnesses to how the liturgy grasped the Shema, even without the Decalogue, as an ancient covenantal ceremony. Indeed, 'This prayer actually constitutes a pledge to take upon oneself the "yoke of the kingdom of God," and is formulated like the loyalty oaths sworn to the sovereign and emperor in the ancient world.'[18]

The third blessing of the Shema liturgy

Although each blessing is involved in persuading the worshipper of its theological grounding, the third blessing makes this explicit. After the aforementioned 'True and firm', a series of asseverations, introduced by the word 'true', are, staccato-like, rattled off:

> True! the God of the world/eternity is our king . . .
> True! You are our God . . .
> True! You are the lord of Your people . . .
> True! You are the first and You are the last . . .
> True! You have redeemed us from Egypt . . .[19]

Cumulatively, they add up to a credo, all proclaimed in the context of the supporting structures of collective memory. Save for the first where God is acclaimed 'our king', they are expressed in the language of direct address: 'You are our God . . .; You are the lord of Your people . . .; You are the first and You are the last . . .; You have redeemed us from Egypt . . .' What better example of prayer as catechism, intoned as praise?

The liturgical antiphons

As the angelic Qedushah/Sanctus and the Song of the Sea conform to Greco-Roman models of royal acclamation by having a single verse or selection divided and recited antiphonally,[20] so did the communal recitation of the Shema verse. Originally, the leader, called *Pores*, said, 'Hear O Israel', and the congregation responded, 'The Lord our God, the Lord is One.' Just as one party did not intone the whole Song of the Sea or one set of angels utter the whole Qedushah/Sanctus verse, so no one party declaimed the whole Shema verse. Indeed, according to one source, the antiphonal performance of the Shema actualized the Sinaitic encounter where Israel originally realized divine sovereignty.[21]

THE AMIDAH[22]

There is no communal or statutory service without an Amidah. As the first such service to emerge after the destruction of the Second Temple, it was designated *Ha-Tefillah*, 'the prayer'. There are different variations for special occasions.[23] The Sabbath and Festival versions each contain seven blessings, whereas the High Holiday *Musaf* comprises nine. The weekday version now consists of nineteen blessings. While still consisting of only eighteen,[24] it became known as *Shemoneh Esreh*, the Hebrew for eighteen, a term still in use. Since the Amidah now comprises nineteen blessings and is recited while standing, the name *Amidah*, 'standing', has rightfully gained in usage.[25]

The Amidah was not created *ex nihilo*. Comprised of elements some of which hark back to the Second Temple period, indeed to the Temple service itself,[26] it crystallizes an extended process of liturgical composition. The number of blessings, topics, and their order, fixed under the auspices of Rabban Gamaliel of Yavneh, became known as the Yavnean order.[27] By mandating a fixed sequence, the tannaitic rabbis formalized the Amidah as liturgy as they did to the Shema and other services.[28]

The meaning of the Amidah is less a reflex of contemporary events,[29] than an expression of its order and structure. The Yavnean order, which is constant throughout the various versions including those of the Genizah,[30] reflects a purposeful collage of units whose overall structure affects the meaning of each blessing. The internal structure consists of an opening and closing triad of blessings with twelve/thirteen middle ones. Efforts to categorize the two triads as praise or thanksgiving and the middle blessings as request have not withstood scrutiny.[31]

The sequence supports the thesis of the Amidah as a prayer for redemption as do its many echoes of biblical redemptive vocabulary. The first blessing goes as follows:

1 Blessed are You, Lord our God and God of our fathers
2 God of Abraham, God of Isaac, and God of Jacob,
3 the God (called) 'great, mighty, and awesome, exalted God'[32]
4 who bestowing loving kindness is creator of all
5 [who mindful of the piety of the patriarchs
6 brings a redeemer to their children's children in love for the sake of His name.][33]
7 King, Helper, Saviour, and Shield.
8 Blessed are You, O Lord, shield of Abraham.

Opening a prayer for redemption, the first blessing addresses God as God was identified to Moses in the burning bush scene of Exodus 3, namely, as announcing the imminent redemption of Israel from Egypt.[34] For the Amidah, the God of the patriarchs is the redeeming God.

The second blessing makes the case for resurrection, mentioning it no less than six times:

1 You are mighty forever, O Lord,
2 *Reviver of the dead* are You, of great saving power.

3 (causing the wind to blow and the rain to fall).
4 You sustain the living with kindness, *reviving the dead* with manifold mercies,
5 {[You] support the fallen, heal the sick, free the fettered.
6 *And maintains His faithfulness with those asleep in the dust.*
7 Who is like You, O Powerful One, who can compare with You?
8 The King who *brings death and life*}[35]
9 and causes salvation to sprout,
10 Faithful are You *to revive the dead*,
11 Blessed are You, O Lord, *reviver of the dead.*

The argument rests on culling the intimations of resurrection which punctuate the course of life. By methodically amplifying the wonders which daily attend us, the blessing enables the worshipper to perceive the divine workings behind the natural course of events, thereby sustaining the hope for resurrection.

In the communal repetition of the Amidah, the third blessing incorporates the Qeddushah/Sanctus. Its concluding verse, 'The Lord shall reign forever, your God, O Zion, for all generations. Hallelujah' (Ps 146:10) serves to acclaim God's sovereignty on earth.

All three initial blessings affirm divine sovereignty. Presenting God as Lord over history, Lord over nature and death, and Lord over heaven and earth bolsters the hope of redemption, as Isaiah says: 'Since . . . the Lord is our King, He will deliver us' (33:22).

The first half of the middle blessings (4–9) presents three accessible dimensions of redemption. The first is the process of personal salvation (4-7): the understanding graciously granted by God in blessing 4 is pressed into the return to Torah and service of God in blessing 5, which sparks the awareness of sin that leads to the seeking of forgiveness in blessing 6, paving the way for the atonement of personal redemption in blessing 7.[36] The other dimensions are physical recovery (8), and agricultural revival (9). Common to all three is a positive reversal of fortunes. The guilty are forgiven, the sick are healed and the earth regains its fertility.[37] Cumulatively, they sustain the hope for the not yet available national redemption.

The second half, from blessings 10–15, delineates the order of national redemption. It commences with the great shofar's blast of freedom, announcing the ingathering of the exiles (10), and continues with the restoration of divine rule through righteous leaders (11), the meting out of appropriate deserts to the righteous and the wicked (12 and 13), the rebuilding of Jerusalem (14) and the return of the Davidic line (15).[38] Since the motifs are all biblical,[39] the distinctive contribution made by this liturgy to the idea of national redemption lies in the particular linguistic formulation, in the sequence of events, and in the uncompromising emphasis on divine involvement, all of which converge to make the point that God alone is the redeemer as opposed to any human redeemer.[40]

Although blessing 16 is only a plea that prayer be answered, its formulation in the abridgement of the Amidah, the *Havinenu*, leans so much on chapter 65 of Isaiah that it also rings with redemptive tones.

Blessings 17 and 18 continue to advance the drama of redemption by focusing on the common motifs of God's return to Zion (17) and the ensuing universal recognition when 'all the living shall acknowledge You' (18).

In its nineteenth blessing, the Amidah ends with peace. This blessing is more a fleshing out of the priestly benediction with its conclusion 'May He grant you peace' (Num 6:24–6), which it follows in the communal repetition, than a continuation of the theme of the Amidah.

The Amidah itself advances from personal (4–7) through national (10–15) to universal redemption (18), each stage involving the progressive realization of divine sovereignty. It appears that blessing 18, with its climax of the universal acknowledgement of God, once concluded the Amidah. The appending of the priestly benediction was intended to enhance the correlation between the synagogue and Temple service.

When the Amidah – with its theme of future redemption – was welded to the end of the liturgy of the Shema – with its theme of past redemption, the memory of past redemption provided the liturgical springboard for prayer concerning future redemption,[41] creating a single integrated rabbinic liturgy.[42]

NOTES

1 See E. Fleischer, 'Studies in the Structural Development of the Piyyutim *ha-me\orot ve-ha-\ahavah*' [Hebrew], *Simon Halkin Jubilee Volume*, Jerusalem, 1975, pp. 367–99, 367–72; and R. Elior, 'From Earthly Temple to Heavenly Shrines: Prayer and Sacred Liturgy in the *Hekhalot* Literature and Its Relation to Temple Traditions' (Hebrew), *Tarbiz*, 1995, vol. 64, pp. 341–80.

2 This part is an abridgement of my 'The Shema^ and Its Rhetoric: From Covenant Ceremony to Coronation', to appear in R. Kimelman, *The Liturgy as Literature: A Historical and Rhetorical Commentary to the Jewish Prayerbook*, London, The Littman Library of Jewish Civilization (forthcoming).

3 For parallel, see C. Newsom, *Songs of the Sabbath Sacrifice: A Critical Edition*, Atlanta, Scholars Press, 1985, pp. 102, 109.

4 See M. Weinfeld, *Deuteronomy 1–11*, (*Anchor Bible* 5), New York, Doubleday, 1991, pp. 257–62.

5 Josephus, *Ant.* 4.8.13 (212); see E. Schürer, *The History of the Jewish People in the Age of Jesus Christ (175 BC–AD 135)*, G. Vermes *et al.* (eds), 3 vols, Edinburgh: T. & T. Clark, 1973–87, vol. 2, p. 455 n. 153; and S. Naeh, and M. Shemesh, 'The Manna Story and the Time of the Morning Prayer' (Hebrew), *Tarbiz*, 1995, vol. 64, pp. 335–40, 335.

6 See E. Fleischer, *Eretz-Israel Prayer and Prayer Rituals As Portrayed in the Geniza Documents* (Hebrew), Jerusalem, Magnes Press, 1988, p. 259 n. 1; and E. Sanders, *Jesus and Judaism*, Philadelphia, Fortress Press, 1986, p. 68.

7 J. Milik and R. de Vaux (eds), *Discoveries in the Judaean Desert VI. Qumran*

Grotte 4, II, Oxford, Clarendon Press, 1977, pp. 52, 59-62, 74–5.

8   See R. Kimelman, 'A Note on Weinfeld's "Grace After Meals in Qumran"',
    JBL, 1993, vol. 112, pp. 695–6.

9   *M. Ber.* 1:3.

10 *Sipre Num.* 115 (Horovitz, 126, line 7), see also R. Ishmael (*Sipre Num.* 112
    [121, lines 9–10]).

11 For the Decalogue, see R. Simeon b. Yohai, *Mek. Tractate Bahodesh, parsha* 6
    (Lauterbach, 2:238); for the Shema, see R. Joshua b. Korha, *m. Ber.* 2:2.

12 See A. Mirsky, *Ha^Piyut: The Development of Post-Biblical Poetry in Eretz
    Israel and the Diaspora* (Hebrew), Jerusalem, Magnes, 1990, pp. 11–17; and L.
    Liebreich, 'The Impact of Nehemiah 9:5-37 on the Liturgy of the Synagogue',
    HUCA, 1961, vol. 32, pp. 227-37.

13 Following Jer 31:35.

14 See Dan 6:27 with S. Tal, *Ha-Siddur Be-Hishtalsheluto*, Jerusalem, Natan Tal,
    1985, p. 65.

15 The remaining part of the blessing consists of interpolations for redemption.

16 See S. Lieberman, *Tosefta Ki-fshutah*, 10 vols, New York, The Jewish
    Theological Seminary, 1955–88, vol. 4, p. 802 n. 61.

17 For the various antiphonal performances, see *b. Hul.* 91a; and 3 (Hebrew
    Apocalypse of) *Enoch*, 38–40, in J. H. Charlesworth (ed.), *The Old Testament
    Pseudepigrapha*, 2 vols, Garden City, NY, Doubleday, 1983–5, vol. 1, pp.
    290–1.

18 See M. Weinfeld, 'The Loyalty Oath in the Ancient Near East', *UF,* 1976, vol. 8,
    pp. 379–414.

19 See N. Wieder, 'An Unknown Ancient Version of the Haftarah Benedictions –
    The Use of \emet to Affirm Important Religious Principles' (Hebrew), in S.
    Elizur (ed.), *Knesset Ezra: Literature and Life in the Synagogue, Studies
    Presented to Ezra Fleischer*, Jerusalem, Yad Izhak Ben Zvi, 1994, pp. 35–46, 41.

20 See I. Knohl, 'A *Parsha* Concerned with Accepting the Kingdom of Heaven'
    (Hebrew), *Tarbiz*, 1984, vol. 53, pp. 11–31, 12.

21 *Deut. Rab.* 1:31.

22 The following is an abridgement of R. Kimelman, 'The Literary Structure of the
    Amidah and the Rhetoric of Redemption', in W. G. Dever and E. J. Wright
    (eds), *Echoes of Many Texts: Reflections on Jewish and Christian Traditions,
    Essays in Honor of Lou H. Silberman*, Brown Judaic Studies, Atlanta, Scholars
    Press, forthcoming, pp. 171–230.

23 See J. Heinemann, *Encyclopedia Judaica*, 2:837–45, s.v., *Berakhah*.

24 On the change, see R. Kimelman, 'Birkat Ha-Minim and the Lack of Evidence
    for an Anti-Christian Jewish Prayer in Late Antiquity', in E. Sanders (ed.),
    Jewish and Christian Self-Definition, Philadelphia, Fortress Press, 1981, vol. 2,
    pp. 226–44, 391–403, which is now being revised; D. Flusser, 'Some of the
    Precepts of the Torah from Qumran (4QMMT) and the Benediction Against the
    Heretics' (Hebrew), *Tarbiz*, 1992, vol. 61, pp. 333–74; and P. W. van der Horst,
    Hellenism–Judaism–Christianity, Kampen, Kok Pharos Publishing House,
    1994, pp. 99–111.

25 The term first appears in *Soperim* 16:9.

26 Semblances of twelve to thirteen of the blessings have appeared elsewhere,
    including *hekhalot* literature; see M. Bar-Ilan, *The Mysteries of Jewish Prayer
    and Hekhalot* (Hebrew), Ramat Gan, Bar Ilan University Press, 1987, pp. 120–
    52, esp. 124 and 152; and D. Flusser, 'The Second Benediction of the Amida and
    a Text from Qumran', *Tarbiz*, 1995, vol. 64, pp. 331–4.

27 See *b. Berakhot* 28b; *Megillah* 17b; and *j. Berakhot* 2:4, 4d, with N. G. Cohen,

'The Nature of Shim^on Hapekuli's Act' (Hebrew), *Tarbiz*, 1983, vol. 52, pp. 547–56.

28 See *t. Berakhot* 2:3–4, and *t. Megillah* 2:1–3.
29 For critiques of such an historical approach, see R. Sarason, 'On the Use of Method in the Modern Study of Jewish Liturgy', in W. Green (ed.), *Approaches to Ancient Judaism: Theory and Practice*, Missoula, MT, Scholars Press, 1978, pp. 97–172; and R. Kimelman, 'Liturgical Studies in the 90s', *Jewish Book Annual*, 1994–5, vol. 52, pp. 59–72, 61–8. For specific critiques of recent historical explanations, see Kimelman, 'The Literary Structure of the Amidah and the Rhetoric of Redemption', op. cit. (note 22), pp. 181–5 (on E. Fleischer); and idem, *Critical Review of Books in Religion 1993*, vol. 6, pp. 434–6 (on T. Zahavy).
30 For the Genizah elements, see Y. Luger, *The Weekday ^Amidah Based on the Genizah* (Hebrew), 2 vols, Ph.D. Thesis, Bar Ilan University, Ramat Gan, 1992.
31 See Kimelman, op. cit. (note 22), pp. 176–9.
32 Translating the divine epithets as vocatives.
33 Missing in Genizah version.
34 As does *Mek., Pisha* 16 (Lauterbach, 1:136).
35 Missing from Genizah version.
36 See A. Marmorstein, 'A Misunderstood Question in the Yerushalmi', *JQR*, 1929/30, vol. 20, pp. 313–20, 319; and E. Bickerman, 'The Civic Prayer for Jerusalem', *HTR*, 1962, vol. 55, pp. 163–85, 172.
37 So strong was the association between agricultural prosperity and redemption that this blessing frequently absorbed pleas for future redemption; see Marmorstein, op. cit., p. 319; and Luger, op. cit., 1:122.
38 For these themes, see Schürer, op. cit., vol. 2, pp. 526–30.
39 For the biblical and extra-biblical models, M. Weinfeld, 'Mesopotamian Eschatological Prophecies' (Hebrew), *Shenaton*, 1978, vol. 3, pp. 263–76.
40 See R. Kimelman, 'The Messiah of the Amidah: A Study in Comparative Messianism', forthcoming in *JBL*.
41 See Kimelman, op. cit. (note 22), pp. 214–16.
42 For the full text of both units, see any standard Jewish prayerbook or J. Heinemann, *Literature of the Synagogue*, New York, Behrman House, 1975, pp. 15–46.

SELECTED BIBLIOGRAPHY

Donim, H., *To Pray as a Jew: A Guide to the Prayer Book and the Synagogue Service*, USA: Basic Books, 1980.
Elbogen, I., *Jewish Liturgy: A Comprehensive History*, ed. R. Scheindlin, Philadelphia, Jewish Publication Society, 1993.
Hammer, R., *Entering Jewish Prayer*, New York, Schocken, 1994.
Heineman, J., *Literature of the Synagogue*, New York, Behrman House, 1975.
——, *Prayer in the Talmud*, Berlin, de Gruyter, 1977.
Kimelman, R., 'Liturgical Studies in the 90s', *Jewish Book Annual*, 1994–5, vol. 52, pp. 59–72.
——, 'The Literary Structure of the Amidah and the Rhetoric of Redemption', in W. G. Dever and E. J. Wright (eds), *Echoes of Many Texts: Reflections on Jewish and Christian Traditions, Essays in Honor of Lou H. Silberman*, Brown Judaic Studies, Atlanta, Scholars Press, pp. 171-230 (forthcoming).
——, *The Liturgy as Literature: A Historical and Rhetorical Commentary to the Jewish Prayerbook*, to be published by The Littman Library of Jewish Civilization.

——, 'The Messiah of the Amidah: A Study in Comparative Messianism', forthcoming in *JBL*.

Liebreich, L., 'The Benediction Immediately Preceding and the One Following the Recital of the Shema^ ', *REJ*, 1966, vol. 125, pp. 151–65.

Reif, S., *Judaism and Hebrew Prayer: New Perspectives on Jewish Liturgical History*, Cambridge, Cambridge University Press, 1993.

Sanders, E., *Jesus and Judaism*, Philadelphia, Fortress Press, 1986.

Schürer, E., *The History of the Jewish People in the Age of Jesus Christ (175 BC–AD 135)*, ed. G. Vermes *et al.*, vol. 2, Edinburgh: T. & T. Clark, 1979.

Tabory, J., *Jewish Prayer and the Yearly Cycle: A List of Articles, Kiryat Sefer*, Supplement to vol. 64, Jerusalem, The Jewish National and University Library, 1992–3.

Weinfeld, M., *Deuteronomy 1–11 (Anchor Bible 5)*, New York, Doubleday, 1991.

Part II

GREEKS AND ROMANS

19

PRAYER IN GRECO-ROMAN RELIGIONS

Larry J. Alderink and Luther H. Martin

Prayer is a prominent feature of Greco-Roman religious life as it is of any religious system in which superhuman power is imagined anthropomorphically in terms of agency. Most fundamentally, prayer is a request made of such divine agents. The significance of the prayer will vary, of course, according to the religious context and to the deity or deities addressed in this context, to the occasion of its utterance and to the specific nature of the request and its formal character.

FORM AND CONTENT OF PRAYER

The structure of Greco-Roman prayers (Gk: *euchai*; Lat: *vota, devotiones*) is typically tripartite: an invocation of deity, a narrative argument justifying the petition of the suppliant and, finally, the request itself. This formal structure may be illustrated already from the early Greek tradition in the Homeric prayer of Achilles to Zeus:

[invocation]

High Zeus, lord of Dodona, Pelasgian, living afar off, brooding over wintry Dodona, your prophets about you living, the Selloi who sleep on the ground with feet unwashed. Hear me:

[justification]

As one time before when I prayed to you, you listened and did me honour, and smote strongly the host of the Achaians, so one more time bring to pass the wish that I pray for.

[request]

For see, I myself am staying where the ships are assembled, but I send out my companion and many Myrmidons with him to fight. Let glory, Zeus of the wide brows, go forth with him to fight. Let glory, Zeus of the wide brows, go forth with him. Make brave the heart inside his breast, so that even Hektor will find out whether our henchman knows how to fight his battles by himself, or whether his hands range invincible only those times when I myself go into the grind of the war god. But when he has beaten back from the ships their clamorous onset, then let him come back to me and the running ships, unwounded, with all his armour and with the companions who fight close beside him.

(*Iliad* 16.233–48)[1]

The invocation deals with a problem characteristic of polytheistic systems that is absent from monotheisms, namely, the choice of the deity to be addressed. In a monotheistic system, of course, the only available deity cannot be misidentified by confusing it with another; however, asking Mars for health or Isis for victory in war could be disastrous for a well-meaning but misinformed suppliant. Any misdirected request will result in failed communication. Hence the need for precision in naming the proper god is at least as deep a need as that expressed through the content of the prayers.

The invocation of Greco-Roman prayers, consequently, may be quite elaborate. In addition to the identification of the deity by name, it may include alternative names for the deity, descriptive predicates of the deity, the sphere of activity, residence and cult-places associated with the deity and references to mythic accomplishments, and even such inclusive precautions as: 'or whatever other name it is lawful to name you' (e.g., Aeschylus, *Agamemnon* 160; Apuleius, *Metamorphoses* 11.2; Macrobius, *Saturnalia* 3.9.10–11). This *theokrasia*, or fluidity of divine nomination, is often referred to as 'syncretism' by those who privilege theological content over cultic practice in the religious systems of Greco-Roman antiquity.

The narrative section might give justification for why this particular deity is considered the appropriate deity to be called upon and why just this deity should now respond. It may include the relationship of the suppliant to the deity, such as previous occasions on which the deity has given aid. In this section, praise and honour were usually offered the deities rather than the expressions of gratitude more characteristic of Jewish and Christian prayer (but see *Chaereas*, Chapter 28 in this volume).

The final section will consist of some favour sought from the god. The specific content of the pagan prayers varies but several themes recur, such as the needs and fears of those praying together with their hopes for support and assistance. Ramsey McMullen points out that pagans generally prayed for health and beauty, for relief and protection, for safety and rescue, and for the needs of the household,[2] in addition, of course, to mastery of one's enemies.

In a system in which agency is hierarchically related, gods rank higher than humans with the result that humans ask and gods grant. Consequently, prayer as a mode of communication in a polytheistic system not only involves identifying the proper recipient of a message but also necessitates negotiation between the participants in the system. This sense of bargaining, clearly exemplified in the prayers of Cato, is expressed in the Roman distinction between *votum*, 'vow' or promise by the suppliant to recognize the deity in an appropriate manner upon compliance with the suppliant's request, and *devotio*, a recompense by the suppliant in advance of the deity's response.

BEHAVIOURS AND ATTITUDES ASSOCIATED WITH PRAYER

Proper behaviour and attitude are required of those who pray. Greeks and Romans stood during prayer, facing and with arms outstretched towards the domain associated with the deity, that is, towards the sky, the sea, or the underworld. Consequently, one of the Christian prayer postures, that of kneeling or prostration, was viewed as curiously 'un-Greek' or 'un-Roman'.

And while there were exceptions, Greek and Roman prayers were almost always spoken aloud (as were Jewish prayers; see 1 Sam 1:12) and in a public context, especially that of sacrifice. By contrast, private or personal prayer, such as that recommended by some Christians (for example, Matt 6:6), tended to be viewed by Greek and Romans as magic, especially when they were offered at night (for example, Mark 1:35; Luke 6:12, 22:41, 55). Apuleius, for example, writes of magic as a 'mysterious', 'loathly and horrible' art that requires 'night-watches and concealing darkness, solitude absolute and murmured incantations' (Apuleius, *Apologia* 47).[3] But this denunciation of magic within the Latin tradition should not be seen as supporting the scholarly habit of distinguishing religion, in which wor-shippers revere and submit to their deity, from magic, in which performers seek to coerce their deity. Submission and coercion are less distinctions between religion and magic, and more differing strategies employed by suppliants in their conduct of communication in an asymmetrical religious framework. For example, the magical appeal to Selene included in this volume (p. 195) contains both submission and coercion. The act of offering sacrifice does not so much 'compel' Selene in the strict sense as display a certain submissiveness which makes the petitioner's dismissal difficult.

While non-discursive practices of religious ritual were prescribed and had to be performed absolutely correctly, what was actually spoken in the accompanying prayers was less fixed. Nevertheless, the words of prayer were carefully considered. The wrong word would be *blasphemia*, an ill use of words which brings harm. But on the other hand, the employment of good words, *euphemia*, is a proclamation of auspicious silence during religious rites. In Plato's *Timaeus*, we find the most general statement about addressing the gods: it is right to seek the aid of the gods and goddesses at the beginning of any undertaking in the hope that the words will be good for both suppliant and deity (*Timaeus* 27c).

THE PLACE OF PRAYER

Important as is the form and practice of pagan prayer for our study, equally significant is their place in the religious life of the Greco-Roman world. Most of the prayers display a combination of reserve and dignity, recognizing the qualities of both the god and the one praying, mentioning both the ability of the god and the need of the petitioner. As the two parties, humans and gods, participate in the exchange of information, the suppliants want good ends for their entire lives and the gods receive their wishes. Both humans and their superhuman agents must recognize their proper domains as well as the needs and abilities under negotiation; both parties must observe the proprieties befitting them. Thus, the pagan prayers require that humans know themselves as much as they know the gods. They operate within a framework of etiquette, in which piety, knowledge of these right relationships (Gk: *eusebia*; Lat: *pietas*), will enable the participants to play their proper roles. In the world of Greco-Roman religions, then, imagination will be a primary requirement in composing and directing prayers. Humans must imagine many deities who can play multiple roles and grant diverse requests; in the face of multiple possible outcomes, prayer is simultaneously a move toward the self-knowledge involved in formulating the suppliant's situation and an act of imagining new and desirable alternatives.

NOTES

1 *The Iliad of Homer*, trans. Richmond Lattimore, Chicago, University of Chicago Press, 1951, p. 336.
2 Ramsey McMullen, *Paganism in the Roman Empire*, New Haven, CT, Yale University Press, 1981, pp. 51–2.
3 *The Apologia and Florida of Apuleius of Madaura*, trans. H. E. Butler, Westport, CT, Greenwood Press, 1970, p. 84.

SELECTED BIBLIOGRAPHY

Bremmer, Jan, 'Greek Hymns', in H. S. Versnel (ed.), *Faith, Hope and Worship: Aspects of Religious Mentality in the Ancient World*, Leiden, E. J. Brill, 1981, pp. 193–215.
Burkert, Walter, *Greek Religion*, Cambridge, MA, Harvard University Press, 1985, pp. 72–5.
Graf, Fritz, 'Prayer in Magical and Religious Ritual', in C. A. Faraone and D. Obbink (eds), *Magika Hiera: Ancient Greek Magic and Religion*, New York, Oxford University Press, 1991.

A. W. Mair, 'Prayer', in James Hastings (ed.), *Encyclopaedia of Religion and Ethics*, New York, Charles Scribners Sons, 1919, vol. 10, pp. 154–205.

Versnel, H. S., 'Religious Mentality in Ancient Prayer', in H. S. Versnel (ed.), *Faith, Hope and Worship: Aspects of Religious Mentality in the Ancient World*, Leiden, E. J. Brill, 1981, pp. 1–64.

20

CATO THE ELDER

C. Robert Phillips, III

INTRODUCTION

The treatise of Cato the Elder (234–149 BC) on farming (*De Agri Cultura*: c. 160 BC) contains several prayers (132, 134, 139, 141); the two presented here hold greatest interest as examples both of Roman prayers and Roman religion. Cato's treatise represents our earliest preserved example of continuous literary prose. His entire outlook was hyper-conservative, favouring social solidarity and traditional values; this outlook appears frequently in the fragments of his voluminous speeches, monographs and history (*Origines*). Even in the conservative context of Roman agriculture, Cato stands out; especially in the work's preface and first two chapters he takes a relentlessly traditional position, accepting no excuses from the farm's manager for vagaries of weather interfering with productivity, and concluding that everything not useful, whether human or animal or material, should be sold: 'best that the farm owner be a seller, not a buyer.'

The prayers' authenticity

Our prayers seem 'fossilized' in Cato – the Roman priestly traditions (see below) carefully conserved them and he apparently repeated them verbatim. Thus their textual problems cannot be solved via the entire treatise's manuscript traditions. Solutions require comparison with other literary and epigraphic texts, analysis of Latin prose rhythms, and frequent appeal to comparative linguistics; the translations here reflect such work but in the interests of intelligibility do not elaborate.

Although Cato writes archaic Latin, many linguistic features of the prayers are archaic even for him. Unlike some reworked documents, (thus Livy 1.12.4–8, 1.32), whose hyper-archaic Latin betrays their nature through frequent misuse of archaic vocabulary and syntax, these prayers can claim authenticity on technical grounds. Moreover, Servius' commentary on

Vergil's *Aeneid* 9.641 quotes from the prayer in Cato 132, noting that the quote came from the Roman pontiffs. Servius means Roman priestly colleges, whose records carefully preserved prayers and rituals from time immemorial; unfortunately, we only possess later antiquarians' (such as Servius) fragmentary notices and random quotes.[1]

There are extant prayers which initially seem earlier,[2] especially a prayer to Mars known from an inscription (*CIL* 1.2) of the Arval Brethren in AD 218. While this is surely an extremely early prayer in origins, it bristles with problems of vocabulary and syntax; it has been so frequently recopied that much is garbled and impossible even speculatively to translate or interpret.[3]

The prayers' style

As just noted, the vocabulary and syntax of these prayers is indisputably older than even Cato's treatise. Various stylistic matters further support this. There is frequent alliteration, especially pairs of alliterative words. There is no attempt to provide a literary series of balanced primary and subordinate clauses; rather, both kinds of clauses appear with equal syntactical importance, providing a choppy effect whether in Latin or translation. All of this also suggests the close connection between early prose and poetry.

The prayers and Roman religion

Many scholars have found it alarmingly easy to dismiss all Roman prayers as evidence for a religion obsessed with ritual and deficient in mythology and belief.[4] Both classicists and non-classicists must share the blame equally, since many have been blinded by the prevalence of 'religions of the book' which proffer both a canonical series of texts and lengthy written theological traditions. Although Roman paganism conserved much religious information in the priestly records, it lacked such canonical texts. Further, it did not preserve a written theological tradition, which has led many to the false conclusion that it had no theology. It is more plausible to observe it did not have a *written* theology – a religion without a theology is a contradiction in terms. Finally and consequently, since the Christian tradition arose in a world of Roman paganism, there has been a triumphalist tendency to take the alleged deficiencies as reason to utilize Roman religion merely as 'background' to the study alleged to be proper, namely, the Christian tradition. In all such cases the study of Roman religion has suffered. Obviously, misunderstandings of belief, ritual and myth in Roman religion have caused this – some clarification of which will now aid in appreciating the theology of Cato's prayers.

Scholars have often complained of the lack of 'myth' in Roman religion and used that to demonstrate its apparent mindless quality in contrast to, say, Greek religion or Christianity, both of which demonstrate mythologies in connection with their rituals and beliefs. But the lack of 'myth' is more accurately viewed as lack of 'myth' of the Greek variety; it is clear that in the nineteenth century, Greek mythology became normative for 'myth' whether in classical studies or elsewhere.[5] More expansive definitions of myth certainly reveal that the Romans had a rich system.

Thus scholars, especially those influenced by the myth–ritual school of interpretation, have readily concluded that Roman rituals were empty because they not only lacked 'myth' but also, as a result, they seemed obsessed with ritual mechanics. Of course, restoring 'myth', as just argued, changes this balance. Because there are no preserved theological treatises, Roman rituals can be seen as mechanical. But the Sanskrit Vedas show even more emphasis on ritual mechanics, and yet contemporary scholars do not claim a theological void there, precisely because lengthy ancient treatises on the meanings of the Vedas have been preserved – and because their 'myths' seem recognizable on the Hellenic model. In addition, much of ritual studies is still mired in the nineteenth century's myth–ritual school; exciting contemporary work bodes well for rethinking the meanings of ritual not as a code to be cracked, but as a part of an entire social system of knowledge.[6]

Finally, consider belief. If Roman religion be found wanting on grounds of myth and ritual, it becomes too easy to claim a lack of belief. Unfortunately, the slippery quality of 'belief' must seriously qualify any attempt to define a culture's religious 'belief'; such attempts are best avoided.[7]

In conclusion, then, these prayers should be taken as parts of a religious system which has, until quite recently, been almost wilfully misunderstood by scholars. The Romans conveyed their religious knowledge in different ways than other better-known religions, and they divided their knowledge under different rubrics, but that does not justify denying them belief or mythology or, as many have done, a religion.

TRANSLATIONS

When clearing a grove (139)

Whether you are a god or goddess[8] for whom this grove (*lucus*)[9] is sacred, since it is your right (*ius*)[10] to receive the sacrifice of a pig for clearing this grove – whether I or someone at my bidding does it, may it be rightly done. Therefore, because of this offering I pray that you be willing and propitious to me, my house, family and children. Therefore let it properly be so (*macte*)[11] because of this sacrificial offering.

To Mars (141)

Father Mars,[12] I pray and request, that you be willing and propitious to me, my house and family. Therefore I have commanded this offering of a pig,

CATO THE ELDER

sheep and ox (*suovetaurilia*)[13]. May you prevent, ward off, and turn away diseases visible and invisible, sterility and destruction, accident, brackish water and inclement weather. And may you allow the fruits and grains and vines and shrubs to grow and turn out well. Too, protect the shepherds and flocks and give safety and health to me, my house, and family. Therefore I have gone over (*lustrandi lustrique*)[14] my fields; as I have said, Father Mars, be properly the recipient (*macte*)[15] of these offerings.

NOTES

1 G. Rohde, *Die Kultsatzungen der römischen Pontifices*, Berlin, Töpelmann, 1936; F. Sini, *Documenti Sacerdotali di Roma Antica*, 2 vols, Sassari, Dessi, 1983.
2 G. Appel, *De Romanorum Precationibus*, Giessen, Töpelmann, 1909, pp. 8–11.
3 E. Courtney, *MUSA LAPIDARIA. A Selection of Latin Verse Inscriptions*, Atlanta, Scholars Press, 1995, pp. 34, 199–204, has most recently grappled with it, but two points need mention. First, even his notes acknowledge the linguistic difficulties. Second, while he is a renowned Latinist, his expertise lies with literature. Specialists in Roman religion do not share his optimism.
4 C.R. Phillips, *Studies in the Roman Religious Experience: Belief, Ritual, Myth*, Baltimore, Johns Hopkins, forthcoming.
5 C.R. Phillips, 'Misconceptualizing Classical Mythology', in M. Flower and M. Toher, *Georgica. Greek Studies in Honour of George Cawkwell*, London, University of London, Institute of Classical Studies, 1991, pp. 143–51.
6 Pascal Boyer, *The Naturalness of Religious Ideas*, Berkeley, University of California, 1994; E. Thomas Lawson and Robert N. McCauley, *Rethinking Religion*, Cambridge, Cambridge University Press, 1990.
7 Rodney Needham, *Belief, Language, and Experience*, Oxford, Blackwell, 1972.
8 'god or goddess': An efficacious prayer had precisely to name the divinity. Although Roman agriculture was rich in specialized gods (*numina* or *indigitamenta*; see note 12), there would inevitably be places where a Roman would recognize an *anonymous* divine presence. Hence this generic phrase; there are epigraphic parallels in Roman agricultural and military contexts. An anonymous divine presence (compare Livy 7.26.4, Vergil, *Aeneid* 8.351–2 and the implicit Christian criticism in *Acts* 17:23) was not uniquely Roman: Aeschylus, *Agamemnon* 160: 'Zeus, whoever he is . . .'.
9 *lucus*: Sacred groves were omnipresent in agrarian Italy; a divine presence was a theological given. For an example, admittedly late and literary, of the perils of ignoring this, Ovid, *Metamorphoses* 8.725–879.
10 *ius*: The word precisely means 'law' in secular legal texts. Its appearance in Roman religious texts (see also the next prayer) has led many to conclude that Roman religion comprised legalistic religious formulae devoid of active thought or belief. This is not so. In archaic Rome, the same socio-economic elite controlled both law and religion; on its view, law and religion constituted parallel methods to ensure the smooth functioning of secular and sacred. The legal reference implies reciprocity, and there is nothing unthinking about equating proper prayer with expected results.
11 *macte*: Even in antiquity this word occasioned debate. Compare Vergil, *Aeneid* 9.641: *macte noua virtute*: '( ) because of your new virtue'. Although Vergil's context is secular, it apparently contains a notion of increase – the divinity receives the proper offering and prayer, the theological stock of divine good will

is increased and the propitiant receives a share. See Kurt Latte, *Römische Religionsgeschichte*, Munich, Beck, 1960, p. 45 n. 2, but certainty on the meaning of *macte* will probably never be possible.

12 'Father Mars': The appearance of Mars in an agrarian context should not startle readers. While Mars appears in later Roman literature as equivalent to the Greek god of war (thus often in Ovid's *Metamorphoses*), Ares, that identification is late and limited to literary contexts of Hellenic antecedents; it has no role in Roman agrarian religion. Vergil's *Georgics* explore this duality, since Vergil portrays agriculture as a struggle with nature, heightening this with frequent military metaphors: the farmer's tools are *arma* (1.160). Such literary uses, while important, do not influence our prayer. Oddly, since Roman religion was especially rich in agrarian spirits (*indigitamenta*), Mars appears in Cato as an omnibus protector of the fields. The fourth-century AD grammarian Servius, in his commentary on Vergil's *Georgics*, preserves (on 1.21) a plausibly authentic list of a dozen such spirits from the early third-century BC annalist Fabius Pictor; it includes Vervactor (first ploughing), and Promitor (corn distribution). In general, see Udo Scholz, *Studien zum altitalischen und altrömischen Marskult und Marsmythos*, Heidelberg, Winter, 1970 with pp. 70–6 on this prayer.

13 *suovetaurilia*: A technical word connected originally with agrarian lustration (next note) festivals in which Mars would, logically, have a role; thus there are the Ambarvalia (lustration of fields; it may well be what Cato describes) and Terminalia (sanctification of field boundaries). See C. Robert Phillips, 'Ambarvalia', in *The Oxford Classical Dictionary*, 3rd ed., 1996, p. 70.

14 *lustrandi lustrique*: Ritual traversal and purification of fields, although in the course of the Republic it was widened to denote purification of an estate, city or group of people. Robert Ogilvie, 'Lustrum Condere', *Journal of Roman Studies* 51, 1961, pp. 31–9.

15 See note 11.

SELECTED BIBLIOGRAPHY

W. Warde Fowler, *The Religious Experience of the Roman People*, London, Macmillan, 1911.

Robert Ogilvie, *The Romans and Their Gods in the Age of Augustus*, London, Chatto & Windus, 1969.

H.H. Scullard, *Festivals and Ceremonies of the Roman Republic*, Ithaca, NY, Cornell, 1981.

Alan Watson, *The State, Law and Religion: Pagan Rome*, Athens, GA, University of Georgia Press, 1992.

21

CLEANTHES – *HYMN TO ZEUS*

William Cassidy

INTRODUCTION

The nature of the text

The source of the text is the fifth-century CE anthology of ancient Greek literary excerpts compiled by Ioannes Stobeus, known to scholars as *Stobaeus*.[1] This is an eclectic work, containing selections from both poetry and prose of the archaic to the Roman periods.

The *Hymn* is written in the epic style of classical Greek poetry. Most late classical and Hellenistic philosophers wrote prose, and Cleanthes followed this general practice. The third-century CE historian of philosophy Diogenes Laertius lists the titles of some fifty works by Cleanthes, some several volumes in length.[2] It has been suggested that the *Hymn* was a poetical interlude in one of his longer works.[3] Unfortunately, little is known of the content or form of these writings.

Cleanthes' use of the epic form for the *Hymn* seems quite appropriate. The *Hymn* is as religious as it is philosophical, thus poetry (to the Greek a 'higher' and more serious form of literature) matches 'the truth to be found in the consideration of the divine'.[4] This form of epic poetry was based on the paradigmatic works of Homer and Hesiod who were imitated by the anonymous authors of the *Homeric Hymns* as well as by myriad other writers. It would seem natural to a religiously minded philosopher such as Cleanthes to employ the form. There are parallels to this attitude in pre-Socratic philosophy: the use of poetic form by Empedocles in his *Purifications* or by Parmenides in his *Proem* are good examples.

Cleanthes and Stoicism

Stoicism, a Hellenistic philosophy,[5] was founded by Zeno (335–263 BCE) around 300 BCE. It gets its name from the *Stoa Poikile* (Coloured Porch), a roofed colonnade in the city centre of Athens that was decorated with paintings and served as the meeting place for this philosophical school. Cleanthes (331–232) was a student of Zeno and succeeded his master as leader of the school from 263 to 232. Astonishing as it may seem for the leader of a philosophical school, he had a reputation for being slow of wit.[6] Cleanthes was nevertheless well-respected at Athens for his industry, his cheerful indifference to poverty, and his moral character. His successor Chrysippus (280–207) was far more brilliant, and, perhaps because of this, little of Cleanthes' work has survived. The longest piece is his *Hymn to Zeus*, which surely contributes to Cleanthes' reputation as the most religious of the Stoics.

The only elements of Stoic philosophy which need concern us here are those connected to religion, such as theories of divinity and nature. Unlike their rivals the Epicureans, the Stoics argued that the Divine is active in the world. While they criticized the sacrifices and practices of traditional Greek religion, they maintained that the gods and goddesses of Greek religion existed, interpreting them, as A. A. Long conceives it, as 'names of natural phenomena (Hera or Juno is "air") which are divine manifestations of the one ultimate deity, Nature, whose name is also Zeus'.[7] It is with this understanding of god that Cleanthes salutes Zeus in the *Hymn*, a deity that is at once the king of the gods and father of men (as was understood in Greek myths and religion), the embodiment of *logos* (reason) that pervades all creation, and the source of all the cosmos.[8] As we shall see, Cleanthes believes it entirely appropriate that we humans praise this god by seeking to follow the divine *logos* through leading lives guided by philosophy.

Philosophical issues in the *Hymn*

It is Zeus the philosophical god, then, who is addressed in the *Hymn*. Cleanthes' view is rather a pantheistic one: Zeus is the source and essence of all. The other deities, in reality allegories of nature, are thus aspects of Zeus, the 'first cause', as Cleanthes puts it in the second line of the poem. The association of law (*nomos*) with Zeus is traditional and is already prominent in early epic poetry. But while the early Greek understanding of Zeus' law refers to traditional customs of the Hellenes, in Stoicism law is universalized. This law is at once the law of nature and law appropriate for guiding human lives, since, for Cleanthes, the universe is entirely unified in Zeus. Law is also rational: it is connected, as Cleanthes puts it, to 'the common reason (*logos*) which flows through everything' (ll. 12–13). Reason is also the 'likeness' (l. 4) that human beings share with Zeus, thus the ideal for humans is to employ their rationality through studying philosophy in order to develop good judgement which will allow them to live in honour according to the divine, rational law of nature which is Zeus (ll. 23–4, 34–5).

Cleanthes, influenced by the pre-Socratic philosopher Heraclitus, uses the image of fire as a central metaphor. Zeus' thunderbolt, which is his traditional weapon in the myths, becomes here the elemental power by which Zeus animates the cosmos. The thunderbolt creates and maintains 'all the works of nature' (l. 11). It is the heat of life and the beacon of reason; the 'divine light' which fuels the stars and the human mind (ll. 12–13). The thunderbolt, no longer a destructive weapon as in Greek myths, is here the force of 'the common reason, which flows through everything', as noted above.[9]

Yet it is possible for humans to resist it. While for Zeus good and evil are harmonized (ll. 19–20), for humans they can remain in polarity. Evil human beings are those who shun reason and seek material goals such as political power, wealth, and sexuality as ends. In pursuing these lesser goals they fail to follow Zeus' divine plan and thus waste their potential in the darkness of bestiality. For Cleanthes evil is the result of human ignorance.[10] The good will seek to follow Zeus' divine reason.

The *Hymn* as a prayer

The poem follows a quite traditional form for literary Greek prayers, which is '*invocatio* (invocation by means of the name, surname, epithets and descriptive predicates), the *pars epica* (in which the suppliant explains why he is calling on this particular god for help, what his relationship with the deity is, and why he thinks he can count on his assistance), and the actual *preces* (the content of the wish)'.[11] The *invocatio* consists of lines 1–3 (Most . . . Hail!), the *pars epica* 3–30, and the *preces* the remaining lines of the poem.

Most of the *invocatio* is quite traditional, and, save for 'first cause of Nature', might have been written by Homer or Hesiod. The *pars epica*, however, is utterly Stoic in spirit. Where a traditional poet, such as those of the *Homeric Hymns*, would have mentioned mythic themes and a pious worshipper would have recounted past sacrifices and past prayers made to the deity, Cleanthes bases his claim for divine assistance on his Stoic understanding of the relationship between Zeus and human beings. The *preces*, the actual request, is universal rather than personal, as befits a philosopher. Though philosophical and literary in form, Cleanthes' *Hymn to Zeus* seems to be a genuinely religious work, the act of a man for whom philosophy is a spiritual as well as an intellectual path.

TRANSLATION[12]

1 Most glorious of immortals, honoured under many names,
  all-powerful forever,
  O Zeus, first cause of Nature, guiding all things through law,
  Hail! For it is just for all mortals to address you,
  Since we were born of you, and we alone share in the likeness
5 Of deity, of all things that live and creep upon the earth.

So I will hymn you and sing always of your strength.
For all the cosmos, as it whirls around earth,
Obeys you, wherever you lead, and it is willingly ruled by you.
For such is the power you hold in your unconquerable hands:
10   The two-forked,[13] fiery, ever-living thunderbolt.
For all the works of nature are accomplished through its blows,
By which you set right the common reason, which flows
Through everything, mixing divine light through things great and
      small.[14]
Nothing is accomplished in this world save through you, O Spirit,
15   Neither in the divine, heavenly, ethereal sphere, nor upon the sea,
Save as much as the evil accomplish on their own in their ignorance.
But you are yet able to make the odd even,
And to order the disorderly; and to love the unloved.
For thus you have fit together into one all good things with the
      bad
20   So that they become one single, eternal harmony.[15]
They flee it, those among mortals who are evil –
The ill-starred, they who always yearn for the possession of
      beautiful things
But never behold the divine universal law. Nor do they hear it,
Though if they hearkened to it, using intelligence, they would
      have a fortunate life.
25   But in their ignorance they rush headlong into this or that evil:
Some pressing on in an aggressive search for popularity and
      renown,
Others in reckless pursuit of wealth,
Others yet in laziness or in sensual pleasure
. . . [16]They are borne hither and thither,
30   All hastening to become the opposite of what they are.
Zeus the all-giver, wielder of the bright lightning in the dark clouds,
Deliver mankind from its miserable incompetence.
Father, disperse this from our soul; give us
Good judgement, trusting in you to guide all things in justice,
35   So that, in gaining honour we may repay you with honour,
Praising your works unceasingly, as is always fitting
For mortals. For there is no greater honour among men,
Nor among gods, than to sing forever in justice your universal
      law.

NOTES

1   The standard edition is H. von Arnim, *Stoicorum veterum fragmenta*, 3 vols,
   Leipzig, 1903–5, vol. 4, indices by M. Adler, Leipzig, 1924. The *Hymn* is

CLEANTHES – *HYMN TO ZEUS*

frag. 537. Critical editions of the Greek text of Cleanthes' *Hymn* will be found in A.C. Pearson (ed.), *The Fragments of Zeno and Cleanthes*, London, C.J. Clay & Sons, 1891, and in Iohannes U. Powell, (ed.), *Collectanea Alexandrina: Reliquiae minores poetarum Graecorum Aetatis Ptolemaicae 323–146 AC*, Oxford, Oxford University Press, 1925. The Greek text, but with minimal critical apparatus, is provided by A.A. Long and David Sedley, *The Hellenistic Philosophers*, 2 vols, Cambridge, Cambridge University Press, 1987. English translations of the complete text are in ibid., in Frederick C. Grant (ed.), *Hellenistic Religions: The Age of Syncretism*, New York, Liberal Arts Press, 1953, and in F.H. Sandbach, *The Stoics*, New York, W.W. Norton & Co., 1975.

2   Diogenes Laertius, VII, 174–5.
3   This suggestion was made by H. von Arnim, op. cit. On it, see A.W. James, 'The Zeus Hymns of Cleanthes and Aratus', *Antichthon*, 1972, vol. 6, p. 29.
4   Sandbach, op. cit., p. 110, summarizing Cleanthes' view as found in frag. 468, von Arnim; see Ludwig Edelstein, *The Meaning of Stoicism*, Cambridge, Cambridge University Press, 1987, p. 34 for discussion.
5   On Hellenistic philosophies in general and Stoicism in particular, see A.A. Long, *Hellenistic Philosophy: Stoics, Epicureans, Sceptics*, 2nd edn, Berkeley and Los Angeles, University of California Press, 1986; Long and Sedley, op. cit.; and Eduard Zeller, *The Stoics, Epicureans and Sceptics*, new and rev. edn trans. by Oswald J. Reichel, New York, Russell & Russell, Inc., 1962. On their relation to religion see Luther H. Martin, *Hellenistic Religions: An Introduction*, New York, Oxford University Press, 1987, and Grant, op. cit. General discussions and interpretations of Stoicism are to be found in Sandbach, op. cit. and Edelstein, op. cit.
6   According to Diogenes Laertius, Cleanthes 'had industry, but no natural aptitude for physics, and he was extraordinarily slow' (VII:168, Loeb translation).
7   Long, op. cit., p. 150.
8   David Sedley puts it a bit differently: that Cleanthes' *Hymn* presents 'a god who is at once the Zeus of popular religion, the ordering fire-god of Heraclitus, and the Stoic providential deity' (Long and Sedley, op. cit., p. 332).
9   Long's discussion of this issue in Stoicism is highly recommended (op. cit., pp. 145–84).
10 On the problem of evil in Stoic philosophy, see Long, op. cit., pp. 169–79 and 181–3; Sandbach, op. cit., pp. 101–8; Long & Sedley, op. cit., *passim*.
11 H.S. Versnel, 'Religious Mentality in Ancient Prayer', in H.S. Versnel (ed.), *Faith, Hope and Worship: Aspects of Religious Mentality in the Ancient World*, Leiden, E.J. Brill, 1981, p. 2. On Cleanthes' *Hymn* as following this form (unlike most philosophers' prayers), see P.A. Meier, 'Philosophers, Intellectuals, and Religion in Hellas', in ibid., p. 233.
12 There are many problems in the Greek text. See the *apparati* in Pearson, op. cit., and Powell, op. cit., for their views. For an extended discussion, those with Latin should consult J.D. Meerwaldt, 'Cleanthea I & II', *Mnemosyne*, 1951, vol. 4, pp. 40–69, and 1952, vol. 5, pp. 1–12. See James, op. cit., on relationships between the text and epic poetry.
13 Thus Pearson, op. cit.; others translate it 'double-edged'.
14 The 'things great and small' are usually interpreted as the heavenly bodies: the sun and stars, but I think it better to leave the application open.
15 'Harmony' is a gloss. The Greek is *logos*, reason.
16 Line 29 contains a lacuna in the Greek text.

137

SELECTED BIBLIOGRAPHY

(For a more extensive bibliography, consult Long and Sedley, vol. 2, pp. 491–510, espec. pp. 493–4 on Cleanthes.)

Edelstein, Ludwig, *The Meaning of Stoicism*. Cambridge, MA, Harvard University Press, 1966.

Grant, Frederick C. (ed.), *Hellenistic Religions: The Age of Syncretism*. New York, Liberal Arts Press, 1953.

James, A.W., 'The Zeus Hymns of Cleanthes and Aratus', *Antichthon* 6, 1972, pp. 28–38.

Long, A.A., *Hellenistic Philosophy: Stoics, Epicureans, Sceptics*, 2nd edn, Berkeley and Los Angeles, University of California Press, 1986.

Long, A.A. and Sedley, D.N., *The Hellenistic Philosophers*, 2 vols, Cambridge, Cambridge University Press, 1987.

Martin, Luther H., *Hellenistic Religions: An Introduction*, New York, Oxford University Press, 1987.

Pearson, A.C. (ed.), *The Fragments of Zeno and Cleanthes*, London, C.J. Clay & Sons, 1891. Reprint edn: New York, Arno Press, 1973.

Powell, Iohannes U. (ed.), *Collectanea Alexandrina: Reliquiae minores poetarum Graecorum Aetatis Ptolemaicae 323–146 AC*, Oxford, Oxford University Press, 1925.

Sandbach, F.H., *The Stoics*, New York, W.W. Norton & Co., 1975.

Versnel, H.S. (ed.), *Faith, Hope and Worship: Aspects of Religious Mentality in the Ancient World*, Leiden, E.J. Brill, 1981.

Zeller, Eduard, *The Stoics, Epicureans and Sceptics*, new and rev. edn trans. by Oswald J. Reichel, New York, Russell & Russell, Inc., 1962 (1st edn 1852).

22

CATULLUS 34: A PRAYER TO DIANA BY C. VALERIUS CATULLUS

Frederick W. Danker

INTRODUCTION

This prayer is one of one hundred and sixteen poems by Gaius Valerius Catullus (*c.* 87–54 BC; hereafter all dates are BC), born at Verona, and one of Rome's most illustrious lyric poets. Little, beyond gleanings from his poetry, is known about his private life. He was not a man of means, and much of his emotional life was futilely expended on a married woman whom he calls Lesbia.

Deceptively simple in its syntax and diction, this hymn is a masterpiece of taut structure, dense in thematic expression, but without obscurity. Goddess Diana is here presented as Rome's patron, and the emotional effect produced by this hymn owes much to the patriotic tone that underlies the overt expression and imagery. From the beginning we are invited to share the Roman spirit, and at the end we realize that Diana's prestige is intimately linked with Rome's interest, whose future lies in her hands. Roman mythology, as exhibited especially in poets, owes much to Greek mythographers, and Diana assumes many of the features associated with Artemis.[1]

Whether the poem was composed for a specific occasion cannot be determined, but the tone of the entire poem evokes the image of a solemn occasion at which tradition would dictate the presence of a priest and a chorus. Carefully chosen words and phrases suggest throughout to the alert Roman auditor or reader the reasons for Rome's greatness and the need for Diana's ongoing providential concern. Unobtrusively embedded in support of the theme are some of the cardinal virtues so highly prized by Roman moralists, including *fides* (fidelity to a trust: Diana); *castitas* (purity and uprightness: the chorus); *pietas* (reverence: the chorus); *frugalitas* (simple style of life: the farmer); and *constantia* (steadfastness of purpose: Diana). All these, of course, are to be emulated by Rome if it is to endure. Thus the hymned petition is unobtrusively sermonic.

Except for line 3, restored by the Renaissance commentator Palladio Fosco,[2] with assistance from another Renaissance editor named Avanzi, who altered Palladio's 'Dianae' to 'Dianam', the poem has suffered little textual uncertainty.

TRANSLATION

In Diana's care are we,[3]
girls and boys, all chaste.
'Diana', we chaste[4] boys
and girls are carolling.

Latona's daughter! Of Jove,
the highest, high offspring,
whom nigh the Delian olive[5]
your mother birthed,[6]

so that mistress[7] you might be
of mountains and verdant
woodlands, secluded wilds
and resounding streams.[8]

In pangs of birth you
are hailed Lucina Juno
You, with Trivia's power, with borrowed
light, as Luna are hailed.[9]

With your monthly career[10]
you space the course of the years[11]
and rude huts of farmers you fill
up with good fruits.[12]

Under whatever name you please,[13]
may you hallowed be,[14] and save,
as ever of old,[15] the race of Romulus
through your goodly aid.[16]

NOTES

1 J. Gaisser, *Catullus and his Renaissance Readers*, Oxford, Clarendon Press, 1993, pp. 97–102.
2 L. Farnell, *The Cults of the Greek City States*, 5 vols, Oxford, Clarendon Press,

1896–1909, II, pp. 425–607; on Artemis see also G. Mussies, 'Artemis', in K. van der Toorn, B. Becking and P. van der Horst, *Dictionary of Deities and Demons in the Bible (DDD)*, Leiden, E. J. Brill, 1995, cols 167–80.

3   On association of boys and girls with Artemis, see Farnell, op. cit., p. 537. The thematic note in line 1 invites expression of associated ideas. Ultimately, Rome's fortunes are the poet's concern, but instead of beginning with an exploration of Roman virtues he focuses on Diana and links loyal 'care' (*fides*) with her. The choral members are her wards.

4   Since observance of purity was important for acceptable rites, Catullus characterizes the members of the chorus as pure and 'chaste' (*integri*). The auditor is expected to identify with the chorus and the Roman ideals it proclaims through praise of Diana. In a sense all Romans are in her custody. Hence the poem begins with recognition of the virtue that finds implicit expression in the climactic petition at the end of the poem. Compare the contrast of a chorus of virgins and boys with the '*profanum volgus*', Horace, *Odes* 3.1–4. If the restoration of the third line is correct (see K. Quinn, *Catullus*, New York, St Martin's Press, 1970, p. 92) we have a strong affirmation of Roman identity. The boys and girls are here presented as Rome's treasure and the hope for her continuing greatness.

5   The religious earnestness or *pietas* with which the poem begins is here wedded to traditional mythology, where three names were as fuel for the enkindled patriotic flame. Diana is closely linked with Jupiter (*Jove*) through wordplay: she is 'great' (*magna*) as offspring of 'greatest' (*maximus*) Jupiter; cf. Ovid, *Epistulae ex Ponto* 4.2.1; for the customary Greek formulation see Pindar, *Nemean* 1.9. She is also implicitly linked with Apollo, the Roman pantheon's major deity, through two skilfully chosen adjectives: 'Latonian' and 'Delian'. Latona would immediately be recognized as mother of Diana and Apollo. For Diana's lineage through Jupiter's liaison with Latona see Ovid, *Metamorphoses* 6.106; Hesiod, *Theognis* 918. Reference to Delos further confirms her association with Apollo, popular at Delos – see Farnell, op. cit., V, pp. 442–4; on Artemis and Delos, pp. 465–6. By avoiding specific mention of Apollo, the poet maintains focus on Diana.

6   In legend Latona gave birth to her illustrious offspring by leaning against an olive tree. This reference provides easy transition to stanza three, which focuses on natural phenomena. For the story see Ovid, *Metamorphoses* 6.333ff. and 13.634–5. Phaedrus 1.19.4 uses the verb '*depono*' of a dog dropping her young, and 1.18.5 of a woman birthing her child. The form '*deposivit*' (cf. Callimachus, *Hymns* 3.25) is one of the few archaic forms used in the poem and enunciates solemnity without challenge to the verbal simplicity that pervades the poem as an expression of children.

7   Cf. Artemis: 'Give me all mountains ... for Artemis seldom goes to a town.' Callimachus, *Hymns* 3.18-19.

8   Catullus heightens Diana's claim on his own public's attention by parading Rome's countryside. In ten beguiling words nature falls under Diana's sway. The appeal to patriotic sentiments is subliminal. Only by maintaining ancient moral standards can Rome keep on the path to greatness.

9   The poet ensures Diana's attention through personal address suggesting three jurisdictions: the earth, the netherworld and the heavens. She is addressed by women in childbirth as Juno Lucina. In Greek mythology Artemis is known also as Eileithyia (Lucina), a goddess subordinate to Hera (Juno) and linked with her in the context of childbirth. Thus Diana becomes associated with the special process of parturition. On Eileithyia see Farnell, op. cit, II, pp. 608-17; cf. Pindar, *Nemean* 7; Horace, *Odes* 3.22.1. In Theocritus 27.29 Eileithyia

brings on birth pangs, but Artemis lightens them, v. 30. Diana is also identified as Trivia, that is, the goddess of the 'crossways', known in Greek mythology as 'Trioditis' or Hecate, who was associated with the netherworld. On association of Artemis with crossroads see Farnell, op. cit., II, 516–17; for the equivalent Greek term *trioditis* see Charicledes 1. In heaven Diana shines as the moon, albeit with light that is not her own. Lucretius 5.575 uses the same terminology: *[lustrans] notho lumine*; the perception can be traced to Parmenides – see Plutarch, *Moralia* 929a; 1116a. With this description Catullus accounts for the moon's waxing and waning. It is misplaced criticism to term the description 'inappropriate', as does W. Kroll, *C. Valerius Catullus*, 5th edn, Stuttgart, Teubner, 1968, on line 15. Diana is powerful, perhaps because of her magical powers, especially important to lovers. Cf. Horace, *Odes* 3.22.4.

10   The mention of the moon permits Catullus to consider Diana's role in Rome's agricultural life. From Italy's farms come the bulk of Rome's armies; cf. Horace, *Odes* 3.6.37–8. Reference to the farmer's 'rude huts' is therefore elegantly economical in patriotic statement. Catullus is himself not given to an extravagant lifestyle, T. Wiseman, *Catullus and his World: A Reappraisal*, Cambridge, Cambridge University Press, 1985, p. 103. Kroll's verdict, op. cit., on line 17, on *rustica* as empty in content misses the point. Catullus can count on readers to infer a contrast between the *frugalitas* or simplicity of life of people of the land and the spiritually decadent life of aristocrats. Diana's identity as moon-goddess is essential to consideration of the farmer's blessings; cf. Horace, *Odes* 4.6.38–40. Her division of the year into appropriate segments bears on the farmer's success; cf. Xenophon, *Memorabilia* 4.4–6 on beneficence bestowed by movements of heavenly bodies.

11   Orderly processing of the year ensures proper times for ploughing, planting and reaping. Through Diana's beneficence, as also Callimachus affirmed of Artemis (*Hymns* 3.1129–31), farmers enjoy the bounties of the earth. But Diana can also inflict terrible plagues and losses on sinners, and especially on renders of the social fabric; see Callimachus, *Hymns* 3.121–8; 133. On the history of Artemis–Diana's association with agriculture, see Farnell, op. cit., II, p. 530.

12   The word 'good' renders *bonum*, which underlies 'goodly' in stanza 6. As with *rustica* ('rude'), Kroll, op. cit., on line 20, inappropriately views this adjective as 'devoid' of content. The verbal echo in effect asks whether such experience of bounty will prevail in the future. The answer is important to Catullus' public who have experienced numerous political–economic oscillations.

13   The customary escape clause of Roman ritual, to cover any inadvertencies in addressing a divinity; see Quinn, op. cit., on line 21. E. Fraenkel, *Aeschylus: Agamemnon*, II, Oxford, Clarendon Press, 1962, pp. 99–100, in connection with Agamemnon 160f cites, *inter alia*, Plato, *Cratylus* 400e; Athenaeus 8.334b. Compare Catullus 40.3; Callimachus, *Hymns* 3.7. It is a common device in spells and incantations; numerous examples in H. Betz, *The Greek Magical Papyri in Translation*, Chicago, University of Chicago, 1986.

14   Diana is approached not only under the numerous names already mentioned, but any other she may prefer. Catullus only asks that she may find herself hallowed (*sancta*), whatever the name be. The use of multiple names for deities has a long history; see J. Bremmer, 'Name', in K. van der Toorn *et al.*, op. cit., cols 1148–9.

15   Diana is revered as a benefactor and asked to continue in that role, 'as ever of old', i.e. in the old way (*antique*). Compare Psalm 24:6. See also the numerous appeals to the billionaire Opramoas based on previous performance, *Inscriptiones Graecae ad Res Romanas Pertinentes*, 4 vols in 3, Chicago, Ares, 1975, no. 738.

16 The precatory moment toward which all the earlier phrases with their names and descriptions have been moving looms large. The verb *sospito* rendered 'save' is an old word and especially appropriate in a petition; it is used mostly in devotional language in the sense 'preserve, defend'. See R. Ellis, *A Commentary on Catullus*, Oxford, Clarendon Press, 1876, p. 93, with his ref. to Livy 1:16. On children's petition for their city's welfare, cf. Horace, *Odes* 1.21; see also O. Kern (ed.), *Die Inschriften von Magnesia am Maeander*, Berlin, W. Spemann, 1900, no. 98, lines 19–31. Echoing line 19, the phrase 'goodly aid' brings the poet's prayer to a close. The repetition effectively enhances the request for renewed beneficence.

SELECTED BIBLIOGRAPHY

Bardon, H., *Catulli Carmina*, Brussels, Latomus, 1970.

Ellis, R., *A Commentary on Catullus*, Oxford, Clarendon Press, 1876.

Gaisser, J., *Catullus and his Renaissance Readers*, Oxford, Clarendon Press, 1993.

Kroll, W., *C. Valerius Catullus*, 5th edn reprint with additions of 3rd edn of 1959, Stuttgart, Teubner, 1968.

Merrill, E., *Catullus*, New Rochelle, NY, Caratzas Brothers, 1976 [1893].

Quinn, K., *Catullus*, New York, St Martin's Press, 1970.

——, Trends in Catullan Criticism', in *Aufstieg und Niedergang der römischen Welt*, I/3, Berlin and New York, Walter de Gruyter, 1973.

Whigham, P., *The Poems of Catullus*, Berkeley and Los Angeles, University of California, 1969.

Wiseman, T., *Catullus and his World: A Reappraisal*, Cambridge, Cambridge University Press, 1985.

23

THE OATH OF AENEAS: VERGIL, *AENEID* 12.176–94

Frances Hickson-Hahn

INTRODUCTION

A literary version of a treaty oath appears in the *Aeneid*, an epic poem on the founding of the Roman nation, written by the Roman poet Vergil (70–19 BCE). Partly because of the *Aeneid*'s many accounts of prayer and ritual, by late antiquity Vergil had acquired a considerable reputation for his expertise in Roman cult. In fact, in Macrobius' *Saturnalia*, a work largely devoted to commentary on the *Aeneid*, one speaker refers to Vergil as *pontifex maximus*, the chief priest of state cult (1.24.16). Despite this reputation, the influence of the Homeric epics on the *Aeneid* is omnipresent even in matters of religion. In the case of prayers, Vergil's choice of language, and sometimes content as well, never represents an exact reproduction of Roman cultic prayer, but sometimes reflects Homeric practice and on other occasions his own poetic artistry. None of the prayers in the *Aeneid* should be viewed as expressions of Vergil's personal religiosity.[1]

Attestation

The text of Vergil's *Aeneid* survives in numerous manuscripts, both ancient and medieval. The main witnesses to this poem are several ancient manuscripts, written in rustic capitals, a format otherwise reserved for inscriptions. The three most important of these manuscripts all preserve Aeneas' prayer: the fifth-century Medici codex (M), the fifth/sixth-century Palatine codex (P) and the fifth/sixth-century Roman codex (R).[2]

Literary context

The speaker of this oath is Aeneas, a survivor of the Trojan war and member of the royal house of Troy, who leads a band of Trojans to Italy where the fates have decreed a new homeland. As in the Roman state, where civil and religious authority were united in magistrates, Aeneas is responsible for all areas of his people's communal life, including the religious. As the chief mediator between the human and divine spheres, he is the dominant figure in the celebration of ritual and offering of prayers. Aeneas' role as speaker of prayers is also part of Vergil's characterization of the Trojan leader as a man of piety (*pius Aeneas*), a moral quality encompassing the fulfilment of obligations to family, country and deities.

In the twelfth and final book of the *Aeneid*, an attempt is made to end a war between Trojans and Italians through single combat by the primary heroes of each side, Aeneas and Turnus. Both sides approve a treaty indicating the terms of victory or defeat and establishing future relations between Trojans and Italians. Prior to combat, Aeneas and King Latinus swear oaths to uphold the terms of that treaty. This oath, like many in Greco-Roman antiquity, is sworn in the context of an animal sacrifice, which frequently functioned as a metaphor for the fate of the man who did not uphold his promises.

Mingling of cultic and literary in Aeneas' oath

Aeneas' oath opens with an invocation of deities to witness the provisions of the treaty. He names three anthropomorphic divinities, Jupiter, Juno and Mars, alongside the elemental powers of sky, earth and water. Jupiter's presence in this invocation is necessitated by his role as the chief deity of the Roman state and, like his Greek counterpart Zeus, the primary god of oaths. From the perspective of Roman cult, the additional invocation of Juno and Mars makes no sense. One would expect to find either the archaic triad of Jupiter, Mars and Quirinus[3] or the later Hellenized triad of Jupiter, Juno and Minerva. From a literary point of view, however, the inclusion of Juno and Mars is significant. Juno is the instigator of this war and a potential threat to the peace of any future Trojan settlement because of her long-standing hatred of the Trojans. Aeneas' parenthetical address to Juno ('kinder now, goddess, I pray') highlights his concerns and motivations for including her in the invocation. As the god of war, Mars is a logical deity to be invoked in a treaty intended to end wars.[4] Roman legend also claims him as the father of the Roman nation through his son Romulus, its founder, a descendant of Aeneas. From the perspective of Greek mythology, Juno follows Jupiter as his wife and Mars follows as their son.

Vergil's manner of presentation of these deities also points to literary models. Roman cult attached the utmost value to the ability to invoke a deity by name and did so whenever possible to ensure that the correct deity was addressed and thus responded. In Aeneas' oath, however, Jupiter is not invoked by name, but rather by the epithet 'all-powerful father'. In some manuscript versions, Vergil also omits the name of Juno and refers to her instead as Jupiter's 'Saturnian wife', that is, the offspring of Saturn.⁵

Aeneas' invocation of the Sun, Earth, Springs and Rivers, and divine powers of the sky and sea reflects the influence of Vergil's Homeric models. The prayer most closely paralleling that of Aeneas is the oath preceding the duel in the *Iliad* between Paris and Menelaus, intended to end the Trojan war and determine which man would take Helen as his wife (3.276–91).⁶ There Agamemnon swears by Zeus, the Sun, Rivers, Earth and those deities who avenge the violation of oaths. The Sun and Earth are common deities in Greek oaths, both literary and cultic, where they regularly appear together.⁷ As omnipresent beings, these two deities were considered especially effective as witnesses. In particular, the Sun, from its heavenly situation, was described as all-seeing. From the perspective of Roman religion, however, although both the Sun and Earth received cult, there is no evidence for their pairing.⁸ Instead, the expected partner for the Sun is the Moon and that of the Earth, the agricultural deity Ceres. In fact, Vergil's description of the Earth as one 'for whom I have been able to endure such great toils', suggests not a divinity at all but simply the Italian country. Aeneas' invocation includes another pair of natural phenomena, Springs and Rivers, probably also deriving from Agamemnon's oath ('Rivers', *Iliad* 3.278). Although both springs and rivers were recipients of Roman cult, usually specific springs or rivers in a particular locale, there is no evidence for their invocation in Roman treaty oaths. Aeneas concludes his invocation with the words 'whatever divine powers there are in the lofty sky, and whatever powers dwell in the blue sea', thus recalling the universal invocations, such as 'all the immortal gods', which typically close a Roman invocation.⁹ With the inclusion of heaven and sea, Aeneas' invocation more explicitly describes the entire cosmos through the tripartite division into heaven, earth and waters.¹⁰ Latinus' oath, which follows immediately after that of Aeneas, commences with a similar invocation of the cosmos: 'I swear by these same elements, the earth, sea and heavens . . .' (12.197).

Vergil's construction of this god-list does not conform to the traditional patterns observable in treaties from Rome, Greece or the Near East. Neither does it follow its nearest Homeric model. In all these sources, the speaker regularly names the chief deity first. Vergil, however, invokes Jupiter third, following the Sun and Earth. In Greece and the Near East, the names of other high gods traditionally appear next, followed by natural elements. Yet Vergil mixes the two categories and inserts the anthropomorphic deities between the Sun/Earth and the Springs/Rivers.

After the invocation of divine witnesses, treaty oaths list the agreed-upon provisions. Among these terms, Aeneas proclaims that he will contribute to any future community the sacred rites and deities which he has brought from Troy. This provision (falsely) links Roman religion with that of the Trojans, thus giving it the sanction of the great heroic period of Greek legend. Following the list of terms, ancient oaths traditionally conclude with a curse invoked by the speaker upon himself and the state he represents should either violate the oath. Vergil, however, omits this section from Aeneas' oath.

Style

Not only does the content of Aeneas' oath follow primarily literary models, but so does its style. It contains no technical phrases and little traditional vocabulary. Unlike Roman cultic prayers, this oath contains no repetition of ideas or use of synonyms.[11] This avoidance of a realistic style may be attributed not only to the influence of the Homeric epics, but also to Vergil's desire to maintain a smooth poetic tone, which would be interrupted by the reproduction of cultic language. Instead, the language of the *Aeneid*, like its narrative, resides outside any actual time or place, in the world of epic poetry.

TRANSLATION

Witness[12] my prayer now, O Sun, together with this Earth, for whom I have been able to endure such great toils, also you, all-powerful father, and you, his Saturnian wife (kinder now, goddess, I pray), and you renowned Mars, father, who direct all wars under your power. I invoke both Springs and Rivers, and whatever divine powers there are in the lofty sky and whatever powers dwell in the blue sea.[13] If by chance the victory goes to Italian Turnus, it is agreed that the conquered will depart to the city of Evander, Iulus will withdraw from the fields and no rebellious followers of Aeneas will afterwards take up arms again or provoke these kingdoms with weapons. But if Victory grants the battle to us (as I think more likely; may the gods confirm this with their power), I will not order the Italians to obey the Trojans nor do I seek kingdoms for myself: let both nations unconquered enter into a lasting treaty with equality. I will bring the sacred rituals and deities; let my father-in-law Latinus hold the military command and his lawful power. The Trojans will build a city for me and Lavinia will give it her name.

NOTES

1 On Vergil's own beliefs, see Bailey, especially pp. 1, 87, 312–13. Although marred by Christianizing assumptions, Bailey's study is probably correct in its conclusion that Vergil's religiosity is to be found in the area of philosophy rather than traditional Greco-Roman polytheism.

2 M = Florentinus Laurentianus 39.1 plus Vaticanus lat. 3225, f. 76; P = Vaticanus Palatinus lat. 1631; R = Vaticanus lat. 3867. On the manuscript tradition, see the introduction to R. A. B. Mynors' Oxford Classical Text, copyright 1969, the edition used by this author.

3 The Greek historian Polybius writes that of the treaties between Rome and

FRANCES HICKSON-HAHN

Carthage, one was sworn by Jupiter Lapis and the others by Mars and Quirinus (3.25.6). Most likely they were all sworn by the complete triad. See Walbank's commentary on Polybius on this passage.

4 Near Eastern treaties frequently include the god of war (Barré: 125).
5 12.178 *coniunx* PRbf: *Iuno* Mω (as appears above 12.156 *Saturnia Iuno*).
6 The winner of the combat between Aeneas and Turnus will wed Lavinia, daughter of Latinus.
7 At *Iliad* 19.259, Agamemnon swears by Zeus, the Earth, Sun and Avenging Goddesses. The pair Sun/Earth also appears in Near Eastern oaths (Barré: 18, 89; Ziebarth: 20–3).
8 Neither is there any evidence for the invocation of the Sun in Roman treaty oaths. There is one reference to Earth as witness of the vow of devotion (Macrobius, *Saturnalia* 3.9.11).
9 E.g. *Corpus Inscriptionum Latinarum* 2.172.
10 The elements heaven and sea frequently appear in god-lists of the Near East. In Hittite treaty lists, the sea almost always appears in a triad of watery elements such as Aeneas invokes: rivers, sea and springs. Similarly, the Carthaginian treaty of Hannibal and Philip of Macedonia likely refers to rivers, lakes/sea and springs (Polybius 7.9.2–3). See Barré: 90–3 and Walbank's commentary on Polybius.
11 cf. the prayer of Scipio Africanus in this volume, pp. 152–3.
12 Vergil's phrase 'be a witness' is unattested in prior Latin and translates the Greek phrase used in Agamemnon's oath at *Iliad* 3.280 (*marturoi este*).
13 The language here recalls a typical Greek formula ('whoever there may be', *hostis pot' estin*). See Hickson: 41.

SELECTED BIBLIOGRAPHY

Bailey, C., *Religion in Virgil*, Oxford, Clarendon Press, 1935.
Barré, M., *The God-list in the Treaty between Hannibal and Philip V of Macedon*, Baltimore, Johns Hopkins University Press, 1983.
Hickson, F., *Roman Prayer Language: Livy and the Aeneid of Vergil*, Stuttgart, Teubner, 1993.
Lehr, H., *Religion und Kult in Vergils Aeneis*, dissertation, Giessen, 1934.
Walbank, F., *A Historical Commentary on Polybius*, Oxford, Oxford University Press, 1957.
Ziebarth, E., *De iureiurando in usu Graeco Quaestiones*, dissertation, Göttingen, 1892.

24

A PRAYER OF SCIPIO AFRICANUS: LIVY 29.27.2–4

Frances Hickson-Hahn

INTRODUCTION

An interesting example of prayer as a literary device appears in the history of the Roman nation written in Latin by the Roman historiographer Livy (c. 59 BCE to CE 17). The speaker is Scipio Africanus, the commander who led Roman troops to defeat the Carthaginian general Hannibal and thus brought an end to the Second Punic War. Scipio is about to set sail from Lilybaeum, Sicily, for the invasion of Africa in 204 BCE. As was customary before setting out on a military expedition, Scipio, as general in command, offers prayer and sacrifice on behalf of the army and the Roman nation.

Attestation

Livy's lengthy (142 books) history, of which thirty-five books survive, was preserved, as it was written, in groups of five and ten books. For books 26–30, from which this prayer derives, the oldest extant manuscript is the Puteanus (P) dating to the first half of the fifth century CE. Independent of the Puteanus and its descendants is the Spirensian tradition, for which witnesses date almost wholly to the thirteenth century and later, but which often provides superior readings.[1]

Scipio Africanus, the legend

Popular stories and even histories of the second century BCE portrayed Scipio as a man unusually favoured by the gods, perhaps in some way divine himself. A major factor in this reputation was Scipio's capture of New Carthage in Spain through an unexpected attack on the city walls in an area thought protected by a lagoon (Polybius 10.8ff.; Livy 26.45.6–9).

This assault was aided by the subsiding of those waters, an event interpreted by Roman troops as evidence of Scipio's favour with Neptune.
Scipio himself may have fostered this interpretation by reference, in a
speech delivered on the previous day, to the god's promised help. The
commander may also have encouraged popular rumours after the event. In
any case, the combination of his military accomplishments with such
stories led to his near-heroization. At some time during the next century,
an extraordinary honour was given to Scipio: his funeral mask was placed
in the Capitoline temple of Jupiter rather than in the atrium of his family's
house where such masks were usually kept (Valerius Maximus 8.15.1;
Appian, *Iberica* 23). Such an unusual honour might have been associated
with the controversial story found in several historians including Livy that
Scipio paid regular visits to the Capitoline temple of Jupiter, where he sat
in silence communing with the god, a highly unusual practice for a Roman
(Livy 26.19.3–9). By the late first century BCE at least, stories about Scipio
had gone far further: Livy reports tales of his mother's impregnation by
Jupiter in the form of a snake (26.19.3–9 and elsewhere). Finally, the *De
Viris Illustr.* adds a story told of Alexander, that a snake crawled over the
newborn child without harming him (49.1–4). Given this unusual
background of religion, myth and superstition, it is quite understandable
that Livy should develop the character of Scipio by assigning him several
prayers (six), including this, one of the lengthiest in Livy's History.

Content

Scipio's prayer opens in the traditional manner with an invocation of those
gods possessing the power to accomplish his requests: 'You gods and
goddesses who inhabit the seas and lands . . .' Scipio does not address the
gods by name. The seas which he will sail and the country where he will land
are foreign and thus he does not know the names of their tutelary deities.
Many ancient peoples, including the Romans, guarded closely the names of
their tutelary deities to limit the ability of enemies to summon those
divinities out of their cities and thus remove their protection. In order to
compensate for ignorance of the names so important to ensure a divine
response, the invocation includes a descriptive clause identifying the divine
domain: 'who inhabit the seas and lands'. Other examples of prayers in such
situations suggest that the speaker would normally specify which seas and
lands were meant more precisely.

Scipio's first petition is for a divine blessing of the acts of his command.
Such a request was traditional in prayers offered at the beginning of military
expeditions.[2] After identifying the object of his petition, Scipio lists those
who are to benefit from his prayer: himself, the Romans and those peoples
with whom Rome maintains political ties. This is a crucial section of a
prayer; failure to name an intended beneficiary would exclude that person or

group from receiving any benefit. Not content with naming four different beneficiaries, Scipio adds a clause more narrowly defining the beneficiaries as those who do in fact follow his own authority and that of Rome. Finally, Scipio specifies the actual request: that his actions may have a successful outcome. Although Scipio presents his request in three separate clauses, their meanings differ little.

In his second petition, Scipio directs his attention to the more present concerns of his listening troops as he requests safety and victory in the upcoming campaign, another traditional feature of prayers offered before military expeditions.[3] Then Scipio elaborates by painting a graphic picture of the returning soldiers, marching into Rome in a triumphal procession, laden with spoils. The words reflect the prayer of thanksgiving offered by victorious generals during the celebration of a triumph.[4] Scipio's prayer reminds us that public prayers served a dual function: to make requests of divine powers and also to shape the attitudes of a human audience. This petition functions in part to encourage the troops by turning their attentions to the glory and physical rewards of victory.

In his closing petition, Scipio again plays on the emotional concerns of his troops as he prays for vengeance. If love of glory and reward were not sufficient motivation for battle, perhaps the desire for revenge would be. Over a period of fourteen years, Hannibal's troops had slaughtered a multitude of Roman soldiers and ravaged the countryside of Italy. By carrying the war to Africa, Roman soldiers at last had an opportunity to inflict on Carthage some of the suffering which their own nation had experienced. They might also hope to rid themselves of the shame of having so long endured an enemy on their doorstep. Such a request for vengeance was in no way incompatible with the principles of Roman religion.

Style

Livy's interpretation of Scipio's prayer is an excellent example of the author's handling of speeches in general. Like other Hellenistic historiographers, Livy's objective was not only to recount historical events but to please his readers through an attractive presentation of the material. That presentation typically included speeches highlighting significant events and characterizing prominent figures. They were not intended as verbatim reports of actual speeches. The same is true of reported prayers. Whenever Livy attributes a prayer of any length to a historical figure, we can feel fairly certain that it is a literary creation. We can also, however, feel comfortable that the structure and general content of that prayer conform to actual Roman practice. Language is a different matter. Livian prayers represent a mixture of technical and literary language, some modelled on earlier authors, some of his own invention. Livy is particularly well known for his careful adaptation of style and diction to suit speakers and situations.

In the case of Scipio's prayer at Lilybaeum, the situation is a formal ritual of state cult; the speaker, a Roman magistrate.

Livy captures the tone of official prayers of the state cult by employing a style characterized by fullness[5] in wording, which results in a rather legalistic tone. One aspect of this fullness is repetition, in its simplest form, the use of quasi-synonymous vocabulary, for example, 'safe and unharmed'. The repetition may be more elaborate; Scipio's prayer contains three separate clauses which repeat the request that his deeds 'turn out favourably'. Another aspect of fullness is the insertion of relative clauses which further identify terms, such as 'gods and goddesses, who inhabit the seas and lands'. The objective of specification is also served by the use of pairs and longer series of words which identify the component parts of a concept. For example, Scipio describes the sphere of Roman influence as 'on land, sea and rivers'. The lengthiest specification of Scipio's prayer is the identification of beneficiaries, which begins 'for myself, for the Roman nation, for the allies . . .'. The fullness of official Roman prayers may reveal something of the Roman attitude toward their deities. There was a pervasive anxiety, it seems, that any omission or inappropriate choice of words might result in the deities' failure to fulfil a prayer's request. The apparent repetitions and specifications may have served as a means of ensuring that the most effective wording was employed. For similar reasons, established technical formulae existed for most common ideas, for example, 'I pray and beseech'. Wording which had proven effective in the past was thought most likely to be effective in the future.

Livy's models for Scipio's prayer were not only official prayers of state cult, but also literary prayers, especially those of poets.[6] This is evident in the use of vocabulary not previously attested in prose prayers, but appearing in poetic prayers.[7] In addition, the triad of tenses of the verb, past, present and future, used in Scipio's petition for a blessing on his command, may illustrate the influence of an earlier Roman poet who used a similar tripartite pattern in a prayer for blessing on the deeds of a character planning revenge (Pacuvius, *Periboea* 297).[8]

To summarize – Scipio's prayer represents an interesting blend of fact and fiction, in the best tradition of the modern historical novel. The speaker and occasion are historical. The language represents the influence of technical and literary sources as well as the creative artistry of Livy himself. Although this prayer should not be quoted as a historical or religious document, with careful analysis it can be a useful text to illustrate content, structure and tone of official Roman prayers.[9]

TRANSLATION

You gods and goddesses, who inhabit the seas and lands, I pray and beseech you that those deeds, which under my command have been accomplished, are being accomplished and will afterwards be accomplished, may turn out favourably and that you may prosper them all and cause them to succeed for myself, for the Roman nation, for the allies and for the Latin peoples who follow the lead, command and authority of the Roman people and of myself on land, sea and rivers. I pray that you may preserve us safe and unharmed by the conquered enemy and that as conquerors together with me these soldiers may return home in triumph adorned with spoils and laden with loot. Grant us the opportunity to avenge our enemies, personal and public. And whatever the Carthaginian people have attempted to do to our state, grant to me and the Roman people the ability to do to the Carthaginian state as an example.

NOTES

1   The most recent edition of book 29 is that of P.G. Walsh, *T. Livius Ab Urbe Condita: Libri XXVIII–XXX*, Leipzig, Teubner, 1986. See the introduction to this volume and to *Ab Urbe Condita: Libri XXVI–XXVII* (ed. Walsh, Leipzig, Teubner, 1982) for a review of the manuscript tradition. To Walsh's bibliography, add M.D. Reeve, 'The Third Decade of Livy in Italy: The Family of the Puteanus', and 'The Transmission of Livy 26–40', *Rivista di Filologio e di Istruzione Classica*, 115, 1987, pp. 129–64 and 405–40.

2   When the emperor Trajan set out against the Dacians in 101 CE, the following prayer was offered: 'may you grant a successful outcome to the acts which he now does and is about to do' (*Corpus Inscriptionum Latinarum* 6.2074.29).

3   E.g. 'may you preserve him [Trajan] safe and bring him home victorious' (ibid., line 31). Prayers offered on behalf of the emperor used words similar to those in republican prayers offered on behalf of the Roman state and people.

4   On the wording of triumphal prayers of thanksgiving see Edward Fraenkel, *Plautinisches im Plautus*, Berlin, 1922. Fraenkel includes Scipio's prayer in his discussion.

5   I take this term from Mark Kiley's discussion of the style of Colossians, which relies in part on the work of Walter Bujard (*Colossians as Pseudepigraphy*, JSOT Press, Sheffield, 1986, pp. 56–7).

6   The surviving fragments of Ennius' *Annales* indicate a significant influence on Livy's history, including its prayers. It is likely that a fragmentary poem on Scipio by Ennius was also influential in Livy's portrait.

7   Livy is the only prose author to use the verb *colere* (inhabit/cherish) in prayers, but there are many instances in poetic prayers. The verb *verruncare* (turn out) is rare, appearing before Livy only in early playwrights (Accius *praetextata* 5–6, 36, Pacuvius *tragedies* 297).

8   'That those things which I have done, am doing and shall do may turn out well' (Pacuvius *tragedies* 297). The likelihood of Pacuvius being Livy's model is increased by the presence of *verruncare* in this fragment (see note 7). By contrast, the authentic Trajanic prayer makes no reference to the past.

9   Neither should this prayer be considered the expression of Livy's own beliefs. On the religiosity of Livy, see Levene, pp. 16–30, with review of primary sources and the scholarly controversy. Levene concludes that 'the search for the "belief of Livy" is illusory'.

SELECTED BIBLIOGRAPHY

Hickson, F.V., *Roman Prayer Language: Livy and the Aeneid of Vergil*, Stuttgart, Teubner, 1993.

Levene, D.S., *Religion in Livy*, Leiden, E.J. Brill, 1993.

Scullard, H.H., *Scipio Africanus, Soldier and Politician*, London, Thames & Hudson, 1970.

Walsh, P.G., *Livy: His Historical Aims and Methods*, Cambridge, Cambridge University Press, 1961.

25

THE ISIS HYMN OF DIODORUS OF SICILY (1.27.3)

Mark Gustafson

INTRODUCTION

Diodorus Siculus intended his *Bibliotheca Historica*, as he tells us (1.4.6; 5.1.4), to be a universal history up to his own day in the mid-first century BCE. Originally consisting of forty books, only books 1–5 and 11–20 are extant complete. The *Bibliotheca* is both the largest surviving Greek history from antiquity and the only surviving large-scale history written in the late republic. Diodorus was not particularly concerned with original scholarship. Rather, he compiled material chosen from the writings of others. As most of these histories are now lost, the information we have from Diodorus is, in many cases, very important. Thus his role as a preserver must not be underestimated. While he has long been seen as a mere copyist, a recent and convincing reappraisal grants Diodorus more responsibility for the ideas and themes of his history than previously allowed.[1]

The first six books, lacking a precise chronology, cover the period before the Trojan war; the first three concern non-Greeks; the first book is about the myths, history and customs of Egypt (1.4.6–7). This is the most complete such account since book two of Herodotus. After a general introduction to the entire work (1.1–11), book one may be divided, roughly, into four parts: religion (11–29); geography (30–41); history (42–68); and laws, customs and dress (69–98). The hymn to Isis thus appears in the first part. Diodorus is especially concerned with Isis and Osiris; he is prone to identify Egyptian gods with Greek; and his viewpoint may be described as euhemeristic (that is, he takes the view of the fourth-century BCE mythographer Euhemerus that the gods were deified mortals and that myths are ultimately historical).[2] The unit consisting of books 1–5 is transmitted by twenty-eight manuscripts belonging to four families, represented by the following: D (Neapolitanus suppl. gr. 4) from the tenth century; C (Vaticanus gr. 130) also from the tenth; V (Vaticanus gr. 996) from the eleventh to twelfth centuries; and L

(Laurentianus 70, 1) from the fourteenth.[3]

Diodorus says that this inscription is from a grave-stele in Nysa in Arabia, written in hieroglyphics (1.27.3), and incomplete, as the rest of the inscription, larger still, had been worn away by time (1.27.6). Is he to be believed? Earlier (1.22.2) he cites the alternative tradition, supported by the hymn from Cyme (in Asia Minor), that Isis was buried at Memphis where she had a shrine near the temple of Ptah-Hephaestus.[4] Diodorus indicates that he was in Egypt some time between 60 and 56 BCE (1.44.1), but that apparent fact does not automatically grant him credibility.[5] A recent view is that Greek thought predominates in this and other Isis hymns, with the lesser influence of Egyptian ideas.[6] But another scholar says, 'the Ichstil [that is, writing from the first person point of view] tells in favour of composition in Greek rather than of translation', and characterizes the hymn as 'Egypto-Greek'.[7] He continues, 'I . . . assume a text written in Greek and shortened by Diodorus or by his source . . .'[8] Still another recent view is that the hymns are entirely Egyptian in background.[9]

The date of this hymn can only be approximated. The time of Diodorus' visit to Egypt, of course, provides something close to the latest possible date for its composition; but the original hymn 'from which the texts given by Diodorus and the Cyme hymn are copied . . . may be considerably earlier'.[10]

Isis is portrayed in this hymn in terms of her relationships: as daughter, wife and sister, mother, and scion of Egypt. She is celebrated also according to her position and her accomplishments: as queen over all, as lawgiver and beneficent provider of food, and as a star in the heavens. For this she has been honoured. Finally, in death she bids Egypt goodbye. This hymn may be, in fact (at least a portion of) the archetype of the Isis aretalogy, but its fully embroidered and enlarged form is probably best viewed in Apuleius, *Metamorphoses* 11.4–6. There Isis addresses Lucius the ass, as she is about to offer him salvation, and tells him of her many names and deeds.

TRANSLATION

I am Isis,[11]
the queen of every land
who was taught by Hermes,
and whatever laws I have ordained,
these no one can abrogate.
I am the oldest daughter of the youngest god, Kronos.[12]
I am wife and sister of king Osiris.
I am the first one to discover corn for humans.
I am mother of the king Horus.
I am she who rises in the star in Canis Major.[13]
The city of Bubastis was founded for me.[14]

Hail and farewell, Egypt that nourished me.

NOTES

1 This is the purpose of the recent study by K.S. Sacks, *Diodorus Siculus and the First Century*, Princeton, Princeton University Press, 1990.
2 For his sources for book one, see F. Chamoux (ed.) (with P. Bertrac (ed.) and Y. Vernière (tr.)), *Diodore de Sicile: Bibliothèque Historique, Livre I*, Paris, Les Belles Lettres, 1993, p. xxiii.
3 ibid., pp. lxxviii–c.
4 A. Burton, *Diodorus Siculus Book I: A Commentary*, Leiden, E.J. Brill, 1972, pp. 115–16.
5 Chamoux, op. cit., p. viii n. 3.
6 D. Müller, *Ägypten und die griechischen Isis-Aretalogien*, Berlin, Abhandlungen der sächs. Akademie der Wissenschaften zu Leipzig, philologisch-historische Klasse, Band 53, Heft 1, 1961, p. 88.
7 A.D. Nock, 'Review of Harder, R., *Karpokrates von Chalkis und die memphitische Isispropaganda*', *Gnomon* 21, 1949, p. 225 (reprinted as 'Graeco-Roman Religious Propaganda', in idem, *Essays on Religion and the Ancient World*, Z. Stewart (ed.), Cambridge, Mass., Harvard University Press, 1972, vol. 2, p. 708).
8 ibid., p. 226 (p. 709). See also Nock, *Conversion*, Oxford, Oxford University Press, 1933, pp. 150–2, regarding P. Oxyrhynchus 1380.
9 Burton, op. cit., p. 116.
10 ibid., p. 115.
11 This hymn of Isis, which Diodorus claims to have recorded from an inscription, corresponds quite closely to the beginning of other Isis hymns in epigraphic form, especially those from Cyme and Ios, as discussed in A. Salaç, 'Inscriptions de Kymé, d'Éolide, de Phocée, de Tralles et de quelques autres villes d'Asie Mineure', *Bulletin de Correspondance Hellenique* 51, 1927, pp. 378–83. It also bears similarities to an inscription from Maroneia, the oldest extant Isis aretalogy, which is treated in detail by Y. Grandjean, *Une nouvelle arètalogie d'Isis à Maronée*, Leiden, E.J. Brill, 1975. There are many other hymn texts for the sake of comparison. See S.K. Heyob, *The Cult of Isis among Women in the Graeco-Roman World*, Leiden, E.J. Brill, 1975, p. 46 n. 39, and J. Charlesworth, (ed.), with M. Harding and M. Kiley, *The Lord's Prayer and Other Prayer Texts from the Greco-Roman Era*, Valley Forge, Trinity, 1994, pp. 243–4.

  This hymn bears many traits (only the most important of which are noted below) similar to those found in other aretalogies. The most immediate and striking is the 'self-predication' in the form of 'I am Isis', discussed in detail by J. Bergman, *Ich bin Isis*, Uppsala, Acta Universitatis Upsalensis, Historia Religionum 3, 1968, pp. 23ff.
12 Kronos corresponds to the Egyptian earth-god Geb, and the epithet 'youngest god' is based on a false etymology, as explained by A. Burton, op. cit., p. 117.
13 The star Sirius-Sothis, on the head of the constellation of the dog, was also called Isis, as indicated in Chamoux, op. cit., p. 65 n. 2, and by J.G. Griffiths (ed.), *Apuleius of Madauros: The Isis-Book (Metamorphoses, Book XI)*, Leiden, E.J. Brill, 1975, pp. 131–2, 143.
14 R.E. Witt, *Isis in the Graeco-Roman World*, Ithaca, Cornell University Press, 1971, p. 101, says that the city of Bubastis in Lower Egypt was the cult centre of the cat-headed goddess whom the Greeks identified with Artemis.

SELECTED BIBLIOGRAPHY

Bergman, J., *Ich bin Isis*, Uppsala, Acta Universitatis Upsalensis, Historia Religionum 3, 1968.
Burkert, W., *Ancient Mystery Cults*, Cambridge, Mass., Harvard University Press, 1987.
Burton, A., *Diodorus Siculus Book I: A Commentary*, Leiden, E.J. Brill, 1972.
Chamoux, F., Bertrac, P. (eds) and Vernière, Y. (tr.), *Diodore de Sicile: Bibliothèque Historique, Livre I*, Paris, Les Belles Lettres, 1993.
Charlesworth, J. (ed.), with Harding, M. and Kiley, M., *The Lord's Prayer and Other Prayer Texts from the Greco-Roman Era*, Valley Forge, Trinity, 1994.
Grandjean, Y., *Une nouvelle arètalogie d'Isis à Maronée*, Leiden, E.J. Brill, 1975.
Griffiths, J.G. (ed.), *Apuleius of Madauros: The Isis-Book (Metamorphoses, Book XI)*, Leiden, E.J. Brill, 1975.
——, 'The Great Egyptian Cults of Oecumenical Spiritual Significance', in A.H. Armstrong (ed.), *Classical Mediterranean Spirituality: Egyptian, Greek, Roman*, New York, Crossroad, 1989.
Heyob, S.K., *The Cult of Isis among Women in the Graeco-Roman World*, Leiden, E.J. Brill, 1975.
Koester, H., *Introduction to the New Testament: Volume One: History, Culture, and Religion of the Hellenistic Age*, Philadelphia, Fortress, 1982.
MacMullen, R., *Paganism in the Roman Empire*, New Haven, Yale University Press, 1981.
Martin, L.H., *Hellenistic Religions: An Introduction*, New York, Oxford University Press, 1987.
Müller, D., *Ägypten und die griechischen Isis-Aretalogien*, Berlin, Abhandlungen der sächs. Akademie der Wissenschaften zu Leipzig, philologisch-historische Klasse, Band 53, Heft 1, 1961.
Nock, A.D., *Conversion*, Oxford, Oxford University Press, 1933.
——, 'Review of Harder, R., *Karpokrates von Chalkis und die memphitische Isispropaganda*', *Gnomon* 21, 1949, pp. 221–8 (reprinted as 'Graeco-Roman Religious Propaganda,' in idem, Z. Stewart (ed.), *Essays on Religion and the Ancient World*, 2 vols, Cambridge, Mass., Harvard University Press, 1972, vol. 2, pp. 703–11).
Sacks, K.S., *Diodorus Siculus and the First Century*, Princeton, Princeton University Press, 1990.
Salaç, A. 'Inscriptions de Kymé, d'Éolide, de Phocée, de Tralles et de quelques autres villes d'Asie Mineure', *Bulletin de Correspondance Hellenique* 51, 1927, pp. 374–400.
Solmsen, F., *Isis among the Greeks and Romans*, Cambridge, Mass., Harvard University Press, 1979.
Witt, R.E., *Isis in the Graeco-Roman World*, Ithaca, Cornell University Press, 1971.

26

WRITTEN IN STONE: A PRAYER TO AUGUSTUS

Dan Schowalter

INTRODUCTION

Much of what we know about the ancient Roman world comes to us by way of inscriptions carved into stone tablets and other monuments. When Roman officials wanted to make a public announcement, it was often read aloud to an assembly, and then posted in the form of an inscription. The vast variety of subjects touched upon in inscriptions gives us great insight into the political, social and religious activities of the Romans. The subject matter of this inscription is an honorific prayer dedicated to the Roman emperor Caesar Augustus and his divine spirit.

Description/publication

This Latin inscription is found on a marble altar 1.1 m high, 0.58 m wide and 0.29 m deep. There are two parts to the inscription, and although it bears striking similarities to other Roman dedications, this is the only known copy. The end of the first inscription is lost, and two lines in the introduction to the second inscription have been erased by chiselling out the letters. The inscription was discovered in 1566. It has been published as part of the nineteenth-century collection of inscriptions known as *Corpus Inscriptionum Latinarum* (*CIL* vol. XII, no. 4333), in *Inscriptiones Latinae Selectae* (*ILS* 112), and in *Documents Illustrating the Reigns of Augustus and Tiberius*, edited by Victor Ehrenberg and A. H. M. Jones. The text and an English translation appear in *Roman Civilization* vol. II, edited by Naphtali Lewis and Meyer Reinhold.

Geographical provenance and date

The inscription informs us that the altar was originally set up in the forum or city centre of Narbo, a Roman colony in southern Gaul (modern day

Narbonne in France). *Colonia Narbo Martius* was established by the Romans in 121 BCE, and it became the home of Julius Caesar's tenth legion some fifty years later. Eventually, Narbo became the capital of the provincial region *Gallia Narbonesis*, and it continued to be an important centre for commerce in the western Mediterranean. The collection of inscriptions from Narbo includes 'over 1300 inscribed and sculptured Roman panels'. Because inscribed altars and rectangular slabs make excellent building materials, most of the inscriptions from Narbo were found in secondary usage in the medieval walls of the town.[1]

The first inscription dates from the time of the altar's construction, and the other recognizes its dedication about a year later. The year of the first inscription is given by the names Titus Statilius Taurus and Lucius Cassius Longinus who are known to have served as consuls during the year 11 CE. Under the Roman republic, the consuls were the chief magistrates of Rome with significant civic and military authority. Under the empire, however, the consulship was chosen and for the most part controlled by the emperor. The exact date of the erection of the altar is said to be ten days before the kalends (first) of October, which falls on 22 September.

Cultural setting

These inscriptions are illustrative of several important aspects of prayer as part of Roman religious practice, and also of the emperor as an object of veneration. They reveal the central role of proper ritual in Roman religion, the intimate connection between religious observance and political life in ancient Rome, and the emperor's essential position at the crossroads between civic and religious life.

The occasion for the erection of the altar is said to be the end of a dispute between the people of Narbo, and the decurions – a council of city officials who were responsible for collecting taxes and other civic matters. Given the vast extent of their empire, it was necessary for the Romans to rely on certain individuals to act as local representatives in many important cities. At times, however, the decurions or other agents of Rome could come into conflict with the inhabitants. As citizens of a Roman colony, the Narbonensians could appeal to the emperor in the event of such a dispute.

The nature of the crisis in Narbo is not stated, but it must have been significant since its resolution by Augustus served as ample reason to honour him with this altar in the centre of town. By placing the altar in a conspicuous place, the Narbonensians were able to show their loyalty and give appropriate thanks to the emperor. At the same time, the altar served as a reminder, especially to the decurions, of Augustus' judgement in the case.

The inscription takes the form of a *votum*, a vow or prayer made to a deity, promising regular ritual observance in return for some divine favour. The classic Roman statement of this reciprocal relationship between human beings and the gods is the Latin phrase *do ut des* which translates as 'I give so that you shall give.' The Romans believed that religious ritual, rightly performed, would ensure the support and favour of the gods. Since different divinities controlled different aspects of life, it was natural for individuals to perform rituals to a variety of deities. Within this polytheistic approach, new and different gods could arise who also demanded the people's attention. In the case of Augustus and emperors after him, their absolute political and military authority was often treated as divine power, and given appropriate homage.

Two phrases in the inscription highlight some of the social divisions in Roman society. The *equites* ('knights') were one of the leading orders in Roman society, usually involved in business and trade. Freedmen were former slaves who had risen in society to the point where they could afford the expense of financing sacrifices like the ones described here. In fact, during the imperial period, freedmen become increasingly influential with the emperor and his family, and members of the senatorial order felt threatened by their growing power.[2]

A further distinction is made between the 'colonists', Roman military veterans who had been settled in the town, and 'inhabitants', the indigenous, non-Roman population of Narbo. In short, the *votum* is a prayer and a promise which involves multiple layers of the complex Roman society.

Structure

In the first inscription, the actual vow comes after a short introduction. The vow is followed by a longer section detailing both the circumstances behind the dedication and the ritual requirements associated with it. A short dedication statement also introduces the second inscription. In this case, however, the vow seems to be extended to include an address to Augustus, rules about use and maintenance of the altar, and a closing statement of the dedication.

Cultic context

In response to the resolution of the crisis with the decurions, the people of the city promise that they will observe a series of public ceremonies on specified dates: the day of Augustus' birth (23 September), the first day of January, the date of his taking control of the empire (7 January), and the anniversary of the resolution of the crisis with the decurions (31 May). On these days, three men from the equestrian order, and three freedmen would each pay for the sacrifice of an animal (probably a bull). These same men would also distribute wine to be poured as a libation and incense to be burned as a sacrifice by the people of the city.

The inscription further states that the people are taking on the obligation to carry out these ceremonies in perpetuity, so that for some time at least, they must have been a permanent part of the religious calendar of the city.

161

The second inscription lays down further stipulations about the mainten-ance and use of the altar. Again, the emphasis is on proper ritual action and following the statutes. It is notable that as shorthand, this inscription defers to regulations found on an altar to Diana on the Aventine Hill in Rome. This must have been a very well-known set of standards in order to serve as a guideline for cultic practices elsewhere.

Theology: portrayal of the deity

Divine honours for Augustus were usually directed toward the *numen*, 'divine spirit' or 'essence', of the emperor. While Augustus usually refused worship of himself as a deity, it was acceptable to recognize and venerate a divine presence which explained his extraordinary success and power. It was as though the earthly accomplishments and authority of Augustus could only be explained as manifestations of a divine nature which he embodied. Of course worship of the *numen* of Augustus also served to enhance his earthly political standing as ruler of the people.

As a human ruler, Augustus held the post of *pontifex maximus* ('high priest'), which meant that he was head of the college of priests, the highest religious position in the empire. Priests were an important part of the fabric of Roman society, since the reading of signs and omens and the proper administration of rituals were deemed essential to most social, political and military activities. The high priest, therefore, was a kind of mediator between the gods and human beings, who had tremendous power to influence civic and individual behaviour.

In the case of Augustus, the earthly office of high priest was complemented by the understanding that he was *divi filius*, or 'son of a god'. This title refers to his uncle and adopted father, Julius Caesar, who had been officially deified by the Roman Senate after his death in 44 BCE. It is often said that the phrase *divi filius* should be translated as a 'son of a divinity', rather than 'son of a god', to indicate that a deified emperor is viewed differently from a traditional god.[3] On the other hand, the Romans could use these terms interchangeably,[4] and when written in Greek the distinction disappeared since the same word (*theos*) was used to describe both the traditional gods, and divinized rulers. The title 'Son of God' was used by early followers of Jesus as well. This usage had its roots in Jewish scripture, but its similarity to imperial nomenclature would not have been lost on residents of the empire.

TRANSLATION OF *CIL* VOL. XII, NO. 4333

Part I

In the consulship of Titus Statilius Taurus and Lucius Cassius Longinus, on the tenth day before the Kalends of October, a vow in perpetuity by the people of Narbo to the Augustan divine essence.

A vow to the Augustan divine essence, undertaken forever by the people of Narbo: May it be good, auspicious, and favourable to the emperor Caesar Augustus, son of god, father of his country, chief priest, holder of the tribunician power for the 34th time, and to his wife, and his children, and his house, to the Roman Senate and people, and to the colonists and inhabitants of the colony Julia Paterna of Narbo Martius, who have obligated themselves to worship his divine essence in perpetuity.

The people of Narbo have placed an altar in their forum, at which every year on the 23rd of September, the day when the good fortune of the era brought him [Augustus] forth as ruler of the world, three Roman knights from the people and three freedmen will sacrifice one victim each, and on that day they will provide for the colonists and inhabitants incense and wine from their own funds in order to worship his divine essence. And on the 24th of September they shall likewise offer incense and wine for the colonists and inhabitants.

Let them also on the first of January offer wine and incense for the colonists and inhabitants. Also on the seventh of January, that day when he began his power over the world, they shall make a prayer with wine and incense and shall sacrifice one animal each, and that same day, shall offer for the colonists and inhabitants incense and wine. And on the 31st of May, because on that day during the consulship of Titus Statilius Taurus and Manius Aemilius Lepidus, the emperor reconciled the people to the decurions, they each shall sacrifice a victim and offer from their own funds, incense and wine for the colonists and inhabitants for an offering to his divine essence. From these three Roman knights and three freedmen, one . . .

Part II

The people of Narbo have dedicated this altar to the divine essence of Augustus . . . by these statutes which are written below.

O divine essence of Caesar Augustus, father of his country, on this day, when I give and dedicate this altar to you, I give and dedicate it by these statutes and limits, as this day I shall publicly state to be the foundation of both this altar and the inscriptions on it: If anyone wishes to clean, decorate or restore it as a free service, it shall be legal and proper to do so. If anyone sacrifices an animal, but does not offer the additional part,[5] nevertheless it shall be considered done properly. If anyone wishes to give a gift to this altar or to enhance it, it is likewise allowed. The statute for such a gift is the same as for the altar. Other statutes for this altar and its inscriptions shall be the same as those on the altar to Diana on the Aventine Hill.

Under these statutes and these limits, just as I have said, I give and dedicate this altar to you, on behalf of the emperor Caesar Augustus, father of his country, chief priest, holder of the tribunician power for the 35th time, of his wife and children and house, of the senate and people of Rome, and of the colonists and inhabitants of the colony Julia Paterna of Narbo Martius, who have obligated themselves to worship his divine essence forever, so that you may be favourable and well-disposed.[6]

NOTES

1 Lawrence Keppie, *Understanding Roman Inscriptions*, Baltimore, Johns Hopkins University Press, 1991, p. 31.
2 The situation was especially bad under the emperor Domitian who ruled from 81 to 96 CE. Pliny the Younger complains that 'while most emperors were masters over their subjects, they were also slaves of their freedmen' (*Panegyricus*, 88.1–3).
3 'The term *divus* was originally not sharply distinguished from *deus* ("god") but from the consecration of Caesar [Julius] onwards it was used almost exclusively (outside poetical texts) of properly consecrated members of the imperial family. This is not to say that *divus* and *deus* were two exclusive categories; rather, *divus* was a subcategory of *deus* and it was thus perfectly possible to refer to a consecrated emperor as *deus*.' Simon Price, 'From Noble Funeral to Divine Cult: the Consecration of Roman Emperors', in David Cannadine and Simon Price (eds), *Rituals of Royalty: Power and Ceremonial in Traditional Societies*, Cambridge, Cambridge University Press, 1987, p. 77.
4 Pliny the Younger refers to divinized emperors with the term *deus* (*Panegyricus*, 10.5, 14.2) and uses the plural of *divus* to refer collectively to all the gods (*Panegyricus*, 94.1).
5 The part referred to (*magmentum*) may be the entrails of the animal.
6 I am grateful to my colleague Christine Renaud for her assistance in preparing this entry.

SELECTED BIBLIOGRAPHY

Gordon, A., *Illustrated Introduction to Latin Epigraphy*, Berkeley, University of California Press, 1983.
Keppie, L., *Understanding Roman Inscriptions*, Baltimore, Johns Hopkins University Press, 1991.
Millar, F., *The Emperor in the Roman World*, Ithaca, NY, Cornell University Press, 1977.
Price, S. R. F., 'From Noble Funeral to Divine Cult: the Consecration of Roman Emperors', in David Cannadine and Simon Price (eds), *Rituals of Royalty: Power and Ceremonial in Traditional Societies*, Cambridge. Cambridge University Press, 1987.
Zanker, P., *The Power of Images in the Age of Augustus*, Ann Arbor, MI, University of Michigan Press, 1988.

27

A SECRET HYMN ABOUT REBIRTH: *CORPUS HERMETICUM* XIII.17–20

Philip Sellew

INTRODUCTION

This hymn celebrating the process of spiritual regeneration is found embedded within a revelation dialogue between the Hellenized Egyptian gods Hermes Trismegistus and Tat (the text known as *Corpus Hermeticum* XIII). We learn that the soul, with the aid of divine powers operative within the enlightened person, can overcome the natural forces in control of our world and achieve immortality. Though the prayer fits comfortably within its surrounding dialogue, it most likely also had an independent use within Hermetic pious circles. By reading or perhaps by chanting the hymn, the initiate could experience, anticipate, or possibly even recall his or her own salvation.

Attestation

The treatise that includes this hymn is part of the *Corpus Hermeticum*, a late collection of Hermetic writings (see below) first gathered in the Renaissance.[1] Eighteen Greek manuscripts contain parts or all of the collection, of which fourteenth-century codices at Florence, Paris and Rome are the most important.[2] During late antiquity and the Middle Ages, some of the treatises were translated into other languages, of which Coptic and Latin provide the most valuable evidence of the original text. This translation relies on the edition of A. D. Nock, along with improvements suggested at various times by Reitzenstein, Scott, Festugière or Copenhaver.[3]

Provenance, date and language

The treatises are thought to stem from Greek-speaking Egypt in Roman and early Christian times. The term Hermetism refers to a popular if now obscure religious movement in Egypt during the periods of Greek and Roman domination. Though ultimately derived from ancient Egyptian thought and practice in significant ways, Hermetic doctrines are expressed in the language and concepts of Hellenistic syncretism. The hymn quoted here may well have its origin as a prayer used in Hermetic worship.[4]

Relation to other works

Hermetic scriptures draw on a bewildering array of intellectual influences, including the popular philosophies of the day (especially Middle Platonism) and the mystery religions, but apparently also the religious thought of both the Greek-speaking Jews resident in Alexandria and a variety of gnostic sects.[5] The treatise that quotes our hymn, for example, displays that particular mixture. We find the disdain for the physical body and the world of sense perception familiar from Platonist and gnostic texts, along with instruction as to how the soul may escape to the divine realm, yet also an almost biblical praise for the god responsible for the created order, who arranged the powers of heaven and earth to support human and divine life.[6]

Literary context within *Corpus Hermeticum* XIII

Tractate thirteen of the Hermetic corpus relates a private conversation between Hermes 'Thrice-Greatest' (the late-antique version of the Egyptian god Toth, patron of learning and wisdom) and his son Tat. While they descend from a mountaintop, Hermes explains how living souls are imprisoned within the realm of death, under the deceitful control of the Zodiac. Traditional lists of vices and virtues help describe how these planetary and stellar forces keep the soul from first realizing its true identity and then mastering the base emotions aroused by sense perception to achieve divine release. The twelve powers of ignorance, grief, incontinence, lust, injustice, greed, deceit, malice, treachery, anger, rashness and wickedness can be overcome by the divine Decade, composed of the seven virtues (knowledge, joy, self-control, steadfastness, righteousness, generosity and truth) as supplemented by goodness, life and light. This salvific process forms the occasion of the prayer of praise included here.

Description and analysis of the hymn

A *prologue* and a *prayer* make up definable sections of the hymn. In the prologue, the hymnist invokes every natural and divine force of the universe, which together comprise the divine All. These natural powers are called upon to hear and heed the prayer that follows. In this first part of the hymn, the creation and its creator are praised using the terms of syncretistic religious monotheism also found in Hellenistic Jewish writers such as Philo of Alexandria, or the Greek translation of the Psalms and prophets.[7] The prayer itself both praises the Decade of divine powers and invokes their participation in overcoming the Duodecad (twelve) zodiacal powers that try to prevent our return to the divine reality above this world. Here the language draws more specifically on imagery known from other initiatory texts, influenced by the cultic expressions of the mystery religions and later Platonism. The names of some divine powers (especially word, light, life, truth) in this prayer may also resonate with key terms deployed by the Gospel of John to reveal the divine identity of Jesus.[8] Some scholars have noticed a tension between the two parts of the hymn, with its praise of creation followed by a rejection of the physical world.[9]

The hymn, though preserved in Greek, does not follow the conventions of ancient Greek cultic verse. Some scholars (notably Scott and Zuntz) have attempted to reconstruct metrical patterns according to the rhythms of Byzantine melody; but the poor state of the transmitted text makes such suggestions difficult to confirm. For this collection the previous translations by Festugière, Grese and Copenhaver have been of greater help than that of Walter Scott, due to his wholesale rearrangements of the Greek text. Scott was justified in his low opinion of the Greek and Latin texts of the Hermetic corpus, but his own emendations have not received much support from other scholars.

TRANSLATION

17 *Prologue*
Let every nature of the world attend to the sound of my hymn.
Open up, O earth;
    may every storm gate[10] open to me.
        Do not shake, O trees.
           I shall now praise the lord of creation,
             the All and the One.
Open, O heavens;
    stay still, O winds.
        Immortal circle of God,
           accept my speech.
For I shall praise the one
        who created everything
        who made the earth solid
        and hung the sky
        and bid the sweet water go
           away from the ocean
           into the inhabited and deserted world,
           for sustenance and creation[11] of all human beings;

who bid fire[12] to appear
    for every purpose
    among gods and humans.
Let us give him praise all together,
    who is high above the heavens,
    the creator of every nature.
He is the eye of the Mind;
    so may he accept the praise of my powers.

18   *Prayer*
O powers that are in me,
    praise the One and the All.
Sing together with my will,
    all you powers within me.
Holy Knowledge, enlightened by you,[13]
    through you I rejoice with my Mind's Joy,
    praising the intelligible Light.[14]
All you powers, sing with me.
And you too, O Continence,[15] join in my praise.
My Justice, praise what is just in me.
My Generosity, praise the All through me.
O Truth, praise the truth.
O Good, praise the good.
Life and Light, my praise comes from you and to you.
I give thanks to you, O Father, Energy of my powers.
I give thanks to you, O God, Power of my energies.
Your Word praises you through me.
Through me receive, O All, by word, a spiritual sacrifice.[16]

19   These things the powers within me
    shout aloud.
They praise the All.
Your will they accomplish,
    your counsel from you, upon you, the All.
Receive spiritual sacrifice from all things,
    O All that is within us;
Save, O Life, enlighten, O Light, inspire.
For Mind shepherds your word.

20   O spirit-bearer, O demiurge,
    you are God.
Your human one shouts out these things
through fire, air, earth, water, spirit –
    through your creatures.
From your Eternity
    I have found blessing

and have rested, as I seek,
   in your counsel.
I saw this blessing by your will.

NOTES

1   For full studies of the hymn and its tractate see K.-W. Tröger, *Mysterienglaube und Gnosis in Corpus Hermeticum XIII*, and W. Grese, *Corpus Hermeticum XIII and Early Christian Literature*.

2   Laurentius 71, 33; Parisinus gr. 1220; Vaticanus gr. 237.

3   R. Reitzenstein, *Poimandres*, Leipzig, Teubner, 1904; W. Scott, *Hermetica*, 4 vols, Oxford, Clarendon Press, 1924-36; A. D. Nock and A.-J. Festugière, *Corpus Hermeticum*, tome II: *Traites XIII-XVIII*, Paris, 'Les Belles Lettres', 1945; B. Copenhaver, *Hermetica*.

4   See the discussion in W. Grese, op. cit., pp. 159–61.

5   See C. H. Dodd, *The Bible and the Greeks*; A.-J. Festugière, *La Révélation d' Hermès Trismégiste*; G. Fowden, *The Egyptian Hermes* and J.-P. Mahé, *Hermès en Haute-Égypte*.

6   For further information on Hermetism see B. Copenhaver, op. cit.; A.-J. Festugière, op. cit.; J.-P. Mahé, op. cit.; and especially G. Fowden, op. cit.

7   See especially C. H. Dodd, op. cit., pp. 240–1, and G. Zuntz, 'On the Hymns in Corpus Hermeticum XIII', pp. 83–5 (= idem, *Opuscula selecta*, pp. 167–9).

8   See the following examples in the hymnic prologue that opens John's gospel (John 1:1–18): *word* used three times in v. 1; *life and light* together in v. 4; *light* in vv. 5, 7, 8; *true light* in v. 9; *word* again in v. 14. Jesus calls himself the *light* of the world and the *light* of life in John 8:12, and the *truth* and the *life* in 14:6.

9   See W. Grese, op. cit., pp. 159, 165–6.

10   R. Reitzenstein alters *ombrou* ('of storm') to *abyssou*: '(gate) of the abyss'.

11   Reading *ktisin*, though some commentators suggest *chresin*, 'use'.

12   I.e., heavenly light, such as the sun.

13   Literally, 'from you'.

14   The light perceived by the Mind.

15   *Enkrateia*, 'self-control'.

16   cf. the *thysian zōsan hagian . . . ten logikēn latreian* mentioned in Rom 12:1. W. Grese translates 'spoken [verbal] sacrifice'.

SELECTED BIBLIOGRAPHY

Copenhaver, Brian P., *Hermetica: The Greek Corpus Hermeticum and the Latin Asclepius in a New English Translation, with Notes and Introduction*, Cambridge, University Press, 1992.

Dodd, C. H., *The Bible and the Greeks*, London, Hodder & Stoughton, 1935.

Festugière, André-Jean, *La Révélation d'Hermès Trismégiste*, 4 volumes, Paris, Lecoffre, 1944–54.

Fowden, Garth, *The Egyptian Hermes*, Cambridge, Cambridge University Press, 1986.

Grese, William C., *Corpus Hermeticum XIII and Early Christian Literature*, Leiden, E. J. Brill, 1979.

Mahé, Jean-Pierre, *Hermès en Haute-Égypte*, 2 volumes, Québec, L'Université de Laval, 1978–82.

Nock, Arthur Darby, and Festugière, André-Jean, *Corpus Hermeticum*, tome II:

Traites XIII–XVIII, Paris, Société d'Édition 'Les Belles Lettres', 1945.

Reitzenstein, Richard, *Poimandres*, Leipzig, Teubner, 1904.

Scott, Walter, *Hermetica*, 4 volumes, Oxford, Clarendon Press, 1924–36.

Tröger, Karl-Wolfgang, *Mysterienglaube und Gnosis in Corpus Hermeticum XIII*, Berlin, Akademie-Verlag, 1971.

Zuntz, Günther, 'On the Hymns in Corpus Hermeticum XIII', *Hermes*, 1955, vol. 83, pp. 68-92. Reprinted in Zuntz, *Opuscula selecta: Classica, Hellenistica, Christiana*, Manchester, Manchester University Press, 1972, pp. 150–77.

28

PRAYER IN CHARITON'S
CHAEREAS AND CALLIRHOE

Mary Lynnette Delbridge

INTRODUCTION

Many of the literary remains we have from the Greco-Roman world reflect the concerns of the educated elite. Not as common, however, are examples of literature belonging to a 'more "popular" cultural context than contemporary "serious" literature'.[1] Chariton's novel, *Chaereas and Callirhoe*, offers us an example of such light, entertaining reading. While a learned audience would have appreciated its allusions to Homer and other classics,[2] the novel's numerous foreshadowings, recapitulations, 'stereotypical scenes, motifs and plots'[3] enabled 'people without critical standards or a wider background of reading'[4] to enjoy the novel as well.

Provenance, language, date, relation to other works, attestation

Chariton identifies himself as the secretary of a rhetor from Aphrodisias, a flourishing cultural centre in southwest Asia Minor.[5] His novel, written in Greek sometime between 50 BCE and 200 CE[6] is the earliest of the five extant and complete romantic novels from the period. We know of it from a thirteenth- or fourteenth-century manuscript located in Florence, three papyri fragments from the second or third centuries CE, and a Coptic palimpsest fragment from the sixth or seventh century. About half of the palimpsest was copied soon after its discovery in 1898 and before it was destroyed by fire.[7]

Literary context – the novel's plot

Chariton's plot does entertain. Chaereas and Callirhoe of Syracuse fall in love and marry. Tricked into thinking his wife has been unfaithful, Chaereas kicks Callirhoe in a jealous fit. She passes out as if dead and is buried.

Robbers find her as she regains consciousness in her tomb and take her across the Mediterranean where they sell her as a slave to wealthy Dionysius. He falls madly in love with Callirhoe who agrees to marry him only when she realizes she is pregnant with Chaereas' child. More travel, intrigue, enslavement and attempts to seduce Callirhoe follow. It takes a war between Egypt and Babylonia for the plot to sort itself out and for Chaereas and Callirhoe to be safely reunited.

Prayers in the novel

Whether Chariton intends it or not, his novel does more than entertain. It introduces us to twenty-three prayers in direct speech from both male and female characters. These prayers address several deities, primarily Tyche (Fortune) and Aphrodite, the primary deity of Chariton's city. These prayers are not highly stylized liturgy or elaborate literary evocations of the deities. Instead, they reflect a more popular piety. By examining them and the following translated prayer in particular, we can deepen our understanding of popular piety in the period.

Our sample prayer takes place after Callirhoe's child is born. Dionysius believes the boy is his own and celebrates the birth at the Aphrodite shrine on his country estate with sacrifice and prayer. After he finishes, Callirhoe asks the crowd to leave the shrine. Accompanied only by her female servant, she takes the child in her arms and holds him up to the statue of Aphrodite as she prays. She is grief-stricken because she believes Chaereas is dead and anxious lest Dionysius discover the true identity of her child. She pours out her feelings and concerns to the goddess. The prayer ends when tears overcome her.

The prayer is one of twelve addressed to Aphrodite. Like the others, it is quite simple with no elaborate appellations or descriptions of Aphrodite's attributes or sphere of power. Callirhoe begins simply, 'O Mistress'. With only one exception, the Aphrodite prayers include petitions. The people praying preface their petitions by reminding Aphrodite of and sometimes thanking her for something she has done for them in the past. In their eyes, Aphrodite's past actions commit her to an ongoing relationship with them. The same is true of this prayer. Callirhoe complains that the goddess has not kept Chaereas safe for her but admits she is grateful to Aphrodite for giving her the child, 'an image' of her husband. She prays for reconciliation with the goddess and for the safety of her child. Her petition reflects the personal concerns which run through all the prayers in the novel. Characters pray for survival and well-being for themselves and their loved ones.

The location of this prayer in the shrine and Callirhoe's posture before the statue of the goddess help reinforce the sense of her relationship with Aphrodite. Ten of the twelve Aphrodite prayers take place in similar locations with the person praying facing or touching a statue of Aphrodite.

Addressing the goddess' statue by prostrating oneself before it, kissing her feet, or grasping her knees underlines the emotional intensity of the supplication[8] and gives a visual and tactile sense of the social relationship and exchange between the superior goddess and the subordinate human being.

This sample prayer also reflects the all-important Greco-Roman concern for honour and shame.[9] Persons have honour when others acknowledge and give them the social status they claim. Males acquire honour when they challenge and dislodge others from their social space and lose honour when they cannot defend their own social position in response to such challenges. Protecting family members, especially females, from outsiders is essential to maintaining one's honour. Females on the other hand contribute to the honour of their families by having 'shame', by being concerned about their status, their reputation and their ability to avoid situations which might bring them dishonour or unwanted sexual attentions. Not surprisingly then, Chaereas and Dionysius pray about the rivals who jeopardize their exclusive claims to Callirhoe while Callirhoe prays about status and compromising sexual situations. In this particular prayer, Callirhoe insists on privacy before she prays. She does so because she cannot afford for others to discover the true paternity of her child but also because she is a woman with modesty and 'shame'. She prays about the status of her child hoping that he will bring honour upon her family, even more than that of her illustrious father, Hermocrates. She laments her second marriage, a burdensome misfortune because it has brought her into sexual contact with a man other than her husband.

Greco-Roman piety

From the twenty-three prayers in Chariton's novel and our sample prayer in particular, we can make some tentative suggestions about popular piety in the Greco-Roman period. First, like the characters of the novel who feel they have been acted upon and have little power to change the fate which Tyche or another deity has chosen for them, popular audiences may believe they have meagre control over or responsibility for the course their lives take. In the face of such helplessness, they desire deities who are more sympathetic to them than Tyche and who will hold her in check.

For Chariton, that deity was Aphrodite. The fact that Chariton commends to his readers the goddess and cult most important to Aphrodisias[10] alerts us to look for the ways local religious loyalties survived and yet were incorporated in the larger cultural and religious mix of the Roman empire. This novel suggests that popular audiences still needed and responded to local cults, that they wanted to see the power of their own deities extolled, and that they wanted their deities to have universal as well as local power.

We can also picture people who did not disembody or intellectualize their prayers but who found shrines, statues and prayer postures essential to their religious life. In Chariton's novel, location and posture are as much a part of the 'form' or 'language' of the prayers as the actual words.

Finally, Chariton's novel suggests that any picture of popular piety must take gender into account. In his portrayals of prayer, females are concerned about their 'shame', their status, their reputations and their sexual exclusivity while males are concerned about their 'honour', protecting what is theirs and responding successfully to challenges from other males. In his narrative world, prayers are not exclusively religious expressions. Instead, they reinforce larger societal ideals for proper male and female behaviour. When we study a prayer therefore, we find ourselves asking how and when it reflects and supports larger cultural ideals and how and when it expresses a religious sentiment in tension with the larger culture. More than likely, we will discover that distinctions between the religious and non-religious aspects of culture are quite blurred, if not altogether non-existent.

TRANSLATION, 3.8.7.2–3.8.9.6

O Mistress, on this child's behalf I thank you; on my own behalf I do not thank you. If you had kept Chaereas for me, then I would be grateful to you on my own account. Still, you have given me an image of my very dear husband and you did not completely take Chaereas away from me. Indeed, for my sake, grant that my son may be more fortunate than his parents and like his grandfather.[11] May he too sail in a general's galley and may people say as he does battle at sea, 'Hermocrates' grandson is mightier than he.' Surely his grandfather will be pleased to have a noble successor and we, his parents, will be pleased even when we are dead. Finally, Mistress, I beseech you, be reconciled to me.[12] I have been sufficiently unfortunate. I have died. I came back to life. I have been taken by pirates. I have gone into exile. I have been sold. I have been enslaved. And I regard my second marriage still more burdensome to me than these other misfortunes. Yet for the sake of all these,[13] I ask one favour from you and through you from the other gods. Preserve my fatherless child.

NOTES

1   T. Hägg, 'Orality, Literacy and the "Readership" of the Early Greek Novel', in Roy Eriksen (ed.), *Contexts of Pre-Novel Narrative: The European Tradition*, Berlin, Mouton de Gruyter, 1994, p. 65.
2   E. Bowie, 'The Readership of Greek Novels in the Ancient World', in James Tatum (ed.), *The Search for the Ancient Novel*, Baltimore, Johns Hopkins University Press, 1994, p. 438.
3   Hägg, op. cit., pp. 53 and 58–66.
4   B. P. Reardon as quoted in Bowie, op. cit., p. 455 n. 26.
5   K. Erim, *Aphrodisias: City of Venus Aphrodite*, Intro. John Julius Norwich,

New York, Facts on File Publications, 1986.

6   B. P. Reardon, *The Form of the Greek Romance*, Princeton, Princeton University Press, 1991, p. 17 n. 3; and T. Hägg, *The Novel in Antiquity*, Oxford, Basil Blackwell, 1983, p. 6.

7   W. Blake (ed.), *Charitonis Aphrodisiensis*, Oxford, 1938, pp. vii–xiii. See also K. Plepelits, *Chariton von Aphrodisias: Kallirhoe*, Stuttgart, Hiersemann, 1976, pp. 21–2 and n. 95.

8   F. T. van Straten, 'Did the Greeks Kneel Before Their Gods?' *Bulletin Antieke Beschaving*, 1974, vol. 49, p. 184. 'Kneeling was in general reserved for urgent prayers, . . . addressed to deities that were close to the common people, and who could be trusted . . . to hear their invocations and come to their aid.'

9   B. Malina, *The New Testament World*, rev. edn, Atlanta, John Knox Press, 1993, pp. 28–54.

10 'In the . . . romances, particular cults are stressed to the exclusion of others.' Xenophon's *Ephesian Tale* gives Artemis and Isis the role played by Aphrodite in Chariton's novel. D. Edwards, 'Acts of the Apostles and Chariton's *Chaereas and Callirhoe*: A Literary and Sociohistorical Study', Dissertation, Boston University, 1987, pp. 89 and 95.

11 The grandfather is Hermocrates, highly honoured for defeating the Athenians.

12 *loipon* can also read: '. . . be reconciled to me *from now on*'.

13 *Anti* used with verbs of entreaty is like *pros* + Gen. and means 'for the sake of'. *Panton* can refer to all the misfortunes Callirhoe has experienced or to all those for whom she prays. Possible translations are: (a) 'Yet for the sake of all these misfortunes, I ask . . .' (b) 'Yet for the sake of all those concerning whom I have prayed, I ask . . .'

SELECTED BIBLIOGRAPHY

Blake, Warren E. (ed.), *Charitonis Aphrodisiensis de Chaerea et Callirhoe Amatoriarum Narrationum Libri Octo*, Oxford, Clarendon Press, 1938.

Bowie, Ewen, 'The Readership of Greek Novels in the Ancient World', in James Tatum (ed.), *The Search for the Ancient Novel*, Baltimore, Johns Hopkins University Press, 1994.

Hägg, Tomas, 'Orality, Literacy, and the "Readership" of the Early Greek Novel', in Roy Eriksen (ed.), *Contexts of Pre-Novel Narrative: The European Tradition*, Berlin, Mouton de Gruyter, 1994.

Malina, Bruce, *The New Testament World: Insights from Cultural Anthropology*, rev. edn, Atlanta, John Knox Press, 1993.

Reardon, B.P., trans., 'Chaereas and Callirhoe', in B. P. Reardon (ed.), *Collected Ancient Greek Novels*, Berkeley and Los Angeles, University of California Press, 1989.

Van Straten, F.T., 'Did the Greeks Kneel Before Their Gods?' *Bulletin Antieke Beschaving*, 1974, vol. 49, 159–89.

29

AN EPHESIAN TALE: PRAYERS TO ISIS AND OTHER GODS

Agneta Enermalm

INTRODUCTION

B. P. Reardon's recent (1989) collection of ancient Greek novels in English translation presents Xenophon's story from the second century CE under the title *An Ephesian Tale*.[1] The tale is of the young and beautiful Anthia and the equally young and handsome Habrocomes who fall in love when they meet in Ephesus, marry and become separated while travelling. Fortunately reunited after many adventures, the couple return to Ephesus where they remain happily together for the rest of their lives. What at first sight looks like a sentimental and unsophisticated love story is rendered in a simple and fairly artless linguistic form.[2]

Provenance and influence

The only manuscript that includes *An Ephesian Tale* gives information of its provenance: one of the scribes introduces himself as 'Demetrius of Melitene', a town on the border between Syria and Armenia.[3] Xenophon's novel is a storehouse of popular motifs; apparently the novel was more readily accepted in the Hellenized parts of the Orient than it was in the West.[4]

Relation to religion

A comparison of Xenophon's novel with the earlier novel by Chariton (*Chaereas and Callirhoe*) reveals a stronger interest in religion. Tomas Hägg says: 'While Chariton's gods may smack of literary personification – of Love, of Chance – in the *Ephesian Tale* we meet the living gods and goddesses of the time: the Ephesian Artemis, the Rhodian Helius, the Egyptian Isis, who threaten, are worshipped and conciliated, and come to the rescue.'[5]

Assemblies go a long way for Chariton: a regular assembly in Syracuse pleads for the marriage of Chaereas and Callirhoe (1.1.11). In Xenophon, the marriage is the result of an oracle by Apollo. This oracle serves as the primary promoting factor in the development of the plot, causing the main actors to travel as far as Egypt to find a turning-point in their misery of constant separation and victimization: 'and beside the waters of the river Nile, to Holy Isis, the Savior, you will afterwards offer rich gifts; but still after their sufferings a better fate is in store.'[6] The story takes off in Ephesus: Habrocomes and Anthia meet as they take part in an Artemisian procession. Love at first sight was caused by the god Eros who was angered at Habrocomes' arrogant disbelief in the power of love. Habrocomes eagerly invokes the god to be benevolent, admitting himself conquered. After their marriage the young couple set out on a journey. On their arrival in Tyre on the Phoenician coast, their radiant beauty makes the inhabitants think they are gods. However, in Tyre they become separated as Habrocomes is thrown into prison for false allegations of adultery. They now have to travel different routes. While they both remain in Egypt, they don't cross paths. But it is here that the story comes to a turning-point, as the oracle of Apollo had predicted. Another oracle, by Apis, the sacred bull of Memphis, confirms: 'Anthia will soon recover her own husband, Habrocomes' (5.4.11). After further travel, they finally meet near the Isis temple in Rhodes. Having returned to Ephesus, the young couple set up an inscription to Artemis commemorating their sufferings and adventures. Thus the story honours the goddess of the city of Ephesus, the 'great Artemis'.[7]

Among the many gods, some are mightier than others; in this novel it is Isis who is supreme. The oracle predicting the destiny of the young lovers mentioned Isis 'the Saviour' just before giving the promise of 'a better fate' (1.6.2). She is the deity preferred by Anthia who develops what one could call a personal faith-relationship with this god. Isis was in a special way the goddess of women in the Greco-Roman world at the time of the novel.[8]

The prayers of the story enhance its dramatic dimension. Close to the turning-point of the drama they become more extensive and intense. The traditional wording and cultic context of the prayers suggest that the author was attuned to religious practices of his time.

TRANSLATION

Prayers to Isis

Anthia visits the temple of Isis in Memphis and laments her situation.[9]

4.3.3   O most mighty[10] of gods,[11] until now I have remained chaste, keeping in mind that I am thine; I have kept my marriage to Habrocomes undefiled. But now I am on my way to India, far

away from the land of Ephesus and far from the remains of
4.3.4   Habrocomes. Therefore, deliver me, miserable woman that I
am, from this situation and give me back to Habrocomes, should
he be alive, or if destiny allows no escape from our lot of dying
apart from one another, let it be that I remain faithful to him,
even if he is dead.

Thus Anthia prays and soon she experiences relief in her distress. But only
temporarily: threatened by Polyidus, the very man who had rescued her, she
takes refuge in the temple and again prays to Isis,

5.4.6   You, O mistress of Egypt, save me again
as you have often come to my assistance;
let Polyidus spare me since I keep myself
chaste for Habrocomes, thanks to you.

Prayer to Apis

Moved by Anthia's prayer, Polyidus is determined to express his love for her
only by looking at her and listening to her voice. Relieved, Anthia renews
her efforts to find Habrocomes by visiting the shrine of Apis.[12] Asking for
oracular guidance, she prays,

5.4.10   O kindest of gods, you who show compassion to all strangers,
have mercy also on me, doomed by an evil fate as I am, and
pronounce to me a true prophecy about Habrocomes. For if I
am still to see him and have him as my husband, I shall continue
to live. But if he is dead, it is best that I too depart from this
painful life.

As Anthia exits from the temple, playing children meet her with the message:
'Anthia will soon recover Habrocomes her husband.'[13]

Prayers to Helius

Separately and without knowing of one another, Anthia and Habrocomes
have arrived at Rhodes which they had once visited together. It is the time of
the Helius festival.[14] The festival is a signal to the reader that the circle is soon
to be closed, because a festival was the occasion for the young couple's first
meeting in Ephesus. Anthia fears that she will have to return to Ephesus
without Habrocomes. She prays,

5.11.4   O Helius, you who watch over the affairs of all people[15] and
neglect me alone, unfortunate woman that I am, when once I
was in Rhodes in full happiness, I worshipped you and offered
sacrifices together with Habrocomes.[16]

178

Anthia's prayer is supplemented by action. She offers a lock of her hair to Helius, sets up an inscription 'on behalf of her husband Habrocomes' and prays for him.[17]

Prayer of thanksgiving to Isis

Two servants of Habrocomes discover the signs of Anthia's presence and inform their master. Appropriately, it is close to the temple of Isis that the young lovers find one another again.[18] Entering the temple, Habrocomes and Anthia say,

> 5.13.4 To you, O most mighty goddess, we owe thanks for our deliverance; thanks to you, O most honourable of all, we have found each other again.

NOTES

1 B. P. Reardon (ed.), *Collected Ancient Greek Novels*, Berkeley/Los Angeles/London, University of California Press, 1989; *An Ephesian Tale* is translated by G. Anderson, pp. 125–69. The Greek text I follow for my translation and comments is the edition by A. D. Papanikolaou, *Xenophon Ephesius*, Leipzig, Teubner, 1973. I have also consulted the Greek–French edition by G. D. Dalmeyda, *Xenophon d' Éphèse*, Paris, Budé, 1926. In support for the second-century dating of the novel, reference has been made to the occurrence of the title 'peace officer' (2.13.3 and 2.9.5), unknown before the time of Hadrian (117–38 CE); see B. E. Perry, *The Ancient Romances: A Literary-Historical Account of their Origins*, Berkeley and Los Angeles, University of California Press, 1967, p. 345.

2 The uneven style has led scholars to regard the work, which is divided into five books, as an abbreviation. For a critical assessment of arguments favouring this hypothesis, see T. Hägg, 'Die Ephesiaka des Xenophon Ephesios – Original oder Epitome?', *Classica et Mediaevalia*, 1966, vol. 27, pp. 118–61.

3 Today the thirteenth-century manuscript is known as codex Laurentinus Soppressi no. 2728; it is kept in the Laurentian Library in Florence. On the manuscript and its provenance, see B. E. Perry, op. cit., p. 344.

4 See T. Hägg, 'The Oriental Reception of Greek Novels', *Symbolae Osloenses*, 1986, vol. 61, pp. 99–131. The tale influenced the English novel after the first printed edition of the Greek text (1726) and its English translation (1727) were published, see G. L. Schmeling, *Xenophon of Ephesus*, Boston, Mass., Twayne Publishers, 1980, pp. 146–53.

5 T. Hägg, *The Novel in Antiquity*, Berkeley and Los Angeles, University of California Press, 1983, p. 26.

6 Anderson's translation, p. 132 (see note 1 above).

7 See 1.11.5 and compare Acts 19:28, 'Great is Artemis of the Ephesians!'

8 See S. K. Heyob, *The Cult of Isis among Women in the Graeco-Roman World*, Leiden, E. J. Brill, 1975.

9 The prospects of her future are dire because a man named Psammis has threatened to take her with him to India.

10 'Most mighty' is preferable to 'greatest' for *megistos*. J. M. Bremer, quoting a hymn to Kouros (second century CE or earlier) that starts *O megiste Koure*,

translates 'most mighty Kouros'; see H. S. Versnel (ed.), *Faith, Hope and Worship*, Leiden, E. J. Brill, 1981, p. 205. H. W. Pleket, in the same volume, warns that one has to distinguish between the poetic use ('greatest') and the cultic use ('most mighty'), p. 180. Among the gods mentioned in Xenophon's novel, Isis alone is called 'greatest' or 'most mighty'.

11 The genitive plural is ambiguous; I prefer 'gods' to 'goddesses' given the role of Isis in the early Roman empire. See R. E. Witt, *Isis in the Graeco-Roman World*, Ithaca, NY, Cornell University Press, 1971, p. 246, who discusses Anthia's prayer and translates 'greatest of the gods'.

12 The sacred bull Apis was worshipped in Memphis as late as the second century CE. Coins from this time often carry the effigy of Apis together with Isis; J. Toutain, 'Le culte du taureau Apis à Memphis sous l'empire romain', *Muséon*, 1916, vol. 1, pp. 193–202.

13 Apis was famous for his clear oracles often revealed by children at play, as both Plutarch (*c.* 50–120 CE) and his contemporary Dio Chrysostom tell us; see Plutarch, *On Isis and Osiris* 356e and Chrysostom, *Discourses* 32.13.

14 In ancient times Helius was the main national god of Rhodes. Pindar (518–438 BCE) recounts the local legend that claimed the island for Helius, calling Rhodes *lachos Aeliou*, 'lot of Helius' (*Olympian Odes* 7.58, ed. B. Snell, Leipzig, Teubner, 1959).

15 This qualification is traditional and attested since Homer (*Iliad* 3.277). This 'watching' role of the Sun god convinces Anthia that ultimate justice will be brought by Helius.

16 On this occasion, they had offered a panoply to the Sun god and a votive tablet with their names.

17 The giving of her hair is an improvised, spontaneous offering that uses for substance what simply is at hand; it serves as an offering of petition. See O. Weinrich, 'Haaropfer und Helios', *Hermes*, 1920, vol. 55, pp. 326–8 for more examples. The whole sequence of action reported in 5.11.4 is a strong appeal to Helius for letting the longtime suffering of Anthia and Habrocomes end in their final reunion.

18 See M. Malaise, 'La piété personnelle dans la religion isiaque', in H. Limet and J. Ries (eds), *L'expérience de la prière dans les grandes religions*, Louvain-la-Neuve, Centre d'histoire des religions, 1980, pp. 109–11. The author discusses Isis' supremacy over Fate. He also notes that, according to numerous testimonies, Isis takes those in love under her guard.

SELECTED BIBLIOGRAPHY

Hägg, Tomas, *The Novel in Antiquity*, Berkeley and Los Angeles, University of California Press, 1983.

Heyob, Sharon K., *The Cult of Isis among Women in the Graeco-Roman World*, Leiden, E. J. Brill, 1975.

Reardon, Bryan P. (ed.), *Collected Ancient Greek Novels*, Berkeley/Los Angeles/London, University of California Press, 1989.

Schmeling, Gareth L., *Xenophon of Ephesus*, Boston, Mass., Twayne Publishers, 1980.

Versnel, H. S. (ed.), *Faith, Hope and Worship: Aspects of Religious Mentality in the Ancient World*, Leiden, E. J. Brill, 1981.

30

A PRAYER TO SARAPIS IN *P. OXY.* 1070

Robert F. Hull, Jun.

INTRODUCTION

The prayer to Sarapis is excerpted from a letter written by a man on a business trip in Alexandria to his wife in Oxyrhynchus.[1] On the basis of its style of handwriting it is dated by its original editor, A. S. Hunt, to the third century, CE.[2] The letter refers to several business and private concerns affecting the wellbeing of the family.

Thousands of private letters written on papyrus have survived in the dry sands of Egypt, where they have been reclaimed from ancient refuse dumps or from mummy cases or 'cartonnage', the ancient equivalent of cardboard. These letters provide information not obtainable anywhere else concerning the daily life of ordinary people living in Egypt from Ptolemaic to Byzantine times (c. 300 BCE to 300 CE). We find letters from family members away from home on business trips, or posted by the military to some distant city. Just as our personal letters often contain such clichéd expressions as 'I hope you are well; I'm doing fine', so did their ancient counterparts. Sometimes a letter will also indicate that its writer has made a visit to a temple and said a prayer on behalf of friends or family back home. These remarks about prayer are always in stereotyped phrases, or prayer 'formulas'. Very occasionally, as in our example, the content of the prayer is summarized or indicated in the letter.

Prayer 'formulas' in the letters

Although most letter-writers make no reference to religion at all, those who do so insert very conventional phrases into the openings or closings of their letters. Typical formulas include: 'above all I pray that you are well'; 'I pray for you every day'; 'I give thanks to the gods.' The standard works on ancient letters have catalogued these formulas,[3] but very little attention has been given to what the use of prayer language may indicate about the personal piety of the writer.[4] Since the language is for the most part formulaic, the prayer references have generally been seen as merely perfunctory and polite conventions. Nevertheless, sometimes these formulas are expanded, adapted and personalized in ways that tell us more about the religious life of the writers. Occasionally we are told that a writer has prayed on a specific occasion, for example 'at the sacrifices of Isis on the night of her birthday',[5] or that the writer will pray or make an act of worship 'tomorrow at the Sarapeum'.[6]

The cultic setting of the prayer

Of the references to prayer in these ancient letters, more of them mention the god Sarapis than any other deity. Sarapis was a Greco-Egyptian god who was understood in Egypt to be identical to Osiris, and to be connected, therefore, with the consort of Osiris, Isis.[7] His association with the Ptolemaic dynasty dates from the time of Ptolemy I (304–282 BCE), who is reported to have installed a huge statue of Sarapis in Alexandria.[8] The god was connected with fertility, and is usually portrayed with a small basket on his head,[9] often decorated with leaves, and carrying a cornucopia in one hand. The cult of Sarapis spread widely in the Mediterranean world during the Ptolemaic and Roman eras. Hundreds of inscriptions honour the god by attributing to him healings, rescue from dangers of travel and protection of children. In these inscriptions he is given such epithets as *euergetēs* (benefactor), *sōtēr* (saviour), *kosmokratōr* (ruler of the world), *basileus* (king), *ploutodotēs* (giver of wealth), *megas* (great), *hypsistos* (highest) and *agathos* (good).[10] In Egypt no other cult was understood to provide such benefactions as that of Sarapis, or Isis/Sarapis. Moreover, Sarapis eventually came to be identified with a number of other Hellenistic deities, including Pluto, Zeus, Asklepios and Dionysos, and endowed with their virtues. During the Roman era Aelius Aristides (second century CE) could write of him:

> He alone is held in honor alike by kings and by private citizens, alike by the wise and the simple, by both great and small. . . . Thus in every circumstance of life he comes on our behalf, and there is no space left unaffected by the workings of this god. Rather, in whatever matters humankind is interested, he too takes an interest, and performs every sort of blessing, beginning with the soul and ending with material wealth.[11]

The cult of Sarapis encouraged daily prayer in the temple.[12] The remains of ancient temples preserve evidence that the worshippers often made an act of worship on behalf of family or friends and left a dedicatory inscription, called a *proskynēma*, to that effect.[13] In our prayer the author's reference to an 'act of worship in the great Sarapeum' may possibly be understood to include having such an inscription made.

TRANSLATION

Aurelios Demareus to Aurelia Arsinoe his sister,[14] greetings. The prayer that I previously made[15] to all the gods[16] for your welfare and that of our child and your brother and your father and your mother and all our friends[17] is now an even greater act of worship[18] in the great Sarapeum.[19] I implore the great god Sarapis concerning your life and that of all our friends and the good hopes held in common by humankind.[20]

NOTES

1   *The Oxyrhynchus Papyri* (a continuing series now under the sponsorship of the British Academy and currently numbering 61 volumes), London, Egyptian Exploration Society (Parts I–XIV Egypt Exploration Fund), 1898– .
2   ibid., Part VII, 1910, p. 227.
3   See Francis X. Exler, *The Form of the Ancient Greek Letter. A Study in Greek Epistolography*, Washington, DC, Catholic University of America, 1923, pp. 103–10.
4   See H. I. Bell, 'Popular Religion in Graeco-Roman Egypt, I. The Pagan Period', *Journal of Egyptian Archaeology*, 1948, vol. 34, pp. 82–97; and B. R. Rees, 'Popular Religion in Graeco-Roman Egypt, II. The Transition to Christianity', *Journal of Egyptian Archaeology*, 1950, vol. 36, pp. 89–100.
5   *Die Bremer Papyri*, ed. U. Wilcken, Berlin, Abhandlungen der Preussischen Akademie der Wissenschaften, Jahr. 1936, no. 15.
6   Ibid., no. 48.
7   The name 'Sarapis' is generally thought to be a combination of 'Osiris' and 'Apis'. See John E. Stambaugh, *Sarapis Under the Early Ptolemies*, Leiden, E. J. Brill, 1972, pp. 36–9.
8   The classic account is in Plutarch, *Isis and Osiris*, 28.
9   Called a *modius*, or *calathos*.
10 Wilhelm Hornbostel, *Sarapis. Studien zur Überlieferungsgeschichte, den Erscheinungsformen und Wandlungen der Gestalt eines Gottes*, Leiden, E. J. Brill, 1973, pp. 26–7.
11 Aristides XLV 18–20, ed. B. Keil, Berlin, Weidmann, 1898, English translation, Stambaugh, op. cit., p. 98.
12 See U. Wilcken, *Grundzüge und Chrestomathie der Papyruskunde*. I, Berlin, Teubner, 1912, p. 123.
13 G. Geraci has catalogued hundreds of examples of these in 'Richerche sul Proskynema', *Aegyptus*, 51, 1971, pp. 3–221.
14 'Sister' is found often in the papyri as a term of endearment for one's wife. This usage may be rooted in the ancient Egyptian practice of brother–sister marriage, but cf. Cant 4:9, 10, 12.
15 This may be a reference to a prayer that Aurelius made before leaving for Alexandria. Further down in the letter (in a part not reproduced above) Aurelius mentions that he has not heard from his wife, despite having written several times. Now, in view of the lack of any communication from home, he prays once more concerning the welfare of the family. We have no reason to imagine some kind of special need of the family; reference to prayers for the welfare of another are commonplace in the papyri.
16 The linking of Sarapis with 'all the gods' reflects the religious syncretism referred to in the introduction.

17 The words 'all' and 'always' appear frequently in the openings of papyrus letters in several stereotyped formulas, such as 'above all I pray that you may be well', or with reference to praying to 'all the gods', 'praying always', or praying for the addressee and 'all' of his or her family or associates; cf. the letters of Paul in the NT (Rom 1:7; 1 Cor 1:2; 2 Cor 1:1; Phil 1:1; 1 Thess 1:2).

18 The word translated 'is an act of worship' is *proskynei*. In the papyri *proskyneō* usually signifies either 'to do an act of worship' (to a deity) or (especially in the Byzantine era) 'to do honour or reverence' to a (human) superior. Both usages are found in the New Testament: to worship God, Matt 4:10; John 4:22–4; Acts 10:25–6; to do reverence to a superior, Rev 3:9. Etymologically the word signifies 'to bend the knee'.

19 Although there were temples dedicated to Sarapis worship in many cities in the Mediterranean world, the 'great Sarapeum' is no doubt the one in Alexandria, where the Sarapis cult was centred during the Hellenistic period. See Samuel Dill, *Roman Society from Nero to Marcus Aurelius*, New York, Meridian, 1956, p. 567.

20 The petition of Aurelius to Sarapis 'for all the good hopes (*chrēston elpidōn*) held in common by humankind' is remarkable, and unmatched in any other letter I have seen. Pagan prayer is sometimes described as being almost wholly self-interested (Ramsey Macmullen, *Paganism in the Roman Empire*, New Haven, Yale University Press, p. 52), yet this petition embraces the general concerns of humankind. It is a question whether a petition so generalizing and pretentious should be taken seriously. Given the description of Sarapis in Aristides (introduction, above), perhaps it should be. Sarapis was widely understood to hold universal sway, and to be able to provide health, wealth and peace. Maybe these are some of the 'good hopes' in the mind of the author of this prayer.

SELECTED BIBLIOGRAPHY

Bell, H. I., 'Popular Religion in Graeco-Roman Egypt, I. The Pagan Period', *Journal of Egyptian Archaeology*, 1948, vol. 34, pp. 82–97.

Exler, Francis X., *The Form of the Ancient Greek Letter. A Study in Greek Epistolography*, Washington, DC, Catholic University of America, 1923.

Hornbostel, Wilhelm, *Sarapis. Studien zur Überlieferungsgeschichte den Erscheinungsformen und Wandlungen der Gestalt eines Gottes*, Leiden, E. J. Brill, 1973.

Hunt, Arthur S. (ed.), *The Oxyrhynchus Papyri Part VII*, London, Egypt Exploration fund, 1910.

Rees, B. R., 'Popular Religion in Graeco-Roman Egypt, II. The Transition to Christianity', *Journal of Egyptian Archaeology*, 1950, vol. 36, pp. 89–100.

Stambaugh, John, *Sarapis Under the Early Ptolemies*, Leiden, E. J. Brill, 1972.

White, John L., *Light from Ancient Letters*, Philadelphia, Fortress, 1986.

31

THE PRAYER IN MENANDER RHETOR 2.445.25–446.13

Edgar Krentz

INTRODUCTION

The third-century rhetorician[1] Menander of Laodicea[2] wrote two works on epideictic oratory that sum up a long rhetorical tradition in masterful fashion. Epideictic orations are speeches that praise or blame a god, an individual, a city, or some other group of people. The first work describes eight types of hymns in praise of gods, while the second discusses the structure and content of seventeen different types of epideictic orations. The last discusses an oration in honour of 'Sminthian Apollo'.[3] To illustrate the type, Menander includes an oration in honour of Sminthian Apollo and inserts into the text instructions on writing such an oration. The Sminthian oration is thus an unusual example of a text commented on by its own writer.

Attestation

Russell and Wilson (1981) suggest that only eight manuscripts deserve attention in reconstructing Menander's text. The most important is Parisinus Graecus 1741, supported by Parisinus Graecus 2423. Six manuscripts make up a second textual tradition. One can safely disregard later manuscripts.[4]

Structure and style

Menander says the oration should begin with a prooemium praising Apollo, the god of speech and leader of the Muses, and asking him to accept the hymn Menander writes, poor though it is in comparison with those of Homer and Pindar. There follows a hymn to the god himself, asking how one should address him (giving a number of possibilities). Next one delivers an account of his birth, an encomium of the country where the oration is given, a description of the power of the god under four categories (archery, prophecy, medicine and music), using traditional mythology to support each category. A description of the god's temple and statue forms the next section. The oration concludes with the god's invocatory titles and a prayer for his continued aid. The text translated here is this laudatory conclusion.

The sentence structure of Menander's Greek is relatively simple, but laced with words that are formal or out of the ordinary. His syntax is simple, but correct. He pays careful attention to word order to ensure that key ideas are stressed, a feature I have tried to reproduce in the translation. Menander's Greek requires the use of relatively short, simple sentences in English, with some attention to reproducing the rhetorical parallelism and emphasis of the original, including the use of some more literary terms rather than simple ones, for example 'address you as' rather than 'call you'.

Sources

Greeks and Romans had no canonical scripture. Instead they had a collection of traditional myths interpreted by poets and dramatists. These myths vary according to local tradition and authorial use. Writers vary them, stressing different points or adding details, to create the desired effect. Thus Menander draws on a variety of Apollo traditions as he writes his Sminthian oration.

Relation to cult

Since this prayer is part of a model oration, there is no evidence that it was ever actually used within the context of an Apollo festival. At the same time, as Adrastus' Sminthiac prayer[5] shows, Menander's prayer has verisimilitude: one could have used it in a Sminthean Apollo festival. It shows that a prayer should both praise the god to whom it is directed and ask for the god's blessings.

Theology of the prayer

This prayer-hymn is a form of praise plus petition. It gives no direct attention to the origins or nature of humankind, has no concept of sin in the Judaeo-Christian sense and exhibits no eschatological hope. Yet it makes clear that human destiny is under the control of Apollo: 'Every city and every land and every nation you control.' Apollo, around whom the chorus of stars dance, clearly controls the universe in which humanity exists. Therefore prayer to Apollo, if properly done, is one way to deal with problems arising from illness, from bad weather and from a fear of the future.

The list of names and titles – a standard feature in prayers, a mode of praising a god for past benefactions – makes clear that Apollo is universally powerful, a protector from disease, a patron of the Muses (and so of music and other arts), a sponsor of oracles about the future, one who controls the heavens and human destiny. Identifying him with Mithras and Horus extends his realm beyond the Greek world, while the Delphian combination of Apollo and Dionysus unites opposites.[6] This provides the basis for the concluding petitions.[7]

Effect on subsequent eras

There is little direct evidence of Menander setting a *norm* for later prayers. He does become a standard author who describes what epideictic orations should be like. Kennedy points out that his two works were still available in tenth- to twelfth-century Byzantium, and that Procopius of Gaza and the church fathers Gregory of Nazianzus, John Chrysostom, and Leo the Wise all delivered epideictic speeches that used the topics and order suggested by Menander.[8] He influences later Christian oratory and homiletics; he may have direct influence on Christian prayer.

TRANSLATION

When you are about to finish your subject, you should use the names of the god [Sminthian Apollo] that recall his deeds as follows:

'Now, O Sminthian and Pythian,[9] from you my speech began and to you it will end. With what titles shall I speak to you? Some people name you Lycian,[10] some Delian,[11] some Akraion, others Actian.[12] The Lacedemonians address you as Amyclaean,[13] the Athenians as Patroan,[14] the Milesians as Branchiate.[15] Every city and every land and every nation do you control; and just as you dance around the heaven having the choruses of stars around you, so you also control the entire inhabited realm of humankind.[16] As Mithras the Persians address you,[17] as Horus the Egyptians (for you lead the seasons [*horai*] in their cycle),[18] as "Dionysus" the Thebans. The people of Delphi honour you with a double name: "Apollo" and "Dionysus".[19] Around you dances the chorus of Muses [text is uncertain],[20] around you are the Thyades [?].[21] From you the moon also receives her ray. The Chaldeans address you as "ruler of the stars". Therefore, whether you rejoice in these appellations or in titles better than these, keep granting that this city may always flourish at the height of blessedness, and that this cultic assembly may forever be joyfully organized for you. And incline favourably also to these words; for from you come both words and city.'[22]

NOTES

1   Professional teacher of the art of rhetoric, persuasive speech.

2 On the Lycus River in Western Asia Minor (modern Turkey).
3 Apollo is one of the pan-Hellenic Greek gods, universally respected throughout the Greek world. Apollo has two sites that transcend local significance: the island of Delos, his birthplace, and Delphi, the seat of his most important oracle. On Apollo and the related mythology see Burkert, (1985), pp. 143–9.
4 No manuscript is without error, as the problem with the text's 'Muses' and 'Thyades' makes clear. The first is a conjecture to make sense of the text; Thyades, which stands in the manuscripts, is a term whose meaning is unknown. It must describe a group close to the Muses, whom we cannot otherwise identify.
5 A literary parallel to the Menander prayer exists in Statius, *Thebaid* 1.696–720.
6 On Apollo's complex role see Rose, (1953), pp. 134–45. Apollo was also the father of Asclepius, the god of medicine.
7 Kennedy, *Greek Rhetoric Under Christian Emperors*, p. 293.
8 ibid., pp. 174, 229, 240, 270.
9 Menander places two titles of Apollo at the head of his prayer: 'Sminthian' ('mouse killer') reminds the auditors that Apollo both caused and averted plague, since the mouse was regarded as an agent of plague. (The title is also tied to a site in Asia Minor.) 'Pythian' ('Python slayer') calls to mind that at Delphi Apollo slew the Python, the dragon who threatened his mother Leto (see the 'Homeric Hymn to Apollo'), and made Delphi his oracular site.
10 The list of names that follows gives significant information about Apollo. 'Lycian' describes Apollo either as a Lycian god from Asia Minor, or as 'wolf-slayer'. The Lyceum at Athens took its name from a nearby precinct of Apollo. The occurrence of the name at the beginning of the list suggests the possible origins of Apollo in Lycia.
11 Delian: Delos is the island where Apollo was born of Leto. For the myth see *Homeric Hymn* 3, 'to Delian Apollo'.
12 Actian: Actium was an important Roman site for the worship of Apollo Patroos.
13 Amyclaean: from the town Amyclae in Laconia, the territory of Sparta.
14 Patroan: protector, from *pater*, 'father'; Athens recognized Apollo as a tutelary, i.e. protective, god.
15 Branchiate: from Branchidai, alternative name for Apollo's oracular site at Didyma in the territory controlled by Miletus. A processional street connected Didyma to the city of Miletus.
16 Apollo was held to be a sun god in later antiquity; Burkert (1985), p. 406 n. 55. That would account for his universal presence.
17 Greeks (and Romans) identified their gods with those of other nations; thus Apollo with Mithras, a saviour god also associated with the sun, chief deity of a Persian mystery religion, found throughout the Roman world by the third century. Statius, *Thebaid* 1.719–20, suggests the same identification.
18 Horus: Apollo, identified as the sun god, controlled the revolution of the sun, as did the Egyptian god Horus. See Plutarch, 'On Isis and Osiris' 61.375F. Menander uses a folk etymology to interpret the significance of the Egyptian name Horus from the Greek term *horai*, 'hours'. See Russell and Wilson (1981), p. 360.
19 Dionysus: on the equation of the god of wine and revelry with Apollo at Delphi see Burkert (1985), pp. 223–5.
20 Apollo plays the lyre (the *phorminx*) and is claimed as patron by poets and bards. When he plays on Mt Olympus, the Muses sing antiphonally and the gods dance for joy. See *Iliad* 1.44–52; 603–4; *Hom. Hymn to Apollo* 3.179–206.
21 The Greek text is uncertain, the significance unclear.

22 The conclusion justifies calling this Sminthian hymn that concludes the oration a prayer.

SELECTED BIBLIOGRAPHY

Burgess, T. C., *Epideictic Literature*, Chicago, Chicago Studies in Classical Philology 3, 1902.

Burkert, Walter, *Greek Religion*, trans. John Raffan, Cambridge, Mass., Harvard University Press, 1985.

Cairns, Francis, 'A Note on the Editio Princeps of Menander Rhetor', *Eranos*, 1987, vol. 65, pp. 138–9.

Dominik, W. J., 'A Generic-Ontological Reading of Adrastus' Sminthiac prayer (Statius, *Thebaid* 1.696–720)', *Scholia*, 1992, vol. 1, pp. 66–78.

Kennedy, George A., *The Art of Rhetoric in the Roman World*, Princeton, Princeton University Press, 1972, pp. 636–7.

——, *Greek Rhetoric Under Christian Emperors*, Princeton, Princeton University Press, 1983, pp. 25–7, 69–70.

Rose, H. J., *A Handbook of Greek Mythology Including Its Extension to Rome*, 5th edn, London, Methuen, 1953.

Russell, D. A. and Wilson, N. G., *Menander Rhetor*, edited with translation and commentary, Oxford, Clarendon Press, 1981.

Solomon, John (ed.), *Apollo: Origins and Influences*, Tucson and London, The University of Arizona Press, 1994.

32

ORPHIC HYMN 13: TO KRONOS

Larry J. Alderink

INTRODUCTION

The text

The standard edition of the Orphic hymns was prepared by W. Quandt in 1955, based on thirty-seven manuscripts dating to the fifteen and sixteen centuries.[1] Because no ancient testimony regarding the Orphic hymns survives, confidence regarding a date of composition is difficult if not impossible; the content and style of the hymns indicate that they may have been composed during the later years of the Roman empire, with the third or fourth centuries CE most likely.[2] Because hymns are sung to three gods whose names appear in inscriptions from the sanctuary of Demeter in Pergamon, Otto Kern and others have considered this city in Asia Minor as a likely place for the writing and use of the hymns.[3]

Orpheus and Orphism

Orpheus was the legendary poet and musician with shamanic powers, whose voice and lyre could charm nature and who journeyed to the underworld. Marginal among the many mysteries and sects in ancient Greece because of its rejection of animal sacrifices, Orphism was an alternative to the Olympian religion of the Greek city.[4]

Orphics appear to have been active by the late sixth century BCE. Herodotus (2.81) mentions certain rituals that are called Orphic and Bacchic, suggesting that the god Dionysus played an important role in Orphic practices. The Orphic hymns were composed and used considerably later, for they lack references to characteristic themes of the Orphism of the classical period. Although Plato (*Laws* 829d–e) and Pausanias (9.30.12) do mention hymns of Orpheus, they refer to a miscellany of poetry that was frequently ascribed to Orpheus in ancient times; the collection of hymns in which our prayer to Kronos is located consists of some eighty-seven hymns with a prefatory address by Orpheus to Mousaios invoking and addressing Zeus and all the gods. Thus we must distinguish earlier from later Orphic religious motifs.

Orphic creation accounts of the fifth and fourth centuries BCE portrayed both the origin of the cosmos and the succession of deities whose rule over the universe culminated in its present lord, Zeus.[5] Soteriological motifs are also prominent in early Orphic materials, as we learn from Aristotle (*De Anima* 1.5.410b) that the Orphic poems of his day distinguished the soul from the body and from Plato (*Cratylus* 400c and *Phaedo* 62b) that the soul was placed in a body as a prisoner guarded by the gods. The Orphic explanation for the entrance of the soul into the body is given by the myth of the dismemberment and eating of the child Dionysus by the Titans. Zeus' thunderbolt reduced the Titans to ashes, from which the human species arose, partly Titanic and partly Dionysiac. A variety of sources provides evidence for an Orphic interest in eschatological matters, with instructions for the soul's journey to the underworld and speaking to the gods upon arrival.[6] Euripides (*Hippolytus* 952–3), Aristophanes (*Frogs* 1032) and Plato (*Laws* 782) mention Orphic initiatory rituals as well as prohibitions on eating meat and sacrificing animals, suggesting that a soul's destiny after death is shaped by its behaviour in its body. Plato (*Republic* 364d–365a) and the Derveni Theogony (16.2–12) offer some hints about early cultic practices and group existence when they mention liturgical texts whose use promised to eliminate guilt, pardon injustices and save from punishment in a life after death.

The Orphic hymns

The Orphic hymns enable us to detect some themes of early Orphism in altered form. Preoccupation with the divine creation of the world and the struggles for power and governance among the gods have receded in favour of connecting deities with the processes of nature. Hymn 10 does address Nature as self-originated and self-sufficient, participating in no one and that in which all participates. Yet in Hymn 55, Aphrodite is the source and controller of everything, and Rhea is addressed in Hymn 14 as the mother of gods and humans and the source of earth and sky. Similarly, the earlier tendency to assimilate the many deities of the Greek pantheon into Zeus in the mythical episode of his swallowing all the other gods (Derveni) or defeating them in conflict (Rhapsodic Theogony) persists in the Orphic hymns by imagining the many gods in one form. Thus, the creator of the world can be called Physis, Rhea, the Titans collectively, Okeanos, or Zeus. A reverse process can also be observed, for one god, particularly Zeus, can stand for all the gods in what we may call syncretistic henotheism.

When Kronos is addressed in Orphic Hymn 13, several typical Orphic features of his character are noticeable. His mental acumen distinguishes him from the more orthodox Hesiodic presentation where he is courageous in eliminating his tyrannical and repressive father but also foolish for losing his throne to his own son and thus repeating his father's mistake (Theogony 154–210 and 453–506). In Hymn 13, Kronos is also addressed as the god in charge of the natural processes of growth and decline, and thus in control of the entire cosmos; even though in other Orphic myths he was replaced by his son, Zeus, here he inhabits the universe he created and rules. The final Orphic theme to appear in Hymn 13 is dual, consisting of the desire for a good life as well as purity at the end of life. The exact content of a good life cannot be identified from any of the Orphic hymns, although Hymn 4, to Ouranos, requests a life of holiness for new initiates. Perhaps early Orphic references to a 'way of life' in Euripides (*Hippolytus* 952–3), Aristophanes (*Frogs* 1032) and Plato (*Laws* 6.782) which mention initiatory rituals as well as a prohibition on eating meat and sacrificing animals are relevant here. The desire for a good death is found in other hymns, such as Hymn 20, where the suppliant asks Zeus to bring a good end to life.

Orphic prayers

Determining the communal and ritual use of a specific hymn, or indeed of the entire collection, is nearly impossible. Throughout the hymns the needs of everyday life are shaped into requests – for crops and food, easy births, safe travels, relief from fears in the night, and peace and health. References to rituals and to favours, particularly the presence of gods in the lives of initiates and celebrants, are common. Clearly those who prayed made specific requests and may very well have offered their prayers in a communal setting.

Prayers figure prominently in ancient Greek rituals, most often providing the words to the rituals they accompany.[7] After preparation through washing and dressing, for example, Penelope asked Athena for protection for Odysseus because he had sacrificed cows and sheep to the goddess (*Odyssey* 4.759–67). Achilles followed a similar pattern when he purified his wine cup before pouring a libation to Zeus and making two requests of him (one was granted, the other denied!). The composition of these prayers is three-fold: invocation or address, reason or justification for a request, and the request proper (*Iliad* 16.225–48).[8] The prayers demonstrate a tendency to offer praise to the deity and to expect favours from them.

TRANSLATION

To Kronos, incense storax

1   Ethereal father of blessed gods and men,

2 subtle of mind, pure, mighty and powerful Titan:
3 You who supervise the growth and decline of all things,
4 unbreakable is your control of the boundless cosmos!
5 O Kronos, father of all beings and creator of time, O Kronos of
    many voices,
6 the child of earth and starry sky,
7 in whom are birth and growth and decline, [you are] the husband
    of Rhea, majestic forethought,
8 you live in every part of the cosmos [as] the ruler of creation,
9 clever and most brave. Hear my suppliant voice,
10 and bring a good life to a blameless end.

NOTES

1 W. Quandt, *Orphei Hymni*, Berlin, Weidmann Verlag, 1955.
2 W.K.C. Guthrie, *Orpheus and Greek Religion*, Princeton, Princeton University Press, 1993, pp. 256–67 and A.N. Athanassakis, *The Orphic Hymns*, Atlanta, Scholars, 1977, pp. vii–viii.
3 O. Kern, 'Das Demeterheiligtum von Pergamon und die orphischen Hymnen', *Hermes*, 1911, vol. 46, pp. 431–46 and W.K.C. Guthrie, op. cit., pp. 259-61.
4 W. Burkert, 'Craft versus Sect: The Problem of Orphics and Pythagoreans', in B.F. Meyer and E.P. Sanders (eds), *Jewish and Christian Self-Definition*, Philadelphia, Fortress, 1982, pp. 1–22; Burkert, *Ancient Mystery Cults*, Cambridge, Mass., Harvard University Press, 1987, pp. 30–53; J.N. Bremmer, *Greek Religion*, Oxford, Oxford University Press, 1994, pp. 88–9.
5 W.K.C. Guthrie, op. cit., pp. 69–147; L.J. Alderink, *Creation and Salvation in Ancient Orphism*, Chico, CA, Scholars, 1981, pp. 25–53; W. Burkert, *Greek Religion*, trans. John Raffan, Cambridge, Mass., Harvard University Press, 1985, pp. 296–98; and M.L. West, *The Orphic Poems*, Oxford, Oxford University Press, 1983, pp. 84–90, 117–21, 215–26 and 234–43.
6 G. Zuntz, *Persephone: Three Essays on Religion and Thought in Magna Graecia*, Oxford, Clarendon Press, 1971, pp. 275–393; S. Cole, 'New Evidence for the Mysteries of Dionysos', *Greek, Roman, and Byzantine Studies*, 1980, vol. 21, pp. 223–38; R. Janko, 'Forgetfulness in the Golden Tablets of Memory', *Classical Quarterly*, 1984, vol. 34, pp. 89–100; K. Tsantsanoglou and G. Parassoglou, 'Two Gold Lamellae from Thessaly', *Hellenika*, 1987, vol. 38, pp. 3–17; H. Lloyd-Jones, *Greek Epic, Lyric, and Tragedy*, Oxford, Clarendon Press, 1990, pp. 80–109.
7 W. Burkert, *Greek Religion*, p. 73.
8 J.M. Bremer, 'Greek Hymns', in H.S. Versnel (ed.), *Faith, Hope and Worship: Aspects of Religious Mentality in the Ancient World*, Leiden, E.J. Brill, 1981; Jan N. Bremmer, op. cit., p. 39, and W. Burkert, *Greek Religion*, pp. 73–5.

SELECTED BIBLIOGRAPHY

Alderink, Larry J., *Creation and Salvation in Ancient Orphism*, Chico, CA, Scholars, 1981.
Anonymous, *Derveni Theogony, Zeitschrift für Papyrologie und Epigraphik*, 1982, vol. 47, pp. 1–12

Athanassakis, Apostolos N., *The Orphic Hymns*, Atlanta, Scholars, 1977.

Bremer, J.M., 'Greek Hymns', in H.S. Versnel (ed.), *Faith, Hope and Worship: Aspects of Religious Mentality in the Ancient World*, Leiden, E.J. Brill, 1981, pp. 193–215.

Bremmer, Jan N., *Greek Religion*, Oxford, Oxford University Press, 1994.

Burkert, Walter, 'Craft versus Sect: The Problem of Orphics and Pythagoreans', in B.F. Meyer and E.P. Sanders (eds), *Jewish and Christian Self-Definition*, Philadelphia, Fortress, 1982, pp. 30–53.

—— *Greek Religion*, trans. John Raffan, Cambridge, Mass., Harvard University Press, 1985.

—— *Ancient Mystery Cults*, Cambridge, Mass., Harvard University Press, 1987.

Cole, Susan, 'New Evidence for the Mysteries of Dionysos', *Greek, Roman, and Byzantine Studies*, 1980, vol. 21, pp. 223–38.

Guthrie, W.K.C., *Orpheus and Greek Religion*, Princeton, Princeton University Press, 1993.

Janko, Richard, 'Forgetfulness in the Golden Tablets of Memory', *Classical Quarterly*, 1984, vol. 34, pp. 89–100.

Kern, Otto, 'Das Demeterheiligtum von Pergamon und die orphischen Hymnen', *Hermes*, 1911, vol. 46, pp. 431–46.

Lloyd-Jones, Hugh, *Greek Epic, Lyric, and Tragedy*, Oxford, Clarendon Press, 1990.

Quandt, W., *Orphei Hymni*, Berlin, Weidmann Verlag, 1955.

Tsantsanoglou, K. and G. Parassoglou, G., 'Two Gold Lamellae from Thessaly', *Hellenika*, 1987, vol. 38, pp. 3–17.

West, M.L., *The Orphic Poems*, Oxford, Oxford University Press, 1983.

Zuntz, Günther, *Persephone: Three Essays on Religion and Thought in Magna Graecia*, Oxford, Clarendon Press, 1971.

33

HYMN TO SELENE–HECATE– ARTEMIS FROM A GREEK MAGICAL HANDBOOK (*PGM* IV 2714–83)

Christopher A. Faraone

INTRODUCTION

This prayer is embedded in a magical recipe which bears the rubric: *Agōgē* ('Spell for Attraction [i.e. of a Lover]'), a popular genre of erotic spell that is almost always designed to force an unwilling female to abandon her family and come to make love to the practitioner. Because it is part of a handbook, the names of the male practitioner and his female target are indicated generically as 'Mr so-and-so' and 'Ms so-and-so' (*ho deina* and *hē deina* respectively). As is true for nearly all Greek prayers, this one is set in the context of a ritual: the recipe directs us to burn Ethiopian cumin and fat from a goat on a roof-top on the thirteenth or fourteenth of the month, while saying the long prayer (the recipe calls it a *logos*[1]) which is translated below. The text is, in fact, composed almost entirely in dactylic hexameters[2] and takes the rhetorical form of a cletic hymn – a type of hymn used to summon a far-off deity to come close, listen to the petitioner and eventually grant his or her request. The papyrus handbook (*PGM* IV) itself dates to the fourth century CE and most probably comes from the personal library of a professional magician working in Upper Egypt.[3] The date of composition for this individual spell is of course earlier, but it is impossible to say how much earlier. The syncretism of Hecate–Selene–Artemis can be dated as early as the late classical period, as can Hecate's association with ghosts and crossroads.[4] The Hellenistic poet Theocritus, moreover, seems to have imitated hymns like this one in his Idyll 2, the first half of which constitutes an elaborate hexametrical incantation that evokes the same triad of goddesses for the same purpose: the erotic arousal of another person.[5] There are three other examples of hexametrical hymns to Selene–Hecate–Artemis in the same handbook: *PGM* IV 2242–2417, 2522–67 and 2786–2870.

The text of this hymn divides neatly into four sections, each of which begins with a summons to Hecate (three out of four of these sections begin with *deur' Hecate* ['Hither Hecate']). The first and third sections are primarily cletic invocations designed to summon the goddess under several different guises from a variety of far-off places, for example: as Baubo she is summoned from Persia; as Artemis from Lydia; and as Ereschigal from Assyria.[6] The second and fourth sections, on the other hand, focus primarily on the immediate goal of the hymn: to drive the female target mad with insomnia so that she abandons her family and comes immediately to the door of the man singing the hymn.[7] It is interesting that in section two, it is Hecate's ghostly companions who are expected to carry out these actions, while in the final section Hecate herself is asked to accomplish the spell.

TRANSLATION[8]

Hither[9] Hecate, giant who protects Dionē,[10] Persian Baubo, Phroune, <goddess>[11] who pours forth arrows, unwedded Lydian, untamed, of noble father, torch-holder, leader who bends down the necks (i.e. of mortals), Kore, hear me, O Artemis, you who have completely closed the gates of unbreakable adamantine and (i.e. you) who even before were the greatest overseer, Lady, earth-cleaver, leader of the hounds, subduer of all, (sc. worshipped) in the streets, three-headed, light-bearing, august virgin,[12] I call you, fawn-slayer, wily lady of the underworld,[13] who appears in many forms.

Hither Hecate, goddess of the crossroads, with your fire-breathing ghosts, you (i.e. the ghosts) who have got as your allotment horrible ambushes[14] and irksome haunts, I call you, Hecate, with those who have died before their time and with those of the heroes, who hissing wildly with anger in their hearts[15] have died without wife or children. You[16] stand above the head {of Ms so-and-so}[17] and take sweet sleep from her. May her eyelids never be closely joined with each other, but rather let her be worn out over her wakeful thoughts about me. And if she is lying down with another man in her embrace, let her push that man away and let her put me (i.e. thoughts of me) down into her heart and let her immediately forsake him and quickly come stand near my doors, subdued in her soul for my wedding bed.

But come, O Hecate of the many names, virgin Kore,[18] come goddess, I command you, O Persephone, guardian and shelterer of the threshing floor, triple-headed <goddess>, who wanders with fiery torches,[19] the cow-eyed one, BOUORPHORBE,[20] all fearful, terrifying,[21] Aktiophi,[22] Ereschigal, NEBOUTOSOUALETH by the gates PUPULEDEDEZO and cleaver of gates.

Hither Hecate of the fiery will, I call you to my incantations,[23] may she, {Ms so-and so} come to my doors driven mad, immediately forgetting the intimacy of her children and parents, and hating the entire race of men and women, except this (sc. race?) of mine, Mr so-and-so,[24] and may she come and stand near holding me alone, subdued in her heart by the strong necessity of love.[25] THENOB TITHELEB ENOR TITHELEB, many named one, KUZALEOUSA PAZAOUS; wherefore, KOLLIDECHMA and SAB set her soul ablaze with tireless fire. Also you Orion and Michael, who sits on high: you hold sway over the seven waters and the earth, by restraining him whom they call the great serpent, AKROKODERE, Lion, Ram, Horus,[26] Adonai, Zeus, DE, Damnameneus, KUNOBIOU EZAGRA. (Add) the usual.[27] Io![28] goddess who rules everything, io! goddess who protects everything, io! goddess who nourishes everything, ZELACHNA, SAAD SABIOTHE NOUMILLON NATHOMEINA, AEIKEINETH, mighty Theseus, Onyx, crafty Damnameneus, avenger, valiant goddess of ghosts, Persian SEBARA AKRA. Hasten immediately and indeed let her come stand near my doors.

NOTES

1 F. Graf, 'Prayer in Magical and Religious Ritual', in C.A. Faraone and D. Obbink (eds), *Magika Hiera: Ancient Greek Magic and Religion*, Oxford, 1991, p. 194, notes that in the magical papyri the designation *logos* is (in this context, at least) always interchangeable with *euchē*, 'prayer'.

2 Dactylic hexameters is the traditional Greek metre for epic narratives (Homer and Hesiod), hymns, oracles and incantations. For an introductory discussion see T.G. Rosenmeyer, M. Ostwald and J.W. Halporn, *The Meters of Greek and Latin Poetry*, New York, 1963, pp. 10–12.

3 *PGM* IV and the several other large magical and alchemical handbooks that comprised the 'Anastasi Collection' were probably all part of a single cache of handbooks owned by a magician living in the neighbourhood of Thebes. See H.D. Betz (ed.), *The Greek Magical Papyri in Translation*, Chicago, 1986, p. xlii; and G. Fowden, *The Egyptian Hermes: A Historical Approach to the Late Pagan Mind*, Cambridge, 1986, pp. 168–74.

4 For the syncretism, see T. Hopfner, 'Hekate–Selene–Artemis und Verwandte in der griechischen Zauberpapyri und auf den Fluchtafeln', in *Pisciculi: Festschriften F.J. Dölger*, Münster, 1939, pp. 125–45. For Hecate's traditional connection with crossroads and ghosts, see S. Iles Johnston, 'Crossroads', *Zeitschrift für Papyrologie und Epigraphik* 88, 1991, pp. 213–20.

5 For the affinities between Theocritus' poem and the Greek tradition of hexametrical incantations, see C.A. Faraone, 'The "Performative Future" in Three Hellenistic Incantations and Theocritus' Second Idyll', *Classical Philology*, 90, 1995, p. 1–15.

6 Many of the names used in this hymn are, in fact, unfamiliar to us. This type of syncretism is the hallmark of Greek hymnody from the Hellenistic period onward, for example the so-called Isis Aretalogies, which assimilate that Egyptian goddess with scores of other goddesses linked to specific cities or lands spread throughout the eastern Mediterranean. In my translation I print

the names of unknown divinities in capital letters. See Graf, op. cit., pp. 189–97, for a discussion of how these so-called *voces magicae* operate like the other comprehensible Greek names and epithets: all are designed ultimately to flatter and persuade the deity.

7 For a detailed analysis of similar spells which aim to torture the victim with sleeplessness, madness and pain, see C.A. Faraone, 'The Wheel, the Whip and Other Implements of Torture: Erotic Magic in Pindar *Pythian* 4. 213-19', *Classical Journal*, 88, 1993, pp. 1–19.

8 Text: K. Preisendanz and A. Henrichs (eds), *Papyri graecae magicae: Die griechischen Zauberpapyri²*, Stuttgart, 1973 (= *PGM*). Unless otherwise noted, I follow the reconstruction of E. Heitsch that appears as 'Hymn 21' in vol. 2 of *PGM* on pages 259–60.

9 The Greek adverb (*deuro*, 'hither') that opens this text is a standard marker of a cletic hymn, see, for example, the opening line of Sappho's famous hymn to Aphrodite: 'Hither [*deuru*, the form in Sappho's Lesbian dialect] to me from Crete to this temple . . .'; see D.A. Campbell, *Greek Lyric*, vol. 1, Cambridge, Mass., 1982, pp. 56–7.

10 Dionē is an alternative name of Aphrodite. Here, however, we would expect it to be a place name or some geographical entity (e.g. 'of Cyprus'), since it is in the genitive case and must have a construction with the noun *medousa* e.g.: 'protectress of Dionē'.

11 Angle brackets indicate words added by Heitsch, op. cit., to restore the metre.

12 This unbroken string of epithets recalls the contemporary 'Orphic hymns' with their long series of divine names and adjectives; in general, see the analyses of three other *PGM* hymns by B. Kuster, *De tribus carminibus papyri parisinae magicae*, Königsberg, 1911. The reference to the opening of the gates and the role of the *episkopos* seems to narrate mythic events in the past, whose effects are however still felt. Thus the phrase *kai prosthen* seems best translated '(you) who even before this were the greatest overseer (i.e. and still are)'.

13 Reading *doloessa* (with Wünsch) and *Aidônaia* (with Reitzenstein); see the apparatus criticus in *PGM*. The papyrus has *loessa audnaia* which does not scan metrically and is not recognizable Greek.

14 The word *hodos* here is literally 'road', but the word does have a specialized hostile meaning, for example 'inroad' or 'ambush', that works best here in parallel construction with *epipompe*, which means 'hostile supernatural attack'.

15 The papyrus indicates that the scribe or his source knew an alternative version of the end of this line. At this point he writes: 'Others (sc. read): holding the form of winds' (i.e. instead of 'holding anger in their hearts').

16 The verbal and participial forms here are plural and must continue to refer to Hecate's companions, the fire-breathing ghosts.

17 These brackets indicate that the word(s) are hyper-metrical, i.e. they can be removed without affecting the metre of the line. Apparently the name of the potential victim was not expected to fit neatly into the hexameter; but see below note 24 where the generic marker *ho deina* seems to fit the metrical line.

18 Literally 'Girl', but also the most common cult name for Persephone, the Queen of the Underworld and a goddess connected with the fertility of grain. See the next line for a reference to the threshing floor and Persephone.

19 E.N. O'Neil in Betz, op. cit., p. 89, translates 'wanders in fire', but I think it is best to envisage Hecate with torches, a common attribute.

20 This word is nonsense in Greek, but part of a well-known *vox magica*; see D.R. Jordan, '*Defixiones* in a Well near the Southwest Corner of the Athenian Agora', *Hesperia*, 54, 1985, pp. 240–1.

21 Following C. Harrauer, *Meliouchos: Studien zur Entwicklung religiöser Vorstellungen in griechischen syncretistischen Zaubertexten*, Wiener Studien Beiheft 11, Vienna, 1987, p. 64, who interprets the two words here (*panphorba pharbara*) as variants of Greek *pamphobera phobera*. She notes, pp. 57–8, that Hecate is called *pamphobera* on a third-century CE *defixio* from Alexandria.

22 Aktiophi(s) occurs in many other places in the *PGM* as an epithet of Selene, but its precise meaning or reference is unknown.

23 At this point the papyrus inserts the following well-known magical formula: MASKELLI MASKELLO PNOUKENTABAO OREOBAZAGRA RHEXICHTHON HIPPOCHTHON PYRIPEGANYX. See Betz, op. cit., p. 336, for discussion and bibliography. As this formula is not metrical and disrupts the hexameters of the hymn, I have excluded it from the translation as a later accretion. This prosaic material was presumably inserted mistakenly by some scribe who did not understand that the reference here to *epaoidai* ('incantations') refers self-reflexively to the hexameters themselves.

24 Here the generic marker *ho deina* fits the metre of the line (see note 17 above).

25 From here to the end of the hymn, the lines are imperfectly hexametrical and the content does not quite fit with what comes earlier. Most notable and jarring is the string of powerful male gods in a prayer ostensibly addressed to a goddess (Hecate). Heitsch does not include them in his text of 'Hymn 21', so I use the text of the *PGM*, loc. cit. Presumably this last section was added at a later time by a redactor. Harrauer, op. cit., pp. 65–6, notes the marked Egyptian or Coptic character of much of this section, e.g. the seven waters (= the seven mouths of the Nile) and the mention of the great serpent (Apophis). See the following note for her analysis of some of the names as Coptic.

26 I follow Harrauer, op. cit., p. 66, who divides MOUISRO into two Coptic words *Moui* ('Lion') and *Sro* ('Ram') and interprets CHARCHAR as a form of Horus' name. As I understand and punctuate the text, the word AKROKODERE is not the name of the 'great serpent', but rather it returns us to the list of powerful male deities such as Horus, Zeus and Adonai.

27 The parenthetical marker here (*koinon*) is shorthand for: 'finish this *logos* with the usual materials', indicating that this string of names was fairly well known to the practitioners of the day.

28 O'Neil, op. cit., translates Io as a name of a deity, but I prefer to see it as the Greek poetic interjection addressed to a divinity in time of great danger or stress. See H. G. Liddell, R. Scott and H.S. Jones, *Greek–English Lexicon*, Oxford, 1968, ad loc.

SELECTED BIBLIOGRAPHY

H.D. Betz (ed.), *The Greek Magical Papyri in Translation*, Chicago, 1986.

C.A. Faraone, 'The Wheel, the Whip and Other Implements of Torture: Erotic Magic in Pindar *Pythian* 4. 213-19', *Classical Journal*, 88, 1993, pp. 1–19.

F. Graf, 'Prayer in Magical and Religious Ritual', in C.A. Faraone and D. Obbink (eds), *Magika Hiera: Ancient Greek Magic and Religion*, Oxford, 1991, pp. 188–213.

C. Harrauer, *Meliouchos: Studien zur Entwicklung religiöser Vorstellungen in griechischen syncretistischen Zaubertexten*, Wiener Studien Beiheft 11, Vienna, 1987.

T. Hopfner, 'Hekate–Selene–Artemis und Verwandte in der griechischen Zauberpapyri und auf den Fluchtafeln', in *Pisciculi: Festschriften F.J. Dölger*, Münster, 1939, 125–45.

B. Kuster, *De tribus carminibus papyri parisinae magicae*, Königsberg, 1911.

34

THE HERMETIC *PRAYER OF THANKSGIVING*, NAG HAMMADI CODEX VI, 7: 63, 33–65, 7

Richard Valantasis

INTRODUCTION

The following prayer comes from the Coptic Nag Hammadi Library discovered in Egypt nearly fifty years ago. The Nag Hammadi Library contains a wide assortment of religious and philosophical material including three texts of Hermetic writings from the Greco-Roman period.

The religion of Hermes Trismegistus

The Roman god Hermes (associated with fertility, travel and oratory) was identified in the Hellenistic and Roman periods with the Egyptian god Toth. The two gods were combined and each became a part of the name Hermes Trismegistus, where the epithet 'Trismegistus' mistranslates 'Toth the Greatest'. This Greco-Egyptian god functions in the literature of this movement as spiritual mentor and guide to the knowledge of the universe.[1]

Hermeticism was an important philosophical religious movement which claimed ancient Egyptian origins, but which seems to have thrived primarily in the first four centuries of our era. This religious movement promulgated an initiation into philosophical religion headed by the god Hermes Trismegistus, 'Hermes the Thrice Great' god, who was the devotees' guide, by combining a kind of gnosticism with philosophical speculation in religious ritual and worship. It was a very popular religion. These religious communities probably consisted of men alone. Because Hermeticism is 'syncretistic' (that is, because it gathers religious myths, philosophical religious concepts, magical practices and liturgical forms from many of the religions which flourished around it) Hermetic literature expresses a wide diversity of mythological, theological, philosophical and religious perspectives all of which are revealed by Hermes Trismegistus or his divine intermediaries. The dialogue between Hermes (or his intermediary) and the initiate is the primary genre of literature of the majority of Hermetic texts. This prayer represents a traditional piece of Hermetic religious practice and seems to be indicative of one style of prayer and the orientation toward worship in these communities.

Hermetic communities

Hermetic religion thrived in the Greco-Roman and Late Antique period among a group of elite, well-educated men. The combination of liturgical and philosophical material indicates that the society of such men not only satisfied their intellectual yearnings, but also addressed their need for male religious association. Hermetic literature survived as the province of male philosophical speculation and religious practice into the Renaissance and following: in 1462, the Greek Byzantine text was given by Cosimo di Medici to Marsilio Ficino for translation into Latin. It became an essential part not only of the Renaissance rediscovery of classical texts, but also of the Renaissance and early modern interest in alchemy and early scientific chemistry. The impact of this Hermetic literature on the western European intellectual tradition has just begun to be appreciated.

The Hermetic prayer

The English translation here comes from the Coptic version found in Codex VI of the Nag Hammadi Library.[2] Codex VI contains three Hermetic writings: 'The Discourse on the Eighth and Ninth' and a large section of the work known as the 'Asclepius', between which stands this prayer. Two other versions of the prayer exist. Papyrus Mimaut (Paris, Louvre, Papyrus 2391) col. XVIII, 591–611 preserves a Greek version that was further edited by K. Preisendanz in his collection of Greek magical papyri. This Greek version was already gathered into a longer magical prayer of which it is a small part. A Latin translation from the Greek also exists in the *Corpus Hermeticum Asclepius* (41b). The prayer forms the conclusion of the 'Asclepius'. The prayer, then, may be understood as an independent piece of Hermetic liturgical tradition that floated from environment to environment and from place to place within the Hermetic literature, but that found its place as the median point between these two texts in the Coptic tradition of Nag Hammadi. Even though its original was in Greek (the original Greek text not having survived except in the very corrupt later magical form in Papyrus Mimaut), it is generally conceded that the Coptic version represents the earliest extant text of the prayer. The material evidence, that is, the date of Codex VI and the rest of the Nag Hammadi Library, seems to come from the early part of the fourth century CE, while the text of the prayer probably comes from the end of the second or beginning of the third century CE.

The narrative envelope

There are actually two different voices in the text which follows. The most notable voice is that of the prayer itself which addresses the deity and makes supplication to the divinity (see below).

The second voice is that of the narrative frame that encloses the prayer: a narrative introduces the prayer and a slightly longer narrative concludes it. The first narrative simply indicates that this is the prayer that the community prayed. The concluding narrative, however, indicates that this prayer had a liturgical function, because it stipulates that after the recitation of the prayer, the people praying embraced each other and went to a sacred, bloodless meal. The narrative clearly places this prayer in the context of a cultic liturgy consisting (among other things presumably) of prayer, a ritual embrace and a sacred meal.

This liturgical function for the prayer provides an interesting perspective on the religious practice of this community. The narrative documents a combination of prayer, a liturgical embrace and a meal – elements which in this context seem to provide a sequence of liturgical performances in which the prayer itself leads into a liturgical embrace or kiss which, in turn, precedes the sacred banquet. The banquet would presumably have not included meat, that is, it is either a vegetarian or a special ritualized meal.

The theology of the prayer

The prayer text does not name specifically as Hermes Trismegistus the deity who is addressed, but rather characterizes the deity with attributes such as the deity who is beyond troubling, and named as 'God' and 'Father'. At the end of the prayer the deity again receives characterization as the deity who is known, who is light, who is the womb of God, who sows, gets pregnant and begets. Such metaphoric address reflects the philosophical orientation of the community: the characterizations of the deity remain abstract and distant. They also provide the deity with functions gendered female – at least according to Greco-Roman medicine – so that this 'Father' also begets, sows and has a womb. This combination of attributes gendered both male and female represents a strategy to understand the deity and the deity's function as comprehensive and beyond traditional categories of sexual distinction. Since the Hermetic community itself consisted only of male participants, this inclusive gender strategy provides a fuller gender representation for the male community in which functions gendered as 'female' are assigned not only to the deity but also to the senior members of the community.[3]

The prayer also expresses three interlocking functions. It presents the deity as bestowing mind, discourse and perception. These in turn allow the initiates to understand, interpret and know the deity. These in turn cause the initiates to rejoice because they have received light (received a revelation of the deity), and because they were divinized. The prayer develops these interconnected themes in such a way as to move from intellectual sight to becoming gods through their prayer. The prayer then concludes with a thanksgiving for the gracious good of the deity and a petition that the initiates not fail in their manner of living.

This summary makes clear that the prayer actually says more about the status of the community addressing the prayer than it does about the manner of praying. The people praying experience themselves as becoming divine themselves. They are enlightened, new creatures who rejoice in their heightened and divinized status. Their petition does not revolve about requests for any other good than being able to persevere in their manner of life. This all seems to reflect the entitled status of those praying and participating in the liturgy and ritual of the community at prayer.

TRANSLATION

This is the prayer that they pronounced:

We give You thanks! Every soul and heart is stretched out to You, O name which cannot be troubled, honoured by the name 'God' and praised by the name 'Father'.

Your fatherly good-will, affection and love (extends) to everyone and to everything. And any teaching there may be that is sweet and plain bestows upon us mind, discourse, (and) perception.[4] Mind (is bestowed) so that we may understand You; discourse, so that we may interpret You; perception, so that we may know You.

We rejoice since we have received light from Your knowledge. We rejoice because You have shown us Yourself. We rejoice because while we were in (the) body, You have made us gods through Your knowledge.

The thanksgiving of the one who reaches to You is one thing: that we know You. We have known You, O noetic light. O life of life, we have known You. O womb of every sowing, we have known You. O womb pregnant with the form of the Father, we have known You. O eternal continuance of the Father who begets, thus have we greeted Your goodness.[5]

There is one wish that we ask: we wish to be preserved in knowledge. And there is one protection that we wish: that we not slip in this kind of life.

When they had pronounced these things in prayer, they kissed each other and they went to eat their sacred, bloodless food.

NOTES

1   See H. Koester, *Introduction to the New Testament*, Philadelphia, Fortress Press, 1982, vol. I, pp. 388–9.
2   The text translated here (as well as the Latin and the Greek versions) is that of P. Dirkse and J. Brashler (eds and trans.), 'The Prayer of Thanksgiving (VI, 7: 63, 33–65, 7)' in Douglas M. Parrott (ed.), *Nag Hammadi Codices V, 2-5 and VI With Papyrus Berolinensis 8502 1 and 4*, Nag Hammadi Studies XI, Leiden, E. J. Brill, 1979, pp. 375–87.
3   This process of gender conflation and its relationship to the community is discussed more fully in my *Spiritual Guides of the Third Century*, Minneapolis, Fortress Press, 1991, pp. 84–6.
4   The philosophical interests of the community form an essential element of the request here. These abstract principles (mind, discourse and perception) contrast markedly with the affectionate and personal language of the introductory phrase of the prayer.
5   The combination of the male and female functions (begetting and womb) underscores the gender dynamic within the theological understanding of the deity and within the community itself. This is very dramatic and strong language metaphorizing the theology of Hermes.

SELECTED BIBLIOGRAPHY

Dirkse, Peter and Brashler, James (eds and trans.), 'The Prayer of Thanksgiving (VI, 7: 63, 33-65, 7)' in Douglas M. Parrott (ed.), *Nag Hammadi Codices V, 2–5 and VI With Papyrus Berolinensis 8502 1 and 4*, Nag Hammadi Studies XI, Leiden, E. J. Brill, 1979, pp. 375–87.

Festugière, A.-J., *La Révélation d'Hermès Trismégiste*, Paris, Société d'edition Les Belles Lettres, 1983.

Mahé, Jean-Pierre (ed.), *Hermès en Haute-Egypt: Les Textes hermétiques de Nag Hammadi et leurs parallèlles grecs et latins*, Québec, Les Presses de l'Université Laval, 1978–82.

Grese, William C., *Corpus Hermeticum XIII and Early Christian Literature*, Leiden, E. J. Brill, 1979.

Nock, Arthur Darby (ed.), *Corpus Hermeticum*, trans. A.-J. Festugière. Paris, S Société d'Édition Les Belles Lettres, 1983.

Preisendanz, Karl and Henrichs, Albert, *Papyri Graecae Magicae*, second edition, Stuttgart, Teubner, 1973, vol. I, pp. 56–96.

Valantasis, Richard, *Spiritual Guides of the Third Century: A Semiotic Study of the Guide–Disciple Relationship in Christianity, Neoplatonism, Hermetism, and Gnosticism*, Harvard Dissertations in Religion, 27, Minneapolis, Fortress, 1991.

Van Moorsel, G., *The Mysteries of Hermes Trismegistus: A Phenomenologic Study in the Process of Spiritualisation in the Corpus Hermeticum and Latin Asclepius*, Utrecht, Drukkerij en Uitgververij, 1955.

Part III

CHRIST TRADITIONS

35

PRAYER IN THE NEW TESTAMENT

Bonnie Thurston

The importance of the Jewish antecedents of the Church's life of prayer can hardly be over-estimated.[1] The earliest Christians prayed at the times and according to the forms established by Temple and synagogue practice (see Acts 2:46; 3:1,11; 5:12–21). Catacomb paintings also suggest that they adopted the most common Jewish position of prayer, standing with arms outstretched and palms upward. Later as the church moved into the Greco-Roman world, its religious forms and practices began to be incorporated into Christianity. And it is the language of Hellenism in which the earliest Church recorded its prayers.

In the New Testament several Greek words are rendered into English by the word 'prayer'. A brief summary of that vocabulary gives some sense of the parameters of prayer in the period which runs roughly from the late 40s CE when Paul wrote his first epistles through the early to mid-second century when the Pastoral and Catholic epistles were probably composed.

Euchē and the words derived from it are the most commonly used words for prayer in the New Testament. Euchē has the dual meaning of 'prayer' and 'vow'. The papyri show that Christian usage follows the classical and includes both senses of the term. In classical usage the word also means 'a wish' or 'aspiration', and it occurs as well in the sense of a curse or a prayer of imprecation. It is used in the Septuagint in the sense of 'a vow' or 'a thing vowed'. In Hellenistic Greek its verb form, *euchomai*, means both 'to pray to God' and 'to wish', thus restricting somewhat the classical usage which includes 'to pray', 'to vow', 'to promise' and 'to profess loudly'. In Hellenistic Greek *proseuchē* means first 'prayer addressed to God', and also has the derived meaning of a place set apart for prayer (an 'oratory'). Every instance of *proseuchē* in the New Testament denotes either 'a prayer' or 'a place of prayer'. The verb form *proseuchomai* means 'to offer prayer' or simply 'to pray'.

The more difficult word for prayer is *deēsis* which seems to mean petition that can be addressed either to God or to humans. In contrast to *proseuchē* which is limited to prayer to God, *deēsis* gives prominence to the expression of personal need. In classical usage the word denotes 'asking' as well as 'wanting' and 'needing'. It is used both in the papyri and the New Testament for 'supplication', but its New Testament usage seems especially to imply entreaty toward God. The verbal form *deomai* derives from the verb *deō*, 'to want or to need'.

New Testament words which imply specific kinds of prayer include but are not limited to *enteuxis* ('meeting with', 'an interview', thus 'intercession'), *eucharistia* ('giving of thanks'), *aitēma* ('what is asked for' or 'petition'), *hiketēria* ('supplication'), *erōtaō* ('to ask' or 'to beseech') and *ainēsis* ('praise').

In summary, where prayer is alluded to in the New Testament, either *proseuchē* (translated by the Vulgate 'oratio') or *deēsis* (translated by the Vulgate 'deprecatio') is usually found. The words often occur together and distinctions are difficult to make although *proseuchē* usually means offering wishes and desires to God and is always restricted to sacred uses, and *deēsis* implies the imploring of grace for any necessity without the restriction that Deity be addressed.[2]

The vocabulary suggests that in the New Testament prayer is understood first as a verbal activity, as the offering up of requests to God, but also includes wider responses to the Deity, including thanksgiving, praising, glorifying and beholding God. Where, then, do we find prayers in the New Testament? The prayer texts occur in three primary contexts: (a) as explicitly spoken prayers of Jesus in the gospels, of the early Christians in Acts and other writings, and of Paul in his letters; (b) as liturgical fragments woven by the writers of the New Testament into their compositions (prayers which in their contexts are not spoken by a named individual or group); and (c) as part of standard Hellenistic epistolary conventions in the epistles.[3] This volume limits itself to actual prayer texts and omits the very interesting passages which are teachings about prayer (for example, Matthew 6:5–8; Mark 11:22–5; Luke 11:1–13, 18:1–14; Col 4:2–4; James 5:13–18; 1 Peter 3:12).

Representatives of the first category of prayer texts, prayers by Jesus and early Christians, included in this volume are the entries on the Lord's Prayer, John 17, Acts 4:24–30 and the selections from Revelation 4 and 5. This last might also be classified as a liturgical fragment; it is presented in the context of heavenly worship. And the Magnificat, Luke 1:46–55, is also a 'hybrid' form as Luke places in the mouth of Mary a prayer with liturgical associations. Other notable examples of prayers of Jesus and the early Christians include Matthew 11:25–6; John 11:41–2; Acts 7:59–60; Ephesians 3:14–21.

Liturgical fragments which have been inserted by New Testament writers into their works either as illustrative of theological points being made or as ejaculatory prayers are particularly interesting since they frequently reflect the Church's earliest christology[4] and because they are among the few clues we have about the earliest Christian worship. Examples included here are

Philippians 2:6–11 and Colossians 1:15–20. Although within the New Testament there are many occurrences of the practice of inserting liturgical materials, most occur in the Pauline corpus, the general epistles and the later Johannine writings.

The one notable category of New Testament prayers absent from this volume is prayers which are standard features of Hellenistic epistles, notably their thanksgivings and closing doxologies and benedictions. Hellenistic letters began with an address giving the name of the sender, addressee, and a greeting wish. This was followed by a thanksgiving and prayer for those addressed, the body of the letter, and finally a conclusion containing personal greetings and a doxology and blessing.[5] Paul followed this form closely in his letters. Philemon provides a concise example: vv. 1–3 are the address, vv. 4–7 the thanksgiving, vv. 8–20 the body and vv. 21–5 the conclusion. Thus, most of the Pauline letters have at the outset a prayer which Paul uses to focus the epistle and to introduce its theme (see for example Romans 1:8ff.; 1 Cor 1:4ff.; 2 Cor 1:3ff.; 1 Thess 1:2ff.) and close with a doxology and/or benediction (see for example Romans 16:25–7; 1 Cor 16:23; Gal 6:8; Phil 4:19–20, 23). This pattern is followed, although more loosely, by 1 Peter, 3 John and the epistolary frame of the Revelation to John. A more complete anthology of New Testament prayers would certainly include representative examples of these important prayer texts.

NOTES

1   For a fuller discussion see Roger Beckwith, 'The Daily and Weekly Worship of the Primitive Church in Relation to its Jewish Antecedents', *Evangelical Quarterly*, 56, 1984; and Sharon Burns, 'The Roots of Christian Prayer and spirituality in Judaism', in A.W. Sakler (ed), *The Journey of Western Spirituality*, Chico, CA, Scholars Press, 1980.
2   The discussion of etymology depends heavily upon an unpublished essay by Burton B. Thurston, Sr., entitled 'A Comparative Summary of Terminology for Prayer in the New Testament'.
3   For a fairly complete listing of all the prayers in the New Testament with devotional commentary see Donald Coggan, *The Prayers of the New Testament*, London, Hodder & Stoughton, 1967. Exhaustive material is contained in James Charlesworth (ed.), *The Lord's Prayer and Other Prayer Texts from the Greco-Roman Era*, Valley Forge, Trinity, 1994.
4   See Jack T. Sanders, *The New Testament Christological Hymns*, Cambridge, Cambridge University Press, 1971.
5   For fuller discussion see Stanley Stowers, *Letter Writing in Greco-Roman Antiquity*, Philadelphia, Westminster, 1986.

SELECTED BIBLIOGRAPHY

Charlesworth, James, 'A Prolegomenon to a New Study of the Jewish Background of the Hymns and Prayers in the New Testament', *Journal of Jewish Studies*, 33, 1982, pp. 264–85.

Cullman, Oscar, *Prayer in the New Testament,* Minneapolis. Fortress, 1995.
Fisher, Fred L., *Prayer in the New Testament,* Philadelphia, Westminster, 1964.
Miller, Patrick D., *They Cried to the Lord: The Form and Theology of Biblical Prayer,* Minneapolis, Fortress, 1994.

36

A JESUS TRADITION PRAYER (Q 11:2b–4; MATT 6:9b–13; LUKE 11:2b–4; *DIDACHE* 8.2)

R. Conrad Douglas

INTRODUCTION

The 'Lord's Prayer' appears in the *Didache* and the Gospel of Matthew (both late first century CE) and Luke (late first to early second century CE). The similarity, often even identity, of the prayer's Greek wording in the three documents indicates a common preceding tradition ('Q').[1] Efforts to translate the present Greek texts into Aramaic have failed.[2] All three documents offer the prayer as a model for Jesus' followers in the context of longer teachings about worship (Matthew, *Didache*) or prayer (Luke). The prayer has continued to be important to theology and piety.[3]

The prayer's structure is chiastic. In Q, addressing God as Father corresponded to asking for right guidance, praying that God's name be made holy corresponded to praying that people might be freed of debts, and the prayer for God's rule corresponded to the prayer for bread. Matthew and the *Didache* preserve this structure but put the petition for God's will in the centre.[4] In Matthew and the *Didache*, a final petition for deliverance from evil contrasts with the Father in the heavens.

The earliest witnesses to the presently accepted text of the Lukan version of the prayer are the Bodmer papyri P[75] (third century) and B (Codex Vaticanus, fourth century). B is also the earliest available text of the Matthean version. Generally, the Lukan text was assimilated to the Matthean version. A weakly attested textual variant at Luke 11:2 has, 'May your holy spirit come on us and purify us.' God's holy spirit is prominent in Luke-Acts but the poor attestation (MSS 162 and 700, Gregory of Nyssa, Maximus of Turin, Marcion before the 'name' petition), the theological language and a possible baptismal setting show that the line was original to neither Q nor Luke. The *Didache* has two Greek texts: H (minuscule discovered in 1873, dated to 1056) and *P. Oxy.* 1782 (very fragmentary, fourth century). *P. Oxy.* 1782 does not contain the prayer. A mid-fourth-century Ethiopic church order contains *Did.* 8.2 as an insertion.

'The Lucan version has preserved the oldest form with respect to *length*; but the Matthean text is more original with regard to *wording*.'[5] A recent painstaking reconstruction of the Q text of the prayer has confirmed this classic observation.[6] The prayer used in Christian worship today follows Matthew's version of the prayer. Some scholars have suggested that the two New Testamental versions belonged to separate traditions. (The versions in Matthew and the *Didache* closely resemble each other.) These scholars believe no single person would have tampered with Jesus' wording.[7]

It is uncertain whether the historical Jesus taught this prayer. The Gospel of Thomas, an early extra-canonical collection of sayings attributed to Jesus, warns against praying (*GosTh* 14).[8] Moreover, one standard criterion for deciding if a saying is 'authentic' (originated with Jesus) is that the saying be something neither Jews of Jesus' time nor early Christians would have coined (criterion of dissimilarity). There are ample instances from Second Temple Jewish literature, within and outside Palestine, of addresses to God as 'Father' (Isaiah 60; *JosAs* 12:8–15 (Burchard); Wis 14:3; Sir 23:1, 4; 51:10; 3 Macc 6:3, 8; 1QH 9,35; 4Q372 1).[9] The earliest Christian mentions of praying to God as 'Abba' ('Father') appear in Paul's epistles to communities outside Palestine and significantly comprising gentile converts (Gal 4:6 and Rom 8:15). 'Abba' appears in the Synoptics only at Mark (14:36), a Gospel perhaps written far from Palestine, probably for gentiles, and some thirty-five years after Jesus. Greek prayers and hymns also refer to God as Father and as king (cf. the references to God's rule in this prayer) and pray for bread, debt forgiveness and rescue from evil. The prayer's address and petitions reflect beliefs unique to neither Jesus nor early Christians. 'Abba' in itself did not connote a special intimacy. As one recent scholar has put it, 'Abba isn't "Daddy".'[10] The prayer's address to God as 'Father' fails to meet the criterion of dissimilarity.

The prayer did reflect the beliefs of Jesus' earliest followers. In Q, belief in God as Father has a Wisdom background. In Q's earliest developments, God as Father cares for the needs of Jesus's followers (cf. Q 6:20–1; 11:9–13; 12:22–32). Apocalyptic Wisdom myth (see especially 1 Enoch) provides the background for the later polemical contrast in Q 11:20–1 between those granted the Father's revelation and those denied it. In Matthean redaction, God as Father symbolizes the author's appeals for communal unity and for demarcation from the community's rivals (For example, 7:21; 13:43; 18:11, 14, 19, 35, 23:9). The unusual aspect of the address in Matthew and the *Didache* is the phrase, 'who are in (the) heaven(s)'. This phrase reflects the theme of heaven as the locus of God's activity which is to be imitated by humans (see also Matt 6:10; 5:16, 45, 48, 7:21; 10:32–3; 12:50 among others).

The following translation is based on a reconstruction of Q. Luke,

Matthew and the *Didache* all differ from it to some extent. The final line of the versions in Matthew and the *Didache* ('but deliver us from evil') summarizes all the preceding petitions. Rescue from evil means God being Father, God's holiness, God's rule, God's will, food, forgiveness, right guidance. The added line reflects the struggle with evil which preoccupies Matthew.[11] Only the *Didache* closes with, 'For yours is the power and the glory forever.' This acclamation's origins are unknown but may lie in meal customs.

TRANSLATION

Q 11:2b-4

2b   Father,
          may your name be made holy;[12]
          may your rule come;
3   our bread which we need[13]
          give us today;[14]
          and free us of our debts,[15]
          as we also free our debtors;[16]
          and do not put us to the test.[17]

NOTES

1   Citations of Q herein are designated by the corresponding Lukan chapter and verse citations.
2   See H. D. Betz, *The Sermon on the Mount: A Commentary on the Sermon on the Mount, Including the Sermon on the Plain (Matthew 5:3-7:27 and Luke 6:20-49)*, ed. A. Y. Collins, Hermenia, Minneapolis, Fortress, 1995, p. 375, and particularly notes.
3   For the period covered by this anthology, see the commentaries by Tertullian, Clement and Cyprian. For the twentieth century, see D. Curzon (ed.), *The Gospels in Our Image: An Anthology of Twentieth Century Poetry Based on Biblical Texts*, New York, Harcourt Brace, 1995, and M. Crosby, *Thy Will Be Done: Praying the Our Father as Subversive Activity*, Maryknoll, NY, Orbis, 1977.
4   The petition for God's will belongs to a Matthean theme (7:21; 12:50; 18:14; 21:31; 26:42) and corresponds to the prayer at 26:42. The petition for deliverance probably depends on Mark 14:38 *par.* Matt 26:42. The correspondences suggest a martyrological nuance in Matt 6:9b–13. Cynics and Stoics also recommended submission to divine will, including death. 'Sanctification of the name' is a traditional Jewish term for martyrdom; see H. H. Ben-Sasson, 'Kiddush ha-Shem and Hillul ha-Shem', *Encyclopaedia Judaica*, 10, 977–86, New York, Macmillan, 1972, cols.
5   J. Jeremias, *The Prayers of Jesus*, trans. J. Bowden *et al.*; SBT 2.6, London, SCM; Naperville, IL, Allenson, 1967, p. 89.
6   S. Carruth and A. Garsky, *Q 11:2b–4, Documenta Q: Reconstructions of Q through Two Centuries of Gospel Research Excerpted, Sorted, and Evaluated*, Leuven, Peeters, 1996.

7 So, for example, J. Jeremias, op. cit., p. 89.
8 See further R. J. Miller, 'The Lord's Prayer and Other Items from the Sermon on the Mount', *Foundations and Facets Forum*, 5, 1989, pp. 177–86.
9 On the last reference, see E. M. Schuller, '4Q 372 1: A Text about Joseph', *RQ*, 14, 1990, pp. 349–76; idem, 'The Psalm of 4Q 372 1 Within the Context of Second Temple Prayer', *CBQ*, 54, 1992, pp. 67–79. See further G. Schelbert, 'Abba, Vater! Stand der Frage', *Freiburger Zeitschrift für Philosophie und Theologie*, 40, 1993, pp. 259–81.
10 J. Barr, 'Abba isn't "Daddy"', *JTS*, 39, 1988, pp. 28–47, against Jeremias, *Prayers*, 90; idem, *New Testament Theology*, New York, Scribner's, 1971, p. 195. See also G. Schelbert, 'Sprachgeschichtliches zu 'abba', in P. Casetti (ed.), *Mélanges Dominique Barthélemy*, OBO 38, Fribourg, Éditions universitaires, 1981, pp. 395–447.
11 The plea belonged to Jewish and Gentile prayers also (see Betz, op. cit., p. 411 and nn. 560–1).
12 This petition reflects a theme of Jewish literature during ancient Gentile invasions and occupations. See Isa 29:23; 57:15; Ezek 20:39; 36:20, 22, 23; 39:7, 25; 43:7, 8; Sir 17:10; 47:10; Wis 10:20; Philo, *Vita Mos.* 2.208; *Spec. Leg.* 4.40; cf. Isa 52:5; Mal 1:6. On purity as a concern for maintaining boundaries and integrity, see M. Douglas, *Purity and Danger: An Analysis of the Concepts of Pollution and Taboo*, London and New York, Routledge, 1992.
13 The Greek word translated here as 'which we need' is unique in all extant Greek literature and documents. Scholars have suggested as translations: 'necessary' (understood either physically or spiritually); 'for the current day'; 'for the coming day'; and 'that which belongs to it'. The succeeding sayings in Q 11:9–13, the reassurance of God's provision in Matt 6:25–33 and the probability that Matthew brought the segment on anxiety in Matt 6:25–33 closer to the prayer (cf. Luke 12:22–31), and the parable of Luke 11:5–8 provide differing contexts which support this translation. A spiritualizing interpretation may have arisen when interpreters such as Origen shifted from physical to spiritual needs. For God as father and people being fed, see Q 11:9–13 and 12:22–32. In Q 6:20–1, the poor receive God's rule and the hungry and thirsty are fed. The announcement in Q 10:9 that God's rule is close follows a series of sayings about food. The sayings complex in Q 12:22–32 tells the audience not to worry about food but to seek God's rule.
14 'Each day' in Luke 11:3 is secondary. Redaction introduced the phrase elsewhere (Luke 9:23 vs. Mark 8:34; Luke 19:47 vs. Mark 11:18). The phrase appears five times in Luke and six times in Acts; Mark and Matthew each have it once. Use of the phrase with an article is unique to Luke. This change accompanies another, not reproducible in English: present tense of 'give' rather than aorist. Both changes generalize the petition.
15 'Sins' is Lukan and jars with 'debtors' in the next line. 'Debt' for 'sin' is unusual in Hellenistic Greek. 'Debts' belongs to the vivid this-worldly imagery characteristic of Q (Betz, op. cit., p.402, comments that the phrase 'comes from law and commerce' and points out that justice in antiquity meant rendering what was due (194–97, citing Aristotle, *Eth. Nic.*). To ask release from debts was to admit an injustice pervading a relationship; to release debts was to act as a beneficent patron (cf. Matt 18:21–35).
16 'As we also' does not mean 'we' cause God to forgive but that 'we' want God's actions and human actions to correspond. The Lukan version ('for') might mean that God should forgive us because we have forgiven others.
17 The Hebrew Bible and Jewish literature witness to the belief that God allows

people to be tested (esp. Abraham in Gen 22:1–19 and Job; see Betz, op. cit., p. 406 nn. 515–16, for a list of passages). The petition probably exemplifies *litotes*; if so, then the Matthean addition, 'but rescue us from evil', makes explicit what the earlier petition implied. The plea does not so much attribute temptation to God as request God's guidance, a commonplace in both Wisdom literature and Gentile philosophy.

SELECTED BIBLIOGRAPHY

In addition to items listed below, see notes. For an extensive bibliography, see M. Harding, 'The Lord's Prayer and Other Prayer Texts of the Greco-Roman Era: A Bibliography', pp. 186–201, in *The Lord's Prayer and Other Prayer Texts from the Greco-Roman Era*, edited by J. H. Charlesworth with M. Harding and M. Kiley, Valley Forge, Trinity, 1994.

Betz, H. D., *The Sermon on the Mount: A Commentary on the Sermon on the Mount, Including the Sermon on the Plain (Matthew 5:3-7:27 and Luke 6:20–49)*, ed. A. Y. Collins, Hermenia, Minneapolis, Fortress, 1995.

Carruth, S. and Garsky, A. *Q 11:2b–4: the Database of the International Q Project. Documenta Q. Reconstructions of Q through Two Centuries of Gospel Research Excerpted, Sorted, and Evaluated*, series editor, S. D. Anderson, Leuven, Peeters, 1996.

37

LUKE 1:46–55 THE MAGNIFICAT

Seung Ai Yang

INTRODUCTION

Luke 1:46b–55, traditionally called the Magnificat after the Latin translation of the first word of the passage, is the first of the four canticles in the Lucan infancy narrative. Together with the other three canticles, namely the Benedictus (sung by Zechariah) in 1:68–79, the Gloria in Excelsis (by the heavenly host) in 2:14 and the Nunc Dimittis (by Simeon) in 2:29–32, the Magnificat has played an important part in Christian liturgy and spirituality.

Origin, language and date

Three different suggestions have been made concerning the origin or the composer of this canticle: (a) Mary, who is mentioned as the speaker in verse 46a; (b) the evangelist Luke; (c) a pre-Lucan hymn. The last suggestion is most plausible because the canticle does not specifically fit Mary's situation.[1] It is difficult to understand why Mary sang, or why Luke composed for her, a hymn praising God only in terms of general salvific action, not referring to the particular event of incarnation, when she just had been greeted as the future mother of the Lord by the future mother of John the Baptist. Therefore, it is reasonable to think that Luke adopted a hymn which was already in use and put it in Mary's mouth. Now the question is where this pre-Lucan hymn originated. Its heavy reliance on the Hebrew Bible (i.e. Old Testament), noticeable similarity to post-biblical Jewish literature,[2] strong Semitic style, and especially its unsuppressed Jewish nationalistic fervour, all strongly suggest a Jewish origin. The next question is whether the song originates from Jews or Jewish Christians. Although this is a very difficult question, especially because of the nature of the ill-defined group of Jewish Christians,[3] the complete lack of christological language[4] as well as the strong nationalistic tone seem to point to a non-Christian Jewish community.[5]

In what language was it originally composed? Although the strong

Semitism of the canticle's language has gained several proponents of a Semitic (either Hebrew or Aramaic) original, it may also reflect a Greek-speaking Jewish environment.[6] Greek seems to be its original language, because the Septuagint, the Greek translation of the Hebrew Bible, often seems to stand behind its biblical allusions.[7] As for the date of its composition, we have no clues to determine this. Its seeming familiarity with the Septuagint, its stylistic resemblance to non-canonical psalms of early Judaism and its inclusion in the Gospel of Luke provide only a broad spectrum, from the second century BCE to the first century CE.

Socio-cultural context and geographical provenance

The canticle reflects the piety of the Anawim, the 'poor ones'. In the Hebrew Bible, this term referred not only to the economically poor but also those who were under oppression for various reasons – physical, political, social or religious.[8] Since the Anawim had to call on God desperately for their salvation from oppression, the term Anawim became more and more connected with religious piety. Thus, in early Judaism sectarians often identified themselves with the Anawim, the pious and humble innocently afflicted, and believed that God would vindicate – or already had vindicated – them as the true remnants of Israel and would also destroy – or already had destroyed – their enemies, the arrogant oppressors. Qumran sectarians expressed a piety of the Anawim especially through their liturgical hymns which resembled the thanksgiving psalms of the Hebrew Bible by form and by language and which sounded like a mosaic of biblical passages. The striking similarity of the Magnificat to the Qumran psalms (in language, style and theology) as well as to the Psalms of Solomon (in vocabulary) shows that it was composed in a Palestinian Jewish community which identified themselves with the Anawim.[9] The similarity also suggests that it may well have been used in a liturgical setting.

Literary and theological context in Luke

Mary, the future mother of the Christ, has just received the news of the incarnation, and she visits Elisabeth, the future mother of John the Baptist. In response to her greetings, Mary sings the Magnificat in which she praises God as the Saviour of the poor – including herself – throughout all time. As the first canticle in the infancy narrative, the Magnificat in the present Lukan narrative sets up the principal theme of Luke's entire two-volume work (Luke and Acts): through Jesus Christ, God has reversed the status of the oppressors and the Anawim and has fulfilled the promise of salvation of Israel, the descendants of Abraham, who are redefined as the poor, the pious who stand in awe of God. Mary is the representative of the Anawim, the true Israel, that is, the Christians.[10]

Its influence in the history of Christianity

The Magnificat has enormously influenced later Christianity, especially in the liturgy. Since the Middle Ages numerous musicians have composed settings for the canticle in various modes.[11] Today, eastern churches sing or pray the Magnificat in the morning service and western churches at evening prayer (Vespers). In recent years, the Magnificat has become a favourite source text for various Christian liberation movements.[12]

TRANSLATION

46 And Mary[13] said:
    My soul extols the Lord,
47 and my spirit rejoices[14] in God my Saviour,[15]
48 for he has looked graciously on the lowliness[16] of his slave girl.[17]
    From now on, indeed, every generation will count me blessed,[18]
49 for the Mighty One has done great things for me.
    And holy is his name.
50 And his mercy is from generation to generation on those who stand
    in awe of him.[19]
51 He has acted powerfully with his arm.
    He has scattered those who are haughty in their innermost
        thoughts.[20]
52 He has pulled down mighty ones from (their) thrones,
    and has lifted up lowly ones.
53 Hungry ones has he filled with good things,
    and rich ones has he sent away empty-handed.[21]
54 He has taken the side of Israel his servant boy,[22]
    remembering (his) mercy,[23]
55 as he spoke to our ancestors;[24]
    (his mercy is) on[25] Abraham and his descendants[26] forever.

NOTES

1 Only one verse (v. 48) seems to be an exception. However, even this verse does not fit exactly the virgin's conception of the Son of God by the Holy Spirit (Luke 1:30–5) but rather seems to allude to a miraculous conception by a barren woman in the Hebrew Bible (e.g. Hannah in 1 Samuel 1 and Leah in Genesis 29–30).

2 For parallels from the canonical Bible see notes 15–23. A handy table including non-canonical early Jewish literature is provided by R. E. Brown, *The Birth of the Messiah: A Commentary on the Infancy Narratives in Matthew and Luke*, new updated edition, New York, Doubleday, 1993, pp. 358–60. The most exhaustive list is found in Paul Bemile, *The Magnificat within the Context and Framework of Lukan Theology*, Regensburger Studien zur Theologie 34, Frankfurt am Main, Peter Lang, 1986, pp. 116–33.

3   The complexity of Jewish communities of the first century as well as that of early Christian communities does not allow a clear picture of this group. In what sense or to what degree were they Jews? In what sense were they Christians?

4   For example, one may well expect here such Christological language as that in Luke 1:32–3, 35, 69; 2:11.

5   The most influential proponent for the canticle's Jewish Christian origin is R. Brown, who identifies the canticle's origin with the Jewish Christian Anawim of Jerusalem (op. cit., pp. 350–5). Against the non-Christian Jewish origin, he points out two Christian themes in the canticle: 'a tremendous sense of salvation accomplished through the House of David' and 'the fulfillment of the covenant with Abraham' (p. 350). This explanation is questionable in two points. (1) Brown's judgement is based on his presupposition that all the canticles in the Lucan infancy narrative originate from the same group. However, the thematic and linguistic similarities among the canticles do not necessarily mean that they were originally 'composed' by the same group. They may reflect Lucan adaptation or at most pre-Lucan adaptation by Jewish Christians who got the canticles from various sources and from whom Luke got them. Actually, in the Magnificat itself there is no reference or even allusion to the House of David, which is strongly present in the Benedictus. (2) Furthermore, it is difficult, if not impossible, to read v. 55 as the reference to 'the fulfillment of the covenant with Abraham', as Brown suggests (p. 350). In fact, the Jewish literary parallels which Brown provides support the canticle's non-Christian Jewish origin rather than Christian origin. Therefore, it is reasonable to conclude that the canticle was originally a Jewish hymn to praise God's past, present and future salvation of Israel. It is important not to confuse two different questions, i.e. source and origin, although it is possible that they sometimes are identical. Most probably Luke came upon the canticle in a Jewish Christian community which preserved and used to sing it.

6   My own experience makes a good analogy. My English, either spoken or written, frequently reveals 'Koreanism' especially with regard to the order of words and idiomatic expressions.

7   For the list of the those passages, see Brown, op. cit., pp. 358–60.

8   Note that the term 'the poor' comes only either first or last in several Gospel passages in referring to the list of the oppressed persons, which especially reflects Isa 61:1–3, where the term 'the poor' comes first, too: Matt 5:3–12// Luke 6:20b–26; Matt 11:2–6//Luke 7:18–23; Luke 4:16–30. 'The poor' is an overarching term which includes all the groups listed.

9   For a comparison between the Magnificat and the Qumran *Hodayot*, see especially, Bemile, op. cit., pp. 105–10.

10   See especially, Luke 8:19–21; 11:27–8; Acts 1:14 for Luke's consistent presentation of Mary as the model of Christian discipleship.

11   See especially, Samuel Terrien, *The Magnificat: Musicians as Biblical Interpreters*, New York/Mahwah, Paulist Press, 1995.

12   A good example of its liberationist interpretation is found in Robert McAfee Brown, *Unexpected News: Reading the Bible with Third World Eyes*, Philadelphia, Westminster Press, 1984, pp. 74–88; or in Bemile, op. cit., pp. 237–53.

13   Three manuscripts of the Old Latin version read Elisabeth for Mary. Three patristic quotations also take Elisabeth as the speaker: Armenian and Latin translations of Irenaeus, *Adv. Haer.* 4.7.1; Jerome's translation of Origen, *Hom. In Luc.* 7; Nicetas of Remesiana, *De psalmodiae bono* 9.11. On the basis of these Latin

traditions, some scholars suggested that originally it read 'Elisabeth' or simply an unidentified 'she' and that later scribes changed the speaker to Mary. However, not only most of the ancient traditions including all Greek manuscripts but also the narrative flow of the Lucan Gospel as a whole support reading Mary as the speaker. On this discussion, see especially, Brown, op. cit., pp. 334–6.

14 Literally, 'has rejoiced' or 'rejoiced'. The verb tense in Greek is aorist. Those who propose a Semitic original of the Magnificat see here a Greek translation of the Hebrew perfect with *waw*-consecutive, which denotes a present meaning. However, the aorist denotes a timeless act as is found in lyrical passages in the LXX (F. Blass, A. Debrunner and R. Funk, *A Greek Grammar of the New Testament and Other Early Christian Literature*, Chicago, University of Chicago Press, 1961, §333.2).

15 Ps 35:9; 1 Sam 2:1–2; Hab 3:18.

16 Notice the same word 'lowliness' is used in v. 52b in an adjectival form as a substantive. Mary is the representative of the lowly.

17 Gen 29:32. Note the contrast between 'slave girl (*doulēs*)' and 'servant boy (*pais*)' (v. 54). They come from the self-designations of Hannah (1 Sam 1:11) and of Abraham (Gen 18:3, 5) in the context of the promise of the miraculous births of Samuel and of Isaac, respectively.

18 Gen 30:13.

19 Ps 103:17.

20 Literally, 'with respect to the thought of their heart'. The heart refers to the centre of one's feeling or thinking.

21 Vv. 51–3 echo various Hebrew Bible passages, e.g., 1 Sam 2:7–8; Pss 89:11; 107:9; Ezek 21:31.

22 Isa 41:8–9.

23 Ps 98:3.

24 Literally, 'fathers'.

25 Most interpreters consider the two phrases, 'to our ancestors (*pros tous pateras hēmōn*)' and 'on Abraham and his descendants (*tō Abraam kai tō spermati autou*)' to be in apposition. The Greek, however, does not allow that interpretation: the simple dative without preposition in v. 55b must be understood as related to the last word 'mercy' in v. 54 and as parallel to v. 50 where the simple dative is also used. The two verses construct an important *inclusio* as the main thesis of the entire hymn.

26 Literally, 'seed', as collective.

SELECT BIBLIOGRAPHY

(For an exhaustive bibliography up to 1992, see Brown 1993.)

Bemile, Paul, *The Magnificat within the Context and Framework of Lukan Theology: An Exegetical Theological Study of Lk 1:46–55*, Regensburger Studien zur Theologie, 34, Frankfurt am Main, Peter Lang, 1986.

Brown, Raymond E., *The Birth of the Messiah: A Commentary on the Infancy Narratives in Matthew and Luke*, new updated edition, New York, Doubleday, 1993.

Coleridge, Mark, *The Birth of the Lukan Narrative: Narrative as Christology in Luke 1–2*, JSNTSup88, Sheffield, JSOT, 1993.

Dupont, J., 'Le Magnificat comme discours sur Dieu', *Nouvelle Revue Théologique*, 102, 1980, pp. 321–43.

Farris, Stephen, *The Hymns of Luke's Infancy Narratives: Their Origin, Meaning and Significance*, JSNTSup 9, Sheffield, JSOT Press, 1985.

Meynet, 'Dieu donne son nom à Jésus: Analyse rhétorique de Lc 1, 26–56 et de 1 Sam 2, 1–10', *Biblica,* 66, 1985, pp. 39–72.

Terrien, Samuel, *The Magnificat: Musicians as Biblical Interpreters,* New York/Mahwah, Paulist Press, 1995.

38

JESUS' 'HIGH PRIESTLY PRAYER': JOHN 17

L. William Countryman

INTRODUCTION

The Gospel of John places this long prayer on the lips of Jesus at the conclusion of his final meal with the disciples, immediately before they go out across the Kidron Valley to the garden where he will be arrested. It has long been called the 'High Priestly Prayer', suggesting that, in it, John's Jesus is interpreting his forthcoming sacrifice of himself on the cross.[1]

The Gospel of John

The Gospel of John, also referred to as 'the Fourth Gospel', is quite different from the other three New Testament gospels. To be sure, it does narrate a life of Jesus, but with many differences of detail and a substantial contrast in the style and substance of Jesus' teaching. Where the Jesus of the other three gospels focuses his teaching on the Kingdom of God, John's Jesus centres his teaching on himself, his identity and mission. He speaks in riddles and in long speeches rather than in the familiar parables and short sayings found in the other three gospels. He makes strong statements about himself, beginning with an emphatic '*I* am . . .' When others ask him questions or make leading statements, his response often appears, on first reading, to have nothing to do with what prompted it.

The Gospel of John is generally thought to have been written near the end of the first century CE. Ancient tradition placed its writing in the vicinity of Ephesus,[2] and the Gospel itself claims that its author was the 'disciple whom Jesus loved' (21:20–4), whom it depicts as companion to Jesus during his last days in Jerusalem. The concluding chapter of the book, which contains this information, may be of later origin than the rest;[3] and it is impossible to be certain of the truth of its claims. Still, it is the earliest evidence that we have. Despite an ancient assumption that this 'beloved disciple' was John the son of Zebedee, however, what is said of him does not appear to match what we know otherwise of that John. Indeed, he is not mentioned in John's narrative until Jesus' final meal with the disciples (13:23).

Various modern suggestions have been made about the book's place of writing, authorship and general intellectual connections. One can at least say that it came from the eastern Mediterranean area and that it emerged from an early Christian tradition of theological reflection, often referred to as 'the Johannine school',[4] that stands alongside the school of Paul as one of the most profound and influential theological expressions of first-century Christianity. The other ancient work most closely related to it is the First Letter of John in the New Testament. Wherever it was actually written, the intellectual 'homeland' of the Gospel was Alexandria. Its christology is related to the wisdom/*logos* speculation to be found in Alexandrian Jewish works such as *Wisdom of Solomon* and Philo's *On the Creation of the World According to Moses*. And there is a connection of style and thought with the pagan Greek works known as the *Corpus Hermeticum*, which embody a mystical (some would say gnostic) appropriation of Platonist philosophy.[5]

Recent scholarship pictures the Johannine community as composed of Greek-speaking Jewish Christians who were involved in a struggle for identity with the authorities of the Jewish communities in which they lived. By the time the Gospel was written, they were being pushed out of the mainstream synagogue community (cf. John 9:22). In response, they seem to have characterized their enemies as enemies of God. These enemies are referred to as *ho kosmos*, 'the cosmos/world'; but also as *hoi Ioudaioi*, 'the Jews (or Judaeans)'. The tensions between the Jewish Christians who made up the Johannine community and the ongoing synagogue community, enshrined as they are in the Gospel of John, have made an unfortunate and unforeseeable contribution to later Christian anti-Judaism.[6]

The Fourth Gospel acquired canonical status among Christians in the second century and kept it despite criticism from those who noticed how different its account of Jesus was from that of the other gospels and from those who may have felt that its doctrine of the Spirit gave too much aid and comfort to Montanism.[7] Because of its status as part of the New Testament, the Gospel of John survives in a great number of Greek manuscripts (its original language); in fact, an early second-century papyrus scrap from Egypt containing a few verses from John is probably the oldest surviving fragment of any New Testament book. The Gospel is also found in ancient translations into Latin, Syriac, Coptic and other languages. While there are some textual variants in chapter 17, they do not affect the meaning of the passage in any substantive way.

The High Priestly Prayer in the context of John's Gospel

John's Gospel interprets the crucifixion and resurrection of Jesus as a 'lifting up', a movement into glory, a return to the God from whom Jesus came (e.g., 3:14, 12:32, 13:2–3). The High Priestly Prayer is particularly concerned with interpreting this process for those whom Jesus would leave behind – his immediate disciples, but also the later Johannine community who formed the original audience for this work. In the prologue of the Gospel (1:1-18), John identifies Jesus as the incarnation of the *logos* (Word) of God, understood as the agent through whom God created the world. He also speaks of Jesus as *Son* of God, intimately related to the Father. In the corresponding language of the prayer (17:1–5), Jesus speaks of being glorified anew with the glory he had before the creation and of returning to his original intimacy with the Father. He and his Father are 'one'. And he promises that, through his return to the Father, his followers will also become 'one' with him and with God.[8]

The style of the prayer is an exalted version of the style that characterizes the rest of the Gospel of John, including both Jesus' discourses and the comments of the evangelist himself. It is circular and repetitive, building its meanings out of an artificially small vocabulary through subtle variations. The prayer is thus stylistically integral with the rest of the Gospel and was probably composed as a part of it. It is difficult to imagine what independent cultic function it could have served apart from its specific role in the Gospel of John. Through its place in this Gospel, it subsequently plays a role in Christian liturgy, but as a reading, not as a prayer.[9]

Relation to other texts

The prayer has literary parallels in other ancient works, but scholars have not been able to agree as to their relative importance. One line of interpretation has suggested a connection with a type of gnostic prayer 'spoken by the [Gnostic] Messenger on his departure from the world'.[10] Another has suggested that we should compare the whole sequence of Last Supper discourses in John, including the Prayer (chs 13–17), with the farewell messages of other biblical worthies, which tend to include at least a reference to prayer and blessing: for example, the farewells of Jacob (Gen 49), Moses (the whole of Deuteronomy, with the blessings in ch. 33), Samuel (1 Sam 12) and Paul (Acts 20:17–38).[11]

Yet, another line of thought links the High Priestly Prayer particularly with the prayers that mark the moment of initiation in two tractates of the *Corpus Hermeticum* – pagan Greek writings that date to a period later than that of John but appear to draw on first-century traditions.[12] This approach has in its favour John's specific linking of the foot-washing and, by implication, the Last Supper discourses (which begin by explaining that action) with Jesus' consciousness that he was returning to union with God (13:1–12). Use of a hermetic model, however, would not have excluded influence from biblical or gnostic models as well.

The theology of the Prayer

The theology of the High Priestly Prayer represents the same sort of Platonizing, Alexandrian Judaism that pervades the Gospel as a whole. John's Gospel assumes that God created the world through an intermediary being, whom he calls Word (*logos*), or Son. John, as a Christian, takes the additional step of identifying this being as incarnate in Jesus.[13] The purpose of this incarnation was to bring God's *logos* back into the created cosmos in a new way. The cosmos was created by God, through the *logos*, but has turned against its creator and must be called back into communion with God. The cosmos is therefore both the object of God's efforts to save it (e.g., 3:16) and the summation of all that is categorically opposed to God (e.g., 17:14).

According to John the incarnation of the *logos* in Jesus gives those who believe in him the opportunity to return to unity with God. This union can be understood in various ways. There is an element of future expectation in it (e.g., 14:1–4), but John is very restrained in his use of future eschatology, particularly as compared to the more apocalyptic stance of the other gospels. For John, unity with God seems to be available rather in the here and now. It is partly a kind of communion of spirit which the believers enjoy in the Church, but it is also a mystical union that the believer can experience now and which will be brought to completion after death. This mysticism is not inherently surprising, since mystical thought was on the rise in late antiquity in Jewish and pagan Greek circles as well as in Christianity. The best-known examples are the Therapeutae and the chariot (or throne) mysticism in Judaism, and the Hermetic writings and the neo-Platonism of Plotinus in paganism. While the primary documentation for all of these except the Therapeutae comes from later than the writing of the Fourth Gospel, their roots at least appear to be coeval with John.

Subsequent influence

The influence of the Gospel of John on later Christian theology has been enormous. It was the first book of the New Testament canon to receive a commentary (by Heracleon, a Valentinian gnostic). And it inspired notable commentaries by Origen, John Scotus Eriugena, and others. Its *logos*-christology was one of the foundations of Nicene orthodoxy regarding the Trinity and the person of Christ. It was regarded, from an early time, as the 'spiritual' gospel, delving into mysteries beyond the more pedestrian synoptics (Matthew, Mark, Luke). Accordingly it was assigned the eagle as its emblem, because the eagle was thought to fly toward the sun with impunity.

The High Priestly Prayer has acquired a particular importance in the twentieth century on account of the Ecumenical Movement. Jesus' prayer that 'they may all be one' has been seen as a mandate for reunification of the disparate Christian denominations. The High Priestly Prayer does not, to be sure, refer literally to the purpose or fate of denominational institutions created only in later eras; indeed, Johannine Christianity seems to have been notable for its relative lack of internal articulation and institutionalization. The internal unity of the Church, however, was undoubtedly an important ideal for the Johannine School (cf. 1 John 2:18–19). And it was of a piece, in the Johannine perspective, with the mystical unity that obtains among the believers and between the believers and God and Jesus.

TRANSLATION[14]

Jesus said these things;[15] and he raised his eyes to heaven and spoke: 'Father, the hour has come.[16] Glorify your son, so that the son may glorify you – (2) just as you gave him authority over all flesh, so that all that you've given him he might give to them – everlasting life.[17] (3) And this is everlasting life – to know you, the only real God, and Jesus Christ whom you sent.[18] (4) I've glorified you on earth by finishing the work you've given me to do; (5) and now glorify me yourself, father, alongside yourself with the glory I had by your side before the cosmos existed.[19]

(6) 'I've revealed your name to the people you gave me out of the cosmos. They belonged to you and you gave them to me; and they've kept your word. (7) Now they know that all the things you've given me are from you, (8) because I've given them the words[20] that you gave me and they themselves have accepted them and really know that they came from you. And they've believed that you sent me. (9) I myself am praying for them. I'm not praying for the cosmos, but for those you gave me, because they're yours.[21] (10) And all things that are mine are yours, and yours are mine; and I've been glorified in them. (11) And I'm no longer in the cosmos, and *they* are in the cosmos, and *I'm* coming to you. Holy father, keep them in your name which you've given me, so that they may be one just as we are one.[22]

(12) 'While I was with them, *I* kept them in your name which you gave me, and I guarded them, and not one of them was destroyed except the son of destruction – so that the writing[23] might be fulfilled. (13) But now I'm coming to you, and I'm saying these things in the cosmos so that they'll have my own happiness brought to the full in themselves. (14) *I've* given them your word,[24] and the cosmos has hated them because they're not from the cosmos, just as *I'm* not from the cosmos. (15) I'm not praying for you to take them out of the cosmos, but to keep them out of the evil. (16) They aren't from the cosmos, just as *I'm* not from the cosmos. (17) Consecrate them in the truth: your word [*logos*] is truth. (18) Just as you sent me into the cosmos, I, too, have sent them into the cosmos. (19) And on their behalf, *I* consecrate myself, so that

they, too, may themselves be consecrated in truth.[25]

(20) 'Not for these only do I pray, but also for those that believe in me through their word, (21) that they may all be one, just as you, father, are in me and I in you, that they, too, may be in us, so that the cosmos may believe that you have sent me.[26] (22) And as for me, the glory you gave me,[27] I have given them, so that they may be one just as we are one, (23) I in them and you in me, so that they may be completed into one, so that the cosmos may recognize that you sent me and have loved them just as you loved me. (24) Father, I want what you have granted me, that where I am they, too, may be with me, so that they may see my glory, which you gave me because you loved me before the foundation of the cosmos. (25) Righteous father, even the cosmos did not know you,[28] but I've known you and these people know that you have sent me. (26) And I have made your name known to them and I will make it known, so that the love with which you've loved me may be in them and I in them.'[29]

NOTES

1 This title for the prayer dates to the sixteenth century, but the idea of treating it in priestly terms is much older; Rudolf Schnackenburg, *The Gospel According to St. John*, trans. David Smith and G. A. Kon, vol. 3, New York, Crossroad, 1982, p. 433.

2 Irenaeus, *Adversus haereses* 3.1.1, cited in Eusebius, *Historia ecclesiastica* 5.8.1–5.

3 There are diverse theories about the compositional history of John's Gospel, with some scholars arguing that it went through a series of editions, involving substantive change in the order of material. The author of ch. 21 may have been largely responsible for the present shape of the rest of the work. See Scott Gambrill Sinclair, *The Road and the Truth: The Editing of John's Gospel*, Berkeley, BIBAL Press, 1994, pp. 1–8.

4 R. Alan Culpepper, *The Johannine School: An Evaluation of the Johannine-School Hypothesis Based on an Investigation of the Nature of Ancient Schools*, SBL Dissertation Series 26, Missoula, Scholars Press, 1975.

5 C. K. Barrett, *The Gospel According to St. John: An Introduction with Commentary and Notes on the Greek Text*, 2nd edn, Philadelphia, Westminster Press, 1978, pp. 27–41. Alexandrian thought was influential throughout the eastern Mediterranean.

6 J. Louis Martyn, *The Gospel of John in Christian History: Essays for Interpreters*, New York, Paulist Press, 1978, pp. 90–121.

7 Hans von Campenhausen, *The Formation of the Christian Bible*, trans. J. A. Baker, Philadelphia, Fortress Press, 1972, pp. 236–40.

8 '... it is unmistakable that this chapter is a summary of the Johannine discourses and in this respect is a counterpart to the prologue', Ernst Käsemann, *The Testament of Jesus: A Study of the Gospel of John in the Light of Chapter 17*, Philadelphia, Fortress Press, 1968, p. 3.

9 The structure of the prayer moves in a general way from Jesus to the disciples to future believers. Various proposals for a more detailed analysis have been inconclusive, but some see the tripartite element as echoing the prayer of Aaron in Lev 16:11–17. See Raymond E. Brown, *The Gospel According to John*

(*xiii–xxi*), The Anchor Bible, Garden City, NY, Doubleday, 1970, pp. 749–51.

10 Rudolf Bultmann, *The Gospel of John: A Commentary*, trans. G. Beasley Murray *et al.*, Philadelphia, Westminster Press, 1971, p. 489.

11 Barnabas Lindars, *The Gospel of John*, New Century Bible Commentary, Grand Rapids, Eerdmans, 1972, p. 516.

12 C. H. Dodd, *The Interpretation of the Fourth Gospel*, Cambridge, Cambridge University Press, 1953, pp. 420–3. Dodd cites in particular *Poimandres* (*CH* 1) and the tractate *On Rebirth* (*CH* 13). He notes that John 17, with its group of disciples, is more communal than the hermetic texts, which depict a 'secret colloquy between the individual and his initiator' (p. 422).

13 Another example of this development in early Christian thought can be found in the Epistle to Hebrews in the New Testament; see especially Heb 1:1–3:6.

14 The translation of John 17 is taken from L. Wm. Countryman, *The Mystical Way in the Fourth Gospel: Crossing Over into God*, rev. edn, Valley Forge, PA, Trinity Press International, 1994, pp. 113–16. It is reproduced here by permission.

15 This transition emphasizes the connection of the prayer with the preceding discourses.

16 Jesus' 'hour' is treated variously in the Gospel as the moment when he can act, the moment when he becomes vulnerable to his enemies, or, as here, the moment when he consummates the purpose of his mission. Here, the phrase echoes its use at the beginning of the Last Supper narrative: 'Before the feast of the Passover, Jesus knew that his hour had come for him to cross over from this cosmos to the father' (13:1). Cf. the Hermetic prayer: 'God, you father, you are the lord, you are the mind. Accept from me the rational sacrifices that you want, for at your will all things are completed' (*CH* 13.21). For John, Jesus' death is an expression of the glory of God 'because self-sacrifice is the expression of love', a topic also raised in 13:1 and brought back at the end of ch. 17; see William Temple, *Readings in St. John's Gospel*, London, Macmillan, 1955, p. 308.

17 The *logos* has had life in him from the beginning and this 'life was the light of human beings' (1:4). The work of Jesus' ministry is thus in continuity with the creative ministry of the pre-existent *logos*.

18 Because the *logos* is the source of life and because the cosmos has turned away from its own origins and imagines that it is somehow its own God, to recognize the *logos* in Jesus is the same as returning to the inexhaustible source of life. Cf. the Hermetic prayer: 'Holy is God who wants to be known and is known to his own' (*CH* 1.31).

19 This is the glory of the *logos*, of whom it can be said both that he was 'with God' and that he 'was God' (1:1–2). The concept of 'glory' in John refers to the manifestation of beauty and power that signals God's presence (equivalent to the Hebrew *shekhinah*), but also to the more idiomatic Greek sense of 'reputation, praise', which means that it is always understood as a gift.

20 The Greek term here is *rhemata*, the more common term for 'words'. *Logos*, while traditionally translated 'word' in John, really means 'speech, the power of speech, reason'.

21 The Gospel of John holds that Jesus was sent to save the cosmos (3:16–17), but its use of the term 'cosmos' is ambivalent. In many cases, as here, 'cosmos' is the name of what is unsalvageable; whatever Jesus succeeds in reclaiming as his own is no longer cosmos.

22 The oneness of Father and Son is such that, even though they can be thought as separate ('The *logos* was with God'), they can also be thought as one ('The *logos* was God', 1:1). In 10:30, John's Jesus asserts his unity with the Father in terms

228

identical to the ones used here in 17:11.

23 Or 'scripture'; ancient Greek had no separate word for 'scripture'. The scripture in question may be Isaiah 57:4 or Prov 24:22 in the Septuagint. John does not cite scripture much and, when he does, it is not always possible to identify what he is quoting; e.g., the quotation in 7:38 has never been satisfactorily identified.

24 The Greek is *logos* here, not *rhema* as in v. 8, suggesting that what Jesus has given them is, in reality, himself.

25 Because the believers have received Jesus' own essence as *logos*, his consecration of himself avails for them, too. Cf. the following from the prayer that concludes *Poimandres*: 'I depart into life and light. You are blessed, father. Your human being wants to consecrate along with you, just as you have granted him all authority' (*CH* 1.32).

26 For the ambiguity of the term 'cosmos', see note 21 above.

27 This is what Jesus has earlier referred to as 'the glory I had by your side before the cosmos existed' (17:5, cf. 24).

28 Since God created the cosmos in the first place, the latter might have been expected to know its maker; but John observes early on that the *logos* 'was in the cosmos, and the cosmos was made through him, and the cosmos did not recognize him. He came to his own property and his own people did not receive him' (1:10–11).

29 The Greek terms for 'love' (*agape* and *agapao*) appear only in the last four verses of the chapter, but they echo the beginning of the Last Supper narrative where John introduces the foot-washing with the words 'having loved his own who were in the cosmos, he loved them to the end' (13:1). 'Love' here is functionally equivalent to the idea of unity with God and with one another. Compare the emphasis in 1 John on love as constituting the Christian community; only those who love their fellow-Christians are in the light (1 John 2:9–11) and those who violate this love by leaving the community are understood as never having been truly part of it in the first place (2:18–19).

SELECTED BIBLIOGRAPHY

Barrett, C. K., *The Gospel According to St John: An Introduction with Commentary and Notes on the Greek Text*, 2nd edn, Philadelphia, Westminster Press, 1978.

Bornkamm, Günther, 'Towards the Interpretation of John's Gospel: A Discussion of *The Testament of Jesus* by Ernst Käsemann', in *The Interpretation of John*, ed. John Ashton, Philadelphia, Fortress Press, 1986, pp. 79–98.

Countryman, L. Wm., *The Mystical Way in the Fourth Gospel: Crossing Over into God*, rev. edn, Valley Forge, Trinity Press International, 1994.

Dodd, C. H., *The Interpretation of the Fourth Gospel*, Cambridge, Cambridge University Press, 1953.

Käsemann, Ernst, *The Testament of Jesus: A Study of the Gospel of John in the Light of Chapter 17*, Philadelphia, Fortress Press, 1968.

Schnackenburg, Rudolf, *The Gospel According to St John*, vol. 3, trans. David Smith and G. A. Kon, New York, Crossroad, 1982.

39

ACTS 4:24–30: PRAYER OF THE FRIENDS OF PETER AND JOHN IN JERUSALEM

Marie-Eloise Rosenblatt

INTRODUCTION

Source and genre

Acts 4:24–30 is a public prayer at a community gathering.[1] The reader can imagine either a memorized prayer chanted in unison, or individual voices praying aloud in succession.[2] The prayer has an explicit biblical character and represents the voice of Jewish Christians in Jerusalem. It is proposed to Luke's largely gentile readership as a model of the heroism of the founding community in Jerusalem.

Theme: vindication of the oppressed minority

The prayer has several features which link it to other moments in Luke-Acts. Reversing a climate of victimization and fear, its mood is victorious gratitude for the release of Peter and John from their interrogation and warning by religious leaders. Acts 4:24–30 vindicates the weak, the powerless and the voiceless, as in the Magnificat and the prayer of the martyrs in Revelation.

There is also a polemic comparing some Jewish elders to gentiles who rage against God's purposes. Psalm 2, quoted in this prayer, celebrates David's military triumph by mocking Israel's enemies who thought they could band together and defeat God and God's anointed on the battlefield. The military victory was celebrated as a theological triumph over gentiles and non-believers as well. In Acts 4, Herod, Pontius Pilate and the priests Caiphas and Annas all belong to the same category: leaders who oppose God's purposes in contrast to the followers of Jesus.[3]

Master–servant christology

Of special note is the prayer's master–servant christology, a theme which casts Jesus as the servant of God, and his followers as servants of Jesus who is master to them. The metaphor of child/servant expresses a hierarchical social relation to Jesus but also the humility of believers in relation to each other. An appealing feature of this christology is its gender-inclusiveness. Both women and men could dominate society as 'masters' as well as suffer social subordination as servants or slaves.[4] Emancipation or manumission of slaves, which involved payment for their release, was a powerful image for describing salvation by Christ.[5] The master–servant (*despotes/pais*) relation reflects a late christology, because the image is clustered in John, Jude, 1 Peter, James and Revelation.[6]

Analysis of five stages of the prayer

Several stages can be discerned in the prayer of Acts 4:24–30. The narrative event controlling it is the healing of the lame man in 3:1-10. This 'sign and wonder' has civil consequences and belongs to the genre of other acts of compassion, to which we can add the healing of the Gerasene demoniac, Mark 5:1–20; the healing of the clairvoyant girl in Acts 16:16–24; and the raising of Lazarus in John 11:1–48. All result in negative civil consequences for the healer.

The prayer, like the sermons and speeches in Acts, is a Lukan composition. Hemer notes that the prayer is 'kerygmatic in content, appropriate to theological analysis, but not a speech in the usual sense, nor attributed to an individual'.[7] Its first movement is a traditional acknowledgement of God as master of all creation, but this has apocalyptic overtones since the language of judgement is linked in the NT with the Maker of the 'heavens, the earth, the sea, and all that is in them'.

Second, the prayer acknowledges, in the reference to Ps 2, that God was the spokesperson for David, king of Israel. It has a political dimension. Acts 4 pits the Lukan community's leaders of Galilean origin against the Judaean authorities. In 'winning the battle', the community invokes divine retribution against its enemies as compensation for unremitting persecution and humiliation. The whole spirit of the passage implies that there will be no appeasement, only resistance.

The third moment leaps from David's anointing as king, in 1000 BCE, to the period immediately following the resurrection of Jesus in the early 30s CE. The execution of Jesus under the leadership of Herod and Pilate is reinterpreted as an event which falls within the providence of God. Mechanical ideas of fulfilment should be rejected, however. Luke places all events within the purview of God's purpose or *boulē* to show how the disciples continue the work God did through Jesus.

The fourth turn in the prayer is a petition for the servants to continue to preach boldly and courageously, despite all the hardships and opposition they might suffer. Peter and John in fact emerged from their interrogation unscathed and unstoppable, galvanized by a force like Paul's *parrhesia* or boldness at the end of Acts.

The fifth element is the acknowledgement of God as healer through the name of Jesus. This theocentric focus satisfies monotheistic interests of Jewish Christians and side-steps a competition between Jesus-healers vs. God-healers. At the end of the prayer, the whole building shakes, in theophanic confirmation which the reader of Acts associates with other moments of divine intervention, such as Pentecost, Peter's being set free from prison and Paul's deliverance from chains.

TRANSLATION

24 Master[8]
   you are the maker of the heavens and the earth and the sea
   and everything in them.[9]

25 Our father David, your servant,[10]
   speaking through the Holy Spirit, said,
   'Why did the gentiles get angry
   and their people hold on to fantasies?

26 The kings of the earth colluded
   and the leaders conspired together
   against the Lord and against his anointed one.'[11]

27 In fact, gathered in this very city[12]
   against your holy child Jesus,[13] the one you chose,[14]
   were both Herod and Pontius Pilate,[15]
   and gentiles joined with the people of Israel.[16]

28 They accomplished the deeds
   which your hand and plan[17]
   ordained to happen.

29 And now, Lord, pay heed to their threats.
   Give to your servants[18]
   full courage[19] to preach your word.

30 Stretch out your hand in healing.[20]
   Let signs and wonders be shown[21]
   in the name of your holy child Jesus.[22]

NOTES

1 The text is the 26th edition of the Nestle-Aland *Novum Testament um Graece*, Stuttgart, Deutsche Bibelgesellschaft, 1983. For commentary and photography plates, see Frederick G. Kenyon, *Chester Beatty Biblical Papyri II/1: The*

Gospels and Acts, Text, London, E. Walker Ltd, 1933; II/2: The Gospels and Acts, Plates, London, E. Walker Ltd, 1934. Setting this data in context is Kurt Aland and Barbara Aland, The Text of the New Testament, trans. Erroll F. Rhodes, 2nd edn revised, Grand Rapids, MI, Eerdmans/Leiden, E. J. Brill, 1987, 1989, pp. 98–9 from 1989 edition.

2   For a theory of the editorial stages of Acts, see M.-E. Boismard and A. Lamouille, Les Acts des Deux Apôtres I: Introduction-Textes, Paris, J. Gabalda, 1990, pp. 3–5, 13, 33, 77–8.

3   David L. Tiede, '"Fighting against God": Luke's Interpretation of Jewish Rejection of the Messiah Jesus', in Craig A. Evans and Donald A. Hagner (eds), Anti Semitism and Early Christianity: Issues of Polemic and Faith, Minneapolis, Augsburg/Fortress, 1993, p. 109.

4   The servant–child relation is part of a larger semiotic field. See William F. Arndt and F. Wilbur Gingrich, A Greek–English Lexicon of the New Testament, 2nd edn, Chicago and London, University of Chicago Press, 1957, 1979, pp. 602–5 from 1979 edition.

5   See the contract from Oxyrhynchus in which Aline, daughter of Komon and widow of Mnesitheus, enacts the manumission of her female slave Euphrosyne. The decree is dated 24–8 August, 86 CE. P. Oxy. 2843.

6   Luke Timothy Johnson, The Acts of the Apostles, Sacra Pagina Series, vol. 5, Collegeville, MN, Michael Glazier/Liturgical Press, 1992, pp. 82–5. Johnson reviews several LXX citations of prophets and psalms in Acts. He notes that the term hagios pais (holy child) is a designation for David and acquires a messianic association when it is attributed to Jesus.

7   Colin J. Hemer, The Book of Acts in the Setting of Hellenistic History, ed. Conrad H. Gempf, Winona Lake, IN, Eisenbrauns, 1990, p. 416 n. 4.

8   The vocative despota from despotes is not the equivalent of 'Lord' (kyrie), but is more accurately translated 'Master' in order to accommodate the household sense of 'servant' (doulos) and 'child' (paidion), which in some contexts is the equivalent of 'slave'. The term despota for 'ruler' or 'lord' is unusual in the NT, with Luke the only exemplar in the canticle of Simeon (Luke 2:29–32): 'Now, Master (despota), you can dismiss your servant (doulon sou).'

9   God as the Maker of creation is formulaic, and occurs in contexts where the speaker is calling down God's powerful judgement to punish unbelievers and political enemies; cf. Acts 14:14, Rev 5:13, 10:6, 14:7.

10 paidos sou = your servant/child David. See 1 Sam 17:32, 34 where the master–servant metaphor moves from secular to sacred meaning. David is servant and son of his father Jesse, 1 Sam 17:58. But in 1 Sam 23:10, David is God's servant and prays to the God of Israel as his master.

11 Ps 2, linked with Ps 110, is cited by the NT writers to legitimate the messianic character of Jesus and his Davidic, kingly role.

12 The reference to Jerusalem is a Lukan focus throughout Acts. One of Luke's purposes is to underline the Jesus movement's origin in Jerusalem. Very likely, this was to counter the de-Judaizing and revisionist historical tendencies of gentile Christian preachers.

13 hagion paida sou = your holy servant/child Jesus; cf. Jude 1:4.

14 chriō = anoint. It is a rare NT use, occurring in Luke 4:18 of Jesus' sense of mission, in Acts 10:38 of Jesus' anointing, and Heb 1:9, cf. Ps. 45:6–7, to Jesus as the one anointed like David; in 2 Cor 1:21 it is Paul's bold claim of a share in God's anointing.

15 The relationship between Herod Agrippa (I) and Pontius Pilate is unique to Luke, who cites the link at the beginning of Jesus' ministry (3:1) and again

during the passion narrative (23:11–12); this locates Jesus within competing forces of Roman occupation and Jewish nationalism.

16 Luke portrays a cooperative venture between gentiles and the people of Israel. Luke's vision of enemies reconciled is anticipated in Simeon's prophetic prayer with its theme of inclusion, 'a light of revelation to the gentiles and the glory of your people Israel' (2:32).

17 *Boulē* = plan or purpose. It is a characteristically Lukan term, not used by other evangelists, and generally refers to God's initiative which can be assented to by human beings, but not resisted, no matter their hostility. See Lk 7:30, 25:51, Acts 2:23, 4:28, 5:38, 13:36, 20:27, 27:12.

18 *doulois sou* = your servants, which could include Peter and John, the praying community itself, and all believers in Jesus.

19 *parrhesia*. The term refers variously to boldness, openness, courage and unstoppable energy. See 2 Cor 7:14, Phil 1:20, John 18:20, Acts 28:31.

20 Stretching out the hand to heal is what Jesus does, as with the leper in Mark 1:41 and the man with the withered arm in Mark 3:5. God's healing power is manifest when the lame man walks at the Beautiful Gate in Jerusalem, Acts 3: 1–8, 4:8–10.

21 *Semeia kai terata* = signs and wonders; sometimes linked with mighty works (*dynamis*). They arouse people's faith and confidence in the doer. See Mark 13:22, Matt 24:24, Ro 15:19, 2 Cor 12:12, Acts 2:22, 2:43, 5:12, 6:8, 7:36, 14:3 and 15:17

22 *hagiou paidos sou* = your holy servant/child Jesus.

SELECTED BIBLIOGRAPHY

Boismard, M.-E. and Lamouille, A., *Les Acts des Deux Apôtres I: Introduction-Textes*, Paris, J. Gabalda, 1990.

Johnson, Luke T., *The Acts of the Apostles*, Sacra Pagina Series, vol. 5, Collegeville, MN, Michael Glazier/Liturgical Press, 1992.

Thurston, Bonnie, *Spiritual Life in the Early Church: The Witness of Acts and Ephesians*, Minneapolis, Fortress Press, 1993. See especially 'The Prayer in Acts 4:23–31', pp. 55–65.

40

PHILIPPIANS 2:6–11

L. W. Hurtado

INTRODUCTION

Paul's authorship of Philippians is not disputed, but the letter is dated variously depending on where and when one places the imprisonment Paul refers to in the letter: Ephesus c. 53–5, Caesarea c. 56–9, Rome c. 59–62. Even the latest date puts the letter within thirty years of the beginning of the Christian movement, making it extremely valuable historically. There is no doubt that Phil 2:6–11 is an original portion of the letter Paul wrote.

Provenance and language

The passage is widely regarded as Paul's adaptation of a Christian ode or hymn originally used in Christian worship, though some argue that Paul himself composed the passage. The compressed expression, the extended concentration on Jesus, the exalted mood of the passage, and the way parts of the passage seem to parallel or balance other parts all suggest strongly either a hymn or a hymn-like composition of exalted prose reflecting the themes of some early Christian praise and worship.

Convinced that Phil 2:6–11 is an adaptation of a hymn, various scholars have attempted to trace its origins, some arguing that the passage is a Greek translation of an Aramaic original (for example Fitzmyer 1988), others concluding that the hymn was composed in Greek among Greek-speaking Jewish Christian circles. In either case, the hymn would derive from a point perhaps significantly earlier than the epistle itself, giving a glimpse of Christian faith and devotional practice within the first decades of Christianity.

Other relevant material

Whatever its origin, if this is a Christian hymn it is perhaps the earliest surviving example. Other NT passages widely thought to incorporate first-century hymns include Col 1:15–20; John 1:1–18; Heb 1:3; 1 Pet 3:18–22 (see Sanders 1971). In Revelation (c. 95 CE), the author gives us hymns sung in heaven, which may also reflect the worship of Christian groups in which he was a participant (see, for example, Rev 5:9–10; 15:3–4). *The Odes of Solomon* are the earliest surviving Christian hymn-collection (c. 100–75 CE). Hymns were one of the earliest and most important forms in which Christian beliefs came to expression (see Hengel 1983), the centre of earliest Christian development of belief being the worship setting in which powerful religious enthusiasm and inspiration promoted the articulation of Christian convictions.

Religious import

The devotional pattern reflected in Phil 2:6–11 consists in celebrating Jesus' actions and significance, associating him with God in striking ways. This concentration on Jesus is characteristic of many early Christian hymns. 1 Cor 14:26; Col 3:16–17; and Eph. 5:18–20 refer to hymns in Christian worship, implying that they stem from Christian inspiration and are heavily concerned with celebrating Jesus. Yet, the reverence of Jesus is never at the expense of God ('the Father'). Jesus is given the divine name/title 'Lord', and the allusion to Isa 45:23 suggests that this term is a Greek equivalent of God's name (YHWH), a breathtaking claim. But God gives Jesus his final exalted status (v. 9), and the universal acclamation of Jesus' divine honour actually serves the glory of God (v. 11). This 'binitarian' devotion, combining reverence for God and Jesus within a monotheistic commitment, involved a tacit or explicit functional subordination of Jesus to 'the Father', even the exalted and glorified Jesus. Early Christian prayers and liturgical formulae such as doxologies characteristically reflect this binitarian pattern as well (for example, see Phil 1:2; 4:6, 19–20).

There has been major scholarly controversy over whether vv. 6–7 portray a 'pre-existent' Christ (existence in heaven prior to earthly/historical existence) who becomes human, with some insisting that these verses are merely poetic description of the self-abasement of the human Jesus (see, for example, Talbert 1967). Most scholars remain persuaded that the hymn does reflect the idea of Christ's pre-existence, making the passage perhaps the earliest explicit evidence of this idea.

TRANSLATION

(5)   Maintain this attitude among yourselves which is given in Christ Jesus.[1]
(6)   Being in the form of God,[2] he did not regard being like God[3] an opportunity to exploit for his own advantage;[4]

(7) but instead he poured himself out,[5]
     taking the form of a slave,[6]
     being born in human likeness.[7]
     And being in human state,[8] (8) he humbled himself,
     becoming obedient to the point of death,
     indeed, death on a cross.[9]

(9) Therefore, God highly exalted him[10]
     and bestowed on him the name above every name,[11]

(10) so that in Jesus' name[12] every knee should bow,
     among heavenly and earthly and under-earth beings,[13]

(11) and every tongue should acknowledge that Jesus Christ is Lord,[14]
     to the glory of God the Father.[15]

NOTES

1 Paul's lead-in statement is important for understanding how vv. 6–11 function
   in the letter. The second part of the sentence has no verb in Greek (literally,
   'which also in Christ Jesus'), and there are two scholarly views: (a) 'in Christ
   Jesus' means 'in the Christian fellowship' (Paul frequently uses the phrase 'in
   Christ' with this meaning, e.g., Rom 16:3–10); (b) the phrase refers to Jesus' own
   actions and attitude. Because both the phrasing ('in Christ *Jesus*') and the
   following verses emphasize Jesus personally, I have chosen the latter option and
   supplied the verb 'given', taking the phrase as introducing the selfless actions of
   Jesus described in vv. 6–11. (Cf. Rom 15:5–6 for a similar reference to Jesus'
   example in ethical exhortation.)

2 'In the form of God' (*en morphē theou*) here means a mode of being like God's.
   Although what being like God is not specified (and such speculation is not part
   of the author's intent), it implies 'pre-existence', some form of (heavenly)
   'existence' of Jesus prior to his earthly life. Contrary to assertions of some, *en
   morphē theou* is *not* simply synonymous for the 'image of God' (*eikōn theou*),
   and thus not simply an allusion to Adam as God's 'image' (Gen 1:26–8). Here,
   'form of God' seems an intended contrast for the 'servant form' (*morphē
   doulou*) of the human Jesus in v. 7.

3 'Being like God' translates *to einai isa theō*, and is a parallel expression to 'in the
   form of God'.

4 'An opportunity to exploit for his own advantage' translates the word
   harpagmos used here in an idiomatic expression (see Hoover 1971). What Jesus
   refuses is not the state of 'being like God' but the self-oriented exploitation of
   this state.

5 'Poured himself out' (*heauton ekenōsen*), or 'emptied himself', probably a
   metaphorical expression for the service-oriented option Jesus chose instead of
   the 'opportunity' rejected in v. 6 (see 2 Cor 8:8–9 for a parallel statement).

6 'Form of a slave' (*morphēn doulou*), contrasts with 'the form of God' (v. 6).
   Though some scholars see Jesus as voluntarily putting himself in subjection as
   slave to hostile (demonic) spiritual powers, there is no basis for this in the text.
   Instead, Jesus is probably to be seen as serving God, here and also in the
   obedience referred to in v. 8.

7 'Being born in human likeness', taking *genomenos* as 'born', the sense it has,
   e.g., in Gal 4:4. 'Human likeness' probably connotes the full human similarity

237

of Jesus, a real incarnation of the pre-existent figure in human mode, and does not imply that Jesus was human in appearance only.

8 The Greek participle *heuretheis* (lit. 'being found') probably has a meaning like the French *se trouver*, and is translated here 'being'. 'Human state' translates *schēmati hōs anthrōpos*, and is a parallel expression for 'in human likeness'.

9 Because these words make the sentence more difficult to fit within the demands of Greek poetical conventions, many scholars consider this reference to the cross to have been inserted by Paul. But earliest Christian hymns may well have been patterned more after the Psalms, and thus be more variable in the length of verse lines than Greek poetry with its emphasis upon syllabic metre. Consequently, this phrase could be an original part of the text of the composition. Death by crucifixion carried a unique horror and ignominy in Greco-Roman society, so a willingness to face such a death constituted a particularly striking degree of obedience.

10 The resurrection of Jesus involved his exaltation to heavenly glory (see, e.g., 3:20–1). See Eph 1:20–3 for a more extended reference to God's exaltation of Jesus.

11 The two possibilities are (a) God makes the name 'Jesus' superior to all others ('bestowed' a metaphor for the new dignity attached to the name), or (b) the title 'Lord' (*Kyrios*) is awarded to Jesus (see comment on v. 11 below). With most scholars, I think the context better supports the latter option. The phrase reflects ancient Jewish honorific language used to refer to the special name of God (YHWH). See Eph 1:21, where Jesus is exalted over all authorities and 'above every name that is named'.

12 The Greek here seems shaped by expressions in the Greek OT (LXX) referring to prayer and praise 'in the name' of God (e.g., Pss 63:4 [62:5 LXX]; 44:8 [43:9 LXX]; 105:3 [104:3 LXX]), and the obeisance referred to in v. 10 is both occasioned by the ritual acclamation of Jesus' name and directed to him.

13 Cf. Rev 5:13 for a synonymous description of universal acclamation. In this verse and the next, there is an allusion to Isa 45:23, where God is to be given universal homage, the wording here adapted to refer to Jesus as object of reverence. The full range of creation (not only hostile powers) is covered in the three spheres mentioned, 'under-earth' referring to the dead and/or infernal powers.

14 The acclamation is a slightly fuller form of the expression 'Jesus is Lord', which is found in Rom 10:9 and 1 Cor 12:3, and widely regarded as an early creedal formula and acclamation that formed a part of earliest Christian worship.

15 Some regard this phrase as added by Paul to the original hymn. Though possible, it is difficult to produce any compelling argument for or against this suggestion.

SELECTED BIBLIOGRAPHY

Fitzmyer, J. A., 'The Aramaic Background of Philippians 2:6 11', *Catholic Biblical Quarterly*, 50, 1988, pp. 470–83.
Hengel, Martin, 'Hymns and Christology', in *Between Jesus and Paul*, London, SCM, 1983, pp. 78–96.
Hoover, R. W., 'The Harpagmos Enigma: A Philological Solution', *Harvard Theological Review*, 64, 1971, pp. 95–119.
Hurtado, L. W., 'Jesus as Lordly Example in Philippians 2:5–11', in P. Richardson and J. C. Hurd (eds), *From Jesus to Paul*, Waterloo, Wilfrid Laurier University Press, 1984, pp. 113–26.

Käsemann, Ernst, 'A Critical Analysis of Philippians 2:5–11', in R. Funk (ed.), *God and Christ: Existence and Province*, New York, Harper, 1968, pp. 45–88.

Martin, R. P., *Carmen Christi*, rev. edn, Grand Rapids, Eerdmans, 1983 (orig. edn, 1967).

Marshall, I. H., 'The Christ-Hymn in Philippians', *Tyndale Bulletin*, 19, 1969, pp. 104–27.

Sanders, J. T., *The New Testament Christological Hymns*, SNTSMS 15, Cambridge, Cambridge University Press, 1971.

Talbert, C. H., 'The Problem of Pre-Existence in Phil 2:6–11', *Journal of Biblical Literature*, 86, 1967, pp. 141–53.

Wright, N. T., 'Jesus Christ is Lord: Philippians 2.5–11', in N. T. Wright (ed.), *The Climax of the Covenant*, Minneapolis, Fortress Press, 1992, pp. 56–98.

41

COLOSSIANS 1:15–20

Bonnie Thurston

INTRODUCTION

Attestation

The hymn is found in the two standard editions of the Greek Testament, Aland (*et al.*) 2nd edition (United Bible Societies, 1968) and Nestle-Aland (Deutsche Bibelgesellschaft, 1983). The latter provides more extensive textual notes and prints vv. 15–18a in verse strophes.

Provenance, authorship, date

The author of Colossians had not visited the church (2:1) which was probably the result of missionary work by Epaphras (1:7–8; 4:12–13) in the Lycus valley. References to the pagan past of the letter's recipients (1:21–2; 2:13) suggest a gentile-Christian community, though Jews were present. The fathers of the church universally accepted Colossians as Pauline; the continuing lively debate about authorship began in the nineteenth century. According to the text, Epaphras brought Paul news of threats to the Church's faith from false teaching (called 'philosophy' 2:8), but its substance can only be inferred from Chapter 2. Whoever wrote the letter and whenever and wherever it originated (we can be no more precise than, 'probably in the latter half of the first century in Asia Minor'), its crucial task is to refute the false teaching.

The text

At the heart of that refutation is the 'Christ Hymn'. E. Norden in *Agnostos Theos* (B. G. Teubner, 1913) was the first to point out on the basis of the repetitions and rhythm of the text that the passage might be a hymn or liturgical text. The shift of pronouns from the surrounding material (first person in vv. 13–14, third in 15–20, first and second in 21–3) and the use of relative constructions that mark liturgical materials support his assertion. Although the original provenance of the material is debated (Käsemann argues it was baptismal, Bornkamm that it was eucharistic), the scholarly consensus is that the passage is an insertion into the letter. If Paul wrote Colossians, vv. 15–20 contain the greatest concentration of words not found elsewhere in Paul, ten non-Pauline expressions and five hapax legomena. Apparently the author made insertions in and amended an already existing hymn. Käsemann observes that only eight of the 112 words need be omitted to remove all Christian references from the hymn.

Several divisions of the text are suggested. Scholars have delineated five strophes of four lines each, a two-fold division of vv. 15–17 and 18–20 and, the most usual division, vv. 15–18a and 18b–20. Thematically the hymn has cosmological material followed by soteriological. Some scholars argue the pre-Colossians hymn is marked with the Semitic stamp of the wisdom tradition, and others that it reflects Hellenistic gnostic redeemer-myth origins. I suggest that it is an example of the author's 'dual purpose vocabulary', material chosen by the author precisely because it had resonances for both Jewish and gentile audiences.

Although much is debated, the purpose of the hymn is clear. The author warns against doctrinal errors in the Colossian Church centring on the way Jesus Christ was understood (2:6–23). The christological hymn establishes the pre-eminence and supremacy of Christ in creation. The author assures the Colossian Christians that all powers in all the creation are subject to Christ's lordship. 'All' appears eight times in the hymn; 'heaven *and* [emphasis mine] earth' twice, at the opening and closing as a framing device to stress that Christ holds supremacy in all of reality. The hymn is introduced at the beginning of the letter because it presents an accurate Christian cosmology in vv. 15–18a, in which Christ in creation is associated with the figure of Wisdom, and a proper soteriology in vv. 18b–20, in which Christ's role in creation is that of reconciler and peacemaker. Christ is identified with God whose purpose in creation was to sum up all things in Christ and to return the whole creation to right relationship with the Divinity through him.

Christ is shown to be above all the heavenly beings in the panoply of those known to persons who formerly practised Hellenistic religions. His pre-eminence in creation and reconciliation is established. The cosmic powers, in the face of which the Colossians are depicted as feeling powerless, had been subdued and pacified by Christ who was before and above them all. As Käsemann noted, only this cosmic Christ could satisfy and overcome the religious concerns of syncretism in the Colossian congregation. In short, the hymn declares that Christ is all the Colossian Christians need.

BONNIE THURSTON

TRANSLATION

1.15 He is the image[1] of the unseen God,
firstborn[2] of all creation
16 For[3] in him[4] all things were created,
in the heavens and upon the earth,
things seen and unseen,
whether[5] thrones, or powers, or rules, or authorities
all things were created through him and for him.
17 And he himself[6] is before[7] all and in him all things cohere.[8]
18 And he himself is the head of his body the church,
who is beginning, first born from the dead,
so that in all he might have first place,[9]
19 that in him all the fullness (of God) delighted to dwell,[10]
20 and through him to reconcile all things in him,
whether things upon the earth or things in the heavens,[11]
making peace through the blood of his cross.[12]

NOTES

1 In 2 Cor 4:4 Paul has referred to Christ 'who is the image of God' (cf. John 1:18). As the image, literally icon, of God, Christ not only shares the reality he represents (according to Hebrews, 'the exact imprint of God's very being', 1:3 NRSV), but stands with the creator apart from the creation. The title *eikōn* here and *archē* in v. 18 are correlative designations of the *logos*.
2 'Firstborn' expresses not only priority, but in the cultural context, supremacy, as F. F. Bruce remarked, 'not only priority but primacy'. Ironically, Philo called Wisdom 'the firstborn son'.
3 The *hoti* conjunction with which the verse opens introduces the opinion of the writer.
4 That all things were created 'in Christ' make him the sphere within which the work of creation takes place (cf. 1 Cor 8:6 which has been called Paul's 'Christianized *Shema*', Deut 6:4) and reinforces the suggestion introduced in v. 1 that Christ appropriates Wisdom's role in creation. (See Prov 8, Sir 24, Wis 7.) Several scholars believe the idea of the pre-existence of Jesus entered Christianity via wisdom speculation (for example, J. D. G. Dunn, *Christology in the Making*, Philadelphia, Westminster, 1980).
5 H. G. Liddell and R. Scott (*A Greek–English Lexicon*, 8th edn, New York, American Book Company, n.d.) suggest *eite* be translated 'whether'. I have done so initially, but substituted the smoother English 'or' for the subsequent three occurrences. Eph 6:12 also depicts a hierarchy in the spiritual realm.
6 Since *autos* is used emphatically, I have translated the word as 'he himself' both here and in v. 18.
7 *Pro* with the genitive can express either time or rank. Here both are appropriate, though perhaps a temporal allusion is to be preferred.
8 Forms of *sunistēmi* are used in Hellenistic philosophy to describe the unity of creation. In the hymn, Christ is the principle of cohesion in the universe.
9 Plato's *Timaeus* conceives of the cosmos as a living being. Several scholars suggest the author added 'the church' here. For Christ as 'head of the church'

242

see also Eph 1:22–3 and 4:15; as 'first born from the dead' see Acts 26:23, Rom 14:9, Rev 1:5; as 'beginning' see Rev 3:14. On the basis of *archē* Burney argued that Col 1:16–18 is a rabbinic exposition of the first word of Genesis. As is usual the *hina* clause expresses purpose. Compare 1:18 and 2:10.

10 The verse makes the christological claim that all of God's essence and power reside in the Christ (cf. 2:9). *Plērōma* suggests not only the 'filling out' of something, but was used in religious texts of late antiquity for the uppermost spiritual world, nearest God. For a full discussion of this very potent term see Lohse (cf. 2:2–3).

11 Martin suggests that 'things upon the earth or things in the heavens' is an addition to amplify the scope of 'all'.

12 Note that the language of this verse is relational. *Apokatallaxai* implies not only reconciliation, but return to a previously unblemished state. Through Christ the creation is returned to its divinely created and determined state. 'Making peace' occurs in Matt 5:9. Scholars suggest 'through the blood of his cross' is an addition. I omit the second *di autou* which the RSV translators retain. (See Bruce Metzger, *A Textual Commentary on the Greek New Testament*, New York, United Bible Societies, 1975.) Repetition of *pas* forms throughout the hymn indicates the superiority of Christ.

SELECTED BIBLIOGRAPHY

Bruce, F.F., 'The "Christ Hymn" of Colossians 1:15-20', *BibSac*, 141, 1984, pp. 99–111.

Burney, C.F., 'Christ as the ARXH of Creation', *JTS*, 27, 1925/6, pp. 160–77.

Käsemann, E., 'A Primitive Christian Baptismal Liturgy', in *Essays on New Testament Themes*, Philadelphia, Fortress, 1982, pp. 149–68.

Lohse, E., *A Commentary on the Epistles to the Colossians and Philemon*, Philadelphia, Fortress, 1971.

Martin, R.P., 'An Early Christian Hymn (Col. 1:15–20)', *EvQr*, 36, 1964, pp. 195–205.

Robinson, J.M., 'A Formal Analysis of Colossians 1:15–20', *JBL*, 76, 1957, pp. 270–87.

Thurston, B., *Reading Colossians, Ephesians, and II Thessalonians*, New York, Crossroad, 1995.

Vawter, B., 'The Colossian Hymn and the Principle of Redaction', *CBQ*, 33, 1971, pp. 62–81.

Wright, N.T., 'Poetry and Theology in Col. 1:15–20', *NTS*, 36, 1990, pp. 444–68.

42

REVELATION 4:8–11; 5:9–14: HEAVENLY HYMNS OF CREATION AND REDEMPTION

Jean-Pierre Ruiz

INTRODUCTION

While some interpreters of the Apocalypse explain the place and function of doxologies in the book on the analogy of the choruses of Greek tragedy,[1] others suggest that the acclamations of Revelation 4 and 5 are patterned after elements of Second Temple Jewish or early Christian liturgy.[2] It is more likely that they are *ad hoc* compositions of the author,[3] who drew upon biblical images in shaping visionary narratives that were intended to be read aloud, perhaps during worship (1:3, 9–10), in the churches of the seven cities (Ephesus, Smyrna, Pergamum, Thyatira, Sardis, Philadelphia, Laodicea) of the Roman province of Asia towards the end of the reign of Domitian (81–96 CE). Evidence of the powerful influence of the imperial Roman court and cult on Asian Christians led David E. Aune to reject the view that Revelation 4–5 mirrors early Christian liturgy and to propose instead the convincing suggestion that the depiction of ceremonial words and deeds in Revelation 4–5 draws on rituals connected with the Roman court.[4]

To deal with the irreconcilably conflicting claims between Christ and the emperor, John's Apocalypse draws from sources that included biblical language and imagery, and from practices of imperial court ceremonial, to equip Christians with resources to resist assimilation. While the language of praise in Revelation 4–5 may not have been drawn directly from the liturgy of the Asian churches, it was intended to be read within their liturgy to reinforce their commitment to Jesus.[5]

The setting of these hymns in Revelation 4–5

Set within the report of a vision of the heavenly throne room, a vision introduced in Rev 4:1 by an invitation for the seer John to ascend through an open door, the acclamations in 4:9, 11; 5:9–10, 12–13 are combined with ritual gestures and cultic objects (prostration [4:10; 5:8, 14]; presentation of gold crowns [4:10], harps and gold bowls full of incense, incense that represents the prayers of the saints [5:8; 8:3–5]). These acclamations and gestures are performed by attendants at God's throne, beginning with the four living creatures (4:8), to whose doxology the twenty-four elders respond (4:10–11). In three expanding choruses of praise that follow, the living creatures and the elders sing together the 'new song' of 5:9–10; then 'myriads of myriads and thousands of thousands' of angels add their voices (5:11), until all creation joins in a hymn (5:13) that concludes with the 'Amen' of the living creatures and elders (5:14).

The throne vision inspired by Daniel 7,[6] into which these acclamations and ritual gestures are set, focuses on the seven-sealed book in the right hand of the one seated on the throne (5:1), on the question raised by the mighty angel in 5:2, 'Who is worthy to open the book and to open its seals?' and on the appearance of the seven-horned, seven-eyed slaughtered lamb (Revelation's most frequent image for Jesus, with twenty-nine occurrences), which unseals it in chapters 6–8.

Relation to other texts

Several of the hymnic acclamations in Revelation 4–5 have been and continue to be used in prayer and in Christian sacred music.[7] Hans Wildberger points out that the Trisagion ('holy, holy, holy') of the Isaian seraphim, the model for the utterance of the living creatures in Revelation 4:8, 'was part of the liturgy in the Jerusalem cult'.[8] In Jewish prayer, the Trisagion forms part of the *Qedushah*, the third blessing of the Amidah, the prayer known as the 'Eighteen Benedictions'. In many Christian liturgies, both eastern and western, the Trisagion appears in the hymn of praise that precedes the anaphora of the eucharistic liturgy. There is evidence for Christian liturgical use of the Trisagion as early as the late first century CE (1 Clement 34:6).

The Trisagion also forms part of the *Te Deum*, a fifth-century Latin hymn of praise to God the Father and to Jesus: '*Tibi omnes angeli, tibi caeli et universae potestates: tibi cherubim et seraphim incessabili voce proclamant: Sanctus, Sanctus, Sanctus Dominus Deus Sabaoth. Pleni sunt caeli et terra maiestatis gloriae tuae.*' In combining praise of God with praise of Christ, the *Te Deum* echoes the pattern of the acclamations in Revelation 4–5.

The structure and theology of the hymns

Within the vision report, the hymnic acclamations have their own consistent configuration.[9] The Trisagion is followed by three acclamations in which

God, then Jesus, and then both God and Jesus are declared worthy.[10] The three-fold pattern of the living creatures' constant (day and night) 'Holy, holy holy', underlined by the three-fold designation of God as the one 'who was and who is and who is to come', is echoed by three-fold patterns in the hymnody that follows. The Trisagion is followed by three 'worthy' acclamations, and the motive clauses associated with the first two of these (4:11 and 5:9–10) contain three members. In 4:11 the elders declare God worthy of glory, honour and power because (a) 'you created everything'; (b) 'through your will they existed'; (c) '[they] were created'. In 5:9–10 the living creatures and elders declare the Lamb worthy to receive and unseal the book, (a) 'because you were slaughtered'; (b) 'you purchased for God by your blood [*those from*] every tribe and language and people and nation'; (c) 'you made them for our God a reign and priests'.

The ascription of similar attributes to God, to Jesus, and then both to God and to Jesus establishes a consistent pattern borne out through the rest of the Apocalypse, a pattern in which the qualities of God are attributed to Jesus. Three attributes are ascribed to God in 4:9 (*doxa, timē, eucharistia*) and in 4:11 (*doxa, timē, dynamis*), the quasi-antiphonal response of the elders following the Trisagion of the living creatures. Seven are ascribed to Jesus in 5:11 (*dynamis, ploutos, sophia, ischys, timē, doxa, eulogia*), an instance of the Apocalypse's tendency towards expansion,[11] while four are ascribed to God and to Jesus in 5:13 (*eulogia, timē, doxa, kratos*). Some attributes are repeated: *doxa* and *timē* appear four times and *dynamis* appears twice.

The first two 'worthy' acclamations establish the theological and christological outlook of Revelation 4–5: in 4:11 God is declared worthy of glory, honour and power as the creator of all things; in 5:9 Jesus is pronounced worthy because of the redemption wrought by his crucifixion. The acclamations of Revelation 4–5 invite the audience to recognize the unity of the divine design as it unfolds both in creation and in redemption.

TRANSLATION

(4:8) And the four living creatures,[12] each of them having six wings, full of eyes inside and all around, do not cease day and night saying,
'Holy, holy, holy[13]
Lord God the omnipotent,[14]
who was and who is and who is to come.'[15]
(9) And as the living creatures give glory and honour and thanks to the one seated on the throne, who lives forever and ever, (10) the twenty-four elders fall down before the one seated on the throne and offer worship to the one who lives forever and ever, and they throw their crowns before the throne,[16] saying
(11) 'Worthy are you, our Lord and our God[17]
to receive the glory and the honour and the power

because you created everything
and through your will they existed and were created.'
(5:9) and they sing a new song,[18] saying,
'Worthy are you to receive the book and to open its seals
because you were slaughtered and you purchased for God[19] by your blood
[*those from*] every tribe and language and people and nation,[20]
(10) and you made them for our God a reign and priests[21]
and they will reign on the earth.'[22]
(11) Then I looked, and I heard the sound of many angels around the throne, and of the living creatures and of the elders, and their number was myriads of myriads and thousands of thousands,[23] (12) saying in a loud voice,
'Worthy is the slaughtered lamb to receive power and wealth and wisdom and strength and honour and glory and blessing.'
(13) and I heard every creature in heaven and on earth and under the earth and in the sea and everything in them, saying,
'To the one seated on the throne and to the lamb,
blessing and honour and glory and might forever and ever.'
(14) Then the four living creatures said, 'Amen', and the elders fell down and worshipped.

NOTES

1   J. W. Bowman, 'The Revelation to John: Its Dramatic Structure and Message', *Interpretation* 9 (1955), pp. 436–53.

2   See S. Läuchli, 'Eine Gottesdienststruktur in der Johannesoffenbarung', *Theologische Zeitschrift* 16 (1960), pp. 359–78.

3   See D. R. Carnegie, 'Worthy is the Lamb: The Hymns in Revelation', in H. H. Rowdon (ed.), *Christ the Lord: Studies in Christology Presented to Donald Guthrie*, Leicester, Intervarsity, 1982, pp. 243–56.

4   D. Aune, 'The Influence of Roman Imperial Court Ceremonial on the Apocalypse of John', *Biblical Research* 28 (1983), pp. 5–26.

5   See D. L. Barr, 'The Apocalypse of John as Oral Enactment', *Interpretation* 40 (1986), pp. 243–56; J. P. Ruiz, 'Betwixt and Between on the Lord's Day: Liturgy and the Apocalypse', *Society of Biblical Literature Seminar Papers*, 1992, pp. 654–72; idem, 'The Apocalypse of John and Contemporary Roman Catholic Liturgy', *Worship* 68 (1994), pp. 482–504.

6   G. K. Beale, *The Use of Daniel in Jewish Apocalyptic Literature and in the Revelation of St. John*, Lanham, University Press of America, 1984, pp. 178–228.

7   The AV text of Revelation 5:12–14 was set to music in the concluding choruses of Georg Friederich Handel's 1741 oratorio, *Messiah*.

8   Hans Wildberger, *Isaiah 1–12: A Commentary*, Minneapolis, Fortress, 1991, p. 265.

9   M. Harris, *The Literary Function of Hymns in the Apocalypse of John*, Ph.D. Dissertation, Southern Baptist Theological Seminary, Louisville, 1988, pp. 310–19.

10 W. C. Van Unnik, 'Worthy is the Lamb: The Background of Apoc 5', in A.

Descamp and A. De Halleux (eds), *Mélanges bibliques en hommage au R. P. Béda Rigaux*, Gembloux, Duculot, 1970, pp. 449–60.

11 R. H. Mounce, *The Book of Revelation*, New International Commentary on the New Testament, Grand Rapids, Eerdmans, 1977, p. 149; W. Bousset, *Die Offenbarung des Johannes*, 6th edition, Göttingen, Vandenhoeck & Ruprecht, 1906, p. 261.

12 The four living creatures combine features of the living creatures in the throne vision of Ezekiel 1–3 (faces: Ezek 1:6, 10; eyes: Ezek 1:18) and the seraphim of Isaiah 6 (6 wings: Isa 6:2).

13 See Isa 6:3; 1 Enoch 39:12; 2 Enoch 21:1.

14 This designation of God is used in Rev 11:17; 15:3; 16:7; 19:6; 21:22.

15 See Rev 1:4, 8.

16 According to Aune, who finds no biblical or extra-biblical Jewish parallel to the elders' gesture, 'The presentation of gold crowns to a sovereign was a ceremony inherited by the Romans from the traditions of Hellenistic kingship. . . . The Roman emperor was customarily presented with gold crowns by the senate (and provincial cities) on the occasions of accessions, consulships, victories and anniversaries' (op. cit., pp. 12–13). Aune cites examples from Arrian (*Anab. Alex.* 7, 23) and from Josephus (*Antiquities* 14, 304) describing the presentation of gold crowns as an act of homage. In other texts, the gesture of removing one's crown and presenting it to another is an act of submission by a defeated ruler to the victor. For example, Tacitus, *Annals* 15, 29: '*Tum placuit Tiridaten ponere apud effigiem Caesaris insigne regium nec nisi manu Neronis resumere*' ('It was then arranged that Tiridates should lay the emblem of his royalty before the statue of the emperor, to resume it only from the hand of Nero' [Loeb Classical Library translation]). Also Cicero, *Pro Sestio* 27, '*Hunc Cn. Pompeius cum in suis castris supplicem abiectum vidisset, erexit atque insigne regium, quod ille de suo capite abiecerat, reposuit*' ('Gnaeus Pompeius, however, when he saw him in his camp a suppliant at his feet, raised him up and replaced the royal diadem which he [*Tigranes*] had cast from his head' [Loeb Classical Library translation]). Because the elders in Revelation 4:10 are not defeated rulers, it is more appropriate to understand theirs as a gesture of homage than as a gesture of concession after defeat.

17 According to Suetonius, the emperor Domitian, during whose reign (81–96 CE) the Apocalypse of John was probably written, claimed the title '*dominus et deus noster*', 'our lord and god' (Suetonius, *Domitian*, 27).

18 See Isa 42:10; Pss 33:3; 40:4; 96:1; 98:1; 144:9; 149:1; Rev 14:3.

19 In place of *ēgorasas tō theō*, the preferable reading, some manuscripts read *ēgorasas tō theō hēmas* or *hēmas tō theō*. See Elisabeth Schüssler Fiorenza, 'Redemption as Liberation: Apoc 1:5f and 5:9f', in *The Book of Revelation: Justice and Judgment*, Philadelphia, Fortress, 1985, pp. 68–81.

20 These terms appear, in varying order, in Rev 7:9; 11:9; 13:7; 14:6. See Dan 3:4, 7, 29; 5:19; 6:25; 7:14.

21 'a reign and priests', first used in Rev 1:6, is an allusion to Ex 19:6, 'you shall be for me a reign of priests'. See Elisabeth Schüssler Fiorenza, *Priester für Gott: Studien zum Herrschafts- und Priestermotive in der Apokalypse*, Neutestamentliche Abhandlungen 7, Münster, Aschendorf, 1972.

22 In place of the future, *basileusousin*, some manuscripts (A, 046, 1006, 1611, 1859, 2020, 2065, 2081, 2138) read the present, *basileuousin*. The first person plural *basileusomen* is attested in one minuscule (2432), in the Clementine Vulgate and in the commentaries of Primasius and Beatus.

23 See Dan 7:10; 1 Enoch 14:22; 40:1; 60:1; 71:8.

SELECTED BIBLIOGRAPHY

Bowman, J. W., *The First Christian Drama: The Book of Revelation*, Philadelphia, Westminster, 1968.

Friesen, S. J., *Twice Neokoros: Ephesus, Asia, and the Cult of the Flavian Imperial Family*, Leiden, E. J. Brill, 1993.

Hurtado, L., 'Revelation 4–5 in the Light of Jewish Apocalyptic Analogies', *Journal for the Study of the New Testament* 25 (1985), pp. 105–24.

Mowry, L., 'Revelation 4–5 and Early Christian Liturgical Usage', *Journal of Biblical Literature* 71 (1952), pp. 75–84.

O'Rourke, J. J., 'The Hymns of the Apocalypse,' *Catholic Biblical Quarterly* 30 (1968), pp. 399–408.

Prigent, P., *Apocalypse et Liturgie*, Cahiers théologiques 52, Neuchâtel, Delachaux & Niestlé, 1964.

Thompson, Leonard L., *The Book of Revelation: Apocalypse and Empire*, New York, Oxford University Press, 1990.

Vanni, Ugo, 'L'Assemblea liturgica "soggetto interpretante" dell'Apocalisse', *Rassegna di Teologia* 23 (1982), pp. 497–513.

43

POST NEW TESTAMENT
CHRISTIAN PRAYERS

Barbara E. Bowe and John Clabeaux

These selected prayers span the period from the late first century to the mid-third century. It is thus not surprising that certain features of the New Testament prayers and hymns appear in these early prayers. For example, there is the sustained reference to Jesus Christ (especially in *Didache* and Ignatius), and the use of doxologies (in *Didache*, *1 Clement*, and the later prayers in *Martyrdom of Polycarp*, *Acts of Peter* and the *Prayer of the Apostle Paul*). However, some of these post New Testament prayers are in fact earlier than the latest of the New Testament documents. The prayers exhibit very different styles, functions, language and theology and thereby testify to the rich diversity in early Christian experience and in the language of prayer in the post New Testament period.

The various selections also differ in their form and structure. Two are explicitly liturgical or cultic prayers: the eucharistic prayers from the *Didache* 9 and 10 and Polycarp's prayer of sacrificial offering of his life at the moment of his martyrdom. Origen's prayer to Jesus the Footwasher may have been used in the context of a footwashing ceremony or some other penitential rite. It has been argued that Johannine Christians used such a ceremony into the second and third centuries.[1] The brief prayer in *Acts of Peter* 10 may allude to expressions from some sort of ceremony for re-admission of apostate Christians into the community. The hymn of Clement of Alexandria may have served as an invitation to worship since it ends with the words, 'escort with simplicity the mighty Son, as a chorus of peace, born of Christ . . . let us sing psalms together to the God of peace'. Finally, the Christian Vespers hymn, *Phōs Hilaron*, was used in the context of a service of light marking the close of the day.

Most of the prayers contain petitions on behalf of the one praying or on behalf of others. Some are simple and direct; others are more elaborate. Petitions for deliverance, mercy, healing and forgiveness abound. Present, too, is the request that God confound those who persecute Christians (especially in the prayer of *Ode of Solomon* 5). And in the selection from *1 Clement*, there are even petitions on behalf of the health, peace, and stability of the emperor. Only one of the selections contains the prayers of women (*Acts of Paul and Thecla*). All the others are (implicitly or explicitly) attributed to or prayed by men, although one cannot dismiss altogether the possibility that women might have prayed them, too. The prayer of Clement of Alexandria, moreover, contains the striking feminine image of Christ the *Logos* nursing at the breast tiny infants who come to him.

Most of the prayers selected are addressed directly to God, or to God through Christ, in keeping with the style of prayer evidenced in the New Testament texts. But two of the latest Christian prayers selected (those from Clement of Alexandria and Origen) address only Christ. In the case of Clement, there are twenty-four different poetic epithets for Christ. The rich symbolism of Clement's language illustrates the imaginative and creative character of early Christian prayer. *Phōs Hilaron* combines invocation first to Christ, then later in the hymn, to the Triune God, then again to Christ.

In several examples included in this section the language of the Christian prayers reflects the style and language of Jewish prayer forms. This influence is seen especially, for example, in the *Ode of Solomon* 5 with its opening *Hodayot* formula, 'I praise you O Lord, because I love you', or in the long prayer of *1 Clement*. This Jewish influence is less pronounced in the later selections, such as the *Acts of Peter*, the *Acts of Paul and Thecla*, Clement of Alexandria and Origen, a fact which attests that Christian prayer increasingly developed its own unique style and vocabulary.

Each of these early Christian prayers (with the exception of the *Ode of Solomon* 5, the *Prayer of Paul the Apostle* and *Phōs Hilaron*) is found embedded within a longer narrative selection, whether a letter (*1 Clement*, Ignatius, *Ephesians* 19, *Martyrdom of Polycarp*), a church order (*Didache*), narrative acts (*Acts of Peter* and *Acts of Paul and Thecla*), a treatise (Clement's *Pedagogue*) or a homily (Origen). The specific functions of these various prayers within their narrative settings are manifold. But wherever prayer language occurs it functions as a means to establish a cohesive bond between parties in the communication.[2] It taps the deep roots of commonly held beliefs and reinforces the symbolic world shared by the speaker/writer and the recipients of the communication. 'Prayer is a primary means of socializing oneself into and participating in such an order of existence.'[3] Hence, in the development of early Christianity, prayer language was an especially powerful tool for the maintenance of a developing Christian self-identity.

A difference in theological and christological content in these prayers reflects the diversity that marked early Christianity from its beginnings. Typically, in most of the selected prayers, God is addressed as holy and sovereign Lord, Creator and Master of the universe, Father of Jesus. The petitioner regularly expresses trust in God's willingness to save and to protect. However, a more intimate and personal God appears in Tryphaena's cry of help for Thecla: 'O God of my child Thecla, help Thecla!'

Christological differences in the selected prayers are even more striking. Compare, for example, the mediating, servant role of Christ in the prayers of the *Didache, 1 Clement* and the *Martyrdom of Polycarp* with the astral speculation of the 'Star Hymn' in Ignatius, or with the gnostic language of the *Prayer of Paul the Apostle* who prays to 'the First Born of the Pleroma of grace'. The multiple metaphors for Christ of Clement of Alexandria, and Origen's focused attention on the Johannine Jesus who is Footwasher, or the simple invocation of *Phōs Hilaron*, 'Joyous Light', show the range and diversity with which Christians could address Christ in prayer. The language of these prayers invites response. A number of the selections include doxologies ascribing glory and praise to God and calling forth an 'Amen' in reply. Believers are meant to be transformed by the prayer: strengthened in their faith, comforted, reassured and summoned.

A chronological development is evident among the prayers which divide roughly into two groups, composed either before or after *c.* 160 CE:

A   *Didache, 1 Clement, Odes of Solomon*, Ignatius and *Martyrdom of Polycarp*

B   *Acts of Peter, Acts of Paul, Prayer of Paul the Apostle*, Clement of Alexandria, Origen and *Phōs Hilaron*

The first group has more resonance with Jewish prayers, except for the 'Song of the Star' in Ignatius which itself exhibits a more unusual form. *Didache, 1 Clement* and the *Ode of Solomon* 5 have many allusions to the Hebrew Bible. All of these prayers as a whole (again with the exception of Ignatius) are directed to God the Creator through Jesus. This orientation in prayer is confirmed especially in the doxologies of the *Didache, 1 Clement* and *Martyrdom of Polycarp*, a form which had its origins in Judaism.

In the second group of prayers only the *Prayer of Paul the Apostle* has a doxology and allusions to the Hebrew Bible are far less frequent. There is a greater tendency to focus on particular incidents from the Christian gospels (Clement of Alexandria and Origen). And in both *Acts of Peter* and *Prayer of Paul the Apostle* it is difficult to determine whether it is to Jesus or to the Father that the various titles refer. Finally, the second group shows greater familiarity with features of Greco-Roman poetry and prayer. For example, Origen's prayer displays structural and rhythmical features of lyric poetry.[4] Clement of Alexandria's prayer mimics the well-documented Greco-Roman characteristic of heaping up epithets for the deity. And *Phōs Hilaron* borrows outright from the ritual hymns of the Isis and Cybele cults. Thus the trend overall is a continual departure from Jewish prayer forms and an increasing acceptance of features from the Greco-Roman classics.

NOTES

1   See the study of John Christopher Thomas, *Footwashing in John 13 and the Johannine Community*, JSNTSup 61, Sheffield, JSOT, 1991, *passim*.
2   See the discussion of 'cohesive language' in G. B. Caird, *The Language and Imagery of the Bible*, Philadelphia, Westminster Press, 1980, pp. 32–6.
3   Harry Maier, 'Ignatius Ephesians 19.1–3', see below, chapter 46, p. 267.
4   However, we cannot be sure whether the 'lyrical artistry' resides with Jerome who translated the Greek into Latin, or whether it was present in the original Greek.

44

1 CLEMENT 59.3–61.3 EPISTOLARY PRAYER IN CLEMENT OF ROME

Barbara E. Bowe

INTRODUCTION

Among the earliest Christian documents outside the New Testament canon, this letter from the Roman church to the church in Corinth provides a valuable witness to Christian life and practice in these two important cities in the latter part of the first century. On the basis of both internal and external evidence, *1 Clement* can be securely dated between *c.* 80 and 120 CE,[1] with a date around the turn of the century the most likely. The occasion which prompted these Roman Christians to write to Corinth was the report that had reached Rome (*1 Clem.* 47.7) of the renewed outbreak of factions and divisions in Corinth. These had been triggered by the deposition of some of the Corinthian presbyters (44.6). In keeping with acceptable rhetorical strategy, the author(s) provides only vague allusions to the exact nature of the dispute and to its cause. However, he considers its effects serious enough to warrant some response from the Roman community in the form of an appeal for the restoration of peace and concord (63.2). The letter was carried to Corinth by couriers from Rome (63.3; 65.1) who no doubt acted as mediators in the dispute. Rome, however, had no power or authority to impose its will on Christians in Corinth, but the letter does offer strong advice and warning should the dispute go unresolved.

The identity of the author(s) remains obscure, but ancient tradition from the time of Eusebius in the early fourth century (*Church Hist.* 3.16.1; 3.38.1) has attributed the letter to 'Clement'. Who this Clement might have been is still uncertain, although many, following the suggestion of J. B. Lightfoot, claim that he was an imperial freedman of the household of Titus Flavius Clemens and a (the?) leader among the Roman presbyters. He might have been the same Clement mentioned by the Shepherd of Hermas (*Vis.* 2.4.3) whose duty it was to send communication from Rome 'to the cities abroad', but this identification is by no means certain. On the other hand, it is certain that he did not function in the role of monarchical bishop, as Irenaeus later claimed (*Against all Heresies*, 3.3.3), since other early sources (notably Ignatius' letter to Rome) confirm that the monarchical episcopate did not exist in Rome until the middle of the second century. Moreover, *1 Clement* uses the terms 'bishops' and 'presbyters' interchangeably and always in the plural.

Whoever the actual author(s) might have been, the world-view and perspective of the letter are unambiguous. The author shares a positive assessment of Roman society and government (*1 Clem.* 61.1–3) and demonstrates a concern for the maintenance of hierarchical order consistent with the prevailing perspective of the well-educated 'social elite' of Roman society.[2] This viewpoint stands in sharp contrast, for instance, with the perspective of the author of a contemporary text, the Book of Revelation, which sees the imperial Roman system as the 'Beast' to be opposed at all costs, even at the risk of death.

1 Clement is preserved in five different manuscripts: Codex Alexandrinus [A], a Greek uncial MS of the fifth century, missing *1 Clem.* 57.7–63.4; Codex Hierosolymitanus (also called, Constantinopolitanus) [C], a Greek minuscule which dates from 1056 CE; a Syriac translation of the New Testament [S] dated to 1170 CE which includes the two so-called letters of Clement; an ancient Latin translation [L], perhaps from the second or third century, now preserved in a medieval MS from the eleventh century; and a Coptic translation [Co] preserved in two different MSS from the fourth and seventh centuries, respectively. In addition, the writings of both Clement of Alexandria and Jerome contain quotations from *1 Clement*. Its importance, especially in early Egyptian Christianity, is signalled by the fact that it was included with the New Testament documents in both the Codex Alexandrinus and in one of the Coptic manuscripts.

Prayer in *1 Clement* – form and function

Prayer language permeates the entire letter from Rome to Corinth and no doubt reflects the liturgical language and ethos prevalent in the Roman community of its day. Doxologies, blessings and thanksgivings, as well as the long petitionary prayer, punctuate the exhortations of this lengthy letter. Prayers such as these function as 'cohesive language' establishing rapport and creating a sense of mutual trust and common ethos between partners in the communication.[3] The long concluding prayer in *1 Clement*, moreover, lends a final, solemn authoritative note to the contents of the entire letter.

The style and theological tone of the prayer are close to Septuagintal language. In fact, this prayer is composed of a veritable pastiche of LXX phrases, praising God as Master, Creator of the ordered universe, helper and protector of creatures. God's sovereignty over all things is praised and celebrated throughout. Especially interesting and instructive are the verses

255

in 60.4–61.2 which offer prayer on behalf of the civil rulers who are seen as God's agents for the establishment of order and harmony on earth. The prayer concludes with a solemn doxology through Jesus Christ 'the high priest and protector of our souls'.

TRANSLATION

59.3   ... to hope[4] in your name, the source of all creation,
Open the eyes of our heart[5] to know you
who alone are the highest among the highest,
[and] who remains holy among the holy;[6]
[you] humble the pride of the arrogant,
nullify the plans of nations,
put the humble on high,
and the haughty [you] humble,
[you] make rich and poor,
kill and bestow life,[7]
[you] alone are the benefactor of spirits[8] and God of all flesh.
You look into the depths[9] and see human endeavours;
you are the helper of the endangered,
the saviour of those without hope,[10]
the creator and guardian over every spirit.
You multiply nations upon the earth,
and from them all you have chosen those who love you
through Jesus Christ your beloved Servant,[11]
through whom you have taught us, sanctified us, given us honour.

59.4   We beseech you, Master, be our helper and defender.[12]
Those who are in distress among us, save,
on the lowly, have mercy,
the fallen, raise up,
to those in need, show yourself
to the sick,[13] grant healing,
those of your people who stray, turn back.
Feed the hungry, ransom our prisoners,
revive the weak,
comfort the fainthearted.
Let all the nations know you, that you are God alone[14]
and that Jesus Christ is your Servant,
and that we are your people and sheep of your pasture.[15]

60.1   For you, through your works, revealed the eternal fabric of the universe;
you, Lord, created the world,
[you are] the faithful one in all generations,

righteous in judgement,
marvellous in might and majesty,
wise in creating,
understanding in establishing what is,
the one who is good in what is observed,
and kind to those who trust in you,
merciful and compassionate;[16]
Forgive us our iniquities and unrighteousness,
    [our] transgressions and faults.

60.2 Do not consider every sin of your servants and handmaids[17]
but cleanse us with the cleansing of your truth
and direct our steps
to walk in holiness of heart
and to do the things that are good and pleasing before you[18]
and before our rulers.

60.3 Yes, Master, make your face shine on us for our good in peace
that we might be sheltered by your mighty hand,
and delivered from all sin by your uplifted arm,[19]
and deliver us from those who hate us unjustly.

60.4 Give concord and peace to us and to all who dwell on the earth,
just as you gave to our ancestors when they called upon you
piously in faith and truth,
when they became obedient to your almighty and glorious[20] name.
[give concord and peace] also to our rulers and governors upon
    the earth.[21]

61.1 You, Master, have given the power of sovereignty to them
through your excellent and indescribable might,
that knowing the glory and honour given to them by you
we might be subject to them, in no way resisting your will:
Give to them, Lord, health, peace, concord, stability,
that they may administer the government which you have
given to them without offence.

61.2 For you, heavenly Master, King of the ages,[22]
give to human agents glory and honour and power over the things
on earth;
Lord, you direct their will according to what is 'good and
pleasing'[23] before you,
that, by administering in peace and gentleness with piety
the power given to them by you, they may find mercy with you.

61.3 You, who alone are able to do these things, and more abundant
good things for us, we praise you through the high priest and

protector of our souls – Jesus Christ – through whom to you be glory and majesty, both now and for all generations and forever and ever. Amen.[24]

NOTES

1 See L. L. Welborn, 'On the Date of First Clement', *Biblical Research*, 1984, vol. 29, pp. 35–54.
2 See James S. Jeffers, *Conflict at Rome. Social Order and Hierarchy in Early Christianity*, Minneapolis, Fortress, 1991, *passim*.
3 See, G. B. Caird, *Language and Imagery of the Bible*, Philadelphia, Westminster, 1980, pp. 32–3.
4 The prayer begins abruptly with an unexpected shift from 'his name' to 'your name' showing the author's unconscious slip into direct address. There is no need to conjecture a missing phrase.
5 Eph 1:18.
6 Isa 57:15.
7 This text combines allusions to: Isa 13:11; Ps 32:10; Job 5:11; 1 Sam 2:7 (Luke 1:53); Deut 32:39; 1 Sam 2:6; 2 Kgs 5:7; Num 27:16.
8 'Benefactor' (*euergetēn*) C; 'creator' (*ktistēn*) Co; 'finder' (*heuretēn*) LS.
9 Sir 16:18, 19.
10 Judith 9:11.
11 cf. Acts 4:27, servant or child.
12 Judith 9:11
13 'sick' (*astheneis*) LSCo; 'godless' (*asebeis*) C.
14 1 Kgs 8:60; 2 Kgs 19:19; Ezek 36:23.
15 Pss. 79:13; 95:7; 100:3.
16 Joel 2:13; Sir 2:11; 2 Chron 30:9.
17 It is striking that such inclusive language appears in this text.
18 Pss. 40:2; 119:133; 1 Kgs 9:4; Deut 12:25, 28; 13:18; 21:9.
19 This verse is another pastiche: see, for example, Ps 67:1; Num 6:25–6; Jer 21:10; Gen 50:20; Exod 6:1.
20 'Glorious' (*endoxō*) LSCo; 'most excellent' (*panaretō*) C.
21 For helpful insights on this verse especially, I thank John Clabeaux.
22 Tobit 13:6, 10; 1 Tim 1:17.
23 Deut 12:25, 28; 13:18.
24 Stanzas for 60.2–61.3 adapted from: S. Légasse, 'La Prière pour les chefs d'état. Antécédents Judaïques et témoins chrétiens du premier siècle', *NovT*, 1987, vol. 29:3, pp. 236–53.

SELECTED BIBLIOGRAPHY

Bowe, Barbara E., *A Church in Crisis: Ecclesiology and Paraenesis in Clement of Rome*, Minneapolis, Fortress, 1988.
——, 'Prayer Rendered for Caesar? 1 Clement 59.3–61.3', in *The Lord's Prayer and Other Prayer Texts from the Greco-Roman Era*, edited by James H. Charlesworth with Mark Harding and Mark Kiley, Valley Forge, PA, Trinity Press International, 1994, pp. 85–99.
Grant, R. M. and H. H. Graham, *First and Second Clement, The Apostolic Fathers*, vol. 2, New York, Nelson, 1965.
Henne, Philippe, *La christologie chez Clément de Rome et dans le Pasteur d'Hermas*,

Paradosis: Études de littérature et de theologie anciennes 33, Fribourg, Editions universitaires, 1992.

Holmes, Michael W. (ed.), *The Apostolic Fathers. Greek Texts and English Translations of Their Writings*, trans. and ed., J. B. Lightfoot and J. R. Hammer, 2nd edn, Grand Rapids, Baker, 1992.

Jaubert, A., *Clément de Rome: Epître aux Corinthiens*, SC 167, Paris, Cerf, 1971.

Jeffers, James S., *Conflict at Rome. Social Order and Hierarchy in Early Christianity*, Minneapolis, Fortress, 1991.

Légasse, S., 'La Prière pour les chefs d'état. Antécédents judaïques et témoins chrétiens du premier siècle', *NovT*, 1987, vol. 29:3, pp. 236–53.

Knopf, R., *Die Apostolischen Väter. Zwei Clemensbriefe*, HNT, Tübingen, Mohr–Siebeck, 1920.

Lightfoot, J. B., *The Apostolic Fathers, Part 1: S. Clement of Rome*, 2nd edn, 2 vols, London, Macmillan, 1890.

Lindemann, Andreas, *Die Apostolischen Väter I Die Clemensbriefe*, HNT 17, Tübingen, Mohr–Siebeck, 1992.

Richardson, Cyril C. (trans and ed.), *Early Christian Fathers*, New York, Macmillan, 1970.

45

THE EUCHARIST PRAYERS FROM
DIDACHE 9 AND 10

John Clabeaux

INTRODUCTION

The *Didache* is the earliest example of a Church Order which we possess.
This genre of early Christian literature included instruction for community
organization, teaching, prayer and praxis. The prayers presented below are
for the community's eucharist or Lord's Supper. Though the precise date for
the work as a whole eludes us, the prayers and the ritual they imply are
among the earliest known. The text is of enormous significance for the study
of the development of Christian liturgy. Parallels between these prayers and
rabbinical Jewish prayers have long been noted. The resolution of the extent
and meaning of these parallels is of great import for the study of Christian–
Jewish relations at the time this text was compiled.

Attestation

The only complete manuscript witness for the prayers of *Didache* 9 and 10 is
manuscript 'H' (for Hierosolymitanus, i.e., Jerusalem) dated 1056 CE.[1] A
Coptic manuscript dated to the fifth century (hereinafter Cop) is incomplete.[2] The most substantial difference between Cop and H is the addition in
Cop of a third prayer – a blessing for ointment. A similar blessing occurs in
the *Apostolic Constitutions*.[3] This last source (*Apostolic Constitutions* 7.25–7)
should not be considered a primary witness to the text of the *Didache*. Its
compiler consistently added to or deleted from the *Didache* to adapt it to
traditions which are certainly later.

Provenance, date and language

Although the *Didache* was used in Egypt as early as the fourth century, a
fact that is demonstrated by its use in the *Apostolic Constitutions*, the place

of its origin was more likely Syria or Palestine for two reasons. First, in *Didache* 9.4 there is a reference to 'bread scattered upon the mountains'; wheat is not grown on mountains in Egypt. Second, the *Didache* has affinities with the pre-Matthean tradition, that is, sayings of Jesus which eventually appeared in the Gospel of Matthew. Current scholarship on Matthew leans toward a Syrian or Palestinian origin for that gospel. Even those scholars who argue for an Egyptian origin of the *Didache* admit that the prayers here in chapters 9 and 10 probably derive from Palestinian Christianity.[4] The original language of our text was Greek, since, as with the canonical gospels, the text of the *Didache* is not easily converted into Aramaic.

There is an emerging consensus to set the date of the *Didache* between 90 and 100 CE, because the author seems not to have known or cited from the canonical gospels.[5] These prayers in *Didache* 9 and 10 probably predate the work itself and may derive from as early as 50–70 CE. The evidence usually adduced for this, namely, the rather primitive character of the service and the low christology it implies,[6] is not at all conclusive. Still, it is yet more unlikely that the author/compiler of the *Didache* has produced an original eucharistic service which he hoped to pass off as traditional.

Relation to other works

Didache's closest affinities are with the Gospel of Matthew. It has been conclusively demonstrated that the author did not have as a literary source the Gospel of Matthew known to us.[7] But the text of the Lord's Prayer in *Didache* 8.2 is very near to that of Matthew. More importantly, the author shows signs of being engaged in a struggle similar to that of the Matthean Community, namely, of differentiating itself from the Judaism emerging in Palestine after the destruction of Jerusalem in 70, while at the same time claiming continuity. Both Matthew and *Didache* seem to be in a relationship of imitative hostility *vis à vis* this 'formative Judaism' as it is called.[8] In both, one sees a sustained concern for ethics, reference to a system of wandering prophets and apostles,[9] and Jewish practices such as fasting on certain days of the week and fixed times for prayer.

In its eucharistic ritual *Didache* stands apart from all canonical works which contain eucharistic material.[10] The *Didache* prayers contain no reference to the Last Supper, no 'words of institution' and no explicit artic-ulation of the saving death of Jesus, although one could argue it is implied in the description of Jesus as 'Servant' by way of Isa 52:13–53:12, a passage known to Christians as the Suffering Servant song. The *Didache* eucharist involves an actual meal.[11] It should be noted, however, that the unusual order in *Didache* 9 of 'cup' and then 'bread' is seen also in Luke 22:14–23 and 1 Cor 10:16.

In terms of genre *Didache* has no real New Testament parallel. As a

Church Order it is more aptly compared to the *Manual of Discipline* or to the *Damascus Document* – both from Qumran. Like those documents it is sectarian literature with a pronounced eschatological emphasis, yet with its frequent references to Christ it is unquestionably Christian. Other parallels with the Qumran literature include the emphasis on 'life' and 'knowledge' as especially valued gifts of God.[12]

While there is a substantial scholarly consensus in favour of the dependence of these prayers on certain rabbinical prayers, namely the Kaddish, the Tenth Benediction and the Birkat ha-Mazon,[13] the verbal parallels are far outnumbered by the highly significant differences between these and the *Didache* prayers. In fact, there is more verbal resonance between the *Didache* prayers presented here and the Lord's Prayer as cited in *Didache* 8.2 than there is with any of the above-mentioned rabbinical prayers.

Literary context in the *Didache*

The context of these eucharistic prayers in the *Didache* are the author's ethical instruction in chs 1–6 and a directive near the end of the work (in 14.2) that the community members should confess sins and reconcile with each other prior to each Sunday eucharist.[14] This helps one to understand why the prayers emphasize so strongly the theme of gathering the community (see 9.4 and 10.5 below), and the 'perfecting' and protection of the community (see 9.5, 10.5 and 10.6 below). Unlike other eucharistic prayers the sacrificial elements are not in focus. Rather the community as 'holy vine' (9.2), 'broken bread' (9.4), the baptized (9.4), the dwelling place of God's name (10.2), the ones 'graced with spiritual food and drink' (10.3), and 'the church . . . made holy' (10.5), is constantly in view.

Use and effect on later writings

In the *Apostolic Constitutions* major changes were made in these prayers which suggest that the later sacramental tradition found them lacking in some ways. Words of institution were added, as were more explicit references to the sacrificial death of Jesus. *Didache*'s simple eucharist was overwhelmed by later streams of tradition evident in the *Apostolic Constitutions*. But what is most striking is the fact that some value must have been found in the *Didache* prayers. The fact that they were put to use by the editor of the *Apostolic Constitutions* and others[15] bespeaks their importance. They expressed concern for the unity of the Christian community as vital to the celebration of the eucharist. Perhaps this is why the *Didache* has enjoyed a resurgence of interest in twentieth-century liturgical reform. If one becomes familiar with the words, one will notice them in a growing number of hymns currently in use in Christian worship.[16]

TRANSLATION

9.1   Now, regarding the Eucharist (Thanksgiving),
      this is how you are to give thanks:

2   First, regarding the cup:
     We thank you, Our Father,[17] for the holy vine[18] of David your
      Servant,
     which you have made known to us through Jesus your servant.[19]
    – To you be glory forever. –[20]

3   Then regarding the broken (bread):[21]
     We thank you, Our Father, for life and knowledge
     which you have made known to us through Jesus your servant.
    – To you be glory forever. –

4   Just as this broken (bread) was scattered upon the mountains
     and, when gathered, became one, so may your church be gathered
     from the ends of the earth into your kingdom.
    – For yours is the glory and the power forever. –

5   But let no one eat nor drink from your Eucharist but those who
     have been baptized into the name of the Lord. For about this too
     has the Lord spoken, 'Do not give what is holy to the dogs'[22]

10.1 But after the meal[23] this is how you are to give thanks:

2   We thank you, Holy Father,[24]
     for your holy name which you caused to dwell in our hearts,
     and for knowledge, faith and immortality
     which you have made known to us through Jesus your servant.
    – To you be glory forever. –

3   You, Master Almighty, have created all things for the sake of your
     name.
    Food and drink you have given to human beings for their
     refreshment,
     that they may give thanks to you.
    But us you have graced with spiritual food and drink
     and eternal life through your servant.

4   Above all things we thank you for you are mighty.
    – To you be glory forever. –

5   Remember, Lord, your church
     to deliver her from all evil and to perfect her in your love.[25]
    Gather her from the four winds,[26] made holy,
     into your kingdom which you have prepared for her.
    – For yours is the power and the glory forever. –

6   Let grace come and let this world pass away!
    – Hosanna to the God of David![27] –
    Whoever is holy, let him (or her) come.
    Whoever is not, let him (or her) repent.

– Marana Tha. Amen. –[28]

7   But as for the prophets, let them give thanks as much as they wish.[29]

NOTES

1   The text of H was largely corroborated by a Georgian translation from an early nineteenth-century manuscript. The problem is, we no longer possess this text, and, since it was obtained in Constantinople, the current resting place of H, the two manuscripts may be related. The scribe of the Georgian translation may have seen H. A list of the Georgian version's variations from a German translation of H is presented by G. Paradse, 'Die Lehre der zwölf Apostel in der georgischen Überlieferung', *Zeitschrift für Neutestamentliche Wissenschaft*, 1932, vol. 31, pp. 111–16. It is also fully represented and discussed by J. P. Audet, *La Didachè: Instructions des Apôtres*, Paris, Gabalda, 1958, pp. 45–50.

2   It begins at *Didache* 10.3 and breaks off for no apparent reason at 12.2. It has been described as a scribal writing exercise. This would account for its abrupt beginning and ending. The best presentation and discussion of the Coptic manuscript is that of F. Jones and P. Mirecki, 'Considerations of the Coptic Papyrus of the Didache', in Clayton Jefford (ed.), *The Didache in Context*, Leiden, E. J. Brill, 1995, pp. 47–87. Currently, many scholars have ceased trying to adjudicate every difference between Cop and H and now simply speak of two recensions of the *Didache*, one represented by Cop and the *Apostolic Constitutions* and the other represented by H and the Georgian translation.

3   The prayer in *Apostolic Constitutions* 7.27 reads: 'Regarding the ointment, this is how you are to give thanks: We thank you, God, Creator of all things, both for the fragrance of the ointment and for eternal deathlessness which you have made known to us through Jesus your servant. For yours is the glory and the power forever.'

4   Arthur Vööbus, *Liturgical Traditions in the Didache*, Stockholm, ETSE, 1968, pp. 169–72 accepts Palestinian Jewish-Christian origin, but warns against a more precise specification of the locale.

5   This was conclusively demonstrated by H. Koester, *Synoptische Überlieferung bei den apostolischen Vätern*, Texte and Untersuchungen no. 65, Berlin, Akademie Verlag, 1957, especially p. 260, and has been confirmed more recently by C. Jefford, *The Sayings of Jesus in the Teaching of the Twelve Apostles*, Leiden, E. J. Brill, 1989.

6   These arguments are summed up by Johannes Quasten, *Patrology*, vol. 1, Utrecht, Spectrum, 5th edn, 1975, pp. 36–7. The weakest element of this evidence is the use of the term *pais theou* (Servant of God) for Jesus. R. Kraft (*The Apostolic Fathers*, vol. 3, *Barnabas and the Didache*, New York, Thomas Nelson & Sons, 1965, p. 75) represents the view that this sort of terminology is similar to the Jerusalem tradition reflected in Acts of the Apostles (see Acts 3:13, 26 and 4:25) and is, therefore, rather primitive. The reader of this anthology, however, will notice that *pais* (Servant) is used for Jesus in *1 Clement* and the *Martyrdom of Polycarp*. Hence the use of that term for Jesus is no proof of an origin in the first generation of the Christian movement.

7   See n. 5.

8   See A. Overman, *Matthew and Formative Judaism*, Philadelphia, Fortress, 1993, for a full description of what is meant by the term 'Formative Judaism'.

9   A. Overman, op. cit., pp. 117–19, notes that in the Matthean Community the system of wandering prophets was on the wane.

10 These include Matt 26:26–9, Mark 14:22–5, Luke 22:15–20, John 6:51–8 and 1 Cor 11:23–5.

11 See *Didache* 10.1, 'after the meal' which when translated more literally is rendered 'after you have been filled'. In 1 Cor 11 the eucharist was held along with an actual meal, but in that passage Paul discourages this procedure.

12 See the Qumran *Manual of Discipline* (1QS) 3.15 and 11.3.

13 See J. Riggs, 'From Gracious Table to Sacramental Elements: The Tradition History of *Didache* 9 and 10', *Second Century*, 1984, vol. 4, p. 91 n. 30. He lists both the supporters of this dependency and those who have opposed it.

14 For a persuasive presentation of this position see A. Milavec, *The Pastoral Genius of the Didache*, Mahwah, Paulist, 1997.

15 A. Vööbus, op. cit., p. 80 cites Athanasius, Serapion of Thumis, the author of the Papyrus of Der Balizeh and at least three Ethiopic eucharists.

16 A short list includes: 'Father We Thank Thee' by F. Tucker, 'We Thank Thee Father' by G. Norbet, 'Life Giving Bread, Saving Cup' by J. Chepponis, 'Seed Scattered and Sown' by D. Feiten and 'One Bread, One Body' (verse 3) by J. Foley.

17 This is the same form of address to God as in the Lord's Prayer in *Didache* 8.2.

18 This expression refers to the Church as People of God. The use of the image in the Hebrew Bible is sufficient source. See Psalm 80:8–18; Jer 2:21; Ezek 17:5–10; 19:10–14; and Hos 10:1 for Israel as 'vine'. See also 4 Ezra 5:23. In Isa 5:1–7 Israel is the vineyard. The Dead Sea Community saw itself as a 'Plantation' or 'Planting' in its *Manual of Discipline* (1QS) 8.5 and *Damascus Document* (CD) 1.7.

19 See Acts 3:13, 26; 4:25, 27 and 30 for the use of this early title for Jesus.

20 Many editors add 'Amen' here and after the doxologies like it. They base this on the presence of 'Amen' in such places in Cop which only contains *Didache* chs 10–11. I have used dashes before and after the doxology to mark it off as a response of the congregation. It may have been said by the presider.

21 Manuscript H reads *klasma* which simply means 'broken'. Some editors suggest that the original reading is the more usual word for bread, *artos*, as it occurs in the *Apostolic Constitutions* and other later prayers. Certainly bread is meant, but the brokenness is in focus here. 'Broken' (*klasma*) is more likely the original reading since it is easier to imagine someone changing it to 'bread' (*artos*) than the other way around.

22 These words occur verbatim in Matt 7:6a.

23 The Greek word is *emplēsthēnai* which means 'to have been filled'. Some translators render it 'after you have been filled'. The important thing is that an actual, substantial meal is indicated.

24 Jesus uses this address in his prayer in John 17:11. Arguments for a literary dependence of *Didache* 9 and 10 on John 17 are insubstantial. Both John and the *Didache* are dependent on ancient liturgical traditions.

25 The call to perfection, also found in Matt 5:48 and 19:21, refers not to ethical perfection but completeness of commitment. See 1 Kings 8:61; and 1:4, the Qumran *Manual of Discipline* (1QS) 1.8–13, and the *Thanksgiving Hymns* of Qumran (1QH) 1.36. In the *Manual of Discipline* (1QS) 8.9 the Qumran Community is referred to as a 'House of Perfection'.

26 See Isa 11:11–12 and Psalm 147:2. For the specific reference to gathering 'from the four winds' at the end of time see Matt 24:31.

27 Cop reads 'house of David', *Apostolic Constitutions* 7.26.5 has 'Son of David'. Both are later attempts to improve the clumsy, but original, expression 'God of David'. Once again, the more difficult reading is to be preferred.

28 See Rev 22:17, 20 and 1 Cor 16:22 for similar 'liturgical dialogue' i.e., statement by the presider with response by the congregation.
29 This 'as much as they wish' (*hosa thelousin* in Greek) may mean either 'as often as they wish', or 'as extensively as they wish'. Context suggests the latter.

SELECTED BIBLIOGRAPHY

(For an exhaustive bibliography see the entry under 'Jefford, Clayton' below.)
Audet, Jean-Paul, *La Didachè: Instructions des Apôtres*, Paris, Gabalda, 1958.
Jefford, Clayton, *The Didache in Context: Essays on Its Text, History and Transmission*, Leiden, E. J. Brill, 1995.
Niederwimmer, Kurt, *Die Didache*, Göttingen, Vandenhoeck & Ruprecht, 1989.
Milavec, Aaron, *The Pastoral Genius of the Didache*, Mahwah, Paulist, 1997.
Riggs, John, 'From Gracious Table to Sacramental Elements: The Tradition History of Didache 9 and 10', *Second Century*, 1984, vol. 4, pp. 83–101.
Vööbus, Arthur, *Liturgical Traditions in the Didache*, Stockholm, ETSE, 1968.

46

IGNATIUS *EPHESIANS* 19.1–3

Harry O. Maier

INTRODUCTION

The 'Star Hymn' appears near the end of Ignatius' *Letter to the Ephesians*, the first of seven letters the bishop of Antioch wrote while *en route* as a prisoner to Rome where he was martyred in *c.* 113 CE. Ignatius' concern in this correspondence was two-fold: to oppose a docetic christology which had taken root in Ephesus and other Asia Minor churches, and to encourage his audience to submit themselves to the oversight of a single bishop. The hymn, with its allusion to the abolition of death in 19.3, as well as the reference to the birth and death of Christ in Ignatius' preface, is clearly anti-docetic. As esoteric teaching (for example, the oxymoronic 'three mysteries of a loud shout') its inclusion by Ignatius must have gone some way toward legitimating him as a spiritual authority and added weight to his exhortations to the Ephesians to submit themselves to the authority of a single bishop.[1] Whether or not Ignatius achieved the desired result by including it, the Star Hymn was to exercise an effect on an audience far wider than the bishop of Antioch's immediate circle of readers: it was one of the most quoted extra-canonical passages in the early Church.[2]

Form and text

There is some disagreement whether the hymn proper (v. 2–3) is pre-Ignatian. Of the many arguments proposed in support of a pre-existing hymn,[3] the presence of stylistic elements and vocabulary typical of hymnody and poetry (chiasmos, homoeoteleuton, parallelism, etc.), as well as vocabulary absent in the rest of the Ignatian correspondence, are the strongest evidence for the theory of a pre-existing hymn,[4] though none of these can exclude the possibility of composition by Ignatius.[5] The hymn has been categorized literarily as belonging to a genre of epiphany hymns, of which certain *Odes of Solomon*, the Magnificat (Luke 1:46–56), the Benedictus (Luke 2:29–32) and

John's Prologue (1:1–5, *passim*) are also alleged as instances.[6] If the existence of such an epiphany genre remains doubtful, it is none the less certainly correct to link the hymn with epiphany themes.[7] Once the hymn with its exotic star imagery is understood as a celebration of and commentary on the appearance of the star of Bethlehem (Matt 2:2–4, 9–10) and its role in signalling the incarnation, the meaning of the star references falls into place.

In the translation below, the division of the hymn into four strophes is based on formal and stylistic elements of the Greek text.[8] The first three strophes take up respectively the star's appearance, its effect on the heavenly bodies, and the results of its epiphany; the fourth provides a concluding theological commentary. It is impossible in an English translation to capture the stylistic elements of the Greek text. This is especially the case in the third strophe, where ll. 2–4 share homoeoteleuton, ll. 2–3 are parallel grammatically, and ll. 1 and 2 as well as 1 and 5 form chiasms. The manuscript tradition presents few differences worthy of note here. The Armenian and Syriac abridgement of the Greek original text omit the verb 'destroyed' (*diephtheireto*) in strophe 2, l. 4, thus altering the connection of nouns and verbs, but its presence in the two definitive Greek manuscripts and their literal Latin translation weigh heavily in its favour, and its presence contributes significantly to the stylistic elements just outlined. A Syriac abridgement of the original Greek manuscript also omits the phrase 'and similarly the death of the Lord' in 19.1, but the phrase is presupposed in the reference to the three loud shouts that follows and is indeed central to the theological assertion of the hymn as a whole, testified by its concluding line. Indeed, 'the *pathos* is the center round which his [Ignatius'] thoughts revolve'.[9]

Theology

Cultural anthropologist Clifford Geertz has defined a religion as 'a system of symbols which acts to establish powerful, pervasive, and long-lasting moods and motivations in men by formulating conceptions of a general order of existence and clothing these conceptions with such an aura of factuality that the moods and motivations seem uniquely realistic'.[10] Prayer is a primary means of socializing oneself into and participating in such an order of existence. Religiously and theologically Ignatius' hymn introduces us to a symbolic world in which religious identity is conceived of as freedom from the constraint and domination of hostile metaphysical forces. It betrays a world in which magic and the power of the stars are believed to affect the course of human affairs, usually adversely (a view widespread in antiquity), and where the mood of those celebrating their identity through the hymn is one of joyous victory over those inimical forces which once held them in bondage. While the cosmic imagery of the hymn is to be located in reflection on the star narrative connected with Jesus' birth, its theological centre is the celebration of the newness which the incarnation, especially Jesus' death, has inaugurated and the victory over the principalities and powers it signals. It thus betrays a decidedly (deutero-)Pauline character, as we shall see.

Some have discerned traces of a gnostic myth of the descending redeemer in the references to the appearance of the star (19.2). While there are certainly parallels between the star imagery and gnostic conceptions,[11] the elaborate theories derived from them (that the hymn is an Ignatian redaction of an earlier gnostic text;[12] that 19.2 represents a gnostic kernel, commented upon by Ignatius in 19.1 and 3)[13] far exceed the bounds of the evidence.[14] The simpler explanation of the star imagery is to be found in reflection on the significance of the birth and death of Jesus, the former heralded by the star.[15] In the passage which immediately follows the hymn (20.1) Ignatius promises to send a second letter to the Ephesians instructing them regarding the life, death and resurrection of 'the new man Jesus Christ'. In 19.2-3, then, we are dealing most probably with the birth story, as is indicated in the references in 19.1 to Mary's virginity and the birth.

Relationship to other literature

The star narrative associated with Jesus' birth was fertile ground for theological reflection and imagination in early Christianity. Alongside Matt 2:2–4, 9–10 two texts are notable. Dating from the mid- to late second century, *The Protevangelium of James* testifies (19.2) that when Mary was giving birth 'a great light appeared in the cave, so that our eyes could not bear it. A short time afterwards that light withdrew until the child appeared, and it went and took the breast of Mary.' (A perhaps later addition to the text (21.2) has one of the Magi report, 'We saw how an indescribably bright star shone among these stars and dimmed them, so that they no longer shone.') The other text, from Clement of Alexandria's *Excerpta ex Theodoto* 69–75, with language strongly reminiscent of our hymn, links the star's appearance with the descent of the redeemer: a 'strange and new star' rose to overthrow 'the old order of the stars, shining with a new light that is not of this world' (74). Behind these passages, including Ignatius' hymn, one may perhaps detect the influence of a sapiential tradition which represented Wisdom as a light more resplendent than the sun and the stars (Wis 7:29–30) or the liberating Word appearing on earth to free God's elect from bondage (Wis 18:14–15).[16]

It is to this latter theme of liberation that the star imagery of Ignatius' hymn is directed, especially in the third strophe (19.3) where the effects of the star's appearance are enumerated. The violent language introduces a sinister note to the more panegyric strains of 19.2, foreshadowed in 19.1 with the references to the hidden incarnation. The connection of the star with magic is anticipated, again, in Matt 2:2–4, 10–11. Tertullian (*On Idolatry* 9) interpreted this passage as heralding the end of the dominion of the stars and magic. Similarly, Origen (*C. Cel.* 1.60) argued the appearance of the star brought an end to the ability of the magi to practise divination, given them by evil spirits. The gnostic *Excerpta ex Theodoto* is also not far from this when it links the appearance of the new and strange star with the overthrowing of 'the old order of the stars'. The belief that heavenly bodies were governed by fallen angels appears in 1 Enoch (18.12–19.3; 21.1–10) and the similarly apocalyptic, second-century *Ascension of Isaiah* describes the firmament and the earth as governed by 'the angels of this world' (10.8–13). Similar to the Ignatian preface to the hymn, Isaiah sees Jesus descending secretly into Satan's dominion, his birth kept silent, his identity during the crucifixion hidden, in order to vanquish the inimical powers (11.1–24). In Ignatius' hymn, Jesus likewise enters alien territory in order to win a decisive victory, in this case over death (19.3).

When Ignatius refers to the events hidden from the 'ruler of this age' in 19.1 he is probably reflecting on 1 Cor 2:6–8, having just quoted 1 Cor 1:20 in 18.1. Paul refers to the probability that Jesus would not have been crucified had 'the governing powers' of this 'passing age' or 'the powers that rule the world' known who Jesus was. It is unclear whether Paul means earthly powers or cosmic ones, but Paul's later canonical interpreters, the writers of Colossians and Ephesians, resolved the ambiguity by identifying them as metaphysical beings, interpreting salvation as freedom from the dominion of cosmic powers (Col 1.13; 2.8, 18–20; Eph 2.1–6; 6.12) and it is in this tradition that Ignatius finds himself when he reflects on the newness of Christian life. As already stated, references to newness recur as the refrain of the first three strophes and this is a theme Ignatius goes on to develop when in Pauline terms he describes Jesus as 'the new man' in 20.1. Whether composed by Ignatius or not, the allusion in the third strophe to God being revealed as a human 'for newness of eternal life' is reminiscent of NT Rom 6:4 and can hardly have been written without that passage or theological orientation in mind.[17] The newness which this hymn proclaims is a newness centred in the new human being Jesus Christ. Again as in the case of Paul and his interpreters, the new state which results from Jesus' death and, in the case of Colossians and Ephesians, ascension, entails a new knowledge. The elect are those who have privileged understanding of the mysteries of God (1 Cor 1:5; 13:2; 2 Cor 2:14; Phil 3:8; Col 2:3; Eph 3:19), an understanding the Star Hymn as a whole presumes and indeed celebrates where it states that with the incarnation came the abolition of ignorance of evil (a theme fully developed in gnosticism).[18] What is unique about this hymn is the way it blends these more Pauline motifs, which constitute its theological centre, with the birth narrative traditions associated with the star.

TRANSLATION

(19.1) Hidden from the ruler of this world were the virginity of Mary and her giving birth and similarly the death of the Lord – three mysteries of a loud shout, accomplished in the stillness of God. (2) How then was this revealed to the world?

> A star shone in heaven outshining all the stars,
> inexpressible was its light
> and its newness caused astonishment.

> All the remaining stars
> with the sun and moon
> joined in chorus to hymn the star;
> its superabundant light was outshining all the others.
> Perplexity arose, whence came this new star so unlike them.

> (3) From that time onward all magic began to be dissolved
> and every bond made to vanish,
> ignorance of evil began to be vanquished,
> the old reign destroyed;
> when God was revealed as a human
> to bring the newness of eternal life.

> What had been purposed by God for completion was inaugurated.
> Henceforth everything was disturbed
> because the overthrow of death was being effected.

NOTES

1. For further discussion of issues of social setting see Harry O. Maier, 'The Charismatic Authority of Ignatius of Antioch', *Studies in Religion/Recherches Sciences Religieuses* 1989, vol. 18, pp. 185–99.
2. See J.B. Lightfoot, *The Apostolic Fathers* (Part 2: Ignatius and Polycarp, vol. 2), Michigan, Baker, 1981, p. 76 for a catalogue of references.
3. The chief ones are presented by C.F. Burney, *The Aramaic Origin of the Fourth Gospel*, Oxford, Clarendon Press, 1922, p. 161; Ernst Lohmeyer, *Kyrios Jesus: Eine Untersuchung zu Phil. 2, 5–11*, Sitzungsberichte der Heidelberger Akademie der Wissenschaften, Philosophisch-historische Klasse 18/4, Heidelberg, 1927/8, p. 64; R.P. Martin, *Carmen Christi*, Cambridge, Cambridge University Press, 1967, pp. 11ff., 310.
4. R. Deichgräber, *Gotteshymnus und Christushymnus in der frühen Christenheit, Untersuchungen zu Form, Sprache und Stil der frühchristlichen Hymnen*, Göttingen, Vandenhoeck & Ruprecht, 1967, pp. 157ff.
5. William R. Schoedel, *Ignatius of Antioch*, Philadelphia, Fortress, 1985, p. 88; Henning Paulsen, *Studien zur Theologie des Ignatius von Antiochien* (Forschungen zur Kirchen- und Dogmengeschichte 29), Göttingen, Vandenhoeck & Ruprecht, 1978, pp. 176f.
6. Gottfried Schille, *Frühchristliche Hymnen*, Berlin, Evangelische Verlagsanstalt, 1965, pp. 117f.
7. Convincingly argued for and documented by Jean Daniélou, *Primitive Christian Symbols*, Baltimore, Helicon, 1964, pp. 102–23.
8. These are more fully discussed by H.F. Stander, 'The Starhymn in the Epistle of Ignatius to the Ephesians (19.2–3)', *Vigiliae Christianae*, 1989, vol. 43, pp. 209–14, whose lead I here follow.

9   Lightfoot, op. cit., p. 78.
10 *The Interpretation of Cultures*, New York, Basic Books, 1973, p. 90.
11 These are more fully outlined by Schoedel, op. cit., p. 91.
12 Heinrich Schlier, *Religionsgeschichtliche Untersuchungen zu den Ignatius-briefen*, Giessen, Töpelman, 1929, pp. 5 32.
13 Hans-Werner Bartsch, *Gnostisches Gut und Gemeindetradition bei Ignatius von Antiochien*, Gütersloh, Evangelischer Verlag, 1940, pp. 156ff.
14 For detailed criticism of the theories of Schlier and Bartsch see Virginia Corwin, *St. Ignatius and Christianity in Antioch*, New Haven, Yale University Press, 1960, pp. 175–88; Robert M. Grant, *Ignatius of Antioch* (The Apostolic Fathers, vol. 4), London, Camden, Toronto, Thomas Nelson, 1966, pp. 49–51.
15 Thus, ibid. and Schoedel, op. cit., pp. 90–1.
16 For fuller discussion of the connection with Wisdom see Alan Cabanassis, 'Wisdom 18:14f.: An Early Christian Text', *Vigiliae Christianae*, 1956, vol. 10, pp. 97–102.
17 Thus W. Bauer, *Die Briefe des Ignatius von Antiochia und der Polykarpbrief* (Handbuch zum Neuen Testament Die Apostolischen Väter II), Tübingen, J.C.B. Mohr, 1920, p. 216.
18 Paulsen, op. cit., pp. 178–9.

SELECTED BIBLIOGRAPHY

Bauer, W., Paulsen, H., *Die Briefe des Ignatius von Antiochia und der Polykarpbrief* (Handbuch zum Neuen Testament Die Apostolischen Väter II), Tübingen, J.C.B. Mohr, 1985.
Corwin, Virginia, *St. Ignatius and Christianity in Antioch*, New Haven, Yale University Press, 1960.
Grant, Robert, *Ignatius of Antioch* (The Apostolic Fathers, vol. 4), London, Camden, Toronto, Thomas Nelson, 1966.
Lightfoot, J.B., *The Apostolic Fathers* (*Part 2: Ignatius and Polycarp*, vol. 2), Michigan, Baker, 1981.
Paulsen, Henning, *Studien zur Theologie des Ignatius von Antiochien* (Forschungen zur Kirchen- und Dogmengeschichte 29), Göttingen, Vandenhoeck & Ruprecht, 1978.
Schoedel, William R., *Ignatius of Antioch*, Philadelphia, Fortress, 1985.
Stander, H.F., 'The Starhymn in the Epistle of Ignatius to the Ephesians (19:2–3)', *Vigiliae Christianae*, 1989, vol. 43, pp. 209–14.

47

ODE OF SOLOMON 5: PRAISE WHILE CONTEMPLATING PERSECUTORS

James H. Charlesworth

INTRODUCTION

The *Odes of Solomon* are forty-two hymns attributed to Solomon, because of his renowned wisdom and especially because of the biblical record which asserts that he composed numerous poetic works. The odes were composed by a Jew who had become a Christian. He most likely lived in the community that produced the Gospel of John.

Praise for deliverance

Odes of Solomon 5 is a psalm for individual deliverance. The flow of this poetic work is as follows: opening praise (5:1), followed by six petitions (5:2–7) and a narrative (5:8–9), then a conclusion (5:10–15) that celebrates the conquering of fear because 'the Lord is with me' (5:15).

The *Odes of Solomon* are preserved in two Syriac manuscripts (tenth and fifteenth centuries CE), one third-century Greek papyrus (Pap. Bod. 11), in a fourth-century Coptic psalmbook (the *Pistis Sophia*), and in the fourth-century Lactantius quoted in Latin two verses from ode 19. Ode 5 is extant in only one Syriac manuscript (fifteenth century) and a Coptic quotation which contains only verses 1 through 11.

Original language and provenance

Any explanation of this ode must be informed by the present consensus on the original language and date of the *Odes of Solomon*.[1] J. A. Emerton and J. H. Charlesworth have stressed that this collection of odes is clearly Christian, originally composed in Syriac[2] and is not to be branded as gnostic.[3] M. Lattke has recently shown that they must antedate *c.* 125 CE.[4]

It is impossible to discern in which country these odes were composed. If Syriac is the original language, then it is somewhere in Syria (which in the first half of the second century would include Galilee). Charlesworth and R. A. Culpepper have indicated that the *Odes of Solomon* neither influenced the composition of the Gospel of John (as Bultmann thought)[5] nor were influenced by it. Rather, both the *Odes of Solomon* and the Gospel of John took shape over a period of time within the Johannine Community (or School).[6] J. Carmignac and Charlesworth independently suggested that the vast and impressive links between the *Odes of Solomon* and the *Thanksgiving Hymns*, as well as the *Rule of the Community* (both from Qumran), raise the probability that they were composed by an Essene converted to Christianity.[7] D. E. Aune used the *Odes of Solomon* to indicate the presence of 'realizing eschatology' in earliest Christianity;[8] which is surely one of the hallmarks of the present ode and of the Gospel of John.

Exegesis of ode 5

With these insights in mind let us turn to an exegesis of ode 5. The ode is thoroughly Jewish. Long ago R. Harris offered the opinion that the ode 'contains a somewhat Jewish section in verses 4–9, with prayer for the discomfiture of one's enemies. If there is a definite Christian feature, it is, perhaps, the garland upon the singer's head ...'[9] Indeed, there is nothing peculiarly 'Christian' about this ode; hence, it seems to derive from an early time when Judaism included those Jews who believed in Jesus, or conceivably some place in the Levant before *c.* 125 CE in which Jews and 'Christians' were on amicable terms. Perhaps the only verse that seems to be peculiarly 'Christian', in distinction from Jewish thought before 135 CE, is 5:3, 'Freely did I receive your grace,/May I live by it.' It is more likely that a Christian than a Jew would express such thoughts; but then the Syriac word can also mean 'goodness' or 'kindness' (the Coptic means 'your judgement'). Here is illustrated the inappropriateness of interpreting these odes without any reference to the history of Jewish theology, especially liturgy.

That point is driven home again when we study how the ode begins: 'I praise you, O Lord,/because ...' Here we find an echo of the *Hodayot* formula with which virtually every one of the *Thanksgiving Hymns* commences. Indeed, that formula, rare outside of the Qumranic hymnbook, is 'I praise you, *Adonai*,/because...'[10] It is wise to ponder the possibility that the Odist uses the formula because he had memorized at least portions of the Qumran hymnbook, the *Thanksgiving Hymns*.

Theology of ode 5

The Odist is profound in his outlook. He stresses the importance of sight.

He prays that his persecutors 'will not see', that 'their eyes' be darkened with obscuring darkness, and that they have no light to see, so that their counsels devolve into dullness. The consistency of the imagery is impressive. Though he most likely did not compose the *Odes of Solomon* in Egypt, he probably would have agreed with a thought articulated by Philo of Alexandria. Philo pointed out that 'hearing' is misleading or deceptive, but sight, by which we discern reality, 'is devoid of falseness'.[11]

The author wants to be delivered from the 'persecutors' who are only generically described and hence cannot be identified with a group within or without early Christianity. There is no reason to equate the 'persecutors' with a synagogal group, which gave rise in other times or places to the phenomenon of expulsion from the synagogue (*aposynagôgos*) found only in John 9:22, 12:42, 16:2). I am not persuaded, however, that the persecutors are only 'the spiritual foes of the Christian', as J. H. Bernard maintained.[12] Research today on Christian origins is far too influenced by anthropology and sociology to be so confident that this ode does not include 'men of flesh and blood'.[13] It is conceivable that the Odist may be thinking about social crises that preceded or included the schism within the Johannine Community. It is insightful to note that the Odist has not described the persecutors as past or even present; they are of the future. Yet, when they come the Lord will be like a protective and securely grounded wreath or crown (ode 5:12–13).

All emotions and thoughts are invested in the Lord, *māryâ*, who is the object of the Odist's 'love' (5: 1), 'hope' (5:2, 10) and salvation (5:11). The reason becomes obvious: the Odist is united with the Lord, 'Because the Lord is with me,/And I with him' (5:15). Hence, the ode concludes with the Hebrew loan word, 'Hallelujah'.

This central, organizing principle of the ode is articulated in numerous ways. The persecutors are painted with 'darkness' (5:5), and for them the Odist asks that they have 'no light' (5:6). Most importantly, they will have what they conspired return 'upon their heads' (5:7); but, the Odist has the Lord upon his head like a crown; that is, the wreath of victory so well known in the first century. Perhaps the community that recited these odes connected this image of unity with the paraenesis on unity that characterizes the Gospel of John in chapters 15–17,[14] and especially the metaphorical use of the vine. Both the vine and the crown symbolize how God has woven, united together, those who adhere to the Lord.

The meaning of the Lord who is like 'a crown upon my head' may be explained by a study of odes 1 and 24. The crown does not sit precariously on the head. It is rather plaited for and within the Odist – and all like him – so that its branches blossom in the individual (1:2). The crown is grounded with deep roots. Thus, the Odist can celebrate that the Lord 'lives' on his head, and 'blossoms' on him. In ode 24 the unparalleled Lordship of the Messiah is depicted as a dove who is over the 'head' (*rîsheh*) of 'our Lord Messiah' because he was 'her head' (*rîshâ*). The paronomasia on 'head' is well known in biblical and Semitic poetry. The sound of the resounding *rîsh* helps unite the thought of ode 24.

What seems appealing about this ode for our present concerns? It seems to be the perception of reality: there are persecutors who 'will come'. There are enemies who devise evil counsels against us, and prepare themselves maliciously (5:9). But the Odist supplies the proper perception by employing the concept of time: they will be found to be impotent (5:9). Those who place their hope on the Lord need not fear, 'shall not die' (5:14), because they are one with the Most High (5:2, 15). Twice the Odist writes *lâ êdhhal*, 'I shall not fear.' The key, the Odist seems to be saying, is to place 'hope' solely on the Lord, and that echoing note opens the petitions and the concluding celebration of the cessation of fear (5:2, 10).

The poetic form of the ode

The ode, like all the others in the *Odes of Solomon*, is modelled upon the poetic form of the Davidic Psalter. Note in the following translation the structuring of thought according to separate bi-cola. Unlike most of the psalms and odes of the Second Temple period (notably the Qumranic *Thanksgiving Hymns*), this ode is constructed in parallel lines (*parallelismus membrorum*), and it is usually step parallelism with an emphasis on the reason for praise or result of a petition.[15] This construction is evident in the pervasive use of 'because', 'for', 'so', and similar result clauses in verses 1, 2, 6, 7 and 11. The Syriac word *metōl*, 'because', appears in 5:1b, 2b, 11a and 15a. The only apparent synonymous parallelism is in the final stichos (5:15), which celebrates the unity between the Odist and the Lord, thus explaining the opening stichos: 'I praise you, O Lord, because I love you.'

The Psalter has also supplied some of the Odist's imagery. In 5:5 the clouding of tormentors' eyes may have been shaped by Psalm 69:22, 'May their eyes grow dim so that they cannot see; . . .' (*TANAKH*).[16] The return of evil conspiracy upon the conspirators may have been shaped by the thoughts of Psalm 69:23, 'May their table be a trap for them', and Psalm 7:16, 'He has dug a pit and deepened it, and will fall into the trap he made' (*TANAKH*). The dismissal of fear because of hope in the Lord in 5:10 was most likely influenced by Psalm 27:1, 'The Lord is my light and my help; whom should I fear?' (*TANAKH*). The thought about not being shaken but standing firm in 5:13 may be inspired by Psalm 30:7, 'I thought "I shall never be shaken", for You, O Lord, . . .' (*TANAKH*).

TRANSLATION

Translation	*Form*
1 I praise you, O Lord; Because I love you.	Opening doxology

Translation	*Form*
2 O Most High, forsake me not, For you are my hope.	Petitions
3 Freely did I receive your grace, May I live by it.	
4 My persecutors will come, But let them not see me.[17]	
5 Let a cloud of darkness fall upon their eyes; And let an air of thick darkness obscure them.	
6 And let them have no light to see, So that they cannot seize me.	

7 Let their counsel become dull,
    So that whatever they have conspired
    shall return upon their own heads.	

8 For they devised a counsel, But it was not for them.[19]	Narrative[18]
9 They prepared themselves maliciously, But they were found to be impotent.	
10 Indeed, my hope is upon the Lord, And I shall not fear.	Celebration
11 And because the Lord is my salvation, I shall not fear.	
12 And he is like a crown upon my head, And I shall not be shaken.	
13 Even if everything should be shaken, I shall stand firm.	
14 And though all things visible should perish, I shall not die;	

15 Because the Lord is with me,
    And I with him.
    Hallelujah.	

NOTES

1 See the bibliography published by M. Harding in J. H. Charlesworth, M. Harding and M. Kiley (eds), *The Lord's Prayer and Other Prayer Texts from the Greco-Roman Era*, Valley Forge, Trinity Press International, 1994, pp. 155–8.
2 Note the pleasing assonance in the opening of the four lines beginning with 5:13, '*w\en . . . \ená\ . . . w\en . . . \ená*'.
3 Charlesworth in *The Old Testament Pseudepigrapha*, Garden City, New York, Doubleday, 1985, vol. 2, pp. 725–34; Emerton in H. F. D. Sparks (ed.), *The Apocryphal Old Testament*, Oxford, Clarendon Press, 1984, pp. 683–7.
4 M. Lattke, 'Dating the *Odes of Solomon*', *Antichthon* (1993), vol. 27, pp. 45–58. E. Azar also stresses that these odes are very ancient. See his *Les Odes de Salomon*, Sagesses chrétiennes, Paris, Éditions du Cerf, 1996, pp. 43–7.
5 R. Bultmann, *The Gospel of John*, trans. G. R. Beasley-Murray, Oxford,

Blackwell, 1971 [from the 1964 edition]. Bultmann rightly saw that the Johannine Prologue is constructed in a fashion similar to that of the *Odes of Solomon*: 'Sometimes both parts of the couplet express one thought (vv. 9, 12, 14b); sometimes the second completes and develops the first (vv. 1, 4, 14a, 16); sometimes the two parts stand together in parallelism (v. 3) , or in antithesis (vv. 5, 10, 11)' (p. 15). See esp. pp. 29–31.

6 Charlesworth and Culpepper, 'The Odes of Solomon and the Gospel of John', *CBQ* (1973), vol. 35, pp. 298–322.

7 J. Carmignac, ' Un qumrânien converti au christianisme: l'auteur des *Odes de Salomon*', in H. Bardtke (ed.), *Qumran-Probleme*, Deutsche Akademie der Wissenschaften zu Berlin 42, Berlin, Akademie-Verlag, 1963, pp. 75–108. Charlesworth, '*Les Odes de Salomon* et les manuscrits de la mer morte', *Revue biblique* (1970), vol. 77, pp. 522–49.

8 D. E. Aune, *The Cultic Setting of Realized Eschatology in Early Christianity*, New Testament Studies 28, Leiden, E. J. Brill, 1972. By 'realizing eschatology' scholars mean the present actualizing of the endtime; that is, the author experiences future rewards (eschatology) in the present time. Thus, the Odist celebrates in the present the joys of the future (perhaps post-resurrection) day.

9 J. R. Harris and A. Mingana, *The Odes and Psalms of Solomon*, Manchester, Manchester University Press, 1920, vol. 2, p. 231. Far more insightful regarding the Jewishness of a 'crown' are the remarks by E. A. Abbott in *Light on the Gospel from an Ancient Poet*, Cambridge, Cambridge University Press, 1912, pp. 19–33. See esp. *Mishnah Aboth* 4.17: 'Rabbi Shimon said: There are three crowns, the crown of the Torah, the crown of priesthood and the crown of kingship. But the crown of a good name excels them all.' See S. R. Hirsch, *Chapters of the Fathers*, trans. G. Hirschler, Jerusalem, Feldheim [1967], 1989, pp. 68–9.

10 See 1QH 2.20, 2.31, 3.19, 3.37, 4.5, 5.5, 5.20, 7.6, 7.26, 7.34, 8.4, 11.3, 11.15 (in the last two occurrences we find \ly in place of \dony; it appears in a modified form only at 4Q511 according to the GC: J. H. Charlesworth *et al.*, *Graphic Concordance to the Dead Sea Scrolls*, Princeton Theological Seminary Dead Sea Scrolls Project, Tübingen, Mohr [Siebeck], Louisville, Westminster/John Knox, 1991, p. 8.

11 *On Flight and Finding* 208 (LCL).

12 J. H. Bernard, *The Odes of Solomon*, Texts and Studies 8.3, London, Cambridge University Press, 1912, p. 55.

13 J. H. Bernard, op. cit., p. 55.

14 I am convinced that these chapters were added to the first edition of the Gospel of John. See J. H. Charlesworth, *The Beloved Disciple: Whose Witness Validates the Gospel of John?*, Valley Forge, Trinity Press International, 1995.

15 When it was not sufficiently clear a Coptic scribe clarifies it [5:8].

16 The translation of the Hebrew Scriptures, the 'Old Testament', is according to *TANAKH*, Philadelphia, The Jewish Publication Society, 1985.

17 R. H. Charles, famous for editing the first collection of the Old Testament Pseudepigrapha into English and the first expert to perceive that the *Odes of Solomon* must be translated as poetry and in parallel lines, translated 5:4 as follows: 'Let my persecutors be overthrown/And not see me . . .' Charles in *Revue of Theology and Philosophy* (1910), vol. 6, p. 223.

18 As M. Franzmann points out, this section of the ode is marked by a shift from the imperfect to the perfect tense. She sees four stanzas: 1–3, 4–7, 8–9 and 10–15. Franzmann, *The Odes of Solomon: An Analysis of the Poetical Structure and Form*, Novum Testamentum et Orbis Antiquus 20, Göttingen, Vandenhoeck & Ruprecht, 1991, pp. 31–9.

19   Here the third-century Coptic text completes the thought with a spurious verse:
     'And they were vanquished although they were powerful.'

SELECTED BIBLIOGRAPHY

Abbott, E. A., *Light on the Gospel from an Ancient Poet*, Cambridge, Cambridge University Press, 1912.

Azar, E., *Les Odes de Salomon: Présentation et traduction*, Sagesses chrétiennes, Paris, Éditions du Cerf, 1996.

Bernard, J. H., *The Odes of Solomon*, Texts and Studies 8.3, London, Cambridge University Press, 1912.

Charlesworth, J. H., *The Odes of Solomon*, Oxford, Clarendon Press, 1973, reprinted by Scholars Press, Chico, CA, 1977.

——, '*Odes of Solomon*', in Charlesworth (ed.), *The Old Testament Pseudepigrapha*, Garden City, NY, Doubleday, 1985, vol. 2, pp. 725–71.

Emerton, J. A., 'The *Odes of Solomon*', in H. F. D. Sparks (ed.), *The Apocryphal Old Testament*, Oxford, Clarendon Press, 1984.

Harris, J. R. and A. Mingana, *The Odes and Psalms of Solomon*, 2 vols, Manchester, London, New York, Manchester University Press, 1916, 1920.

Lattke, M., *Die Oden Salomos in ihrer Bedeutung für Neues Testament und Gnosis*, 3 vols, Göttingen, Vandenhoeck & Ruprecht, 1979–86.

Winterhalter, R., *The Odes of Solomon: Original Christianity Revealed*, St Paul, MN, Llewellyn Publications, 1985.

48

ACTS OF PAUL AND THECLA 28–31

Jeffrey A. Trumbower

INTRODUCTION

The *Acts of Paul and Thecla* (abbreviated *APT*) is one of the Christian Apocryphal Acts dating probably from the middle of the second century. It forms part of a larger work, *The Acts of Paul*, but it often circulated separately and was quite popular in antiquity and the Middle Ages. The story is first mentioned by the Latin theologian Tertullian (*c.* 200 CE), but he disapproves of its contents because it exalts a woman who preaches and baptizes (he thinks such activities are inappropriate for women), and because the work is not by Paul (*De Baptismo* 17).[1] The text survives in eleven Greek manuscripts dating from the tenth to the fourteenth centuries, and is also found in Latin, Syriac, Armenian, Slavic, Arabic and Coptic versions. The critical Greek text underlying the translation here is that of Lipsius,[2] with consultation of Vouaux.[3] An English translation of the whole work may be found in Schneemelcher, who also provides detailed information about the manuscript tradition and about the relationship between *APT* and the larger *Acts of Paul.*[4]

The tale concerns a woman named Thecla from the city of Iconium in Asia Minor, who is converted to Christianity and the virgin life by Paul, and who must endure two near-martyrdoms and a number of other trials before a glorious career of preaching and teaching ending with a peaceful death. In the passage translated here, Thecla has just been condemned to the beasts in the city of Pisidian Antioch for publicly humiliating a ruffian named Alexander, after he tried to violate her virginity by force. A wealthy kins-woman of the emperor named Tryphaena has befriended Thecla. The tale is probably not historical, though there was a Queen Tryphaena in Paul's day, but the evidence associates her with Thrace and Pontus, not with Pisidian Antioch.[5]

It is not known whether the character Thecla is based on a historical person, but a cult devoted to her was quite strong in Asia Minor in late antiquity. She is the key spokesperson for the Christian virgin life in a third-century work, *Symposium of the Ten Virgins*, by Methodius of Olympus, patterned after Plato's *Symposium*. She is considered a heroine by Gregory of Nyssa in the fourth century, when he reports that at the birth of his learned sister Macrina, a vision appeared to their mother proclaiming the baby's secret name to be Thecla, signifying that Macrina would choose the same type of life as the famous virgin (*Life of St Macrina* 2.24–31).

There are four prayers in *APT* 28–31, all uttered by women: the crowd of pagan women cries out to God in 28, Thecla prays for Tryphaena's dead daughter Falconilla in 29, Tryphaena prays for God to help Thecla in 30, and Thecla prays for Tryphaena in 31. All four prayers are efficacious in the story: the women of the city see justice done when Thecla is set free (*APT* 38), Tryphaena declares that her dead child now lives (*APT* 39), Thecla is indeed saved by God from the beasts as Tryphaena had requested (*APT* 33–6), and God does grant a reward to Tryphaena as Thecla converts her and the majority of the maidservants in her house (*APT* 39).

One of these prayers deserves special comment: Thecla's intercession for the dead pagan Falconilla. It is similar to the prayer of the martyr Perpetua in her diary contained in *The Martyrdom of Perpetua and Felicitas*, 7–8.[6] In that early third-century text, right before her own martyrdom, Perpetua prays for the posthumous salvation of her presumably unbaptized brother Dinocrates who had died of a tumour at age 7. At first she sees him in torment, disfigured, thirsty and unable to drink. After her prayer she sees him playing and able to drink. Both Thecla and Perpetua are portrayed as having a special intercessory power just before their executions. Such power is commonly associated with martyrdom, so much so that Cyprian, bishop of Carthage from 249 to 258 CE, felt that the martyrs were too free in granting forgiveness to apostates; their pronouncements challenged his own authority as bishop (Cyprian, *Epistles* 9, 27, and elsewhere). Rather than forgive living baptized apostates, however, Thecla and Perpetua use their power to intercede for non-Christians already long dead (compare Paul's cryptic 'baptism on behalf of the dead', 1 Cor 15:29, and Judas Maccabeus' prayer for sinful dead soldiers, 2 Macc 12:42–4). The idea that Dinocrates was not a baptized Christian was later of great concern for Augustine, who believed that prayers for the unbaptized dead could not be efficacious, even if offered up by a martyr as holy as Perpetua (Augustine, *On the Nature and Origin of the Soul*, I.10.12, II.10.14 and III.9.12).[7]

TRANSLATION

(28) As the beasts led the procession, Thecla was bound to a fierce lioness, and Queen Tryphaena followed close behind. While Thecla was

seated upon her, the lioness licked her feet, and the entire crowd was amazed. The charge written on her inscription read: Sacrilege. The women, however, along with their children, cried out from above, 'O God! An unholy judgement has come forth in this city!'[8] After the procession, Tryphaena again took Thecla into her care, for her deceased daughter Falconilla had said to her in a dream, 'Mother, you shall have the abandoned stranger Thecla in my stead, in order that she might pray on my behalf and I might be transferred to the place of the righteous.'[9]

(29) Therefore, when Tryphaena took her in after the procession, she mourned because Thecla was going into battle with the beasts on the next day, but at the same time she loved her earnestly like her own daughter Falconilla. She said, 'My second child Thecla, come pray on behalf of my daughter, that she might live forever,[10] for this I saw while sleeping.' So Thecla, without delay, raised her voice and said, 'O my God, the Son of the Most High, who is in heaven,[11] grant to her according to her wish, that her daughter Falconilla might live forever.' After Thecla said these things, Tryphaena mourned as she contemplated such beauty being thrown to the beasts.

(30) When dawn came, Alexander came to take Thecla away, for he himself was responsible for the games. He said, 'The governor has taken his place and the crowd is clamouring for us. Hand over the combatant that I might take her away!' But Tryphaena cried out, 'Grief for my Falconilla has come upon this house a second time, and there is no one to help – no child, for she is dead, and no kinsman, for I am a widow. O God of my child Thecla, help Thecla!' Her outburst caused Alexander to flee.

(31) The governor then sent soldiers so that Thecla might be brought. Tryphaena did not withdraw, but taking Thecla's hands she led her out saying, 'My daughter Falconilla I delivered to the tomb; you, Thecla, I deliver to the beasts.' Thecla wept bitterly and groaned to the Lord, 'Lord God in whom I believe, in whom I took refuge, who saved me from the fire, grant a reward to Tryphaena, who has shown sympathy for me your servant, because she has kept me pure.'

NOTES

1 Some have argued that Tertullian is referring, not to our text, but rather to a now lost pseudepigraphon which was attributed to Paul and which mentioned Thecla. See S. L. Davies, 'Women, Tertullian, and the Acts of Paul', in D. R. MacDonald (ed.), *The Apocryphal Acts of the Apostles, Semeia*, vol. 38, Atlanta, Scholars Press, 1986, pp. 139–44.

2 R. A. Lipsius (ed.), *Acta Apostolorum Apocrypha*, Leipzig, Hermann Mendelssohn, 1891.

3 L. Vouaux, *Les Actes de Paul et ses Lettres Apocryphes*, Paris, Letouzey, 1913.

4 W. Schneemelcher, 'Acts of Paul', in idem (ed.), *New Testament Apocrypha*, trans. R. Wilson, Louisville, Westminster/John Knox Press, vol. 2, 1992, pp. 213–70.

5 See R. Hanslik, 'A. Tryphaena', in Konrat Ziegler and Walther Sontheimer (eds), *Der Kleine Pauly*, Stuttgart, Alfred Druckenmüller, 1964, vol. 1, column 415.

6 English translation in H. Musurillo, *The Acts of the Christian Martyrs*, Oxford, Clarendon Press, 1972, pp. 106–31.

7 For more on all these issues, see F. J. Dölger, 'Antike Parallelen zum leidenden Dinocrates in der Passio Perpetuae', in idem, *Antike und Christentum*, Münster, Aschendorff, 1930, vol. 2, pp. 1–40.

8 Tertullian (*Apology* 17.5–6) notes that pagans often utter short prayers and other statements to 'God'; this does not mean they have become exclusive Christian monotheists, but rather it reflects the philosophical notion of a divine unity underlying various individual deities. Tertullian takes this as evidence that all people have a natural inclination toward monotheistic worship.

9 Just where is Falconilla thought to be when she appears to her mother? Perhaps she is an unsettled spirit wandering the earth, perhaps she is in some kind of intermediate place, or perhaps the author had in mind a conception of the different levels of Hades similar to that found in Luke 16:19–31, one level for the righteous and another for the wicked. The key difference would be that Falconilla, through Thecla's intercession, will be able to cross from one side to the other, contra Luke 16:26, where Abraham says, 'No one can cross from there to us'. In line with Luke's rigidity on this issue is *2 Clement*, an anonymous Christian sermon roughly contemporary with *APT*, which states that one cannot hope for a chance at salvation after death: 'Once we have departed this world, we can no longer confess there or repent any more' (*2 Clem.* 8:3). For a view more similar to *APT*, see the *Martyrdom of Perpetua and Felicitas* 7–8, discussed above in the introduction.

10 Several manuscripts omit 'forever'.

11 The addressee in this prayer varies widely in the Greek manuscripts. Manuscript A reads: 'God of the fathers, son of the most high'; B: 'God most high, eternal God'; C: 'God most high'; E: 'My God, son of the most high, who is in heaven'; F and H: 'Lord God who made the heaven and the earth, son of the most high, Lord Jesus Christ'. Lipsius followed E. The Latin manuscripts read 'God of heaven, son of the most high'. In the Syriac and Armenian versions Thecla prays only to the Father here. In the Coptic version, she prays to 'God of Heaven, Son of the Most High'. See O. von Gebhardt, *Passio S. Theclae Virginis. Die lateinischen Übersetzungen der Acta Pauli et Theclae, nebst Fragmenten, Auszügen und Beilagen*, Leipzig, Hinrichs, 1902, pp. CI–CII. For the Coptic text, see C. Schmidt (ed.), *Acta Pauli aus der Heidelberger koptischen Papyrushandschrift nr. 1*, Hildesheim, Georg Olms, 1965.

SELECTED BIBLIOGRAPHY

Hayne, L., 'Thecla and the Church Fathers', *Vigiliae Christianae* 1994, vol. 48, pp. 209–18.

Lipsius, R. A. (ed.), *Acta Apostolorum Apocrypha*, Leipzig, Hermann Mendelssohn, 1891.

MacDonald, D. R. (ed.), *The Apocryphal Acts of the Apostles, Semeia*, vol. 38, Atlanta, Scholars Press, 1986.

Ruether, R. R., 'Mothers of the Church: Ascetic Women in the Late Patristic Age', in

R. R. Ruether and E. McLaughlin (eds), *Women of Spirit: Female Leadership in the Jewish and Christian Traditions*, New York, Simon & Schuster, 1979, pp. 71–98.

Schneemelcher, W., 'Acts of Paul', in idem (ed.), *New Testament Apocrypha*, trans. R. Wilson, Louisville, Westminster/John Knox Press, 1992, vol. 2, pp. 213–70.

Vouaux, L., *Les Actes de Paul et ses Lettres Apocryphes*, Paris, Letouzey, 1913.

49

POLYCARP'S FINAL PRAYER
(*MARTYRDOM OF POLYCARP* 14)

Frederick W. Weidmann

INTRODUCTION

The so-called *Martyrdom of Polycarp* (*Mart. Pol.*) is an account of the martyrdom of Polycarp, bishop of Smyrna, along with eleven other Christians. It was recorded in letter form and sent from Polycarp's church at Smyrna in Asia Minor (modern-day Turkey) to a Christian community at Philomelium, also in Asia Minor. It has been called 'the first of the martyr acts,'[1] and its influence on other ancient martyrdoms and on the modern study of ancient Christianity is large.

Attestation

Mart. Pol. is known through two separate text traditions, the Ps.-Pionian and the Eusebian. The former has been preserved through manuscript editions of readings about holy women and men; the latter within Eusebius' *Church History* (*HE*).[2] These text traditions differ at points and many scholars believe that details were added to the Ps.-Pionian tradition after Eusebius had produced his work.[3] *Mart. Pol.* is also known in several language versions besides its original Greek.[4]

Date and provenance

Mart. Pol. purports to have been produced within Polycarp's Christian community at Smyrna and there are no compelling reasons to doubt that.

The date of Polycarp's execution and, secondary to that, of the martyrdom account is debated.[5] The earliest possibility, based on both internal and external evidence, is 154–5 CE; more probably, 155–6. The latest date proposed is 177. Polycarp's execution almost certainly occurred during the early or middle part of this (approximately) twenty-year window, with the martyrdom being written and circulated soon after. The later one places Polycarp's execution the more difficult it is to account for *Mart Pol.*'s influence on other martyrdoms, the earlier one places *Mart. Pol.* the more difficult it is to account for its 'anti-rigorist (probably anti-Montanistic) element '.[6]

Relationship to authoritative writings

The narrator asserts that Polycarp's is a 'martyrdom according to the gospel' (*Mart. Pol.* 1.2).[7] *Mart. Pol.* contains eighteen apparent quotations from, or allusions to, Jesus' passion as recounted within the canonical gospels.[8]

Regarding the Hebrew Bible/Old Testament, within the final prayer may be found allusions to Israelite cult sacrifice (as discussed, for example, in Lev and Num), the Servant Songs of Isaiah, and The Prayer of Azariah and the Hymn of the Three Youths in the Septuagint version of Daniel ('DanLXX').[9]

There are also likely allusions to other early Christian literature, notably the so-called 'First Letter of Clement' (*1 Clem.*) and the letters of Ignatius, bishop of Antioch. Among Ignatius' letters are one to Christians at Smyrna and another specifically to Polycarp.

Use of early Christian liturgical traditions, as preserved in the *Didache* (*Did.*) and elsewhere, is suggested by certain phrases within the prayer.

Polycarp and other early Christian literature

Polycarp's own *Letter to the Philippians* (Pol. *Phil.*) has been preserved. According to Irenaeus, bishop of Lyons, who was raised in Smyrna, Polycarp also wrote several other works.[10]

A so-called 'Life of Polycarp', whose value for reconstructing Polycarp's life is minimal, is found in one of the ancient manuscripts containing *Mart. Pol.*[11] Were the 'Life' and *Mart. Pol.* part of an ancient collection of works by and about Polycarp which has since been lost?[12]

Irenaeus includes discussion of Polycarp in several writings,[13] and his comments remain influential. Irenaeus' 'Letter to Florinus' contains the earliest extant report of Polycarp's personal association with John and other apostles, a report whose accuracy is questioned.[14] The relationship to John is central to another (untitled) document which is preserved in the Harris Collection of Coptic papyri.[15] Further comments on Polycarp can be found in the writings of Tertullian, Jerome, (pseudo-)John Chrysostom, and in the *Martyrdom of Pionius* (*Mart. Pion.*), about a Smyrnaean Christian arrested on the anniversary of Polycarp's martyrdom.

Polycarp at prayer

That Polycarp should offer a final prayer before his execution is consistent both with martyrological convention[16] and with the character of Polycarp as he is remembered. *Mart. Pol.* 5.1 states that 'night and day' Polycarp was 'doing nothing other than praying . . .'. Upon his capture, Polycarp 'prayed' aloud 'for two hours' (*Mart. Pol.* 7.3).[17]

Prayer was part of the Christian tradition which Polycarp had received and, in turn, passed on. The Smyrnaean bishop repeatedly urges others to pray (Pol. *Phil.* 4, 7, 12). Meanwhile, Ignatius' *Letter to the Smyrnaeans* (Ign. *Smyrn.* 11) recalls the prayer of that community, while his *Letter to Polycarp* advocates 'unceasing prayers' (Ign. *Pol.* 1).[18]

Polycarp's final prayer (*Mart. Pol.* 14) is most simply categorized by the Petition ('Let me be received') which occurs approximately at its midpoint.[19] Previous to that there is an Address which places 'God', 'Jesus Christ', and 'all the family of those who are just' in their proper cosmological order. Following the Address, and preceding the Petition, Polycarp affirms God through a Blessing and, in turn, asserts God's own affirmation of him ('you have considered me worthy'). The final prayer form employed is that of Doxology.

Besides making a petition, the prayer structures the universe, describes, affirms and praises God, recalls the stories of Jesus Christ and Polycarp, and reminds the hearer of that tradition of Christian formation and exhortation which runs through Polycarp. As memorial to Polycarp, edification to Christians and object of critical study, *Mart. Pol.* 14 continues to challenge and fascinate.

Narrative context

Mart. Pol. 14 records Polycarp's final prayer prior to execution. It follows Polycarp's request that his executioners not use nails since 'the one granting it that I endure the fire will grant that I remain undisturbed in the fire even without the security you derive from the nails' (*Mart. Pol.* 13.3).

TRANSLATION

14.1 So they did not nail him down, but they bound him. After he had placed his hands behind his back and been bound up for sacrifice like a distinguished ram from a great flock, a whole burnt offering prepared and acceptable to God, he looked up into heaven[20] and said:

> O Lord, the all-powerful[21] God, the father of your beloved and blessed servant,[22] Jesus Christ, through whom we have received knowledge about you,[23] the God of angels and of powers and of all creation, also of all the family of those who are just, who live in your presence,[24]

2   I bless you[25] because you have considered me worthy of this day and hour[26] to receive a share among the number of

martyrs in the cup[27] of your Christ, for the resurrection of eternal life – of both soul and body[28] – in the immortality[29] of the Holy Spirit. Let me be received among them in your presence this day through[30] a rich and acceptable sacrifice,[31] just as you have prepared and revealed[32] beforehand, and brought to fulfilment, O unlying and truthful God.[33]

3   On account of this and concerning all things I praise you, I bless you, I glorify you[34] through the eternal and heavenly high priest,[35] Jesus Christ, your beloved servant, through whom to you, with him and the Holy Spirit, be glory both now and throughout the coming ages.[36] Amen.

NOTES

1   Wm. R. Schoedel, 'Polycarp of Smyrna and Ignatius of Antioch', *ANRW*, 1993, vol. II.27.1, p. 355. *Mart. Pol.* is generally considered to represent the earliest and most authentic stratum of martyrdoms.

2   *HE* IV.15.1–45.

3   See Boudewijn Dehandschutter, 'The Martyrium Polycarpi: A Century of Research', *ANRW*, 1993, vol. II.27.1, pp. 486–8, and Schoedel, op. cit., pp. 350–4. The Ps.-Pionian text is readily available in editions of 'The Apostolic Fathers' and other collections (see Selected Bibliography below); the Eusebian text is found in editions of Eusebius' *Church History*. Conventionally, a simple reference to the 'Martyrdom of Polycarp' is to the Ps.-Pionian tradition; so herein.

4   See Dehandschutter, op. cit., pp. 489–90.

5   See Dehandschutter, op. cit., pp. 497–503 and Schoedel, op. cit., pp. 354–5. Not mentioned by either is the short and helpful discussion in Gary A. Bisbee, *Pre-Decian Acts of Martyrs and Commentarii*, Harvard Dissertations in Religion 22, Philadelphia, Fortress, 1988, pp. 119–21.

6   Schoedel, op. cit., p. 351; see *Mart. Pol.* 4 (= *HE* IV.15.7–8). 'Montanism' or 'New Prophecy', a Christian movement characterized by spiritual enthusiasm and belief in the imminent end of the world, began in Asia Minor *c.* 160–70.

7   A statement not found in the Eusebian tradition. All translations of ancient literature herein are mine.

8   Leslie W. Barnard, 'In Defense of Pseudo-Pionius' Account of Polycarp's Martyrdom', in Patrick Granfield and Josef A. Jungmann (eds), *Kyriakon: Festschrift Johannes Quasten*, 2 vols, Münster, Aschendorff, 1970, vol. 1, p. 195.

9   DanLXX 3:24–88; the relationship of *Mart. Pol.* to DanLXX is discussed in Gerd Buschmann, *Martyrium Polycarpi – Eine formkritische Studie: Ein Beitrag zur Frage nach der Entstehung der Gattung Märtyrerakte*, BZNW 70, Berlin, Walter de Gruyter, 1994, pp. 262–6, 275–9.

10 Irenaeus, 'Letter to Florinus' (in *HE* V.20.8).

11 Parisinus gr. 1452 (G).

12 So, for example, J.B. Lightfoot, *The Apostolic Fathers Clement, Ignatius, and Polycarp: Revised Texts, with Introductions, Notes, Dissertations and Translations* (orig. pub. 1885–90), Peabody, MA, Hendrickson, 1989, vol. II.3, p. 424. Dehandschutter, op. cit., p. 491, finds the suggestion 'very unconvincing'.

13 *Against Heresies* 3.3.4 (= *HE* IV.14.3–7), 5.33.4 (= *HE* III.39.1); 'Letter to Florinus' (= *HE* V.20.4–8); 'Letter to Victor' (= *HE* V.24.11–17).

14 *HE* V.20.6; see Frederick W. Weidmann, *The Martyrdom of Polycarp, Bishop of Smyrna in Ancient Christian Literature: A Re-evaluation in Light of Previously Unpublished Coptic Fragments*, Yale University Dissertation 1993, Ann Arbor, UMI, 1994, pp. 193–204.

15 For critical edition, translation and commentary see Weidmann, op. cit.

16 Which *Mart. Pol.* likely influenced; see *Martyrdom of Carpus, Papylus, and Agathonice* 41, 46; *Acts of the Scillitan Martyrs* 15, 17; *Mart. Pion.* 21.8–9; *Acts of Justin* 6. See also the canonical gospels for Jesus' sayings while on the cross; also Stephen, *Acts* 7:59ff.

17 See also the Harris Fragments, p. 64r, line 3, in Weidmann, op. cit., pp. 37, 56; and the 'Life', chs 30–1.

18 Similarly Ign. *Pol.* 7; in Ign. *Smyrn.* 6 the 'heterodox' are associated with lack of prayer.

19 Some have called the prayer a 'Thanksgiving' (J. A. Robinson, 'Liturgical Echoes in Polycarp's Prayer', *Expositor*, 1899, fifth series, vol. 9, p. 65–6; Theofried Baumeister, *Die Anfänge der Theologie des Martyriums*, Münsterische Beiträge zur Theologie, Münster, Aschendorff, 1980, p. 299) but Polycarp nowhere speaks a word of 'thanks'.

20 'He looked up into heaven' does not appear in the Eusebian tradition.

21 cf. *Mart. Pion.* 8.3. In *HE* IV.15.32, 'all-powerful' modifies the previous use of 'God': 'acceptable to the all-powerful God'.

22 The Greek word *pais* ('servant') may also be translated 'child'; see Barnard, op. cit., pp. 200–1. *Pais* is used consistently for 'servant' in the Septuagint version of the Servant Songs of Isaiah; for 'my servant ... my beloved' see Isa 52:13 (quoted in Matt 12:18); in Isa 43:10, as in *Mart. Pol.* 14.1, *pais* is linked with 'knowledge'.

23 cf. *Mart. Pion.* 8.3. For 'servant' and 'knowledge', see *1 Clem.* 59.2 (similarly *Did.* 9); *1 Clem.* 59.3 includes a wordplay about 'the beloved servant, through whom [God] instructed us' ('instruct' [*paideuo*] is a cognate of 'servant' [*pais*]); cf. Prov 3:11, Heb 12:6, Rev 3.19.

24 'A favorite expression in assertions and oaths which call upon God...', BAGD, 270b. DanLXX 3.52ff. orders the cosmos similarly; see also Apuleius, *Metamorphoses* 11.5.

25 cf. Mark 6:41 and par. Ancients often 'blessed' the Divinity, BAGD 322a; cf. *Mart. Pol.* 19.2 (not in the Eusebian tradition).

26 See *Mart. Pol.* 8.1. For 'the hour', see Luke 22:14 (the Last Supper); Mark 14:35, 41 and Matt 26:45 (prayer at the Garden); Luke 22:53 (the arrest); also John 4:23, 5:28, 12:23, 27, 13:1, 16:32, 17:1. For 'you have considered me worthy of this day and hour' as a liturgical formulation, see Robinson, op. cit., p. 70.

27 For 'the cup' as eucharistic imagery, see Mark 14:23 and par. (incl. 1 Cor 11:25–8), *Did.* 9, Justin's 'First Apology' 66; see also Mark 14:36 and par., Mark 10:35ff. and par.

28 For 'fleshly and spiritual' see Ign. *Smyrn.* 12.2.

29 cf. *Mart. Pol.* 17.1, 19.2 (not recorded in the Eusebian tradition), Ign. *Pol.* 2.3.

30 That is, 'by way of'; the Greek preposition *en* expresses instrumentality.

31 For similar imagery see DanLXX 3:39–40; Polycarp equates his martyrdom with a sacrifice, but does not ask that it be received as recompense (DanLXX 3:39) or expiation (see 4 Macc 6:29).

32 'In a vision', while Polycarp was 'praying' (*Mart. Pol.* 5.2, 12.3); cf. Ign. *Pol.* 2.2.

33 See Ps 31:5 (quoted in part by Jesus, Luke 23:46).

34 See DanLXX 3:26. Polycarp practises what he preached ('Should we suffer ... let us glorify [God]'; Pol. *Phil.* 8.2).

35 Pol. *Phil.* 12.2.
36 This doxology may reflect a later (than *c.* 160) formulation; though see Justin's 'First Apology' 65.3. For discussion, see J. A. Robinson, 'The "Apostolic Anaphora" and the Prayer of St Polycarp', *JTS*, 1920, vol. 21, pp. 102–4; Barnard, op. cit., p. 200; and Buschmann, op. cit., pp. 34–5.

SELECTED BIBLIOGRAPHY

(For an extensive bibliography see the entry under 'Dehandschutter, Boudewijn' below.)

Barnard, Leslie W., 'In Defense of Pseudo-Pionius' Account of Polycarp's Martyrdom', in Patrick Granfield and Josef A. Jungmann (eds), *Kyriakon: Festschrift Johannes Quasten*, 2 vols, Münster, Aschendorff, 1970, vol. 1, pp. 192–204.

Buschmann, Gerd, *Martyrium Polycarpi–Eine formkritische Studie: Ein Beitrag zur Frage nach der Entstehung der Gattung Märtyrerakte*, BZNW 70, Berlin, Walter de Gruyter, 1994.

Dehandschutter, Boudewijn, 'The Martyrium Polycarpi: A Century of Research,' *ANRW*, 1993, vol. II.27.1, pp. 485–522.

Lightfoot, J. B., *The Apostolic Fathers Clement, Ignatius, and Polycarp: Revised Texts, with Introductions, Notes, Dissertations and Translations*, 2 parts in 5 vols (orig. pub. 1885–1890), Peabody, MA, Hendrickson, 1989.

Musurillo, Herbert, *The Acts of the Christian Martyrs*, Oxford, Clarendon Press, 1972.

Robinson, J. A., 'Liturgical Echoes in Polycarp's Prayer', *Expositor*, 1899, fifth series, vol. 9, pp. 63–72.

——, 'The "Apostolic Anaphora" and the Prayer of St Polycarp', *JTS*, 1920, vol. 21, pp. 97–105.

——, 'The Doxology in the Prayer of St Polycarp', *JTS*, 1923, vol. 24, pp. 141–4.

Schoedel, Wm. R., *Polycarp, Martyrdom of Polycarp, Fragments of Papias*, Robert M. Grant (ed.), The Apostolic Fathers: A New Translation and Commentary, vol. 5, Camden, Thomas Nelson & Sons, 1967.

50

PRAYER OF THE APOSTLE PAUL FROM THE NAG HAMMADI LIBRARY

Deirdre Good

INTRODUCTION

Provenance, author, date

The Prayer of the Apostle Paul (hereafter Pr. Paul), originally composed in Greek, is preserved only in a Coptic text now part of the collection of writings called the Nag Hammadi Library.[1] Pr. Paul is the front flyleaf of the first Codex, known as the Jung Codex. Since the handwriting resembles that of the conclusion of the last text of Codex I, rather than the handwriting at the beginning of the Codex, it is quite likely that the scribe added Pr. Paul to the collection after he (or she) finished the Codex. As in many ancient manuscripts, the title is placed at the end of the text.

The Coptic language renders late Egyptian into Greek. Thus, the Coptic alphabet consists of Greek letters and several letters from late Egyptian for sounds Greek did not make. Pr. Paul is written in the Subachmimic dialect of the Coptic language.

Most of Codex I was exported from Egypt by Albert Eid, a Belgian antiquities dealer in Cairo, and offered for sale unsuccessfully in New York in 1949. In 1952, Eid's widow, Simone, sold it to the Jung Institute of Zurich whereupon it was renamed the 'Jung Codex'. Jung's interest in Gnosticism was well known from his writings. The whole Codex is now in the Coptic Museum in Cairo.

The alleged author of Pr. Paul is a prominent apostle in the history of the earliest Christian communities. We know about Paul from his epistles, written in Greek in the first century and collected in the New Testament. These letters mention Paul's prayers, and although the specific wording of the present text is not recorded in the New Testament, Pauline phrases recur frequently. The author of Pr. Paul knew the Pauline epistles.

The date of the prayer is uncertain. The collection in which it was found took its final shape in the mid-fourth century. Pr. Paul probably dates to the mid-second century since the form of Christianity it assumes, namely, Valentinian Gnosticism (explained below), was widespread at that time.

In form and content, Pr. Paul resembles prayers in a collection of Hermetic texts known as the *Corpus Hermeticum* and in Christian magical papyri.[2] The similarity of the beginning of the prayer to that of the hymn in the First Stele of Seth, also in the Nag Hammadi Library, suggests a common source.

Valentinian Gnosticism

Of the writings of Valentinus, a brilliant intellectual of the second century, we have only fragments and possibly one longer work, *The Gospel of Truth*. Valentinus was a Christian who revised the classic gnostic myth in light of the categories of emerging orthodoxy particularly by means of allegory. However, of the writings of his followers, the so-called school of Valentinian gnosticism, we have many treatises. Valentinian Gnostics thought highly of the apostle Paul. He sanctioned the use of allegory to interpret scripture (Gal 4:22–7). He wrote obliquely of a personal vision in which he was 'caught up into Paradise and heard things that are not to be told' (2 Cor 12:2–4). Thus, it is not surprising to find a prayer attributed to him in a collection of writings, most of which belong to the Gnostic schools of thought.

The name 'Gnostic', connected to the Greek verb 'to know', meant intuitive or mystical awareness of one's divine origin in spite of one's present imprisonment in the human condition or material existence. Gnostic discovery of the divine within oneself might seem to reduce the 'otherness' of God, and thus the point of prayer. Indeed, some Gnostic texts decry prayer. But these critical comments seem to be the exception rather than the rule. Within the Nag Hammadi Library, for example, there are many kinds of prayers. Amongst the vocal prayers are the prayer of the martyr James (*Second Apocalypse of James*) and the prayer of repentance by which a soul turns to God the Father (*Exegesis on the Soul*). Both of these, like Pr. Paul, are written in the first person singular. Amongst the non-vocal prayers are the vowel sounds of the Gospel of the Egyptians. Presumably these sounds, written out in the text, were meant to be chanted. Readers of the Nag Hammadi texts are also encouraged to pray. Thus, even if Gnostic self-knowledge consists of awareness of the divine within oneself, this does not imply complete identification with divinity. There remains enough awareness of the otherness of God to make possible articulate and inarticulate prayer to God and (in Christian gnostic contexts) to the Son.

Composition and theology of the prayer

It is not clear to whom the prayer is addressed. The title 'Redeemer' could refer to any one of several redeemer figures in non-Christian Gnostic redemption stories: Seth, or Sophia, for example. In light of the Christian nature of this prayer, however, it could be a title for God.

The prayer itself is a petition for redemption, insight, perfection and revelation. In view of its location on the front flyleaf of the first book of the Nag Hammadi collection, it is possible to read the entire prayer as a petition to God for understanding from the erstwhile reader of the library. On the other hand, the position of the prayer might simply suggest that a scribe copied a prayer into an available space on the inside cover.

Most frequent is the use of the imperative: 'Give', 'Grant', 'Reveal', 'Place ...' in direct address to God. Greek loan words are relatively frequent throughout the prayer, mostly as nouns and adjectives. However, two Greek verbs occur in the petitions: 'Give' and 'Grant'. The latter is used to describe the free and gracious giving of a favour by God, for example in Philippians 1:29, 'You have graciously been granted [aorist passive] the privilege of suffering for Christ.'

The request to 'grant what no angel-eye has seen, and no archon-ear has heard' is an allusion to the powers of the lower world that wish to keep humanity ignorant of its divine origins. Beyond them lies true reality, the divine world. The phrases themselves recur in a well-known passage from Paul's first letter to the Corinthians, found in the New Testament. Paul cites the passage 1 Cor 2:9 as a scriptural quotation. The source is unknown. *The Gospel of Thomas* 17 quotes the same phrases as a saying of Jesus:

> I will give you what no eye has seen and what no ear has heard
> And what no hand has touched, and what has never occurred to the
> human mind

This is closer to the petitionary context of the phrases in Pr. Paul.

In light of these three texts, we can speculate about the composition of this petition. The author of Pr. Paul knows that the phrases 'what no eye has seen, nor ear heard, nor the heart of human conceived ...' derive from a Pauline context. That same author has shaped them into a petition by prefacing them with the verb 'Grant ...'. In the composition of prayers it is common to preface verbs of petition to phrases. This is how the third part of Pr. Paul was composed. *Gospel of Thomas* 17 shows that a Christian divine figure, Jesus, could offer to disciples or readers 'what no eye has seen ...'. *Gospel of Thomas* 17 is an interim stage between 1 Cor and Pr. Paul. The use of the Greek verb in Pr. Paul confirms that the petition was originally composed in Greek. Thus, a Pauline citation of scripture, attributed to a divine figure in *Gospel of Thomas*, is made into a request to the divine by 'Paul' in

Pr. Paul. The request is for insight that can only be revealed by the divine rather than acquired by human effort.

TRANSLATION

[*Approximately two lines are missing.*]
[your] light, give me your mercy!
My Redeemer, redeem me for I am yours; the one who has come from
   you.
You are my mind; give me birth![3]
You are my treasure house; open for me!
You are my light-world;[4] take me to you!
You are rest; [5] give me the perfect thing that cannot be grasped!
I entreat you, the One Who Is and who first existed in the name exalted
   above every name,[6] through Jesus Christ, [the Lord] of Lords, the
   King of the aeons;
Give me your gifts, of which you do not repent, through the Son of
   Man, the Spirit,
the Paraclete of truth[7],
Give me authority when I ask you;
Give healing for my body when I ask you through the Evangelist, and
   redeem my eternal light-soul and my spirit. And the first-born of
   the Pleroma of grace – reveal him to my mind!
Grant what no angel-eye has seen and no archon-ear heard and what
   has not entered into the human heart which came to be angelic and
   (modelled) after the image of the psychic God when it was formed
   in the beginning,[8] since I have faith and hope.
And place upon me your beloved, elect, and blessed greatness, the
   First-born, the First-begotten, and the [wonderful] mystery of your
   house; [for] yours is the power [and] the glory and the praise and the
   greatness for ever and ever. [Amen.]
Prayer of Paul (the Apostle). In Peace. Christ is holy.

NOTES

1   *The Nag Hammadi Library in English*, ed. J. M. Robinson, San Francisco,
   Harper & Row, 1988.
2   *The Greek Magical Papyri in Translation*, 2 vols, ed. H. D. Betz, Chicago Press,
   University of Chicago, 1992; *Corpus Hermeticum*, 4 vols, ed. A. D. Nock, tr.
   A.-J. Festugière, Paris, Budé, 1945–54.
3   The idea of divine generation and hence parentage is found in many Christian
   gnostic texts. See Jorunn Jacobsen Buckley and Deirdre Good, 'Sacramental
   Language and Verbs of Generating, Creating, and Begetting in the Gospel of
   Philip', *Journal of Early Christian Studies* (forthcoming, 1997).
4   The 'light-world' is the Gnostic place of origin. See The Apocryphon of John

(NHC II, 1) 3, 18; 4, 20–1 in *The Nag Hammadi Library in English*, ed. Robinson, pp. 106–7.

5   The idea of 'rest' comes from the description in Genesis of God's 'rest' after the six days of creation. However, the Gospel of Truth, also part of Codex 1, has an extended discussion of the theological metaphor of rest. See the (forthcoming) Ph.D. dissertation of Judith Wray, 'Rest as a Theological Metaphor in the Epistle to the Hebrews and the Gospel of Truth', Union Theological Seminary, 1997.

6   Compare the hymn to Christ in Philippians 2:9–10.

7   The Greek term Paraclete, in English, Counsellor, occurs in John 14:16–17a; and 15:26a where it is used by the author of the fourth gospel to describe the Spirit as an alter-ego of the resurrected Jesus. The Paraclete reminds the disciples of past events and leads them into all truths. In Pr. Paul, the term Paraclete is one of several titles given to Jesus.

8   The idea that humankind reflects the image or likeness of God derives from Gen 1:26–7. In Pr. Paul, the same idea is retold from a Gnostic perspective: the human being is formed by lesser beings, the material (or hylic) archons (or rulers) who seek to mould it in their image and thus keep it imprisoned in matter. However, a higher god, in this text identified as 'psychic' (or having to do with soul), unbeknownst to the archons, implants a divine spark in the human creature. Once this dormant element is awakened, the human recalls its true origins and sees beyond material life to recall its true home, that is, 'what no angel-eye has seen, and no archon-ear has heard'. The prayer thus functions to remind the speaker of his or her (divine) origins.

SELECTED BIBLIOGRAPHY

Attridge, Harold, 'Paul, Prayer of the Apostle', in David Noel Freeman (ed.), *The Anchor Bible Dictionary*, Garden City, NY, Doubleday, 1995, vol. V, p. 205.

Evans, Craig, Webb, Robert and Wiebe, Richard (eds), *Nag Hammadi Texts and the Bible*, New Testament Tools and Studies, vol. 18, Leiden, E. J. Brill, 1993, pp. 1–4.

MacRae, George, 'Prayer and Knowledge of Self in Gnosticism', in Daniel Harrington and Stanley Marrow (eds), *Studies in the New Testament and Gnosticism*, Wilmington, DE, Michael Glazier, 1987, pp. 218–36.

Mueller, Dieter, 'The Prayer of the Apostle Paul', in Harold Attridge (ed.), *Nag Hammadi Codex I* (The Jung Codex), Nag Hammadi Studies 22, Leiden, E. J. Brill, 1985, pp. 5–11.

—— 'The Prayer of the Apostle Paul', in James M. Robinson (ed.), *The Nag Hammadi Library in English*, 3rd edn, San Francisco, Harper & Row, 1988, pp. 27–8.

51

HYMN OF THE HOLY CLEMENT TO CHRIST THE SAVIOUR

Clement of Alexandria, *Pedagogue* 3. 12. 101. 4

Annewies van den Hoek

INTRODUCTION

Date, provenance and type of writing

The *Pedagogue* of Clement of Alexandria was written in Greek around 190 CE in Alexandria in Egypt, one of the most important and learned cities of the eastern part of the Roman empire. The work consists of three books. The hymn occurs at the end of the third book, forming a poetic conclusion to the work which is otherwise prose. The hymn is the only known poetic creation by Clement, and, more importantly, one of the first examples of such poetry in an early Christian ambience.

It has much in common with other poetry of Roman imperial times of non-Christian character, particularly in its use of metre. Gnostic Christian literature of slightly earlier date also offers similar compositions. The most important examples are a 'Psalm' of Valentinus and the so-called 'Psalm of the Naasenes.'[1] The name 'Psalm' is slightly misleading, since they too were metrical, unlike the Psalms and other poetry of the Jewish tradition. Some of the apocryphal acts, such as the *Acts of John* and the *Acts of Thomas*, also yield hymnal material of significance.[2] Clement's hymn remains difficult to fit into any recognized category of Christian literature, perhaps since it is among the first examples of Christian poetry that is not based on models from the Psalms.

The hymn has also been referred to as a poem and at other times as a prayer, and the ambiguity in nomenclature reflects the uncertainty of its function in antiquity. It remains unknown whether the work was composed for and employed by Christian congregations in Alexandria as a communal song or whether it was a more private literary creation of the author, written to embellish the concluding part of his *Pedagogue*.

Manuscript tradition

The most important manuscript of the *Pedagogue* (and of its predecessor, the *Protrepticus*) is the famous tenth-century 'Arethas Codex' in the Bibliothèque Nationale in Paris (Codex Paris. graec. 451),[3] written at the request of bishop Arethas of Caesarea in Cappadocia. The Codex is incomplete since forty folia at the beginning of the first book and the poem or hymn at the end of the third book are missing.[4] Some direct copies of the Arethas Codex, however, have survived.[5] They are of a slightly younger date (eleventh and twelfth century) and do show the poem at the end of book three. Thus it can be convincingly argued that the poem would have been included if that part of the Arethas Codex had survived.[6] The title given to the poetic conclusion, 'Hymn of the Holy Clement to Christ the Saviour', is presumably not original but dates at least as far back as the time of the Arethas Codex.

Important editions

The major critical edition is by Otto Stählin in the Corpus of Berlin.[7] The works of Clement have been translated into many modern languages, but the commentary made by Henri-Irenée Marrou in the French editions of *Sources Chrétiennes* is outstanding and indispensable for the study of the hymn.[8] The first English translation of the *Pedagogue* was made in 1868 by William Wilson and published in the *Ante-Nicene Christian Library*, volume 4, which edition was reprinted as volume 2 in the *Ante-Nicene Fathers*.[9] The editors felt obliged to expand the original text of the hymn in order to conform to the contemporary conception of poetry, which required rhyme. Clement's hymn was not, however, rhymed, and the technique was not used in antiquity, when poetry was primarily a matter of rhythmic patterns, or metre. A more recent translation was made by Simon P. Wood in the series of the *Fathers of the Church*, volume 23; again in this case the wording of the hymn was treated freely, although rhyme was not used.[10]

Authenticity

The authenticity of the hymn has been questioned from time to time, primarily because of its absence from the Arethas Codex. There is, however, no serious reason to doubt that the work is Clement's. Many of the characteristic words and images found in the *Protrepticus* and the earlier parts of the *Pedagogue* recur in the hymn. In addition, the three preceding chapters lead up to the final hymn in a natural way.[11] A profound knowledge of classical literature is also apparent in the hymn, and Clement's prose output is similarly learned. Literally thousands of quotations of and allusions to a broad range of Greek literature can be found in Clement's work, and as such it has become an important source for our knowledge of lost literary works. Many words in the hymn are related to the vocabulary of Homer, Aeschylus, Sophocles, Euripides, Pindar, Menander and Callimachus, all writers active long before Clement's time, and their locutions sound somewhat archaic in the context of the later Roman empire.

Literary context

The hymn is closely related to the preceding books of the *Pedagogue*, and many words and concepts that occur earlier are repeated in the hymn at the end. The three books are diverse in approach. While the first book deals with ethical issues in a general and theoretical way, books two and three discuss particular problems of daily life, such as details of eating and drinking habits, dress codes, hairstyles and even make-up. This makes the *Pedagogue* an important document for the student of everyday life and artifacts in antiquity, since many household goods from pots and pans to inlaid furniture are discussed as well.[12] Clement offered his readers a guidebook for a Christian existence in the context of pagan civilization.

Literary contents

The image of the pedagogue as a teacher does not primarily derive from a Christian tradition but draws heavily on Greek and pagan customs. The pedagogue was originally a slave who guides or accompanies the child from home to school and back again but whose title also took on the meaning of a private, household teacher. He became an almost legendary figure in Greek literature, as the now beloved, now ridiculous companion and mentor of a boy. The figure is often depicted in Greek and Roman art, and his female counterpart, the old nurse, is equally well known; both also stood as emblems of dedication and lifelong commitment. The pedagogue may have been servile in origin, but the concept eventually became emancipated and could represent a dignified profession. The pedagogue occurs in metaphoric terms in some of the letters of Paul: for example, when he states that the law had been a pedagogue until the arrival of Christ.[13] In Clement's *Pedagogue*, however, it is Christ himself to whom this image is applied.

Thus the *Logos* or Christ functions as a pedagogue, whose main task it is to instruct the children and to improve their souls. They are cherished and fed with products such as milk, but the pedagogue can also administer bitter food whenever it is necessary to be severe with the children in order to save their souls. It is clear that the audience of the *Pedagogue* consisted of people who were insiders and therefore baptized, or about to be. In an earlier work, the *Protrepticus*, Clement had aimed at a different audience, namely non-Christian Greeks whom he encouraged to accept the Christian message and to convert to Christianity.

The hymn does not quote any specific biblical texts, but some of the images, such as the good shepherd, the fisherman, the way and the light, can be associated with gospel passages. Echoes of Greek literature, particularly poetry, are far more evident than biblical references. Clement himself is clearly trying to be poetic, and the many archaic words show that he is going out of his way to write in a style of earlier times. The metre consists of anapestic monometers with some alterations.[14] The anapest was a metrical verse which was very common in Clement's time.[15] Some of the themes which he had treated in his prose recur in the hymn, but he occasionally substitutes more poetic words for his usual vocabulary, and at times he even coins new words.

Composition

The hymn is addressed to Christ, the Pedagogue or the *Logos*, and strings of metaphoric epithets in the vocative case are applied to him. Christ, for example, is called 'shepherd, ploughman, helm, bridle' in uninterrupted sequence. The grammatical structure in these passages is quite simple, the long list of epithets being followed by a short imperative construction. Another feature of Clement's technique is the use of often quite contrived or consciously poetic adjectives that begin (in the Greek original) with the letter alpha. This phenomenon is called in grammatical terms a privative alpha, or alpha privans. It reverses the original meaning of the word into its opposite.[16] In English these adjectives can be rendered by making use of the prefix un- or the suffix -less.[17] The repetition of these adjectives with privative alpha is so insistent that it gives a dominant sonorous tone to the poem, which has its parallels in ancient rhetorical technique. These adjectives and the strings of epithets, some of which are rather unusual, give the text a somewhat artificial flavour. The translation, given below, tries to reflect these characteristics and preserve the contrived tone.

After the initial epithet series, a prayer begins,[18] and the focus shifts from addressant to addressees, the children, who are depicted in terms of a gathering. They are compared to a chorus, who are assembled; they are the object of the pedagogue's guidance. The chorus then begins to sing in line 11, changing the focus back again on Christ, who is hymned in epithetical terms; some of the images are new and others are repeated. This scheme of, on the one hand, Christ being addressed and, on the other, the chorus singing his praises, continues for most of the hymn, but in line 48 the children become the subject themselves. When Clement introduces the inclusive first person plural seven lines later, it becomes clear that he identifies the children with the Christian community as whole. The 'we', as a chorus of peace, sings the final exhortation, and rhetorically the hymn returns to its beginning, since many of the same adjectives are taken up again.

Usc and effect on later writers

It has been suggested that the hymn served as a song for the Alexandrian Christian community to which Clement belonged; such speculations are intriguing but unverifiable. In support of the idea it could, for example, be argued that the use of the plural at the end of the hymn indicates that Clement had the community in mind while writing it. The absence of information on the early Alexandrine liturgy, however, makes it impossible to confirm that the poem was used for formal worship. The hymn apparently did not enjoy much celebrity in antiquity, since it is not quoted or even echoed by other ancient writers,[19] nor did it find a place in later liturgies. The poem was not, however, a purely private work or intended for a circle of literati. The *Pedagogue* as a whole however was certainly meant for everyday use as a guide for living by Christian readers, and the poem was addressed to this audience.

TRANSLATION

1   Bridle of untamed foals,
     wing of unerring birds,[20]
     unwavering helm of ships,[21]
     shepherd of royal lambs,
5   gather your
     artless children[22]
     to sing in a holy way
     and give unfeigned praise[23]
     with unsullied lips
10   to Christ, the children's guide.
     King of saints,
     all-taming word
     of the most high Father,
     ruler of wisdom,
15   ever joyful support
     for the mortal race
     in toil and pain.
     Saviour Jesus,
     shepherd, ploughman,
20   helm, bridle,
     heavenly wing,
     of the most holy flock,
     fisher of men,

of those saved
25 from the sea of evil,[24]
luring with sweet life
the chaste fish
from the hostile tide.
Holy shepherd
30 of sheep of the *Logos*,
lead, O king,
the unharmed children;
the footprints of Christ,
are the path to heaven.
35 Ever-flowing word,
unlimited age,[25]
everlasting light,
source of mercy,
artisan of virtue
40 of those who praise God
with their holy life.
Christ Jesus,
heavenly milk
pressed from the sweet breasts
45 of the bride,
gracious gifts[26]
of your wisdom.
The tiny infants
with tender mouths,
50 suckled
at the nipple of the *logos*
and filled
with the dewy Spirit.
Let us sing together[27]
55 to Christ, the king,
artless praise
and truthful songs,
holy wages
for the teaching of life.
60 Let us escort with simplicity
the mighty son,
as a chorus of peace,
born of Christ,
temperate people;
65 let us sing psalms together
to the God of peace.

ANNEWIES VAN DEN HOEK

ACKNOWLEDGEMENT

With many thanks to my husband John Herrmann for his help on the translation of the hymn and to the members of the Boston Area Patristic Group for their comments.

NOTES

1 See Ernst Heitsch, *Die griechischen Dichterfragmenten der römischen Kaiserzeit*, Göttingen, Vandenhoeck & Ruprecht, 1963, vol. I, pp. 155–9.
2 Johannes Quasten, *Patrology*, Utrecht-Antwerp, Spectrum Publishers, 1966, vol. I, p. 158.
3 For a description, see the editio major in the Corpus of Berlin: Otto Stählin, *Clemens Alexandrinus. Protrepticus und Paedagogus*, Die griechischen christlichen Schriftsteller, vol. 12 (3. Aufl. von Ursula Treu), Berlin, Akademie – Verlag, 1972, pp. XVI–XXXIX.
4 The text begins at *Ped*. I 96, 1.
5 A tenth- or eleventh-century codex now in Modena, Codex Mut. graec. III D 7, no. 126, and a twelfth-century codex in the Laurenziana in Florence, Codex Laur. graec. V 24.
6 Also the transitional phrase from *Ped*. III 101, 3 is still present in the Arethas Codex.
7 See above, note 3.
8 Claude Mondésert, Henri-Irenée Marrou, Chantal Matray, *Le Pédagogue III*, Sources Chrétiennes, vol. 158, Paris, Éditions du Cerf, 1970.
9 W. Wilson, *The Writings of Clement of Alexandria*, The Ante-Nicene Christian Library, vol. 4, Edinburgh, T. & T. Clark, 1868. This edition has been reprinted in *The Ante-Nicene Fathers*, vol. 2, Edinburgh, T. & T. Clark, 1885, and repr. Grand Rapids, Eerdmans, 1986.
10 Simon P. Wood, *Christ, the Educator, The Fathers of the Church*, vol. 23, Washington, DC, Catholic University of America Press, 1954.
11 See particularly *Ped*. III 101, 3.
12 See also the excellent study on this subject by P. J. G. Gussen, *Het leven in Alexandrië volgens de cultuurhistorische gegevens in de Paedagogus (Boek II en III) van Clemens van Alexandrië*, Assen, Van Gorcum, 1955.
13 Gal 3: 24.
14 For a full and graphic explanation, see H.-I. Marrou and J. Irigoin, in Claude Mondésert, Henri-Irenée Marrou, Chantal Matray, *Le Pédagogue III*, Sources Chrétiennes, vol. 158, Paris, Éditions du Cerf, 1970, pp. 204–207.
15 For comparisons, see Ulrich von Wilamowitz-Moellendorf, *Griechische Verskunst*, Berlin, Weidmannsche Buchhandlung, 1921, pp. 133–4.
16 See Herbert Weir Smyth, *Greek Grammar*, Cambridge, Mass., Harvard University Press, 1984, p. 249, no. 885.
17 See, for example, in lines 1–6: untamed, unerring, unwavering, artless.
18 See line 5.
19 The words themselves have not surfaced in later authors but the format may have inspired others. About a hundred years later, Methodius of Olympus concludes his *Symposium* with a hymn, the introduction of which slightly reflects the transitional passage in the *Pedagogue*.
20 The 'wing' is used as image for the ascension to God; see line 21 where Clement speaks of the 'heavenly wing'.

21 'Ships' is a conjecture because of metre and content; the MSS have the Greek word for 'children'.
22 The simplicity and innocence of the children is one of the central themes of the *Pedagogue*. The gathering evokes a chorus, a word that appears at the end of the hymn.
23 Possibly influenced by 1 Pet 2: 2 (Isa 53: 9)
24 This image probably refers to baptism.
25 Age not measured by time.
26 The 'milk' as gift may also have liturgical overtones.
27 The emphasis in the hymn again changes back from Christ to the faithful in a final exhortation.

SELECTED BIBLIOGRAPHY

Editions of the hymn

Heitsch, Ernst, *Die griechischen Dichterfragmente der römischen Kaiserzeit*, Göttingen, Vandenhoeck & Ruprecht, 1963, vol. I, pp. 157–9.
Mondésert, Claude, Marrou, Henri-Irénée and Matray, Chantal, *Le Pédagogue III*, Sources Chrétiennes, vol. 158, Paris, Éditions du Cerf, 1970.
Stählin, Otto, *Clemens Alexandrinus. Protrepticus und Paedagogus*, Die griechischen christlichen Schriftsteller, vol. 12 (3. Aufl. von Ursula Treu), Berlin, Akademie-Verlag, 1972.

For an introduction to Clement and the *Pedagogue*

Marrou, Henri-Irénée and Harl, Marguerite, *Clément d'Alexandrie. Le Pédagogue*, Livre I, Sources Chrétiennes, no. 70, Paris, Éditions du Cerf, 1949, pp. 7–96.
Stählin, Otto, *Mahnrede an die Heiden; Der Erzieher, Buch I–III; Welcher Reiche wird gerettet werden?*, Bibliothek der Kirchenväter, 2. Reihe, Bd. 7–8, München, Kösel-Verlag, 1934; repr. Nendeln/Liechtenstein, Kraus Reprint, 1968, pp. 9–67.

For the hymn

Dihle, Albrecht, *Greek and Latin Literature of the Roman Empire. From Augustus to Justinian*, London and New York, Routledge, 1994, pp. 381–4.
Lattke, Michael, *Hymnus. Materialen zu einer Geschichte der antiken Hymnologie*, Freiburg Schweiz, Universitätsverlag, 1991; for Clement, see pp. 278–81 (with an exhaustive bibliography, including translations).
May, Gerhard, 'Der Christushymnus des Clemens von Alexandrien', in H. Becker and R. Kazynski (eds), *Liturgie und Dichtung*, St Ottilien, EOS Verlag, 1983, vol. I, pp. 257–73.

52

ORIGEN'S PRAYER TO JESUS THE FOOTWASHER

Angela Russell Christman

INTRODUCTION

Origen (*c.* 185–*c.* 254 CE), the great third-century Christian theologian, utters this prayer to Jesus the Footwasher in his Fifth Homily on Isaiah.[1] As one of the premier theologians of the early Church, Origen is perhaps most well known as the author of the treatise *On First Principles*. However, Origen's greatest contribution to the Church is surely to be found in his exegesis, which has come down to us in the form of commentaries and homilies.[2] In his commentaries Origen treats the biblical text in exhaustive detail. In contrast, his homilies are less detailed and more pastoral in nature, in so far as they are tailored to the needs of the congregation and the constraints of preaching. The Fifth Homily on Isaiah exemplifies these characteristics, for Origen's primary concern is to explain to his congregants how they too might contemplate the things revealed to the prophet in the vision recounted in Isaiah 6. Origen elucidates for his audience what it means to see God, and how they might share the prophet's experience.

Provenance, date, language and manuscript tradition

Origen delivered this homily in Caesarea in Palestine, also known as Caesarea Maritima, sometime after 239,[3] most probably at a liturgical gathering during the week which included both the baptized and the catechumenate.[4] He delivered the homily in his native language, Greek, and stenographers transcribed it as he preached. Unfortunately, we do not possess the homily in the original language; it survives only in Jerome's Latin translation, completed *c.* 380.[5]

Jerome's translation of Origen's homilies on Isaiah survives in over fifteen manuscripts which date from the ninth to the fifteenth centuries. In these manuscripts, the Isaiah homilies are grouped with Jerome's translations of

Origen's homilies on Jeremiah and Ezekiel. For this particular part of the Fifth Homily on Isaiah there are no significant textual differences in the manuscript tradition.[6]

Theology and function

That Origen would pray to Jesus specifically as footwasher in a homily on Isaiah might seem unusual.[7] However, central to Origen's theology is the concept of salvation as the process of the soul's purgation. The biblical text for this homily, Isaiah 6, which describes the cleansing the prophet receives from the seraphim's burning coal, is for Origen an instance of such purgation. Moreover, John 13, the account of Jesus washing his disciples' feet, is one of Origen's favourite texts for discussing the soul's cleansing.[8] Thus it is not surprising that he brings John 13 into relation to the prophet's cleansing in Isaiah 6:6.

In this homily, after quoting Isaiah 6:1–3, Origen explains to his congregation that in order to see the vision which Isaiah saw, one must call upon Jesus. It is the advent of Jesus which enables the Christian to see the mysteries revealed to the prophet. Paraphrasing the text of Isaiah 6:6–7, Origen prays that he may receive the cleansing given to the prophet: 'I pray that "Seraphim may be sent to me" and "cleanse my lips with a coal held with tongs" . . .' This desire for the purgation experienced by Isaiah prompts Origen to observe that although the prophet's uncleanness was limited to his lips, his own is more pervasive: 'I fear that I have an unclean heart, unclean eyes, unclean ears, and unclean mouth. As long as I sin with all these, I am unclean.' As examples of such uncleanness, Origen quotes Matthew's gospel. Unclean eyes exist when he looks with lust at a woman (cf. Matt 5:28) and an unclean heart when 'evil thoughts, adultery, fornication, false witness' proceed from his heart (cf. Matt 15:19). Here the notion of sinful or sinless feet arises through Origen's quotation of Isaiah 52:7: 'How beautiful are the feet of those who preach peace, of those who preach good tidings!' Origen shares with the congregation his own fear that his feet, unlike the beautiful feet of Isaiah 52:7, run toward evil and are unclean. Acutely aware of his own sinfulness, Origen asks, 'Who cleanses me? Who washes my feet?' and answers these questions with this prayer to Jesus as footwasher.

Since Origen preached without a manuscript, the prayer was probably composed extemporaneously. Moreover, it lacks a doxology or any sort of formal ending, perhaps because of its placement in the middle of a homily. However, Origen does not simply move from this prayer back to the subject of the homily, the vision of God. Rather, he shares with the congregation his own fears that God will spurn his prayer.[9] From this, he sets out a brief discussion of the question of God's hearing prayers that is clearly aimed at reassuring both himself and his congregation that God does indeed hear and respond to their prayers.

The homiletical context of Origen's prayer to Jesus as footwasher shows that the prayer arises out of his desire to be cleansed and thereby experience the vision of God. Moreover, when Origen beseeches Jesus for cleansing on his own behalf, he also gives us a glimpse of his response to the biblical text, specifically Isaiah 6 and John 13. However, this homiletical context suggests not only that the prayer expresses Origen's request for himself, but also that it serves as an exemplar for his audience, the Christian community at Caesarea. Through the example of this prayer and the numerous others scattered throughout his homilies, Origen teaches his congregation that the proper response to the word of God always involves prayer. Moreover, the prayer's placement within this homily gives concrete manifestation to Origen's view that biblical exegesis always has the ultimate goal of drawing both exegete and audience God-ward.

TRANSLATION

Jesus, come.
I have dirty feet.
Become[10] a servant for my sake.
Pour your[11] water into your basin.[12]
Come, wash my[13] feet.
I know what I say is brash, but I fear the threat you uttered:
'If I do not wash your feet, you have no part in me.'[14]
Therefore, wash my feet so that I may have a part in you.
But why do I say, 'Wash my feet'?
Peter can say this. He had no need except that his feet be washed;
He was clean through and through.
Indeed, though I was washed once, I need that baptism which the Lord
       spoke of:
'I have another baptism to be baptized with.'[15]

NOTES

1 For a solid, accessible biography of Origen see Joseph Wilson Trigg, *Origen: The Bible and Philosophy in the Third-century Church*, Atlanta, John Knox Press, 1983. For general treatments of Origen's homilies and preaching, see Joseph T. Lienhard, S.J., 'Origen as Homilist', in David G. Hunter (ed.), *Preaching in the Patristic Age*, New York, Paulist Press, 1989 and Thomas K. Carroll, *Preaching the Word*, Wilmington, Delaware, Michael Glazier, Inc., 1984. For a discussion of prayer in the homilies, see Daniel Sheerin, 'The Role of Prayer in Origen's Homilies', in Charles Kannengiesser and William L. Petersen (eds), *Origen of Alexandria*, Notre Dame, Indiana, University of Notre Dame Press, 1988.

2 For the seminal contribution of Origen to the development of Christian exegesis in the patristic period, see Manlio Simonetti, *Biblical Interpretation in the Early Church*, Edinburgh, T. & T. Clark, 1994, pp. 39–48, and Trigg, *Origen*

(especially pp. 120–9) and *Biblical Interpretation*, Wilmington, Delaware, Michael Glazier, 1988.

3   There is disagreement among scholars as to the dating of Origen's homilies. Origen preached without a manuscript, but at some point he allowed shorthand writers to copy the homilies as he preached, thus preserving them. In his *Ecclesiastical History* (6.36), Eusebius of Caesarea explains that Origen did not allow this to be done until he was over 60, which would place the homilies after 245. While some scholars accept Eusebius' report, others date the homilies to the period from 239 to 242, concluding that Eusebius' comment is motivated by his desire to portray Origen in the best light. For a helpful summary of this debate, see Lienhard, 'Origen as Homilist'.

4   On the liturgical context of Origen's homilies, see Lienhard, 'Origen as Homilist'.

5   For the dating of Jerome's translations, see J. N. D. Kelly, *Jerome*, New York, Harper & Row, 1975, pp. 76–7.

6   The critical text of the Isaiah homilies is printed in *Die griechischen christlichen Schriftsteller* (hereafter *GCS*), vol. 33, Leipzig, 1925. For a listing of the various manuscripts, see *GCS* 33, XXVIII–XXXI.

7   Those who are familiar with Origen's treatise *On Prayer* may also be surprised that the prayer is directed to Jesus. In *On Prayer* 15–16, Origen explains that Christians ought not pray to anything 'generated'. Rather, they should pray only *to* the Father, although they may pray *through* the Son. Despite this assertion in *On Prayer*, Origen does not hesitate in his homilies to direct prayer to Jesus.

8   Although Origen often quotes or alludes to John 13 when discussing spiritual cleansing, this is the only passage I know of in which he *prays* to Jesus as footwasher. Other passages in which Origen refers to Jesus' washing his disciples' feet include his exegesis of Lamentations 1.9 ('Her uncleanness is before her feet ...'), his *Commentary on John* and his *Homily 6 on Joshua*. In these passages Origen relates Exodus 3:5 and Joshua 5:15 to John 13, the account of Jesus washing his disciples' feet. He draws an analogy between Moses and Joshua taking off their shoes when they stood on holy ground, and Jesus washing the soul's 'feet'. Both the Old Testament imagery of removing shoes and the New Testament imagery of footwashing symbolize the cleansing necessary for the soul to have a part in Jesus. I am grateful to Joseph W. Trigg for bringing these passages to my attention.

9   Origen's comment here implies that although his prayer to Jesus as footwasher lacks a doxology or formal ending, he considered that he had uttered a complete prayer. Indeed, he refers to it as a *benedictio* (*GCS* 33, 265.7).

10   Two manuscripts have 'may you become'.

11   One manuscript omits 'your'.

12   cf. John 13:5.

13   One manuscript omits 'my'.

14   cf. John 13:8.

15   cf. Luke 12:50; Mark 10:38–39.

SELECTED BIBLIOGRAPHY

Carroll, Thomas K., *Preaching the Word*, Wilmington, Delaware, Michael Glazier, Inc., 1984.

Kelly, J. N. D., *Jerome: His Life, Writings, and Controversies*, New York, Harper & Row, 1975.

Lienhard, Joseph T., 'Origen as Homilist', in David G. Hunter (ed.), *Preaching in the Patristic Age: Studies in Honor of Walter J. Burghardt, S.J.*, New York, Paulist Press, 1989.

Sheerin, Daniel, 'The Role of Prayer in Origen's Homilies', in Charles Kannengiesser and William L. Petersen (eds), *Origen of Alexandria: His World and His Legacy*, Notre Dame, Indiana, University of Notre Dame Press, 1988.

Simonetti, Manlio, *Biblical Interpretation in the Early Church: An Historical Introduction to Patristic Exegesis*, Edinburgh, T. & T. Clark, 1994.

Trigg, Joseph Wilson, *Origen: The Bible and Philosophy in the Third-century Church*, Atlanta, John Knox Press, 1983.

——, *Biblical Interpretation*, Wilmington, Delaware, Michael Glazier, 1988.

53

SHEPHERD PRAYER – *ACTS OF PETER* 10

Robert Stoops

INTRODUCTION

In *Acts of Peter* 10, the apostle Peter intercedes on behalf of a Roman Senator named Marcellus. Peter's prayer draws heavily on biblical imagery of the shepherd, calling upon God to accept Marcellus into the flock of believers. This literary prayer is designed to support the author's belief that repentant apostates can return to the Church. It also reflects the freedom with which prayers were composed in second-century Christianity.

Attestation

Although the *Acts of Peter* was composed in Greek, most of it, including this prayer, survives only in Latin. The translation from the third or fourth century is preserved only in a sixth- or seventh-century manuscript in the north Italian town of Vercelli (Codex Vercellenses CLVIII). The codex adds material from the *Acts of Peter* to the end of the Pseudo-Clementine *Recognitions*.[1] The martyrdom section also survives in three Greek manuscripts and numerous translations, including Syriac, Coptic and Armenian. These Martyrdoms and the single vellum leaf of a Greek manuscript (*P. Oxy.* 849) show that the Latin translation follows the original closely.

Date and provenance

The *Acts of Peter* was probably written during the third quarter of the second century in northern Asia Minor. Some have argued that material dealing with lapsed believers, including the shepherd prayer, was inserted in the early third century.[2] However, the issue is closely linked to the primary concern: competition. Believers and potential believers are drawn away by the false wonders Simon Magus performs. The author wants to demonstrate that a return to faith is possible for apostates.

Relation to the canon

The *Acts of Peter*, like other early Christian apocrypha, follows the genre of the canonical gospels and Acts but makes use of significantly different traditions. New Testament texts are alluded to frequently, but they are not treated as scripture. The author felt free to change their details, so that Peter first confronts Simon Magus in Jerusalem rather than Samaria. In *Acts of Peter* 20 Peter characterizes written gospels as the best humans could do, suggesting that oral tradition was still preferred over written sources. In contrast, Septuagint passages are explicitly cited as scripture. They function as proof texts in the speeches attributed to Peter, which speeches may rely on testimony collections.

Cultural setting

The *Acts of Peter* is not theologically sophisticated; it juxtaposes gnostic and orthodox traditions without comment. Its concerns are practical. Writing in a period of relative peace and prosperity, the author wants to demonstrate that Christ is the most powerful of potential benefactors.[3] Within the narrative, the miracles worked through Peter both elicit conversions and confirm the faith of the believers. The text was meant to have a similar effect on its audience.

Literary function

The shepherd prayer appears near the middle of a section focused on the Roman Senator Marcellus. His story deals with both the role of human patrons and the possibilities of forgiveness.[4] *Acts of Peter* 8 introduces Marcellus as a former benefactor who had supported the believers in Rome financially, even in the face of imperial opposition. By the time Peter arrives in Rome, Marcellus has been seduced by Simon Magus, and most of the believers have followed his example, abandoning Christ in favour of Simon. When Peter expels Simon from Marcellus' house with help from a talking dog, the senator repents and begs Peter to intercede for him.[5]

Peter responds with the shepherd prayer. The prayer opens with a doxology addressed to God, the Father. The doxology employs traditional, elevated language and concludes with an 'Amen'. The intercession is addressed to the shepherd, who may be either the Father or Christ. Both are called Lord in the doxology, and the author elsewhere fails to distinguish clearly among the persons of the Trinity. The pattern of alternating praise and petition is as old as the psalms and is common in both Jewish and Christian prayers. Here, as usual, the elements of praise express the basis for the petitioner's confidence.

The terms of praise draw on the rich tradition of shepherd imagery, which has been applied to God from very early times. It is present in early psalms, developed by the prophets, and employed frequently in the parables of Jesus. Part of its power, here and elsewhere in early Christian experience, is its ability to link Christ to God, David and other shepherd figures in Israel's history. The reference to scattered sheep is rooted in Ezekiel 34:11–16 but applied to the followers of Christ in the gospels, especially in the prediction at the Last Supper (Mark 14:27 and parallels). It suggests apostasy, which is particularly important to the author's concern in this section. However, the identification of the sheep as wandering recalls the parables. The mention of error and ignorance suggests a gnostic understanding, in which going astray would represent birth into the material world and being found would symbolize a return to the spiritual realm or conversion.[6] However, the motif of gathering suggests that reassembling the community is the primary concern and that the issue is larger than Marcellus' conversion.

Use in worship

The author of *Acts of Peter* has combined traditional imagery, scriptural language and the formal elements of prayer to create this literary prayer, which demonstrates the propriety of accepting either converts or repentant *lapsi* into the church. The references to the specific details of the Marcellus story make it unlikely that the shepherd prayer preserves a fixed prayer for the reception of converts or repentant apostates. However, the prayer's efficacy in reinforcing the author's ideas requires that it be recognizable as an appropriate prayer. Both the structure of the prayer and the shepherd motifs were probably familiar from the prayer practice of the author's community.

Other prayers in the *Acts of Peter* connected with the miracles do not follow fixed formulae either, although some motifs, such as a reference to witnesses, appear repeatedly. The prayers contained in popular Christian narratives such as the *Acts of Peter* and the *Acts of Paul* appear to have been constructed for their particular literary contexts, which suggests that occasional prayers were freely composed in the second century. It is likely that prayer was understood to be guided by the spirit rather than by prayer books or fixed liturgy. The efficacy of the intercession is not tied to any Church offices that Peter might hold; rather, it is grounded in the authoritative teachings of Jesus and the genuineness of Marcellus' repentance, documented by his anguish and tears.

Theology of the shepherd prayer

The language of the shepherd prayer in *Acts of Peter* 10 covers both the reception of converts and the forgiveness of apostates. The importance of these issues for the author is documented by the effort expended on them here. New Testament allusions are particularly dense in this section. Peter, himself, is treated as the prime example of one whose faith was weak but later confirmed. Indeed, Marcellus, in his request to Peter, even mentions Peter's failed attempt to walk on water. Placing the argument in the mouth of the apostle also helps to secure the audience's acceptance of the polemic. Couching it as a prayer implies that the argument has been laid before God. Divine acceptance of the exegesis is implied by Peter's embrace of Marcellus.

Prayer language is also used to frame didactic material in *Acts of Peter* 37–8, where the content of Peter's speech is explicitly identified as special instruction. Praise addressed to the Cross of Christ as Peter stands before his own cross, marks the moment as sacred but also conveys some content. It has been suggested that a liturgical source identifying the outstretched arms of the orant with the arms of the cross lies behind this section of the *Acts of Peter*.[7] However, the parallels with the *Odes of Solomon* which are cited are too general to demonstrate dependence on a particular tradition. The prayers in the *Acts of Peter* probably reflect the use of public prayer as a means of instruction as well as an instrument of devotion in early Christianity.

Later use

While the *Acts of Peter* influenced a number of later Christian writings,[8] the focus of Christian apocryphal literature shifted toward the issues of martyrdom and asceticism, so the shepherd prayer did not influence later literature. The Vercelli version of the *Acts of Peter* was eventually supplanted by derivative versions of the martyrdom, which did not include the shepherd prayer. Nevertheless, the prominence of the shepherd image in Christian art of the third and fourth centuries demonstrates its continued popularity in the early church, where it reminded the faithful of Christ's ability and willingness to care for his own.

TRANSLATION

Peter said in a loud voice: Glory and honour to you, our Lord, Omnipotent God, Father of our Lord Jesus Christ.[9] To you be praise, glory, and honour for ever and ever, Amen![10] Since you have now fully strengthened and established us in yourself in the sight of all witnesses, Holy Lord, confirm Marcellus and bestow your peace on him and his house today. For you alone are able to restore all those who are lost or wandering. We entreat you, Lord, Shepherd of the sheep which once were scattered but now shall be gathered together by you,[11] receive Marcellus also as one of your lambs. Do not permit him to revel in error or ignorance any longer,[12] but receive him into the number of your sheep. Accept the one who asks you with sorrow and tears.

NOTES

1 It is likely that some episodes have been dropped from the beginning of the work. The text of the *Acts of Peter* is available in R. Lipsius, *Acta Apostolorum Apocrypha I*, Leipzig, Hermann Mendelssohn, 1891; reprinted, Hildesheim, Georg Olms, 1959, pp. 45–103, and in L. Vouaux, *Les actes de Pierre*, Paris, Letouzey et Ané, 1922.

2 G. Poupon, 'Les "Actes de Pierre" et leur remaniement', *Aufstieg und Niedergang der römischen Welt*, 1988, vol. 2, 25/6, pp. 4374–7, and C. Thomas, 'Word and Deed: The *Acts of Peter* and Orality', *Apocrypha*, 1992, vol. 3, pp. 136–43.

3 R. Stoops, 'Patronage in the *Acts of Peter*', *Semeia*, 1986, vol. 38. pp. 91–100.

4 Stoops, op. cit., pp. 96–8, and 'Christ as Patron in the *Acts of Peter*', *Semeia*, 1991, vol. 56, pp. 152–3.

5 Marcellus identifies himself as one who has fallen away (*lapsus*) from the Lord and his promises. It does not ultimately matter whether Marcellus is considered a lapsed believer or simply someone who failed to convert. His seduction by Simon is blamed for the apostasy of most of the Roman Christians, and their return is connected to his reception into Christ's flock.

6 cf. Gospel of Thomas 107.

7 Brian McNeil, 'A Liturgical Source in Acts of Peter 38', *Vigiliae Christianae*, 1979, vol. 33, pp. 342–6.

8 The *Acts of Peter* shares many motifs with the *Acts of Paul* in particular, although debate continues concerning the direction of influence.

9 The first Latin term translated here as 'honour' should normally be translated as 'renown' or possibly 'splendour', but it is likely that the underlying Greek employed the familiar term. The piling up of titles is typical of the *Acts of Peter*, although the frequent use of the address 'Lord' may belong to the translation rather than the original text.

10 The triple combination of 'praise, glory, and honour' is paralleled only in 1 Pet 1:7 in a different context. However, the terms appear frequently in pairs in New Testament doxologies. The doxology concludes with a formulation, literally 'throughout the ages of ages', that is common because it is rooted in the psalms.

11 In Ezekiel 34:11–16 the scattered sheep are the people of Israel, and the shepherd reference shifts between God and the human king. The image is transferred to the Church with Christ as the shepherd in Mark 14:27 and parallels, and again, somewhat differently, in John 10:11–16. It is difficult to tell which person of the Godhead is addressed in this part of the shepherd prayer, and it probably did not matter to the author, whose theology seems to be closer to modalism than to the doctrine of the Trinity which was formulated later.

12 The term 'revel' (*bacchari*) suggests a comparison with the ecstatic dimensions of Dionysian rituals. The equation of error with ignorance has a gnostic ring but is not exclusively gnostic.

SELECTED BIBLIOGRAPHY

Ficker, G., *Die Petrusakten. Beiträge zu ihrem Verständnis*, Leipzig, Barth, 1903.

Lipsius, R., *Acta Apostolorum Apocrypha I*, Leipzig, Hermann Mendelssohn, 1891, reprinted Hildesheim, Georg Olms, 1959.

McNeil, B., 'A Liturgical Source in Acts of Peter 38', *Vigiliae Christianae*, 1979, vol. 33, pp. 342–6.

Parrott, D., *Nag Hammadi Codices III, 3–4 and VI, with Papyrus Berolinensis 8502, 1 and 4*, Leiden, E. J. Brill, 1979.

Perkins, J., 'The Social World of the *Acts of Peter*', in J. Tatum (ed.), *The Search for the Ancient Novel*, Baltimore, Johns Hopkins University Press, 1994, pp. 285–307.

Poupon, G., 'Les "Actes de Pierre" et leur remaniement', *Aufstieg und Niedergang der römischen Welt*, 1988, vol. 2, 25/6, pp. 4363–83.

Schmidt, C., *Die alten Petrusakten im Zusammenhang der apokryphen Apostelliteratur nebst einem neuentdeckten Fragment*, TU 9.1, Leipzig, J. Hinrichs, 1903.

——, 'Studien zu den alten Petrusakten', *Zeitschrift für Kirchengeschichte*, 1924, vol. 43, pp. 321–48; 1926, vol. 45, pp. 481–515.

——, 'Zur Datierung der alten Petrusakten', *Zeitschrift für die neutestamentliche Wissenschaft*, 1930, vol. 29, pp. 150–5.

Schneemelcher, W., 'The Acts of Peter', in W. Schneemelcher (ed.), *New Testament Apocrypha II: Writings Relating to the Apostles, Apocalypses and Related Subjects*, trans. R. Wilson, Cambridge, Clarke\Louisville, Westminster, 1992, pp. 271–85.

Stoops, R., 'Patronage in the *Acts of Peter*', *Semeia*, 1986, vol. 38, pp. 91–100.

——, 'Christ as Patron in the *Acts of Peter*', *Semeia*, 1991, vol. 56, pp. 143–57.

Thomas, C., 'Word and Deed: The *Acts of Peter* and Orality', *Apocrypha*, 1992, vol. 3, pp. 125–64.

Turner, C., 'The Latin Acts of Peter', *Journal of Theological Studies*, 1931, vol. 32, pp. 119–33.

Vouaux, L., *Les actes de Pierre. Introduction, Textes, Traduction et Commentaires*, Paris, Letouzey et Ané, 1922.

54

THE *PHŌS HILARON*

R. Garland Young

INTRODUCTION

The *Phōs Hilaron* is a Christian vespers hymn of great antiquity. Used in the eastern Church from about the third century, it went unnoticed by Christians in the west until the seventeenth century, when it was translated into English. Since that time it has been used in a wide variety of hymn collections spanning a variety of Christian traditions. The *Phōs Hilaron* is an excellent example of the enduring quality of ancient Greek hymnody for modern Christian liturgy.

Attestation, date and provenance

The oldest extant manuscript for *Phōs Hilaron*, Codex Monacensis, dates from the twelfth or thirteenth century, but it is all but certain that the hymn is much older.[1] St Basil (*c.* 330–79 CE), in *On the Spirit* 73, reports knowledge of an unnamed hymn which uses the line, 'We praise the Father, Son, and Holy Spirit of God' (see lines 7 and 8 of the translation below). But Basil does not mention the hymn's author or source. He does mention, however, that the hymn was sung at the lighting of the lamps at eventide. The tradition of Basil may be corroborated by his brother, Gregory of Nyssa (*c.* 330–95 CE). Recounting the death of his sister Macrina, Gregory reports that on her deathbed Macrina recited to herself a hymn of thanksgiving that was sung at the evening lamp-lighting (*On the Life of the Holy Macrina* 985).

In other traditions in the eastern Church the hymn's authorship has been associated with Sophronius (*c.* 560–638 CE), archbishop of Jerusalem from 634–638 CE.[2] Yet some scholars have suggested that Sophronius, who lived during a period of significant hymn composition in the Greek Church, merely recovered and reworked a much older text of the *Phōs Hilaron*.[3] If the traditional attestation of the hymn is reliable, the text we have today may be based on an original as old as the third century. Given the testimony of

Cappadocian fathers such as Basil and Gregory as well as its connection with Sophronius, the hymn may have originated in Syria or Cappadocia.

The hymn's connection with biblical tradition

Although the hymn contains no direct quotes from the New Testament, much of its key vocabulary mirrors the Christian scriptures. The most notable image of the hymn is, of course, that of light. The New Testament abounds with epithets which associate God and Christ with light, especially in the fourth Gospel.[4] Hence, it seems natural that the hymn-writer would employ this provocative metaphor in worship at eventide, when the lighting of lamps reminded believers of the steadfast presence of Christ even in a world of darkness. Lines 2 and 3 of the hymn, which proclaim Jesus Christ as 'immortal', 'holy' and 'blessed', call to mind the exalted language of 1 Tim 6:15–16.[5]

More unusual is the expression *hilaron* ('joyous' or 'cheerful') in line 1. While not used of God or Christ in the New Testament, the term was widely employed in Greek mystery cults of Isis and Cybele in the celebration of the Hilaria, the Day of Cheerfulness.[6] The author of the hymn apparently wants to challenge pagan assertions about the source of spiritual enlightenment by co-opting the term *hilaron* and applying it to Jesus Christ.

Use of the hymn in Christian hymnody

The *Phōs Hilaron* has been in almost constant use in the eastern Orthodox vespers since it first appeared in late antiquity. By contrast, it was largely unknown in the western Church until the seventeenth century, when Archbishop Ussher took notice of the ancient Greek hymn.[7] Its translation into English soon followed Ussher's citation of the *Phōs Hilaron*, and in 1754 it appeared in a book of Moravian hymns.[8]

In the nineteenth and twentieth centuries the *Phōs Hilaron* has been set to music in a grand variety of hymnals and worship guides in several western Christian settings, including the Anglican, Episcopalian, Lutheran, United Church of Christ and the Roman Catholic traditions.[9] In recent years the hymn has been appropriated as part of the Order of Vespers in the Lutheran church as a result of ecumenical dialogue with other traditions. This service, called the Lucernarium or Service of Light, recalls what may have been the hymn's earliest significance. The hymn is read as a prose piece during the introduction of candles during the service. Set at day's end, the Lucernarium vividly recalls the imagery of Christ as the light of the world (John 8:12), boldly proclaimed in the New Testament and beautifully signalled by the opening line of the *Phōs Hilaron*.[10]

TRANSLATION

Joyous Light of holy glory
Of the immortal heavenly Father,
Holy, blessed
Jesus Christ,
As the sun goes down
And we see the evening light
We sing a hymn to God – Father, Son,
And Holy Spirit.
You are always worthy
To be sung by auspicious[11] voices,
Son of God, Giver of life.
That is why the world glorifies you.

NOTES

1 The text of Monacensis is reproduced in W. Christ and M. Paranikas, *Anthologia Graeca Carminum Christianorum*, Hildesheim, Georg Olms Verlagsbuchhandlung, 1963, p. 40.

2 See the reference in John Julian, *A Dictionary of Hymnology*, second revised edition with supplement, New York, Dover Publications, 1957, p. 894.

3 Eleanor M. Irwin, 'PHOS HILARON: The Metamorphoses of a Greek Christian Hymn', *Hymn*, 1989, vol. 40, p. 7.

4 Matt 4:16 (Isa 9:2 LXX); Luke 2:32; John 1:4, 9; 8:12; 9:5; 12:36, 46; 1 Tim. 6:16; 1 John 1:5; Rev 22:5.

5 The adjective *athanatou* ('immortal') in line 2 of the hymn parallels the noun form *athanasian* ('immortality') in 1 Tim 6:16. And *makaros* ('blessed') in line 3 reflects the alternative form *makarios* in 1 Tim 6:15.

6 See the *Oxyrhynchus Papyri*, 14, 1380, 190–220, which describes Isis as the 'mistress of light' who 'brings the sun from rising to setting'. The only New Testament use of this term, 'for God loves a cheerful giver' (2 Cor 9:7), is not relevant here, since the term describes the believer and not God.

7 The earliest printed version was Archbishop James Ussher, *De Romanae Ecclesiae Symbolo Vetere*, London, 1647, pp. 43–5.

8 The first English translation was made by Samuel Woodford, *Paraphrase upon the Canticles and Some Select Hymns of the New and Old Testament with other occasional compositions in English verse*, London, 1679. The Moravian hymnbook, *A Collection of Hymns of the children of God in all ages, from the beginning till now*, London, 1754, no. 190, preserves the first version of *Phōs Hilaron* set to music under the title, 'Thou lightsome day, the joyful shine'.

9 See the exhaustive list of renaissance to modern settings (thirty-five in all, fourteen dating since 1899) of the *Phōs Hilaron* in Irwin, 'PHOS HILARON', pp. 10–11.

10 For the hymn's use in Lutheran observance of the Lucernarium, see Timothy J. Keyl and Frank C. Senn, 'Phōs Hilaron: Joyous Song of the Light', *Currents in Theology and Mission*, 1986, vol. 13, pp. 354–7.

11 Codex Monacensis reads *aisiais* ('auspicious'), while an early printed version reads *hosiais* ('pious'; H. A. Daniel, *Thesaurus Hymnologicus*, Leipzig, E. Anton, I. A. Bartii and J. T. Loeschke, 1841–6, vol. iii, p. 5).

SELECTED BIBLIOGRAPHY

Irwin, M. Eleanor, 'PHOS HILARON: The Metamorphoses of a Greek Christian Hymn', *Hymn*, 1989, vol. 40, pp. 7–12.

Keyl, Timothy J. and Senn, Frank C., 'Phōs Hilaron: Joyous Song of the Light', *Currents in Theology and Mission*, 1986, vol. 13, pp. 354–7.

Wellesz, Egon, *A History of Byzantine Music and Hymnography*, London, Oxford, 1949.

GLOSSARY

alabarch: an Egyptian office, controller of customs

allegory: the expression by means of symbolic figures and actions of truths about human existence

anapest: a metrical foot consisting of two unstressed syllables followed by one stressed syllable

anaphora: the major prayer in the central part of the Catholic eucharist extending from 'The Lord be with you. . . . Lift up your hearts . . .' to the 'Through him, with him, in him . . . all honour and glory is yours forever.' The *Sanctus* is part of the anaphora

antiphon: a psalm, anthem or verse sung in alternate stages by differing groups or individuals

apocalypse: a genre of literature containing a narrative framework in which a revelation is mediated by an otherworldly figure to a human recipient

apocryphal: lit., 'hidden'. Literature deemed unsuitable for use in liturgical setting. Ironically, this literature is often similar in some respects to texts which are canonical, and in every case provides the historian with a valuable window into a variety of beliefs and practices in a period

Ashkenazic: pertaining to one of the two major divisions of Jews, namely the Eastern European Yiddish-speaking Jews. The other group is called Sephardic.

bi-colon: two rhythmical units of an utterance, each containing a series of from two to not more than six feet, having a principal accent and forming part of a line

canonical: belonging to that collection of literary texts which are judged to be useful guides for the beliefs and practices of a group

chiasmus: a literary formation established by the positioning of parallel elements such that elements at an equal distance from a literary unit's centre are similar to each other; named for the Greek letter CHI, similar in shape to the English letter X

Decalogue: lit., the 'ten words'; the ten commandments

deliberative: a type of rhetoric concerned with the feasibility of a chosen course of action

docetic Christology: a way of talking about Jesus of Nazareth which asserts that he only *seemed* (Gk: *dokein*) to be human

doxological: pertaining to praise

epideictic: the rhetoric of praise or blame

epigraphic: pertaining to inscriptions

eschatology: teaching about the 'last things'. The focus of eschatology is that time in the future when the course of history will be changed to such an extent that one can speak of an entirely new state of reality

forensic: rhetoric intent on bringing the hearers to a decision concerning a person or issue

Genizah: the storeroom of a Cairo synagogue where approximately 200,000 fragments of Hebrew texts were discovered in the late 1800s

Hasmonean: the period from 134–63 BCE which followed the Maccabean rule in Israel and which, together with it, comprised a brief window of independence of Israel from foreign domination

hekhalot literature: Jewish mystical literature which emanates from the third to the seventh century CE. It describes ascent to the celestial spheres during which the seer reports visions of God's chariot or throne

hendiadys: the expression of an idea by the use of usually two independent words connected by *and*

hieroglyphics: a system of writing mainly using pictorial characters

homoeoteleuton: a similar ending of words or lines, often giving rise to accidental error in the transmission of manuscripts

invocation: in a prayer context, address to and naming of a deity

isosyllabic: words having an equal number of syllables

Levant: the regions bordering the eastern Mediterranean Sea, extending from western Greece to western Egypt

litotes: understatement, especially that in which an affirmative is expressed by means of the negative of its contrary, e.g. *not bad at all*

liturgical: pertaining to public, communal prayer life; from the Greek word for 'service'

Maccabean era: a period of successful resistance of Jews against their Seleucid (Greek) overlords. The period began around 167 BCE and witnessed the successive influence of the Maccabee brothers Judas, Jonathan and Simon (who was murdered in 134 BCE). This period probably witnessed the foundation of the Essene community on the northwest corner of the Dead Sea

midrashim: explorations of the underlying significance of a Bible text. Halakhic midrash extracts principles of Jewish law from the Bible text. Haggadic midrash constitutes a running commentary on the Bible text, incorporating maxims, ethical teachings, homilies, anecdotes and folklore

Mishnah: the collection of mainly legal Jewish traditions written down around 200 CE. The collection became part of the Talmud

modalism: that teaching about the Christian God which asserted as early as Praxeas in 210 CE that God is one, indivisible and simple. Modalists insisted that the Father himself entered the Virgin's womb and died on the cross

monometer: a line of verse consisting of a single metrical foot

Montanism: a lay movement in Asia Minor in the latter half of the second century CE, emphasizing apocalyptic expectations, the continuing prophetic gifts of the Spirit, and strict ascetic discipline

morphology: that part of language study concerned with inflection, derivation and compounding

narrative: in a prayer context, the recounting of past benefits and relationship with a deity, recited as basis of the present appeal for continued good

orthography: that part of language study dealing with letters and spelling

oxymoron: a combination of contradictory or incongruous words

palimpsest: a parchment or tablet used one or more times after earlier writing has been erased

panegyric: formal or elaborate praise

peroration: the concluding part of a discourse

Peshitta: a translation of the Bible into Syriac well established by the early fifth century CE

proposition: in a prayer context, the content of a request made of a deity

pseudepigraphic: lit., falsely ascribed writing. Literature whose actual author is different from the purported author

Sanctus: (Lat. 'holy'). The three-fold acclamation of God 'Holy, holy, holy' in Isaiah 6; referred to in Hebrew as the Qedushah/Kedushah and in Greek as the Trishagion

Second Temple era: the period marked by the presence of the temple rebuilt in Jerusalem after the return of the exiles from Babylon after 539 BCE. This temple was destroyed by the Romans in 70 CE

Septuagint: Greek version of the Old Testament/Hebrew Bible

shofar: a kind of trumpet, usually a ram's horn, used in certain Jewish liturgies

syncretism: the combination of different forms of belief or practice

Talmud: the authoritative body of Jewish tradition, comprised of both Mishnah and rabbinic discussion of Mishnah (*gemara*), completed around the sixth century CE

tannaitic: designating the period of activity of scholars of the oral law of Judaism, extending from approximately 20 CE to 200 CE

testament: a genre of literature in which a revered figure, soon before his death, gives instructions and predictions about the future to those gathered around him. In some cases, the figure also prays for those left behind

Vorlage: (Ger.) model, pattern, prototype

Vulgate: A translation of the Bible into Latin effected by Jerome in the late fourth century CE

Yavneh: also Yabneh/Jamnia: an academic gathering of rabbis under the leadership of Johannan ben Zakkai and later Gamaliel II who shaped the course of Judaism in the period following the destruction of the Second Temple in 70 CE

INDEX

When the words in the index are presented with their modifiers, the modifiers occur in alphabetical order. Thus, 'Angels, around throne' precedes 'Angels, during persecution'. In some entries there may be overlap between the sense cited simply by page number and that contained in the modifications.

Plutarch 2, 71, 97, 142, 180, 183, 188
poetry xiii, 5, 12, 18–9, 21, 33, 36, 56–7,
84, 93, 100, 108, 118, 129, 133–4,
137, 139, 147, 190, 197, 213, 238,
243, 252, 267, 276, 296–7, 299
Pontius Pilate 87, 88, 230, 232–3
postures for prayer: bound 287;
kneeling 125, 175n8; outstretched
arms 312; prostration 125, 173;
standing 115, 125; vs.
intellectualizing 173
praise:
  JUDAICA
   and debate over Amidah 115; and
Hymn on Occasions for Prayer
33–7 *passim*; and trust 81; angelic
28–32; as catechism 114; for
answering petition 23; fruit of
36n7; imperative mood and, in
hymnic genre 16n5; inadequate
83; in third person or participial
form 70n2; mode of, disclosed 82;
of Israel's God 14, 21; of
Jerusalem 22n21; of Judith 61; of
Leah 101; of (mother) Zion 20,
80; part of petitionary prayer 40;
promise to 27n23; response to
providence 90; serve and 26;
superior to literal sacrifice 90;
twice a day 10; with angels 28–31
passim; with personal testimony
80
  GREEKS AND ROMANS
   and honor 124; and petition 192;
of Apollo 185–6; of creator/
creation 166; of Diana 141n4; of
divine One and All 168; of
intelligible Light 168; through
following divine logos 134
  CHRIST TRADITIONS
   and commitment to Jesus 244;
and doxology 320; and exalted
prose 235; and panegyric 321; and
petition 310; and power, glory,
greatness 294; and shepherd
imagery 311; artless 301; followed
by Amen 252; for salvation of
Israel 219n5; glory and honor
312, 313n10; God with holy life
301; in New Testament 208; in
Odes of Solomon and *Hodayot*
251, 274; in the name of God

238n12; of Father Son and Spirit
315; of God and Christ 245;
opening *Ode of Solomon* 5 273;
reason for 276; through the high
priest 258, 288; *see also* bless,
doxology, glorify
priest(s) 32, 40, 49, 60, 61, 86, 144, 162;
and chorus 139; angels as 28–9; at
Qumran 29; Christ, high 222–9
passim, 256, 258, 288, 290n35; Eli 75;
Emperor as 162–4; high, as Logos
101; Moses, Aaron and Samuel 76;
Pentephres, Egyptian 67; reign and
246–8
private 15, 39–40, 42, 49, 65, 71, 101,
125, 139, 166, 181, 182, 297–8, 300
prophets 17, 20, 21, 44, 57, 123, 167,
233, 261, 264, 311
proposition 2, 123, 321
protection 56–7, 72, 75, 124, 150, 182,
192, 203, 262
psalms vii, xiii, 10–11, 14–16, 18, 28, 30,
39, 70–1, 217, 233, 238, 250, 278–9,
310, 313; and imagery of Odist 276;
and shepherd imagery 311;
collections of, at Qumran 11, 217;
Greek translation of 167; in the lofty
heights 29; non-Biblical, at Qumran
9; not model for Clement's hymn,
296; of lament 55; of Naasenes 296;
of Valentinus 296; Scroll 18–22; to
God of peace 301; unceasing prayer
in 34; wisdom 11
Pseudepigrapha vii, xi, xix, 38–41, 47,
51, 52, 57–8, 65, 71–2, 76–8, 84–5,
89, 105, 118, 277, 278–9
pseudepigraphic 9, 153n5, 321
public 3, 27, 37, 40, 49, 104, 125, 142,
151, 153, 159, 161, 230, 312, 320

Qumran vii, xi, xii, xiv, xix, xx, 9–19,
21–2, 24, 26–7, 29, 31–7, 43–4, 47,
51, 54–7, 70, 109, 117–18, 217, 219,
262, 265, 274, 278

rabbinic viii, 9, 10, 12, 26, 27, 34, 37, 70,
94, 108, 117, 243, 322
rabbis 10, 36, 37, 115, 322
redemption x, 11, 20, 27, 108–10, 112,
115–19, 244, 246, 248, 293
reign of God: focus of Jesus' teaching
222; in Q11 212–14; pledge to

42–5, 47, 49, 50, 53, 61, 63, 75, 80, 84, 90–1, 101, 104, 129, 162, 186, 202, 204, 210–11, 214, 217–18, 220, 225, 243, 245, 250, 268, 274, 278, 293, 305, 311, 313, 317, 318

thunderbolt: of Zeus, disseminating light of reason 135–6

time xvii, 1, 10, 15, 18, 19, 24, 27, 33–4, 37, 42, 45, 48, 55, 59, 67, 73–4, 80, 82–3, 86–7, 93, 123, 129, 147, 150, 156, 160–1, 163–4, 176–80, 182, 186, 193, 196, 199, 212, 217, 223, 225, 242, 254, 260–1, 265, 269, 271, 274, 276, 278, 282, 292, 297–9, 303, 310, 315, 320

times of prayer: at Qumran 33–7 passim; celebrating Augustus 161; coordinated with Temple sacrifice 42n; debate over thrice-daily 41n3; dusk 111; fixed daily 42n3; habitual and daily 60; morning 117n5; morning and evening 108; night 125; unceasing 246

titles for Apollo 186; for God 61; see also epithets

Titus 86, 160, 162–3, 254

Torah xx, 17, 48, 56, 89, 109, 112, 118, 278; blessing for 108; deeper meaning of 100; gift of 111; knowledge of 24; laws within 102; return to 116

tragedy xii, 100, 193–4, 244

transgression see sin

treaty: oath 144, 146; see also covenant

trials 25

true: and firm 113, 114; You 114

truth: characteristic of God 288;

characteristic of songs 301; consecrated in 226; invocation to 168; learning 76; one of seven Hermetic virtues 166; Paraclete of 294

two world conception 81

Vespasian 86

virtues: piety, courage, self-control 89; Roman 139; seven, of Hermetism 166

Vorlage 43, 46, 322

Vulgate 46n4, 49, 59, 73, 208, 248n22, 322

wicked 15, 77, 80, 82–3, 95, 116, 283

widow 60–2, 71, 233, 282, 291

wilderness 21–2, 35, 76, 104

wisdom 38–9, 70, 76, 83, 89, 100, 102, 110, 166, 223, 242, 247, 269, 272, 300–1; background to 'God as Father' 212; day created in 111; literature 215n17; of Solomon 273; of your grace 69; psalms 11; speculation and Christology 223; tradition 241

word: courage to preach 232; dependence on Word 82; Jesus as 224; kept your 226

Yavneh 40, 115, 322

Zeus viii, 1, 123–4, 131, 133–8, 145–6, 148, 182, 191–2, 197, 199

Zion vii, xiii, 11, 19, 20–2, 63, 80–1, 85, 116–17